COMPENDIUM OF MODERN FIREARMS

A COMPENDIUM OF THE WEAPONS AND EQUIPMENT USED BY THE WORLD'S COUNTERTERRORIST UNITS

PUBLISHED BY

R. TALSORIAN GAMES, INC.

D1219367

STAFF

✳✳✳
Written By   Kevin Dockery
✳
Researched By   Kevin Dockery
✳✳✳
From An Idea By   Bill Fawcett
Kevin Dockery
✳
Edited By   Derek Quintanar
✳✳✳
Art Direction   Matt Anacleto
✳
Graphic Design &   Grant Kono
Layout By
✳✳
Illustrations   Bill Warhop
✳✳✳
Additional   Shon Howell
Illustrations   Grant Kono
Matt Anacleto
✳
Photography   Kevin Dockery
✳✳
Computer   Tim Lasko
Probability
Generation
✳✳✳
Technical   A. Peters
Assistance
✳
Cover   Kevin Dockery
Photography
✳✳✳
Cover Design   Matt Anacleto
✳

R. TALSORIAN GAMES, INC.

Published by R. Talsorian Games Inc.
P.O. Box 7356 Berkeley, CA. 94707
Copyright © 1991 by
William Fawcett & Associates
Edge of The Sword™ is a trademark of
R. Talsorian Games Inc. All Rights Reserved
under the Universal Copyright Code.

ABOUT THE AUTHOR

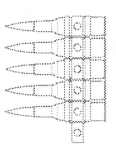
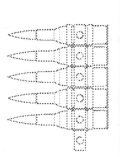
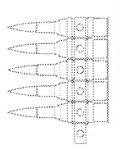

Kevin Dockery was born on October 12, 1954 in the Detroit, Michigan area. He joined the U.S. Army in May of 1972, and received antique weapon training at both the Smithsonian Institute and Colonial Williamsburg, Virginia. While an armorer for the President's guard in Washington, D.C., he did custom pistol work and achieved Class III Gunsmith classification. Kevin has served in the National Guard and as a private gunsmith in Michigan in the years since.

A graduate of Oakland University in 1980 with a degree in communications, his thesis was *The Morrow Project*, a post-holocaust RPG (and his introduction into the gaming field with Timeline Ltd.). He currently lives in southeast Michigan as a custom knife and swordsmith, as well as consulting on many publications in the Special Forces and firearms fields. Kevin's most recent book is *Seals in Action*, a history of the U.S. Navy Sea-Air-Land teams. He was also a civilian contractor to a multi-service unit during Operation Desert Storm.

COMPENDIUM OF MODERN FIREARMS

EDGE OF THE SWORD VOL. 1

A Compendium of the Weapons and
Equipment Used by the World's Counterterrorist Units

CHAPTER 1

PISTOLS

istols, as both revolvers and autoloaders are referred to, are among the most universal weapons found in the hands of counterterrorist groups throughout the world. With their small size and power, today's pistols are increasingly more common, even in those elite military units in whose parent armies pistols

are relatively rare. New weapons developments, especially in autoloaders, increased dramatically in the 1970's stimulated by the requirements put out in requests for new weapons by European militaries. In the United States, the JSSAP trials for a new US military handgun caused several new designs to become available.

The general trend is for police agencies, especially in North America, to use revolvers while military agencies almost universally use autoloader designs. The revolver has the advantage of relative mechanical simplicity with its concurrent mechanical reliability; the ability to fire a second round in the case of a misfire, and the capacity to be easily produced in very powerful calibers. Along with the ability to use the most powerful of cartridges, revolvers are also able to effectively utilize the widest range of loadings available for a given caliber. The simplicity of a revolver's operation allows training in its use to be equally simplified.

On the disadvantage side, revolvers are relatively bulky and large, especially through the cylinder. The six round cylinder of the revolver is probably its weakest point with the limited ammunition capacity greatly reducing the volume of fire that can be delivered in a short time and slowing reloading.

Autoloaders, most often erroneously referred to as "automatics", have the advantages of a relatively large magazine capacity and easy reloading that results in a very high volume of fire being available. The larger ammunition capacity also allows more targets to be engaged in a shorter time without reloading. The flat design of most autoloaders also allows concealed carry to be more easily accomplished. On the disadvantage side, autoloaders are much more mechanically complex and have a greater range of jams than a revolver. Jams in an autoloader normally require both hands to clear. In a revolver most jams can be

"cleared" by just pulling the trigger and bringing a fresh round into line. Those more severe interruptions often result in the weapon being completely out of action and requiring professional attention. Modern ammunition design has greatly lessened the possibility of jams and misfires for all classes of weapons and has greatly increased reliability.

The small size of handguns allow them to be used in very close quarters, such as an aircraft cockpit, where other, longer, firearms would be a distinct disadvantage if not impossible to quickly maneuver. Other advantages include easy use with one hand while the other may be otherwise occupied. All of these reasons and more will result in the handgun being seen in the hands of counterterrorist and military forces for the foreseeable future. ●

For information on using the Probability Tables, see Appendix C.

▼ Steyr GB

CARTRIDGE	9x19mm
OPERATION	Gas-delayed blowback
TYPE OF FIRE	Semiautomatic, Double-action
RATE OF FIRE (SS)	40 rpm
MUZZLE VELOCITY	336 m/s (1102 fps)
MUZZLE ENERGY	507 J (374 ft/lb)
SIGHTS	Open, non-adjustable w/luminous inserts
FEED	18 round removable box magazine
WEIGHTS:	
WEAPON (EMPTY)	0.845 kg
WEAPON (LOADED)	1.190 kg
MAGAZINE (EMPTY)	0.122 kg
MAGAZINE (LOADED)	0.340 kg
SERVICE CARTRIDGE	12 g
BULLET	8 g
LENGTHS:	
WEAPON OVERALL	21.6 cm
BARREL	13.6 cm
SIGHT RADIUS	16.4 cm
STATUS	Production completed
SERVICE	Commercial sales
COST	$500.00

The GB was designed as a replacement pistol for the Austrian military, a competition it lost to the Glock 17, and as such was intended for a very rugged environment where overall size was not a major consideration. The gas-delayed blowback feature of the GB was developed from a WW II German design for a simple semiautomatic rifle, the VG-1 (also referred to as the Barnitske system after its inventor). The gas-delay system of the GB uses the barrel as a stationary piston with the slide acting as a moving cylinder. Upon firing, propellant gasses enter the cylinder through bleed holes in the barrel, and while the gas pressure is high, prevent the slide from opening until the bullet has left the barrel and pressures have reached a safe level. The advantages of this type of system are its mechanical simplicity and a self-regulating feature. The system uses only the pressures generated by the firing round and automatically varies itself to match them, regardless of bullet weight or velocity. The GB does not have a conventional safety. Instead, it has a decocking lever on the slide that lowers the hammer on a loaded chamber. With the hammer lowered, the firing pin is locked in place and will not move until the hammer is cocked either by pulling the trigger, double-action mode, or manually with the thumb, single-action mode. The Steyr GB (the GB stands for Gazbremser or Gas Brake in English), is a very strong and reliable weapon with excellent ergonometrics incorporated into its design. This allows it to be accurate and comfortable to shoot. The safety system prevents there being any switch to be released before firing. Simply point the weapon and pull the trigger. The gas system of the GB allows for any type of 9x19mm ammunition to be used. It also cushions the recoil, adding to the weapon's firing comfort and increasing its accuracy in rapid fire. The sight system includes luminous dots that are simply aligned in a row to allow for aiming in low light conditions. The squared off and checkered front of the trigger guard add to the security of a two handed hold. One of the drawbacks of the GB is that it is relatively large, which makes it somewhat difficult to shoot for people with small hands and limits its concealability. Several Austrian and U.S. police agencies issue or use the Steyr GB and it has seen good sales in the U.S. and abroad.

ASSESSMENT	7/8 IN @ 25 YDS
WEAPON	STEYR GB
AMMO	9x19mm NATO Ball
DISPERSION ANGLE	.0551404 degrees, .980273 NATO mils.

Range	Group Circle Width (mm)	Probability (0<p<.099) (m)			
		Body	**Head**	**Hand**	**Bullseye**
5.0	4.812	0.990	0.990	0.990	0.990
10.0	9.624	0.990	0.990	0.990	0.990
15.0	14.436	0.990	0.990	0.990	0.989
20.0	19.248	0.990	0.990	0.990	0.965
25.0	24.059	0.990	0.990	0.990	0.931
50.0	48.119	0.990	0.990	0.981	0.738
75.0	72.178	0.990	0.990	0.929	0.591
100.0	96.238	0.990	0.981	0.862	0.488
125.0	120.297	0.990	0.958	0.795	0.415
150.0	144.357	0.990	0.929	0.733	0.360

DAMAGE 23/.16

▼ Glock 17

CARTRIDGE	9x19 mm
OPERATION	Short recoil, Double-action only
TYPE OF FIRE	Semiautomatic
RATE OF FIRE (SS)	40 rpm
MUZZLE VELOCITY	350 m/s (1148 fps)
MUZZLE ENERGY	500 J (369 ft/lb)
SIGHTS	open, non-adjustable
FEED	17 round removable box magazine
WEIGHTS:	
WEAPON (EMPTY)	.620 kg
WEAPON (LOADED)	.865 kg
MAGAZINE (EMPTY)	.041 kg
MAGAZINE (LOADED)	.245 kg
SERVICE CARTRIDGE	12 g
BULLET	8 g
LENGTHS:	
WEAPON OVERALL	18.8 cm
BARREL	11.4 cm
SIGHT RADIUS	16.5 cm
STATUS	Current, production
SERVICE	Austrian military and police forces, some U.S. police and security forces, commercial sales.
COST	$450.00

This pistol uses the familiar Browning locking system where the barrel is cammed down from the locked position by a slot in the barrel engaging a stud in the frame. The fact that the Glock is made from only 33 different components including those of the magazine makes for the least possible number of breakdowns of the action, resulting in a very reliable weapon. The weapon is fired by means of a striker that is not cocked until the trigger has been pulled 5mm (which also unlocks the automatic firing pin lock). The trigger must be pulled to activate the weapon as there is a small lever in the center of the trigger that locks it in place until the lever is pressed, preventing the Glock from accidental discharge.

The receiver of the Glock is made from a synthetic polymer plastic, stronger than steel but with only 14% of steel's weight. The Glock 17 has stirred a great deal of controversy with its plastic receiver, resulting in the mass media referring to it as a "plastic" pistol and calling for a ban on the type. In fact, the Glock has more steel in its construction than many other pistols and its ability to pass airport metal detectors is due more to human error than any transparency of the weapon. Media hysteria aside, the Glock is a very well built weapon with a notable record of reliability during testing. The trigger-actuated safety system prevents accidental discharges while allowing the Glock to be very fast to get into action since there is no safety to switch off separately.

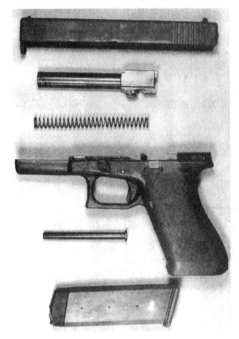

ASSESSMENT	1.25 IN @ 25 YDS
WEAPON	Glock 17
AMMO	9x19mm NATO Ball
DISPERSION ANGLE	.0802041 degrees, 1.42585 NATO mils.

Range	Group Circle Width (mm)	Probability (0<p<.099) (m)			
		Body	**Head**	**Hand**	**Bullseye**
5.0	6.999	0.990	0.990	0.990	0.990
10.0	13.998	0.990	0.990	0.990	0.990
15.0	20.997	0.990	0.990	0.990	0.954
20.0	27.997	0.990	0.990	0.990	0.900
25.0	34.996	0.990	0.990	0.990	0.842
50.0	69.991	0.990	0.990	0.934	0.602
75.0	104.987	0.990	0.973	0.837	0.459
100.0	139.983	0.990	0.934	0.744	0.369
125.0	174.978	0.987	0.887	0.663	0.308
150.0	209.974	0.973	0.837	0.596	0.264

DAMAGE 24/.15

▼ HP-35, Browning Hi Power

CARTRIDGE	9x19mm
OPERATION	Short recoil
TYPE OF FIRE	Semiautomatic
RATE OF FIRE (SS)	40 rpm
MUZZLE VELOCITY	350 m/s (1148 fps)
MUZZLE ENERGY	500 J (369 ft/lb)
SIGHTS	open, non-adjustable
FEED	13 or 20 round removable box magazine

WEIGHTS:

WEAPON (EMPTY)	0.810 kg
WEAPON (LOADED)	0.986 kg w/13 rds
MAGAZINE (EMPTY)	(13 rd) 0.072 kg (20 rd) 0.102 kg
MAGAZINE (LOADED)	(13) 0.176 kg (20 rd) 0.342 kg
SERVICE CARTRIDGE	12 g
BULLET	8 g

LENGTHS:

WEAPON OVERALL	20 cm
BARREL	11.8 cm
SIGHT RADIUS	15.9 cm
STATUS	Production
SERVICE	In service with and/or produced by;

Argentina, Australia, Bangladesh, Barbados, Belgium, Botswana, Burundi, Burma, Cameron, Canada, Chad, Chile, Denmark, Dominican Republic, India, Indonesia, Ireland, Jamaica, Jordan, Lebanon, Luxembourg, Malawi, Malaysia, Mozambique, Netherlands, New Zealand, Nigeria, Oman, Panama, Rwanda, Saudi Arabia, Sierra Leone, Singapore, South Africa, Taiwan, Tanzania, Thailand, Togo, Trinidad & Tobago, Tunisia, Uganda, United Arab Emirates, United Kingdom, Venezuela, Zaire, and Zimbabwe. Also large international commercial sales.

COST $450.00

The Browning Hi Power was the last design of John M. Browning and contained all the improvements he had developed from his earlier work. The barrel is locked into the slide of the Browning by ribs on the top of the barrel engaging slots in the slide. When the slide moves to the rear, the barrel is cammed downward by a slot in the underside of the barrel engaging a cam in the frame. This cam-slot arrangement allows the Browning to be simple and rigid in design. There is normally a magazine safety in the Browning that prevents the hammer from being released by the sear if the magazine is not fully seated in the weapon. The double-column design of the Browning's magazine allows the weapon to have a large number of rounds available while still being manageable in size. The Browning Hi-Power is probably the most popular pistol among counter-terrorist organizations. Very prolific, 47 countries either produce or issue the Browning to their forces, this pistol has also seen widespread commercial sales in the U.S.A. and other countries. The extended 20 round magazine gives the Hi-Power excellent firepower but makes the weapon hard to conceal. The magazine safety is also considered excessive by many users but it can be easily removed. The popularity of the Hi-Power is being extended with the introduction of the Mark 2 version as well as a double-action variant.

WEAPON HP-35
AMMO 9X19
DISPERSION ANGLE .162009 degrees, 2.88016 NATO mils.

Range	Group Circle Width (mm)	Probability (0<p<.099) (m)			
		Body	**Head**	**Hand**	**Bullseye**
5.0	14.138	0.990	0.990	0.990	0.990
10.0	28.276	0.990	0.990	0.990	0.898
15.0	42.414	0.990	0.990	0.989	0.781
20.0	56.552	0.990	0.990	0.966	0.680
25.0	70.690	0.990	0.990	0.932	0.598
50.0	141.379	0.990	0.932	0.740	0.366
75.0	212.069	0.972	0.834	0.593	0.262
100.0	282.759	0.932	0.740	0.490	0.204
125.0	353.448	0.884	0.660	0.417	0.167
150.0	424.138	0.834	0.593	0.362	0.141

DAMAGE 24/.15

▼ HP Browning Mark 2

WEIGHTS:

WEAPON (EMPTY)	0.875 kg
WEAPON (LOADED)	1.051 kg
STATUS	Production
SERVICE	Belgian police forces, and commercial sales
COST	$500.00

Essentially the same weapon as the Browning Hi-Power with an enlarged thumb safety that can be used by either right or left handed users (the original was right hand only), an enlarged pair of sights that are easier to see quickly, more anatomically shaped grips, and a hard, phosphated, anti-glare finish that wears well. The Mark 2 is a utilitarian pistol that should see wide use and good sales with military and police organizations though its commercial sales may be limited by the rather ugly look of the new finish.

▼ BDA -9S

CARTRIDGE	9x19mm
OPERATION	Short recoil
TYPE OF FIRE	Semiautomatic, Double-action
RATE OF FIRE (SS)	40 rpm
MUZZLE VELOCITY	356 m/s (1168 fps)
MUZZLE ENERGY	505 J (373 ft/lb)
SIGHTS	open, non-adjustable
FEED	14 round removable box magazine
WEIGHTS:	
WEAPON (EMPTY)	.850 kg
WEAPON (LOADED)	1.088 kg (w/14 rds)
MAGAZINE (EMPTY)	(14 rd) 0.070 kg
MAGAZINE (LOADED)	(14 rd) 0.238 kg
SERVICE CARTRIDGE	12 g
BULLET	8 g
LENGTHS:	
WEAPON OVERALL	20 cm
BARREL	11.8 cm
SIGHT RADIUS	17.6 cm
STATUS	Production
SERVICE	Not known
COST	$400.00

This is a new pistol design based on the very successful Browning Hi-Power. The most obvious change from the Hi-Power is that the BDA-9S is double action and has a trigger-operated firing pin lock that prevents firing unless the trigger is pulled. In place of a thumb safety there is a decocking lever that allows the hammer to be safely lowered on a loaded chamber without using the trigger. The front of the trigger guard is shaped for two handed shooting and the magazine release can be easily changed from right to left handed operation. The BDA-9 series uses the basic Browning style of locked breech as well as having a general resemblance and the magazine safety. This is a new release from FN and has not yet seen a great deal of use. The design is sound and has some excellent features including the interchangeability of magazines with the Browning Hi-Power. There is also a spring ejector that works on the magazine throwing them clear of the weapon when they are released. Overall the BDA-9 series lends itself very well to quick operation combined with the reliability of a proven design.

WEAPON	BDA-9S
AMMO	9X19
DISPERSION ANGLE	.154106 degrees, 2.73966 NATO mils.

Range	Group Circle Width (mm)	Probability (0<p<.099) (m)			
		Body	**Head**	**Hand**	**Bullseye**
5.0	13.448	0.990	0.990	0.990	0.990
10.0	26.897	0.990	0.990	0.990	0.909
15.0	40.345	0.990	0.990	0.990	0.798
20.0	53.793	0.990	0.990	0.971	0.699
25.0	67.241	0.990	0.990	0.941	0.617
50.0	134.483	0.990	0.941	0.757	0.381
75.0	201.724	0.977	0.849	0.611	0.274
100.0	268.966	0.941	0.757	0.508	0.213
125.0	336.207	0.896	0.678	0.433	0.175
150.0	403.448	0.849	0.611	0.376	0.148

DAMAGE 24/.15

▼ BDA-9C

CARTRIDGE	9x19 mm
OPERATION	Short recoil
TYPE OF FIRE	Semiautomatic, Double action
RATE OF FIRE (SS)	40 rpm
MUZZLE VELOCITY	350 m/s (1150 fps)
MUZZLE ENERGY	490 J (361 ft/lb)
SIGHTS	Fixed, non-adjustable iron
FEED	7 or 14 round removable box magazine
WEIGHTS:	
WEAPON (EMPTY)	0.708 kg (0.770 kg)
WEAPON (LOADED)	0.847 kg w/ 7 rds (1.008 kg w/14 rds)
MAGAZINE (EMPTY)	0.055 kg (7 rd), 0.070 kg (14 rd)
MAGAZINE (LOADED)	0.139 kg (7 rd), 0.238 kg
SERVICE CARTRIDGE	12 g
BULLET	8 g
LENGTHS:	
WEAPON OVERALL	17.3 cm
BARREL	9.6 cm
SIGHT RADIUS	15.2cm
STATUS	In production
SERVICE	Commercial sales

This is a variant of the BDA-9S pistol. The 9C is the compact model with a shortened slide assembly and frame. The reduced size of the grip allows for a special shortened 7 round magazine to be used for maximum concealability. The normal 14 round magazine may also be used. The concealability of the BDA-9C is excellent but some comfort and control is sacrificed for the shortened grip. Fitting the slide assembly of the 9C to the frame of the 9S results in the medium version of the BDA family, the 9M.

WEAPON BDA-9C
AMMO 9x19
DISPERSION ANGLE .162009 degrees, 2.88016 NATO mils.

Range	Group Circle Width (mm)	Probability (0<p<.099) (m)			
		Body	Head	Hand	Bullseye
5.0	14.138	0.990	0.990	0.990	0.990
10.0	28.276	0.990	0.990	0.990	0.898
15.0	42.414	0.990	0.990	0.989	0.781
20.0	56.552	0.990	0.990	0.966	0.680
25.0	70.690	0.990	0.990	0.932	0.598
50.0	141.379	0.990	0.932	0.740	0.366
75.0	212.069	0.972	0.834	0.593	0.262
100.0	282.759	0.932	0.740	0.490	0.204
125.0	353.448	0.884	0.660	0.417	0.167
150.0	424.138	0.834	0.593	0.362	0.141

DAMAGE 24/.15

▼ Knife Pistol Type 86

CARTRIDGE 5.7x17mmR
OPERATION Manual
TYPE OF FIRE Double-action, multi barrel
RATE OF FIRE (SS) 8 rpm (4 rds in 3 seconds)
MUZZLE VELOCITY 250 m/s (820 fps)
MUZZLE ENERGY 81 J (60 ft/lb)
SIGHTS Fixed, non-adjustable iron
FEED 1 round per barrel, 4 barrels
WEIGHTS:
WEAPON (EMPTY) 0.464 kg (0.504 kg w/scabbard)
WEAPON (LOADED) 0.478 kg
MAGAZINE (LOADED) 0.014 kg (4 rounds)
SERVICE CARTRIDGE 3.5 g
BULLET 2.6 g
LENGTHS:
WEAPON OVERALL 26.2 cm
BARREL 8.6 cm
BLADE 14 cm

SIGHT RADIUS 6.4 cm
STATUS In production
SERVICE Unknown, some commercial sales

This is a very unconventional design for a handgun which comes from an unusual source, the Norinco Arsenal in the People's Republic of China. The single-edged blade has four deep grooves, two on either side, to allow passage of bullets fired from the mechanism in the weapon's grip. To fire the weapon the knurled ring (safety) at the front of the grip is rotated to the left, which can be done with the thumb of the firing hand, uncovering a red dot and unlocking the trigger. The trigger extends below the weapon and is pulled by the normal finger with the thumb of the firing hand braced against the upper pivot of the trigger. With the arm extended and rotated with the wrist up the sights on the grip may be used but the weapon is intended for very close use. The end cap of the grip contains the firing mechanism and is unscrewed for reloading. With the endcap removed a long pull on the trigger will eject the fired cartridge cases.

WEAPON Knife/Pistol
AMMO 5.7x17mmR
DISPERSION ANGLE .185717 degrees, 3.30164 NATO mils.

Range	Group Circle Width (mm)	Probability (0<p<.099) (m)			
		Body	Head	Hand	Bullseye
5.0	16.207	0.990	0.990	0.990	0.981
10.0	32.414	0.990	0.990	0.990	0.863
15.0	48.621	0.990	0.990	0.980	0.735
20.0	64.828	0.990	0.990	0.947	0.630
25.0	81.034	0.990	0.990	0.905	0.549
30.0	97.241	0.990	0.980	0.859	0.485
35.0	113.448	0.990	0.965	0.813	0.434
40.0	129.655	0.990	0.947	0.770	0.392
45.0	145.862	0.990	0.927	0.729	0.357
50.0	162.069	0.990	0.905	0.691	0.328

DAMAGE 7/0.03

▼ CZ-75 • CZ-85

☞ continued on next page

☞ *CZ-75 • CZ-85 continued*

CARTRIDGE	9x19 mm
OPERATION	Short recoil
TYPE OF FIRE	Semiautomatic
RATE OF FIRE (SS)	40 rpm
MUZZLE VELOCITY	369 m/s (1212 fps)
MUZZLE ENERGY	544 J (401 ft/lb)
SIGHTS	Fixed, non-adjustable iron
FEED	15 round removable box magazine
WEIGHTS:	
WEAPON (EMPTY)	0.980 kg
WEAPON (LOADED)	1.180 kg
MAGAZINE (EMPTY)	0.020 kg
MAGAZINE (LOADED)	0.200 kg
SERVICE CARTRIDGE	12 g
BULLET	8 g
LENGTHS:	
WEAPON OVERALL	20.3 cm
BARREL	12 cm
SIGHT RADIUS	16 cm
STATUS	In production
SERVICE	Commercial sales

This pistol was developed by Czechoslovakia for the export market because they do not use the 9x19mm round in their military. The operating system is taken from several earlier weapons with the locking system being a modified Browning design and the firing mechanism being similar to the Walther designs. The result of this combination is an accurate and reliable design that has not yet been adopted by any major group.

WEAPON	CZ-75
AMMO	9x19
DISPERSION ANGLE	.158057 degrees, 2.80991 NATO mils.

Range	Group Circle Width (mm)	Probability (0<p<.099) (m)			
		Body	Head	Hand	Bullseye
5.0	13.793	0.990	0.990	0.990	0.990
10.0	27.586	0.990	0.990	0.990	0.903
15.0	41.379	0.990	0.990	0.990	0.790
20.0	55.172	0.990	0.990	0.968	0.689
25.0	68.966	0.990	0.990	0.937	0.608
50.0	137.931	0.990	0.937	0.749	0.374
75.0	206.897	0.975	0.841	0.602	0.268
100.0	275.862	0.937	0.749	0.499	0.208
125.0	344.828	0.890	0.669	0.424	0.171
150.0	413.793	0.841	0.602	0.369	0.144

DAMAGE 25/.16

CARTRIDGE	9x19 mm
OPERATION	Retarded blowback
TYPE OF FIRE	Semiautomatic
RATE OF FIRE (SS)	40 rpm
MUZZLE VELOCITY	350 m/s (1148 fps)
MUZZLE ENERGY	488 J (360 ft/lb)
SIGHTS	Fixed non-adjustable iron
FEED	15 round removable box magazine
WEIGHTS:	
WEAPON (EMPTY)	1.090 kg
WEAPON (LOADED)	1.365 kg
MAGAZINE (EMPTY)	0.095 kg
MAGAZINE (LOADED)	0.275 kg
SERVICE CARTRIDGE	12 g
BULLET	8 g
LENGTHS:	
WEAPON OVERALL	20.3 cm
BARREL	11.4 cm
SIGHT RADIUS	15.8 cm
STATUS	Out of production
SERVICE	This is a French service sidearm as well as being sold commercially.

Though officially adopted by the French Services, the P-15 has also seen wide use through its commercial sales. The unusual locking system has the barrel rotating to release the slide with the pistol then operating as a blowback weapon. The complex trigger mechanism is prone to wear when used by unfamiliar operators (the magazine safety being especially so). All of this aside, the P-15 has excellent handling qualities and shoots well. The extended magazine capacity puts it in the same class as the Browning Hi Power, but the relatively poor sights, hard trigger pull, and difficulty in cocking the slide has kept the P15 from greater commercial success.

WEAPON	MAB PA-15
AMMO	9x19
DISPERSION ANGLE	.162009 degrees, 2.88016 NATO mils.

Range	Group Circle Width (mm)	Probability (0<p<.099) (m)			
		Body	Head	Hand	Bullseye
5.0	14.138	0.990	0.990	0.990	0.990
10.0	28.276	0.990	0.990	0.990	0.898
15.0	42.414	0.990	0.990	0.989	0.781
20.0	56.552	0.990	0.990	0.966	0.680
25.0	70.690	0.990	0.990	0.932	0.598
50.0	141.379	0.990	0.932	0.740	0.366
75.0	212.069	0.972	0.834	0.593	0.262

☞ *continued*

Range	Group Circle Width (mm)	Probability (0<p<.099) (m)			
		Body	Head	Hand	Bullseye
100.0	282.759	0.932	0.740	0.490	0.204
125.0	353.448	0.884	0.660	0.417	0.167
150.0	424.138	0.834	0.593	0.362	0.141

DAMAGE 24/.15

▼ Manurhin MR73 Gendarmerie

CARTRIDGE	9x33 mmR
OPERATION	Manual
TYPE OF FIRE	Double action revolver
RATE OF FIRE (SS)	24 rpm
MUZZLE VELOCITY	w/7.6 cm bbl 385 m/s (1262 fps), w/10.2 cm bbl 410 m/s (1344 fps), w/13.2 cm bbl 428 m/s (1405 fps), w/15.2 cm bbl 468 m/s (1534 fps), w/20.3 cm bbl 504 m/s (1653 fps)
MUZZLE ENERGY	w/7.6 cm bbl 757 J (558 ft/lb), w/10.2 cm bbl 858 J (633 ft/lb), w/13.2 cm bbl 938 J (692 ft/lb), w/15.2 cm bbl 1119 J (825 ft/lb), w/20.3 cm bbl 1299 J (958 ft/lb)
SIGHTS	Adjustable, open iron
FEED	Swing out 6 round cylinder
WEIGHTS:	
WEAPON (EMPTY)	0.880 kg w/6.4 cm bbl, 0.890 kg w/7.6 cm bbl, 0.950 kg w/10.2 cm bbl, 1.050 kg w/13.2 cm bbl, 1.070 kg w/15.2 cm bbl, 1.170 kg w/30.3 cm bbl
WEAPON (LOADED)	0.976 kg w/6.4 cm bbl, 0.986 w/7.6 cm bbl, 1.046 kg w/10.2 cm bbl, 1.146 kg w/13.2 cm bbl, 1.166 kg w/15.2 cm bbl, 1.266 kg w/20.3 cm bbl
MAGAZINE (LOADED)	0.096 kg (6 rds)
SERVICE CARTRIDGE	16 g
BULLET	10.3 g
LENGTHS:	
WEAPON OVERALL	19.5 cm w/6.4 cm bbl, 20.5 cm w/7.6 cm bbl, 23.3 cm w/10.2 cm bbl, 26.4 cm w/13.2 cm bbl, 28.3 cm w/15.2 cm bbl, 33.4 cm w/20.3 cm bbl
BARREL	7.6, 10.2, 13.2, 15.2, or 20.3 cm

SIGHT RADIUS	11.7 cm w/7.6 cm bbl, 14.2 cm w/ 10.2 cm bbl, 17.2 cm w/13.2 cm bbl, 19.2 cm w/15.2 cm bbl, 24.3 cm w/20.3 cm bbl
STATUS	In production
SERVICE	French forces and government agencies

The Manurhin is the first revolver developed and produced in France since 1892. The MR-73 models were created to answer a demand for good quality revolvers for use by the French police forces and especially the elite presidential security units. Until the advent of the Manurhin design, the demand was filled with custom produced Smith & Wessons and the MR-73 has borrowed heavily from the S&W design. An interchangeable cylinder is available for the MR-73 allowing 9x19mm ammunition to be used, but because of its relative inaccuracy in firing and some difficulties in extraction, this option is rarely used. With an excellent trigger pull and quality manufacturing, the MR-73 has gone a long way toward converting many Europeans to the use of a revolver although automatic pistols have been popular there for a long time. The GIGN are particularly pleased with the Gendarmerie Model of the MR-73 because of its adjustable sights and its availability in different barrel lengths.

WEAPON	MR-73 w/10.2 cm bbl
AMMO	9x33R SWC
DISPERSION ANGLE	.173863 degrees, 3.0909 NATO mils.

Range	Group Circle Width (mm)	Probability (0<p<.099) (m)			
		Body	Head	Hand	Bullseye
5.0	15.172	0.990	0.990	0.990	0.986
10.0	30.345	0.990	0.990	0.990	0.881
15.0	45.517	0.990	0.990	0.985	0.758
20.0	60.690	0.990	0.990	0.957	0.655
25.0	75.862	0.990	0.990	0.919	0.573
50.0	151.724	0.990	0.919	0.715	0.346
75.0	227.586	0.965	0.813	0.567	0.247
100.0	303.448	0.919	0.715	0.466	0.191
125.0	379.310	0.866	0.634	0.395	0.156
150.0	455.172	0.813	0.567	0.342	0.132

DAMAGE w/7.6 cm bbl 20/.55, w/10.2 cm bbl 22/.58, w/13.2 cm bbl 23/.61, w/15.2 cm bbl 25/.66, w/20.3 cm bbl 27/.71

▼ Walther PP

Range	Group Circle Width (mm)	Probability (0<p<.099) (m)			
		Body	Head	Hand	Bullseye
5.0	15.172	0.990	0.990	0.990	0.986
10.0	30.345	0.990	0.990	0.990	0.881
15.0	45.517	0.990	0.990	0.985	0.758
20.0	60.690	0.990	0.990	0.957	0.655
25.0	75.862	0.990	0.990	0.919	0.573
50.0	151.724	0.990	0.919	0.715	0.346
75.0	227.586	0.965	0.813	0.567	0.247
100.0	303.448	0.919	0.715	0.466	0.191
125.0	379.310	0.866	0.634	0.395	0.156
150.0	455.172	0.813	0.567	0.342	0.132

DAMAGE 20/.10 (9x17), 17/.06 (7.65x17)

CARTRIDGE 9x17 mm or 7.65x17 mmSR
OPERATION Blowback
TYPE OF FIRE Semiautomatic, double-action
RATE OF FIRE (SS) 30 rpm
MUZZLE VELOCITY 291 m/s (955 fps)(9x17mm), 290 m/s (951 fps)(7.65x17mmSR)
MUZZLE ENERGY 260 J (192 ft/lb)(9x17mm), 199 J (147 ft/lb)(7.65x17mmSR)
SIGHTS Fixed, non-adjustable iron
FEED 7 round (9x17 mm), 8 round (7.65x17 mmSR) removable box magazine
WEIGHTS:
WEAPON (EMPTY) 0.690 kg (9x17mm), 0.695 kg (7.65x17 mmSR)
WEAPON (LOADED) 0.809 kg (either)
MAGAZINE (EMPTY) 0.051 kg (either)
MAGAZINE (LOADED) 0.119 kg (9x17mm), 0.114 kg (7.65x17mmSR)
SERVICE CARTRIDGE 9.7 g (9x17 mm), 7.9 g (7.65x17mmSR)
BULLET 6.2 g (9x17 mm), 4.6 g (7.65x17 mmSR)
LENGTHS:
WEAPON OVERALL 17.3 cm
BARREL 9.9 cm
SIGHT RADIUS 11.3 cm
STATUS In production
SERVICE Wide commercial sales
COST $600.00

Although originally produced in 1929, the Walther PP still sees widespread use and excellent commercial sales because of its solid, practical design. With several design changes between 1929 and today, the PP has not yet been shown inferior to other, more modern, designs. The handling qualities and speed of use all add to the weapon's overall appeal. A major drawback of the PP is that the largest cartridge which its straight blowback design can safely handle is the rather low powered 9x17mm round.

WEAPON Walther PP
DISPERSION ANGLE .173863 degrees, 3.0909 NATO mils.

▼ Walther PPK • PPK/S

Walther PPK with safety set to fire

CARTRIDGE 9x17mm or 7.65x17mmSR
OPERATION Blowback
TYPE OF FIRE Semiautomatic, Double-action
RATE OF FIRE (SS) 30 rpm
MUZZLE VELOCITY 291 m/s (955 fps)(9x17mm), 290 m/s (951 fps)(7.65x17mmSR)
MUZZLE ENERGY 260 J (192 ft/lb)(9x17mm), 199 J (147 ft/lb)(7.65x17mmSR)
SIGHTS Fixed, non-adjustable iron
FEED 6 round (9x17mm) or 7 round (7.65x17mmSR) removable box magazine (PPK/S 7 round <9x17mm> or 8 round <7.65x17mmSR>)
WEIGHTS:
WEAPON (EMPTY) 0.590 kg (0.680 kg <9x17mm>, 0.675 kg <7.65x17mmSR> PPK/S)
WEAPON (LOADED) (0.792 kg <9x17mm>, 0.782 kg <7.65x17mmSR> PPK/S)
MAGAZINE (EMPTY) (0.044 kg <PPK/S>)
MAGAZINE (LOADED) (0.112 kg <9x17mm>, 0.107 kg <7.65x17mmSR> PPK/S)
SERVICE CARTRIDGE 9.7 g (9x17mm), 7.9 g (7.65x17mmSR)

BULLET	6.2 g (9x17mm), 4.6 g (7.65x17mmSR)
LENGTHS:	
WEAPON OVERALL	15.5 cm
BARREL	8.4 cm
SIGHT RADIUS	11 cm
STATUS	In production
SERVICE	Widespread commercial sales
COST	$500.00

The PPK is a shortened version of the Walther PP and shares all of its excellent characteristics. The PPK/S is a hybrid between the PPK and the PP which was developed to pass the restrictions of the American Gun Control Act of 1968. The PPK/S used the shorter barrel and slide of the PPK with the larger frame of the PP. With the advent of American produced PPKs, the PPK/S will gradually disappear.

ASSESSMENT	PPK/S 9x17mm 3 1/8 in @ 15m
WEAPON	PPK/S
AMMO	9x17mm
DISPERSION ANGLE	.301757 degrees, 5.36458 NATO mils.

Range	Group Circle Width (mm)	Probability (0<p<.099) (m)			
		Body	**Head**	**Hand**	**Bullseye**
5.0	26.333	0.990	0.990	0.990	0.914
10.0	52.667	0.990	0.990	0.973	0.706
15.0*	79.000	0.990	0.990	0.910	0.558
20.0	105.333	0.990	0.973	0.836	0.458
25.0	131.667	0.990	0.945	0.765	0.387
50.0	263.333	0.945	0.765	0.515	0.217
75.0	395.000	0.855	0.619	0.383	0.151
100.0	526.667	0.765	0.515	0.304	0.115
125.0	658.333	0.686	0.439	0.251	0.093
150.0	790.000	0.619	0.383	0.214	0.078

* indicates range for which data was supplied

DAMAGE 20/.10 (9x17), 17/.06 (7.65x17)

▼ Walther P1 • P38

Walther P1

Walther P38 (wartime manufacture)

CARTRIDGE	9x19mm
OPERATION	Short recoil
TYPE OF FIRE	Semiautomatic, Double-action
RATE OF FIRE (SS)	32 rpm
MUZZLE VELOCITY	369 m/s (1212 fps)
MUZZLE ENERGY	544 J (401 ft/lb)
SIGHTS	Fixed, non-adjustable iron
FEED	8 round removable box magazine
WEIGHTS:	
WEAPON (EMPTY)	0.772 kg (0.879 kg P-38)
WEAPON (LOADED)	0.970 kg (1.077 kg P-38)
MAGAZINE (EMPTY)	.102 kg
MAGAZINE (LOADED)	0.198 kg
SERVICE CARTRIDGE	12 g
BULLET	8 g
LENGTHS:	
WEAPON OVERALL	21.8 cm
BARREL	12.4 cm
SIGHT RADIUS	18 cm
STATUS	In production
SERVICE	West Germany, Chile, Norway, Portugal, and extensive commercial sales
COST	$900.00

The P38 was another German design to survive World War II. After 1957, the P38 was again made in West Germany with an alloy frame instead of the earlier steel frame. The lightweight alloy frame weapon was adopted by the new German army, designated as the P1. The P38 and the P1 versions both share the same double action trigger mechanism of the Walther PP as well as the safety system which drops the cocked hammer on a locked firing pin when the weapon is put on safe.

WEAPON	P1
AMMO	9x19
DISPERSION ANGLE	.154106 degrees, 2.73966 NATO mils.

☞ continued on next page

☞ *Walther P1 continued*

Range	Group Circle Width (mm)	Probability (0<p<.099) (m)			
		Body	Head	Hand	Bullseye
5.0	13.448	0.990	0.990	0.990	0.990
10.0	26.897	0.990	0.990	0.990	0.909
15.0	40.345	0.990	0.990	0.990	0.798
20.0	53.793	0.990	0.990	0.971	0.699
25.0	67.241	0.990	0.990	0.941	0.617
50.0	134.483	0.990	0.941	0.757	0.381
75.0	201.724	0.977	0.849	0.611	0.274
100.0	268.966	0.941	0.757	0.508	0.213
125.0	336.207	0.896	0.678	0.433	0.175
150.0	403.448	0.849	0.611	0.376	0.148

DAMAGE 25/.16

▼ Walther P5

CARTRIDGE	9x19mm
OPERATION	Short recoil
TYPE OF FIRE	Semiautomatic, Double-action
RATE OF FIRE (SS)	24 rpm
MUZZLE VELOCITY	346 m/s (1138 fps)
MUZZLE ENERGY	480 J (354 ft/lb)
SIGHTS	Fixed, non-adjustable iron
FEED	8 round removable box magazine
WEIGHTS:	
WEAPON (EMPTY)	0.795 kg
WEAPON (LOADED)	0.993 kg
MAGAZINE (EMPTY)	0.102 kg
MAGAZINE (LOADED)	0.198 kg
SERVICE CARTRIDGE	12 g
BULLET	8 g
LENGTHS:	
WEAPON OVERALL	18 cm
BARREL	9 cm
SIGHT RADIUS	13.4 cm
STATUS	In production
SERVICE	Adopted by the Netherlands, Baden-

Wurttemburg, and Rheinland-Pfalz police departments as well as commercial sales

COST $1,100.00

This is the latest development of the Walther P38 series. Though internally much the same as the P38 with several parts being interchangeable, the P5 is externally very different. One of the points of difference is the very high level of safety of the P5. The firing pin of the P5 cannot be struck by hammer until the trigger is pulled to the end of its travel where it lifts the firing pin into the hammer's path. The trigger mechanism is not engaged until the slide is fully forward and locked, adding to the overall safety of the weapon. There is a decocking lever above the left grip which will lower the hammer safely on a loaded chamber. The end result of this design is a weapon that can be safely carried with the hammer down on a chambered round and put into action quickly by just pulling the trigger with no other safeties to be released.

WEAPON	P5
AMMO	9x19
DISPERSION ANGLE	.16596 degrees, 2.9504 NATO mils.

Range	Group Circle Width (mm)	Probability (0<p<.099) (m)			
		Body	Head	Hand	Bullseye
5.0	14.483	0.990	0.990	0.990	0.988
10.0	28.966	0.990	0.990	0.990	0.892
15.0	43.448	0.990	0.990	0.988	0.773
20.0	57.931	0.990	0.990	0.963	0.672
25.0	72.414	0.990	0.990	0.928	0.590
50.0	144.828	0.990	0.928	0.732	0.359
75.0	217.241	0.970	0.827	0.584	0.257
100.0	289.655	0.928	0.732	0.482	0.200
125.0	362.069	0.878	0.651	0.409	0.163
150.0	434.483	0.827	0.584	0.355	0.138

DAMAGE 24/.15

▼ Heckler & Koch P9S

CARTRIDGE	9x19mm (11.43x23mm)
OPERATION	Delayed blowback

	TYPE OF FIRE	Semiautomatic, Double-action
	RATE OF FIRE (SS)	27 rpm (21 rpm)
	MUZZLE VELOCITY	350 m/s (1148 fps (260 m/s <853 fps>)
	MUZZLE ENERGY	500 J (361 ft/lbs) (504 J <364 ft/lbs>)
	SIGHTS	Fixed, non-adjustable iron
	FEED	9 round (7 round) removable box magazine

WEIGHTS:

WEAPON (EMPTY)	0.848 kg (0.789 kg)
WEAPON (LOADED)	1.030 kg (1.014 kg)
MAGAZINE (EMPTY)	0.074 kg
MAGAZINE (LOADED)	0.182 kg (0.225 kg)
SERVICE CARTRIDGE	12 g (21.5 g)
BULLET	8 g (15 g)

LENGTHS:

WEAPON OVERALL	19.2 cm
BARREL	10.2 cm
SIGHT RADIUS	14.7 cm
STATUS	In production
SERVICE	West German police forces, wide commercial sales
COST	$1,300.00

This is the pistol branch of the Heckler and Koch weapons family. Using the roller-locked system of the HK weapons, the P9S is available in two calibers, 9x19 or 11.43x23mm. The relatively small magazine capacity in 9mm puts the P9S at a disadvantage to other modern 9mm's, but the fact that it is available in 11.43mm makes it one of the few modern pistols in that caliber. The P9S is hammer fired with the hammer being enclosed by the rear of the weapon. The lever just behind the trigger can be used to lower the hammer on a chambered round or to cock the hammer for a single action first shot. Though an excellent modern design, the placement of the magazine latch at the bottom rear of the grip greatly slows reloading and the location of the cocking/decocking lever prevents the magazine catch from being placed behind the trigger.

WEAPON	P9S
AMMO	9x19
DISPERSION ANGLE	.162009 degrees, 2.88016 NATO mils.

Range	Group Circle Width (mm)	Probability (0<p<.099) (m)			
		Body	Head	Hand	Bullseye
5.0	14.138	0.990	0.990	0.990	0.990
10.0	28.276	0.990	0.990	0.990	0.898
15.0	42.414	0.990	0.990	0.989	0.781
20.0	56.552	0.990	0.990	0.966	0.680
25.0	70.690	0.990	0.990	0.932	0.598
50.0	141.379	0.990	0.932	0.740	0.366
75.0	212.069	0.972	0.834	0.593	0.262

☞ continued

Range	Group Circle Width (mm)	Probability (0<p<.099) (m)			
		Body	Head	Hand	Bullseye
100.0	282.759	0.932	0.740	0.490	0.204
125.0	353.448	0.884	0.660	0.417	0.167
150.0	424.138	0.834	0.593	0.362	0.141

DAMAGE 24/.15 (9x19), 23/.26 (11.43x23)

▼ VP70M · VP70Z

VP70M

CARTRIDGE	9x19mm
OPERATION	Recoil
TYPE OF FIRE	Selective w/three shot burst (Semiautomatic)
RATE OF FIRE (SS)	40 rpm (A) 100 rpm (CYCLIC) 2200 rpm
MUZZLE VELOCITY	360 m/s (1180 fps)
MUZZLE ENERGY	520 J (376 ft/lbs)
SIGHTS	Fixed, non-adjustable iron
FEED	18 round removable box magazine

WEIGHTS:

WEAPON (EMPTY)	0.816 kg (Stock 0.458 kg)
WEAPON (LOADED)	1.131 kg (1.589 kg w/stock attached)
MAGAZINE (EMPTY)	0.099 kg
MAGAZINE (LOADED)	0.315 kg
SERVICE CARTRIDGE	12 g
BULLET	8 g

LENGTHS:

WEAPON OVERALL	20.3 cm (54.4 cm w/stock attached)
BARREL	11.6 cm
SIGHT RADIUS	17.5 cm
STATUS	Out of production
SERVICE	Commercial sales

This very large 9mm pistol is a double action-only attempt to make a controllable machine pistol. With the buttstock attached, the VP70M is capable of firing a controlled 3 round burst at a very high cyclic rate. Without the buttstock, the VP70M acts as a normal autoloading pistol. The VP70Z is made for more general civilian sales and is unable to take the buttstock/selector switch combination. The large size of the VP70 allows it to take an 18 round magazine,

☞ continued on next page

☞ *VP70M • VP70Z continued*

making it a considerable handful of firepower. The trigger mechanism only allows for double action firing with the trigger needing a full pull along its length of travel to cock and fire the weapon, except for the burst at full automatic. This length of trigger pull prevents the VP70 from needing any other mechanical safety because the weapon is not held in a cocked position. Another point of the VP70 design is that it was the first commercially produced pistol to have the frame made completely of plastic casting manufacture which lightens the weapon considerably.

ASSESSMENT	3rd Burst 12.25in @ 10 yd
WEAPON	VP-70
AMMO	9x19mm NATO Ball
DISPERSION ANGLE	1.99237 degrees, 35.4199 NATO mils.

Range	Group Circle Width (mm)	Probability (0<p<.099) (m)			
		Body	Head	Hand	Bullseye
5.0	173.885	0.988	0.888	0.666	0.310
10.0	347.769	0.888	0.666	0.422	0.169
15.0	521.654	0.768	0.518	0.306	0.116
20.0	695.538	0.666	0.422	0.240	0.089
25.0	869.423	0.584	0.355	0.197	0.072
50.0	1738.845	0.355	0.197	0.104	0.036
75.0	2608.268	0.253	0.136	0.070	0.024
100.0	3477.690	0.197	0.104	0.053	0.018
125.0	4347.113	0.161	0.084	0.043	0.015
150.0	5216.535	0.136	0.070	0.036	0.012

DAMAGE 25/.15

▼ Heckler & Koch P7M8

CARTRIDGE	9x19mm
OPERATION	Gas-retarded blowback
TYPE OF FIRE	Semiautomatic, auto-cocking
RATE OF FIRE (SS)	24 rpm
MUZZLE VELOCITY	351 m/s (1152 fps)
MUZZLE ENERGY	491 J (362 ft/lb)
SIGHTS	Fixed, non-adjustable iron
FEED	8 round removable box magazine
WEIGHTS:	
WEAPON (EMPTY)	0.794 kg
WEAPON (LOADED)	0.959 kg
MAGAZINE (EMPTY)	0.069 kg
MAGAZINE (LOADED)	0.165 kg
SERVICE CARTRIDGE	12 g
BULLET	8 g
LENGTHS:	
WEAPON OVERALL	17.1 cm
BARREL	10.5 cm
SIGHT RADIUS	14.8 cm
STATUS	In production
SERVICE	West German police and border guards, U.S. police agencies and wide commercial sales
COST	$900.00

This weapon has several design features unique to it alone and center around its cocking system. The front strap of the grip is pulled in by the fingers of the firing hand, cocking the striker and releasing the locked firing pin. Pulling the trigger operates the weapon normally as long as the cocking lever is held in. By releasing the lever, the firing pin is locked and decocked and the weapon cannot accidentally fire. When the last round is fired, the slide locks back and is released by squeezing the cocking lever a second time. The locking system of the P7 series is also unique to the design. The system consists of a pressure cylinder below the chamber that fills with gasses from the fired shell. A tight fitting piston at the front of the cylinder prevents the slide from moving until pressure in the system lowers to safe levels. This locking system automatically adjusts to the type of round being fired, resulting in an extremely reliable design.

WEAPON P7M8

AMMO 9x19
DISPERSION ANGLE .162009 degrees, 2.88016 NATO mils.

Range	Group Circle Width (mm)	Probability (0<p<.099) (m)			
		Body	Head	Hand	Bullseye
5.0	14.138	0.990	0.990	0.990	0.990
10.0	28.276	0.990	0.990	0.990	0.898
15.0	42.414	0.990	0.990	0.989	0.781
20.0	56.552	0.990	0.990	0.966	0.680
25.0	70.690	0.990	0.990	0.932	0.598
50.0	141.379	0.990	0.932	0.740	0.366
75.0	212.069	0.972	0.834	0.593	0.262
100.0	282.759	0.932	0.740	0.490	0.204
125.0	353.448	0.884	0.660	0.417	0.167
150.0	424.138	0.834	0.593	0.362	0.141

DAMAGE 24/.15

▼ Heckler & Koch P7PT8

Heckler & Koch P7PT8 showing the (blue) identifying circle at the muzzle

CARTRIDGE 9x19mmPT
OPERATION Blowback w/gas assist
TYPE OF FIRE Semiautomatic, auto-cocking
RATE OF FIRE (SS) 24 rpm
MUZZLE VELOCITY 400 m/s (1312 fps)
MUZZLE ENERGY 34 J (25 ft/lb)
SIGHTS Fixed, non-adjustable iron
FEED 8 round removable box magazine
WEIGHTS:
WEAPON (EMPTY) 0.720 kg
WEAPON (LOADED) 0.818 kg
MAGAZINE (EMPTY) 0.069 kg
MAGAZINE (LOADED) 0.098 kg
SERVICE CARTRIDGE 3.6 g
BULLET 0.42 g
LENGTHS:
WEAPON OVERALL 17 cm
BARREL 10.5 cm
SIGHT RADIUS 14.8 cm

STATUS In production
SERVICE Commercial sales
COST $900.00

This is the same weapon as the standard P7M8 but it has been modified to use the plastic bulleted training ammunition. In order to function with the low power ammunition, the P7M8PT does not have the gas locking system of the P7 family but uses a floating chamber which acts as a gas assist for operation. Firing full power 9x19mm ammunition would destroy the weapon and would probably result in injury to the firer. The light plastic bullet results in a very short, 8 meter lethal range with a maximum range of only 125 meters. This limited range allows the P7M8PT to be used where there are limited range facilities or in a situation where overpenetration is an extreme danger, such as in an aircraft.

ASSESSMENT 10 cm group at 8 meters
WEAPON P7M8PT
AMMO 9x19mm Plastic ball
DISPERSION ANGLE .716189 degrees, 12.7322 NATO mils.

Range	Group Circle Width (mm)	Probability (0<p<.099) (m)			
		Body	Head	Hand	Bullseye
2.0	25.000	0.990	0.990	0.990	0.924
4.0	50.000	0.990	0.990	0.978	0.725
6.0	75.000	0.990	0.990	0.921	0.577
8.0*	100.000	0.990	0.978	0.851	0.475
10.0	125.000	0.990	0.953	0.782	0.403
12.0	150.000	0.990	0.921	0.719	0.349
14.0	175.000	0.987	0.887	0.663	0.308
16.0	200.000	0.978	0.851	0.614	0.276
18.0	225.000	0.966	0.816	0.571	0.249
20.0	250.000	0.953	0.782	0.533	0.227

* indicates range for which data was supplied
DAMAGE 2/.10

▼ Heckler & Koch P7M13

☞ continued on next page

☛ *Heckler & Koch P7M13 continued*

CARTRIDGE	9x19mm
OPERATION	Gas retarded blowback
TYPE OF FIRE	Semiautomatic, auto-cocking
RATE OF FIRE (SS)	39 rpm
MUZZLE VELOCITY	351 m/s (1152 fps)
MUZZLE ENERGY	491 J (362 ft/lb)
SIGHTS	Fixed, non-adjustable iron
FEED	13 round removable box magazine
WEIGHTS:	
WEAPON (EMPTY)	0.850 kg
WEAPON (LOADED)	1.131 kg
MAGAZINE (EMPTY)	.125 kg
MAGAZINE (LOADED)	0.281 kg
SERVICE CARTRIDGE	12 g
BULLET	8 g
LENGTHS:	
WEAPON OVERALL	17.5 cm
BARREL	10.5 cm
SIGHT RADIUS	14.8 cm
STATUS	In production
SERVICE	Commercial sales
COST	$1,100.00

This is an enlarged magazine capacity version of the P7 weapon family and it works in much the same way as the P7M8. There is an insulating block in the forward upper section of the trigger guard to protect the firing finger from the heat of the gas locking cylinder.

WEAPON	P7M13
AMMO	9x19
DISPERSION ANGLE	.162009 degrees, 2.88016 NATO mils.

Range	Group Circle Width (mm)	Probability (0<p<.099) (m)			
		Body	**Head**	**Hand**	**Bullseye**
5.0	14.138	0.990	0.990	0.990	0.990
10.0	28.276	0.990	0.990	0.990	0.898
15.0	42.414	0.990	0.990	0.989	0.781
20.0	56.552	0.990	0.990	0.966	0.680
25.0	70.690	0.990	0.990	0.932	0.598
50.0	141.379	0.990	0.932	0.740	0.366
75.0	212.069	0.972	0.834	0.593	0.262
100.0	282.759	0.932	0.740	0.490	0.204
125.0	353.448	0.884	0.660	0.417	0.167
150.0	424.138	0.834	0.593	0.362	0.141

DAMAGE 24/.15

▼ Heckler & Koch P7K3

CARTRIDGE	(A) 9x17mm, (B) 7.65x17mmSR (C) 5.7x17mmR
OPERATION	Blowback
TYPE OF FIRE	Semiautomatic, auto-cocking
RATE OF FIRE (SS)	24 rpm
MUZZLE VELOCITY	(A) 291 m/s (955 fps), (B) 292 m/s (960 fps), (C) 283 m/s (927 fps)
MUZZLE ENERGY	(A) 263 J (195 ft/lb), (B) 205 J (151 ft/lb), (C) 103 J (76 ft/lb)
SIGHTS	Fixed, non-adjustable iron
FEED	8 round removable box magazine
WEIGHTS:	
WEAPON (EMPTY)	(A) 0.748 kg, (B) 0.757 kg, (C) 0.771 kg
WEAPON (LOADED)	(A) 0.850, (B) 0.847 kg, (C) 0.852 kg
MAGAZINE (EMPTY)	(A, B) 0.052 kg, (C) 0.060 kg
MAGAZINE (LOADED)	(A) 0.102 kg, (B) 0.090 kg, (C) 0.081 kg
SERVICE CARTRIDGE	(A) 9.7 g, (B) 7.9 g, (C) 3.5 g
BULLET	(A) 6.2 g, (B) 4.8 g, (C) 2.6 g
LENGTHS:	
WEAPON OVERALL	16 cm
BARREL	9.7 cm
SIGHT RADIUS	13.9 cm
STATUS	In production
SERVICE	Commercial sales
COST	$600

This is the most recent model in the P7 series and seems to be intended more for the civilian than for the military markets. The 9x17mm version is of interest to those countries which still use that rather light round for their high ranking military officers and police organizations. The K3 weapons do not have the gas reloading system of the other P7 weapons and are safely able to operate with low power ammunition. The K3 operates in the same manner as the other P7s and is comparably safe and easy to operate.

WEAPON P7K3
DISPERSION ANGLE .190986 degrees, 3.39531 NATO mils.

Range	Group Circle Width (mm)	Probability (0<p<.099) (m)			
		Body	**Head**	**Hand**	**Bullseye**
5.0	16.667	0.990	0.990	0.990	0.979
10.0	33.333	0.990	0.990	0.990	0.856
15.0	50.000	0.990	0.990	0.978	0.725
20.0	66.667	0.990	0.990	0.943	0.620
25.0	83.333	0.990	0.990	0.898	0.539
50.0	166.667	0.990	0.898	0.681	0.321
75.0	250.000	0.953	0.782	0.533	0.227
100.0	333.333	0.898	0.681	0.435	0.176
125.0	416.667	0.839	0.599	0.367	0.143
150.0	500.000	0.782	0.533	0.317	0.121

DAMAGE (A) 20/.10, (B) 18/.07, (C) 8/.04

▼ UZI Pistol

CARTRIDGE 9x19mm
OPERATION Blowback
TYPE OF FIRE Semiautomatic
RATE OF FIRE (SS) 40 rpm
MUZZLE VELOCITY 350 m/s (1148 fps)
MUZZLE ENERGY (337 ft/lbs)
SIGHTS Adjustable, open iron
FEED 20, 25, or 32 round removable box magazines
WEIGHTS:
WEAPON (EMPTY) 1.890 kg
WEAPON (LOADED) 2.290 kg w/20 rds
MAGAZINE (EMPTY) 0.160 kg (20 rd), 0.200 kg (25 rd), 0.220 kg (32 rd)
MAGAZINE (LOADED) 0.400 kg (20 rd), 0.500 kg (25 rd), 0.604 kg (32 rd)
SERVICE CARTRIDGE 12 g
BULLET 8 g
LENGTHS:
WEAPON OVERALL 24 cm

BARREL 11.5 cm
SIGHT RADIUS 17.5 cm
STATUS In production
SERVICE Commercial sales
COST $600.00

This is a pistol version of the UZI submachinegun and as such, is not capable of full automatic fire. All controls and general operation remain the same for the pistol as they are for the submachinegun and all weapons use the same magazines. Described by some people as having the best aspects of a pistol and an electric drill, the UZI pistol is quite a handful and the firer must get accustomed to its unusual balance. The availability of large capacity magazines makes the UZI useful where its small size and maneuverability would be an asset.

ASSESSMENT 4 in @ 25 yd
WEAPON UZI Pistol
AMMO 9x19mm NATO Ball
DISPERSION ANGLE .25565 degrees, 4.54489 NATO mils.

Range	Group Circle Width (mm)	Probability (0<p<.099) (m)			
		Body	**Head**	**Hand**	**Bullseye**
5.0	22.310	0.990	0.990	0.990	0.944
10.0	44.619	0.990	0.990	0.986	0.764
15.0	66.929	0.990	0.990	0.942	0.619
20.0	89.239	0.990	0.986	0.882	0.515
25.0	111.549	0.990	0.967	0.819	0.439
50.0	223.097	0.967	0.819	0.574	0.251
75.0	334.646	0.897	0.680	0.434	0.175
100.0	446.194	0.819	0.574	0.347	0.135
125.0	557.743	0.745	0.495	0.289	0.109
150.0	669.291	0.680	0.434	0.248	0.092

DAMAGE 24/.15

▼ Desert Eagle

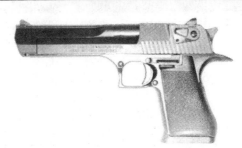

CARTRIDGE 9x33mmR (10.92x33mmR)
OPERATION Gas
TYPE OF FIRE Semiautomatic
RATE OF FIRE (SS) 27 rpm (24 rpm)

☞ continued on next page

☞ *Desert Eagle continued*

MUZZLE VELOCITY	376 m/s (1235 fps), (443 m/s <1455fps>)
MUZZLE ENERGY	725 J (535 ft/lb), (1530 J <1128 ft/lb>)
SIGHTS	Fixed, non-adjustable iron
FEED	9 round (8 round) removable box magazine
WEIGHTS:	
WEAPON (EMPTY)	1.653 kg (1.780 kg)
WEAPON (LOADED)	1.913 kg (2.091 kg)
MAGAZINE (EMPTY)	0.116 kg
MAGAZINE (LOADED)	0.260 kg (0.311 kg)
SERVICE CARTRIDGE	16 g (24.4 g)
BULLET	10.3 g (15.6 g)
LENGTHS:	
WEAPON OVERALL	26.9 cm
BARREL	15.2 cm
SIGHT RADIUS	21.6 cm
STATUS	In production
SERVICE	Commercial sales
COST	$600.00 ($700.00)

In its 10.92mm (.44 magnum) version, this is the most powerful autoloading pistol easily available, but with the 10 round capacity of the 9x33mmR version, it is still in a class by itself. A very large weapon, the Eagle is uncontrollable unless the firer has large hands. To convert the 9mm to the 10.92mm version requires only the replacement of the barrel, magazine, and bolt with ones of the desired caliber. The gas system of the Eagle limits the type of bullets that can be fired and requires a high minimum velocity for dependable operation. The weapon requires strong hands to operate the controls with the slide stop needing the use of both thumbs to release a locked back slide.

WEAPON	Desert Eagle
DISPERSION ANGLE	.146203 degrees, 2.59917 NATO mils.

Range	Group Circle Width (mm)	Probability (0<p<.099) (m)			
		Body	**Head**	**Hand**	**Bullseye**
5.0	12.759	0.990	0.990	0.990	0.990
10.0	25.517	0.990	0.990	0.990	0.920
15.0	38.276	0.990	0.990	0.990	0.815
20.0	51.034	0.990	0.990	0.976	0.717
25.0	63.793	0.990	0.990	0.950	0.636
50.0	127.586	0.990	0.950	0.775	0.397
75.0	191.379	0.981	0.863	0.630	0.286
100.0	255.172	0.950	0.775	0.526	0.223
125.0	318.966	0.908	0.697	0.450	0.183
150.0	382.759	0.863	0.630	0.392	0.155

DAMAGE 20/.53 (9x33 SWC),

28/1.15 (10.92x33 SWC)

Beretta M84

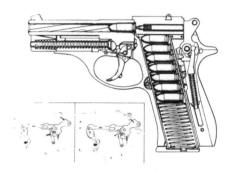

Beretta M84 cross section

CARTRIDGE	7.65x17mmSR (9x17mm)
OPERATION	Blowback
TYPE OF FIRE	Semiautomatic, Double-action
RATE OF FIRE (SS)	36 rpm (39 rpm)
MUZZLE VELOCITY	300 m/s (984 fps) (280 m/s <918 fps>)
MUZZLE ENERGY	213 J (157 ft/lb), (241 J <178 ft/lb>)
SIGHTS	Fixed, non-adjustable iron
FEED	12 round (13 round) removable box magazine
WEIGHTS:	
WEAPON (EMPTY)	0.616 kg (0.606 kg)
WEAPON (LOADED)	0.765 kg (0.786 kg)
MAGAZINE (EMPTY)	0.054 kg
MAGAZINE (LOADED)	0.149 kg (0.180 kg)
SERVICE CARTRIDGE	7.9 g (9.7 g)
BULLET	4.8 g (6.2 g)
LENGTHS:	
WEAPON OVERALL	17.2 cm
BARREL	9.7 cm
SIGHT RADIUS	12.4 cm
STATUS	Out of production
SERVICE	Commercial sales
COST	$500.00

These two models of the Beretta are almost exactly the same except for caliber. The large magazine capacity makes these Berettas the most capable of their class of weapon, while still retaining a small size for concealability.

ASSESSMENT M84, 2.15 in @ 7 yd
WEAPON Beretta M84
AMMO 9x17mm
DISPERSION ANGLE .492383 degrees, 8.75348 NATO mils.

Range	Group Circle Width (mm)	Probability (0<p<.099) (m)			
		Body	Head	Hand	Bullseye
5.0	42.969	0.990	0.990	0.988	0.777
10.0	85.938	0.990	0.988	0.891	0.528
15.0	128.906	0.990	0.948	0.772	0.394
20.0	171.875	0.988	0.891	0.670	0.313
25.0	214.844	0.971	0.830	0.588	0.259
50.0	429.688	0.830	0.588	0.358	0.139
75.0	644.531	0.693	0.446	0.256	0.095
100.0	859.375	0.588	0.358	0.199	0.072
125.0	1074.219	0.508	0.299	0.163	0.058
150.0	1289.063	0.446	0.256	0.137	0.049

DAMAGE 18/.07 (7.65x17), 19/.09 (9x17)

▼ Beretta M1951

CARTRIDGE 9x19mm
OPERATION Short recoil
TYPE OF FIRE Semiautomatic
RATE OF FIRE (SS) 32 rpm
MUZZLE VELOCITY 350 m/s (1148 fps)
MUZZLE ENERGY 488 J (360 ft/lb)
SIGHTS Fixed, non-adjustable iron
FEED 8 round removable box magazine
WEIGHTS:
WEAPON (EMPTY) 0.813 kg
WEAPON (LOADED) 0.966 kg
MAGAZINE (EMPTY) 0.057 kg
MAGAZINE (LOADED) 0.153 kg
SERVICE CARTRIDGE 12 g
BULLET 8 g
LENGTHS:
WEAPON OVERALL 20.3 cm
BARREL 11.4 cm
SIGHT RADIUS 14 cm
STATUS Out of production
SERVICE Italian, Egyptian, and Israeli military, Nigerian police and commercial sales

This is the first of the modern postwar Berettas produced in Italy. The 9x19mm chambering put the M1951 in competition with other 9mm's of its time, with the streamlined design and excellent shooting qualities giving it an edge in several markets. Though out of the commercial market at present, the M1951 was the direct ancestor

of the present Beretta Model 92 series and is still showing good service with several armies.

ASSESSMENT 3.25 in @ 25 yd
WEAPON Beretta M1951
AMMO 9x19mm NATO Ball
DISPERSION ANGLE .208029 degrees, 3.6983 NATO mils.

Range	Group Circle Width (mm)	Probability (0<p<.099) (m)			
		Body	Head	Hand	Bullseye
5.0	18.154	0.990	0.990	0.990	0.971
10.0	36.308	0.990	0.990	0.990	0.831
15.0	54.462	0.990	0.990	0.970	0.694
20.0	72.616	0.990	0.990	0.927	0.589
25.0	90.770	0.990	0.985	0.877	0.509
50.0	181.540	0.985	0.877	0.650	0.299
75.0	272.310	0.939	0.753	0.503	0.211
100.0	363.080	0.877	0.650	0.408	0.163
125.0	453.850	0.813	0.568	0.343	0.132
150.0	544.619	0.753	0.503	0.295	0.112

DAMAGE 24/.15

▼ Beretta M92SB • M92SB-C

CARTRIDGE 9x19mm
OPERATION Short recoil
TYPE OF FIRE Semiautomatic, Double-action
RATE OF FIRE (SS) 45 rpm (39 rpm)
MUZZLE VELOCITY 390 m/s (1280 fps)
MUZZLE ENERGY 606 J (447 ft/lb)
SIGHTS Fixed, non-adjustable iron
FEED 15 or 20 round (13 round) removable box magazine
WEIGHTS:
WEAPON (EMPTY) 0.872 kg (0.780 kg)
WEAPON (LOADED) 1.158 kg w/15 rds (1.035 kg w/13 rds)
MAGAZINE (EMPTY) 0.106 kg (15 rd), 0.156 kg (20 rd), (0.099 kg <13 rd>)
MAGAZINE (LOADED) 0.286 kg (15 rd), 0.396 kg (20 rd), (0.255 kg <13 rd>)

☞ continued on next page

☛ *Beretta M92SB • M92SB-C continued*

SERVICE CARTRIDGE	12 g
BULLET	8 g
LENGTHS:	
WEAPON OVERALL	21.7 cm (19.7 cm)
BARREL	12.5 cm (10.9 cm)
SIGHT RADIUS	15.5 cm (14.6 cm)
STATUS	In production
SERVICE	Italian military and commercial sales
COST	$650.00

This is a modified version of the Beretta M92 and was submitted to the U.S. trials for a new service pistol. The principal changes are the additions of a safety catch on the slide (both sides), which locks the firing pin and the movement of the magazine catch to just behind the trigger guard. With these modifications, the M92SB is seeing excellent commercial sales and wide usage. The M92SB-C is a shortened version of the standard pistol with the overall length and grip length reduced considerably. The reduced grip length results in the 92SB-C having a smaller magazine capacity than the standard 92SB but the compact model can take the larger magazines when necessary.

ASSESSMENT	124 grain flatnose 1 inch @ 15 yds (same rd, 2.9 in. @ 50 ft)
WEAPON	Beretta M92SB-C
AMMO	9x19mm NATO Ball
DISPERSION ANGLE	.135344 degrees, 2.40612 NATO mils.

Range	Group Circle Width (mm)	Probability (0<p<.099) (m)			
		Body	**Head**	**Hand**	**Bullseye**
5.0	11.811	0.990	0.990	0.990	0.990
10.0	23.622	0.990	0.990	0.990	0.935
15.0	35.433	0.990	0.990	0.990	0.838
20.0	47.244	0.990	0.990	0.982	0.745
25.0	59.055	0.990	0.990	0.960	0.665
50.0	118.110	0.990	0.960	0.801	0.421
75.0	177.165	0.986	0.884	0.659	0.305
100.0	236.220	0.960	0.801	0.554	0.239
125.0	295.276	0.924	0.725	0.475	0.196
150.0	354.331	0.884	0.659	0.416	0.166

DAMAGE 27/.17

▼ Beretta Model 92F • Model 92F-C

WEIGHTS:	
WEAPON (EMPTY)	0.859 kg (0.801 kg)
WEAPON (LOADED)	1.145 kg (1.056 kg)
MAGAZINE (EMPTY)	0.106 kg (15 rd), (0.099 kg <13 rd>)
MAGAZINE (LOADED)	0.286 kg (15 rd), (0.255 kg <13 rd>)

SERVICE CARTRIDGE	12 g
BULLET	8 g
STATUS	In production
SERVICE	U.S. Military, wide commercial sales
COST	$700.00

This is the final version of the 92 series which was adopted by the U.S. government as the M-9 service pistol. The magazine base of the 92F is reinforced over earlier versions with the slide safety also automatically lowering a cocked hammer when put on safe. The front of the trigger guard is squared and serrated to assist in a firm two-handed grip. The entire weapon, except the grips, is covered with a teflon derivative coating for protection and lubrication. The C version is a more compact variation of the 92F and follows the same outline as the M92 SB-C version.

ASSESSMENT	2 in @ 25 yd
WEAPON	Beretta M92-F
AMMO	9x19mm NATO Ball
DISPERSION ANGLE	.127825 degrees, 2.27245 NATO mils.

Range	Group Circle Width (mm)	Probability (0<p<.099) (m)			
		Body	**Head**	**Hand**	**Bullseye**
5.0	11.155	0.990	0.990	0.990	0.990
10.0	22.310	0.990	0.990	0.990	0.944
15.0	33.465	0.990	0.990	0.990	0.854
20.0	44.619	0.990	0.990	0.986	0.764
25.0	55.774	0.990	0.990	0.967	0.685
50.0	111.549	0.990	0.967	0.819	0.439
75.0	167.323	0.989	0.897	0.680	0.320
100.0	223.097	0.967	0.819	0.574	0.251
125.0	278.871	0.935	0.745	0.495	0.206
150.0	334.646	0.897	0.680	0.434	0.175

DAMAGE 27/.17

▼ Beretta Line Thrower

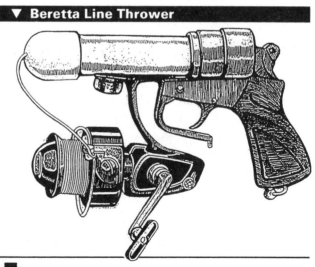

CARTRIDGE	7.65x15mmR
OPERATION	Manual
TYPE OF FIRE	Single shot
RANGE	50 m
SIGHTS	None
FEED	Single round
WEIGHTS:	
WEAPON (EMPTY)	0.590 kg (Pistol w/o line thrower reel, line, or weight
WEAPON (LOADED)	0.920 kg
LENGTHS:	
WEAPON OVERALL	21.3 cm
BARREL	14.5 cm
STATUS	In production
SERVICE	Commercial sales

This pistol is a slightly modified 1 inch (25 mm) flare projector and is intended to launch a soft nylon weight with a line attached. The weight is connected to a standard fishing reel held under the barrel, the reel containing 70 meters of 0.45 mm fishing line with a breaking strength of 33 kilograms. The nylon weight is projected by a blank cartridge that is loaded into the breech with the aid of a chamber adaptor. The reel can be used to draw back the weight after launch or a heavier rope can be drawn to the target by the line attached to the weight.

WEAPON	Beretta Line Thrower
DISPERSION ANGLE	1.90968 degrees, 33.95 NATO mils.

Range	Group Circle Width (mm)	Probability (0<p<.099) (m)			
		Body	Head	Hand	Bullseye
10.0	333.333	0.898	0.681	0.435	0.176
20.0	666.667	0.681	0.435	0.249	0.092
30.0*	1000.000	0.533	0.317	0.173	0.062
40.0	1333.333	0.435	0.249	0.133	0.047
50.0	1666.667	0.367	0.204	0.108	0.038

* indicates range for which data was supplied

▼ SIG P220

CARTRIDGE	(A) 9x19mm, (B) 11.43x23mm, (C) 7.65x19mm, (D) 9x33mmSR
OPERATION	Short recoil
TYPE OF FIRE	Semiautomatic, Double action
RATE OF FIRE (SS)	40 rpm
MUZZLE VELOCITY	(A) 345 m/s (1131 fps), (B) 245 m/s (803 fps), (C) 365 m/s (1198 fps), (D) 355 m/s (1165 fps)
MUZZLE ENERGY	(A) 544 J (349 ft/lb), (B) 446 J (329 ft/lb), (C) 397 J (293 ft/lb), (D) 527 J (389 ft/lb)

SIGHTS	Fixed, non-adjustable iron
FEED	(A, C, D) 9 round (B) 7 round removable box magazine
WEIGHTS:	
WEAPON (EMPTY)	(A, D) 0.750 kg, (B) 0.730 kg, (C) 0.765 kg
WEAPON (LOADED)	(A) 0.918 kg, (B) 0.951 kg, (C) 0.941 kg, (D) 0.940 kg
MAGAZINE (EMPTY)	(A, C) 0.080 kg, (B, D) 0.070 kg
MAGAZINE (LOADED)	(A) 0.188 kg, (B) 0.221 kg, (C) 0.176 kg, (D) 0.190 kg
SERVICE CARTRIDGE	(A) 12 g, (B) 21.5 g, (C) 10.7 g, (D) 13.3 g
BULLET	(A) 8 g, (B) 15 g, (C) 6 g, (D) 8.4 g
LENGTHS:	
WEAPON OVERALL	19.8 cm
BARREL	11.2 cm
SIGHT RADIUS	16 cm
STATUS	In production
SERVICE	(A) In service with the Swiss military, all models are seeing good commercial sales
COST	$700.00

This is a Swiss design made in West Germany to avoid the strict Swiss export regulations. The weapon is made to the most modern requirements with the extensive use of precision metal stampings keeping the individual cost relatively low. The lever behind the trigger on the left side is used to lower the hammer on a chambered round with the lever immediately above the left grip being the slide release. The wide range of available calibers makes the P220 very competitive in today's market.

ASSESSMENT	2.85 in @ 25 yds (11.23x23mm)
WEAPON	SIG P220
AMMO	11.23x23mm Ball
DISPERSION ANGLE	.180459 degrees, 3.20816 NATO mils.

Range	Group Circle Width (mm)	Probability (0<p<.099) (m)			
		Body	Head	Hand	Bullseye
5.0	15.748	0.990	0.990	0.990	0.983
10.0	31.496	0.990	0.990	0.990	0.871
15.0	47.244	0.990	0.990	0.982	0.745
20.0	62.992	0.990	0.990	0.951	0.641
25.0	78.740	0.990	0.990	0.911	0.559
50.0	157.480	0.990	0.911	0.702	0.336
75.0	236.220	0.960	0.801	0.554	0.239
100.0	314.961	0.911	0.702	0.454	0.185
125.0	393.701	0.856	0.620	0.384	0.151
150.0	472.441	0.801	0.554	0.332	0.128

☞ continued on next page

☞ *SIG P220 continued*

DAMAGE (A) 24/.15 (9x19), (B) 21/.25
(11.43x23), (C) 22/.10 (7.65x19), (D)
24/.16 (9x33SR)

▼ SIG P226

CARTRIDGE	9x19mm
OPERATION	Recoil
TYPE OF FIRE	Semiautomatic, Double-action
RATE OF FIRE (SS)	40 rpm
MUZZLE VELOCITY	345 m/s (1132 fps)
MUZZLE ENERGY	475 J (350 ft/lb)
SIGHTS	Fixed, non-adjustable iron
FEED	15 round removable box magazine
WEIGHTS:	
WEAPON (EMPTY)	0.750 kg
WEAPON (LOADED)	1.025 kg
MAGAZINE (EMPTY)	0.095 kg
MAGAZINE (LOADED)	0.275 kg
SERVICE CARTRIDGE	12 g
BULLET	8 g
LENGTHS:	
WEAPON OVERALL	19.6 cm
BARREL	11.2 cm
SIGHT RADIUS	16 cm
STATUS	In production
SERVICE	Swiss and Federal German police forces, wide commercial sales
COST	$750.00

This is an improved version of the P220 which was developed for the U.S. service trials. The magazine catch has been moved from the bottom of the grip, the normal European location, to the rear of the trigger guard, the preferred American position, where it can be switched from side to side. The magazine capacity has also been increased with most other aspects remaining the same as the earlier P220. The P226 does not have the range of calibers of the P220, being only available in 9x19mm.

ASSESSMENT	1.9 in @ 50 ft 123 grain FMJ @ 1194 fps
WEAPON	SIG P226
AMMO	9x19mm NATO Ball

DISPERSION ANGLE .180459 degrees, 3.20816 NATO mils.

Range	Group Circle Width (mm)	Probability (0<p<.099) (m)			
		Body	**Head**	**Hand**	**Bullseye**
5.0	15.748	0.990	0.990	0.990	0.983
10.0	31.496	0.990	0.990	0.990	0.871
15.0	47.244	0.990	0.990	0.982	0.745
20.0	62.992	0.990	0.990	0.951	0.641
25.0	78.740	0.990	0.990	0.911	0.559
50.0	157.480	0.990	0.911	0.702	0.336
75.0	236.220	0.960	0.801	0.554	0.239
100.0	314.961	0.911	0.702	0.454	0.185
125.0	393.701	0.856	0.620	0.384	0.151
150.0	472.441	0.801	0.554	0.332	0.128

DAMAGE 24/.15

▼ SIG P230

SIG P230: Note the decocking lever just in front of the grip plate and the takedown lever ahead of the trigger

CARTRIDGE	(A) 9x18mm, (B) 9x17mm, (C) 7.65x17mmSR
OPERATION	Blowback
TYPE OF FIRE	Semiautomatic, Double-action
RATE OF FIRE (SS)	40 rpm
MUZZLE VELOCITY	(A) 320 m/s (1050 fps), (B, C) 300 m/s (984 fps)
MUZZLE ENERGY	(A) 335 J (247 ft/lb), (B) 277 J (204 ft/lb), (C) 213 J (157 ft/lb)
SIGHTS	Fixed, non-adjustable iron
FEED	(A, B) 7 round, (C) 8 round removable box magazine
WEIGHTS:	
WEAPON (EMPTY)	(A) 0.690 kg, (B) 0.460 kg, (C) 0.465 kg
WEAPON (LOADED)	(A) 0.801 kg, (B) 0.568 kg, (C) 0.578 kg
MAGAZINE (EMPTY)	(A, B) 0.040 kg, (C) 0.050 kg
MAGAZINE (LOADED)	(A) 0.111 kg, (B) 0.108 kg, (C) 0.113 kg
SERVICE CARTRIDGE	(A) 10.2 g (B) 9.7 g (C) 7.9 g
BULLET	(A) 6.6 g (B) 6.2 g (C) 4.8 g

LENGTHS:

WEAPON OVERALL	16 8 cm
BARREL	9.2 cm
SIGHT RADIUS	12 cm
STATUS	In production
SERVICE	Several Swiss police units and commercial sales
COST	$500.00

This is the pocket pistol member of the SIG weapons family. It is considerably smaller and more streamlined than the P220 or P226. The P230 is operated in the same manner as the P220 and any person who is familiar with one will have little trouble with the other. An unusual chambering for the P230 is the 9x18mm, also known as the 9mm Ultra or 9mm Police. This round is a better loading of the Soviet 9x18mm cartridge which will not operate in the P230.

ASSESSMENT	3.2 in @ 50 ft w/ Geco 9x18mm 90 gr FMJ @ 1044 fps
WEAPON	SIG P230
AMMO	9x18mm Police
DISPERSION ANGLE	.180459 degrees, 3.20816 NATO mils.

Range	Group Circle Width (mm)	Probability (0<p<.099) (m)			
		Body	**Head**	**Hand**	**Bullseye**
5.0	15.748	0.990	0.990	0.990	0.983
10.0	31.496	0.990	0.990	0.990	0.871
15.0	47.244	0.990	0.990	0.982	0.745
20.0	62.992	0.990	0.990	0.951	0.641
25.0	78.740	0.990	0.990	0.911	0.559
50.0	157.480	0.990	0.911	0.702	0.336
75.0	236.220	0.960	0.801	0.554	0.239
100.0	314.961	0.911	0.702	0.454	0.185
125.0	393.701	0.856	0.620	0.384	0.151
150.0	472.441	0.801	0.554	0.332	0.128

DAMAGE (A) 22/.11 (9x18 Police), (B) 21/.10 (9x17), (C) 18/.07 (7.65x17)

▼ PSM

CARTRIDGE	5.45x18mm
OPERATION	Blowback
TYPE OF FIRE	Semiautomatic, Double-action
RATE OF FIRE (SS)	24 rpm
MUZZLE VELOCITY	315 m/s (1033 fps)
MUZZLE ENERGY	129 J (95 ft/lb)
SIGHTS	Fixed, non-adjustable iron
FEED	8 round removable box magazine

WEIGHTS:

WEAPON (EMPTY)	0.415 kg
WEAPON (LOADED)	0.500 kg
MAGAZINE (EMPTY)	0.045 kg
MAGAZINE (LOADED)	0.085 kg
SERVICE CARTRIDGE	5 g
BULLET	2.6 g

LENGTHS:

WEAPON OVERALL	16 cm
BARREL	9.1 cm
SIGHT RADIUS	11.5 cm
STATUS	In production
SERVICE	Soviet civil and military security forces

This is a very new Soviet weapon of which relatively little is known here in the West. The PSM, like the Makarov before it, owes much to the earlier Walther PP design from Germany. The small bullet of the PSM loses a lot of its possible effectiveness due to the low muzzle velocity of the weapon; this is the pistol's greatest drawback. The slim design of the PSM is indicative of the designer's intention for the weapon to be very concealable.

WEAPON	PSM
AMMO	5.45x18
DISPERSION ANGLE	.173863 degrees, 3.0909 NATO mils.

Range	Group Circle Width (mm)	Probability (0<p<.099) (m)			
		Body	**Head**	**Hand**	**Bullseye**
5.0	15.172	0.990	0.990	0.990	0.986
10.0	30.345	0.990	0.990	0.990	0.881
15.0	45.517	0.990	0.990	0.985	0.758
20.0	60.690	0.990	0.990	0.957	0.655
25.0	75.862	0.990	0.990	0.919	0.573
50.0	151.724	0.990	0.919	0.715	0.346
75.0	227.586	0.965	0.813	0.567	0.247
100.0	303.448	0.919	0.715	0.466	0.191
125.0	379.310	0.866	0.634	0.395	0.156
150.0	455.172	0.813	0.567	0.342	0.132

DAMAGE 12/.13

▼ P6

P6 with extension supressor attached to muzzle

P6 stripped (without front supressor extension)

CARTRIDGE	9x18mm
OPERATION	Manual
TYPE OF FIRE	Slide action repeater
RATE OF FIRE (SS)	24 rpm
MUZZLE VELOCITY	290 m/s (951 fps)
MUZZLE ENERGY	274 J (202 ft/lb)
SIGHTS	Fixed, non-adjustable, iron
FEED	eight round removable box magazine
WEIGHTS:	
WEAPON (EMPTY)	0.972 kg (0.156 kg front suppressor only)
WEAPON (LOADED)	1.098 kg
MAGAZINE (EMPTY)	0.045 kg
MAGAZINE (LOADED)	0.126 kg
SERVICE CARTRIDGE	10.2 g
BULLET	6.6 g
LENGTHS:	
WEAPON OVERALL	19.5 cm (29.7 cm w/front suppressor)
BARREL	9.1 cm
SIGHT RADIUS	13 cm
STATUS	In production
SERVICE	Soviet Spetsnaz

This pistol has been specifically designed for suppressed firing and is presently issued in the Soviet forces. Developed around the Makarov pistol, the P6 has an integral suppressor body built around the barrel which has been ported to insure a subsonic bullet. The slide has a manual latch that locks it shut during firing, eliminating most of the mechanical noise. The latch is pressed with the non-firing hand and the slide is drawn back and released for reloading. The sights are raised in the rear so that the sight picture clears the body of the suppressor. The P6 is able to be operated with just the integral suppressor with some amount of sound suppression but it is not very efficient. An additional extension suppressor is issued with the weapon that attaches to the muzzle by a slip ring that fits just inside the muzzle of the integral suppressor and locks in place from a plunger underneath the barrel. The extension suppressor significantly reduces the sound signature, making the P6 an efficiently suppressed weapon. The extension suppressor is carried in a pocket in the holster and several of these weapons obtained from Afghanistan have been picked up without the extension. The entire weapon and suppressor assembly can be maintained by the operator in the field.

WEAPON	P6
AMMO	9x18
DISPERSION ANGLE	.16596 degrees, 2.9504 NATO mils.

Range	Group Circle Width (mm)	Probability (0<p<.099) (m)			
		Body	**Head**	**Hand**	**Bullseye**
5.0	14.483	0.990	0.990	0.990	0.988
10.0	28.966	0.990	0.990	0.990	0.892
15.0	43.448	0.990	0.990	0.988	0.773
20.0	57.931	0.990	0.990	0.963	0.672
25.0	72.414	0.990	0.990	0.928	0.590
50.0	144.828	0.990	0.928	0.732	0.359
75.0	217.241	0.970	0.827	0.584	0.257
100.0	289.655	0.928	0.732	0.482	0.200
125.0	362.069	0.878	0.651	0.409	0.163
150.0	434.483	0.827	0.584	0.355	0.138

DAMAGE 20/.10

▼ M1911A1

M1911A1: Note the base pad extending from bottom of magazine

CARTRIDGE	11.43x23mm
OPERATION	Short recoil
TYPE OF FIRE	Semiautomatic
RATE OF FIRE (SS)	35 rpm
MUZZLE VELOCITY	252 m/s (830 fps)

MUZZLE ENERGY	502 J (370 ft/lb)
SIGHTS	Fixed, non-adjustable iron
FEED	7 round removable box magazine
WEIGHTS:	
WEAPON (EMPTY)	1.049 kg
WEAPON (LOADED)	1.271 kg
MAGAZINE (EMPTY)	0.071 kg
MAGAZINE (LOADED)	0.222 kg
SERVICE CARTRIDGE	21.5 g
BULLET	15 g
LENGTHS:	
WEAPON OVERALL	21.9 cm
BARREL	12.8 cm
SIGHT RADIUS	16.5 cm
STATUS	In production by various makers
SERVICE	U.S. Military service weapon, vast commercial sales and duplication
COST	$400.00

This is the famous ".45" which has been used by the U.S. Government for over 70 years. Though claimed by many to be inaccurate, the military M1911A1 must put all of its rounds into a 7.46 inch circle at 50 yards for it to remain in service. The heavy use received by military-issue weapons can "wear out" a pistol in a relatively short time, but the M1911A1 has proven itself an extremely reliable and accurate weapon in well trained hands. Target tuned or customized versions are often able to put all of their rounds into a circle of 2 inches or less in diameter at 50 yards. The drawback of these target model M1911A1's is that they cannot accept the same amount of dirt and abuse as the military model and will start malfunctioning much sooner than the more tolerant military weapon.

ASSESSMENT	1.5 in @ 15 yd (Colt Mk IV Government), 3 in @ 25 m (Custom M1911A1)
WEAPON	M1911A1
AMMO	11.43x23mm Ball
DISPERSION ANGLE	.236853 degrees, 4.21071 NATO mils.

Range	Group Circle Width (mm)	Probability (0<p<.099) (m)			
		Body	**Head**	**Hand**	**Bullseye**
5.0	20.669	0.990	0.990	0.990	0.956
10.0	41.339	0.990	0.990	0.990	0.790
15.0	62.008	0.990	0.990	0.954	0.647
20.0	82.677	0.990	0.990	0.900	0.542
25.0	103.346	0.990	0.975	0.842	0.464
50.0	206.693	0.975	0.842	0.602	0.268
75.0	310.039	0.914	0.707	0.459	0.188
100.0	413.386	0.842	0.602	0.369	0.144
125.0	516.732	0.771	0.522	0.308	0.117
150.0	620.079	0.707	0.459	0.265	0.099

WEAPON	Colt Mk IV Government (commercial M1911A1)
AMMO	11.43x23mm 230 gr FMJ Ball
DISPERSION ANGLE	.158691 degrees, 2.82117 NATO mils.

Range	Group Circle Width (mm)	Probability (0<p<.099) (m)			
		Body	**Head**	**Hand**	**Bullseye**
5.0	15.200	0.990	0.990	0.990	0.986
10.0	30.400	0.990	0.990	0.990	0.880
15.0	45.600	0.990	0.990	0.985	0.757
20.0	60.800	0.990	0.990	0.956	0.654
25.0*	76.000	0.990	0.990	0.918	0.572
50.0	152.000	0.990	0.918	0.714	0.346
75.0	228.000	0.965	0.812	0.566	0.246
100.0	304.000	0.918	0.714	0.466	0.191
125.0	380.000	0.865	0.633	0.394	0.156
150.0	456.000	0.812	0.566	0.341	0.132

WEAPON	M1911A1 CUSTOM
AMMO	11.43x23mm Ball
DISPERSION ANGLE	.174179 degrees, 3.09652 NATO mils.

Range	Group Circle Width (mm)	Probability (0<p<.099) (m)			
		Body	**Head**	**Hand**	**Bullseye**
5.0	13.848	0.990	0.990	0.990	0.990
10.0	27.697	0.990	0.990	0.990	0.903
15.0	41.545	0.990	0.990	0.990	0.788
20.0	55.394	0.990	0.990	0.968	0.688
25.0	69.242	0.990	0.990	0.936	0.606
50.0	138.484	0.990	0.936	0.747	0.372
75.0	207.726	0.974	0.840	0.600	0.267
100.0	276.968	0.936	0.747	0.497	0.208
125.0	346.210	0.889	0.667	0.423	0.170
150.0	415.452	0.840	0.600	0.368	0.144

* indicates range for which data was supplied
DAMAGE 22/.27

▼ Detonics Combat Master

A field stripped Detonics Combat Master

CARTRIDGE	11.43x23mm
OPERATION	Short recoil
TYPE OF FIRE	Semiautomatic
RATE OF FIRE (SS)	30 rpm
MUZZLE VELOCITY	238 m/s (780 fps)
MUZZLE ENERGY	422 J (311 ft/lb)
SIGHTS	Fixed, non-adjustable iron
FEED	6 or 7 round removable box magazine
WEIGHTS:	
WEAPON (EMPTY)	0.820 kg
WEAPON (LOADED)	1.010 kg w/6 rds
MAGAZINE (EMPTY)	0.061 kg (6 rd), 0.071 kg (7 rd)
MAGAZINE (LOADED)	0.190 kg (6 rd), 0.222 kg (7 rd)
SERVICE CARTRIDGE	21.5 g
BULLET	15 g
LENGTHS:	
WEAPON OVERALL	17.1 cm
BARREL	8.9 cm
SIGHT RADIUS	10.1 cm
STATUS	In production
SERVICE	Commercial sales
COST	$700.00

This is a highly modified, commercially produced variation of the M1911A1 pistol. The Detonics is much smaller than its government issue predecessor but it shares many of the same characteristics. The sharp slope at the back of the slide and the rear sight being moved forward are to facilitate cocking the loaded weapon with a thumb drawn across the rear of the slide. The grip safety of the M1911A1 has been retained, though in a much smaller form. The Detonics uses a 6 round magazine that fits flush with the base of the grip or it may use the 7 round M1911A1 magazine that will fit and feed but protrude from the base of the grip.

ASSESSMENT	3 in @ 15 yd, two hand hold, standing
WEAPON	Detonics Combat Master
AMMO	11.43x23mm Ball
DISPERSION ANGLE	.317381 degrees, 5.64234 NATO mils.

Range	Group Circle Width (mm)	Probability (0<p<.099) (m)			
		Body	**Head**	**Hand**	**Bullseye**
5.0	27.697	0.990	0.990	0.990	0.903
10.0	55.394	0.990	0.990	0.968	0.688
15.0	83.090	0.990	0.990	0.899	0.540
20.0	110.787	0.990	0.968	0.821	0.441
25.0	138.484	0.990	0.936	0.747	0.372
50.0	276.968	0.936	0.747	0.497	0.208
75.0	415.452	0.840	0.600	0.368	0.144
100.0	553.936	0.747	0.497	0.291	0.110
125.0	692.420	0.667	0.423	0.241	0.089
150.0	830.904	0.600	0.368	0.205	0.075

DAMAGE 21/.24

▼ Ruger GS-32N

CARTRIDGE	9x33mmR
OPERATION	Manual
TYPE OF FIRE	Double-action revolver
RATE OF FIRE (SS)	24 rpm
MUZZLE VELOCITY	385 m/s (1262 fps)
MUZZLE ENERGY	758 J (559 ft/lb)
SIGHTS	Fixed, non-adjustable iron
FEED	6 round cylinder
WEIGHTS:	
WEAPON (EMPTY)	0.964 kg
WEAPON (LOADED)	1.060 kg
MAGAZINE (LOADED)	0.096 kg (6 rds)
SERVICE CARTRIDGE	16 g
BULLET	10.3 g
LENGTHS:	
WEAPON OVERALL	19.7 cm
BARREL	7 cm
SIGHT RADIUS	15 cm
STATUS	In production
SERVICE	U.S. military, police, and government agencies, commercial sales

COST $300.00

This is the military version of the Ruger Speed-Six revolver. The GS model is available chambered for either 9x33mmR or 9x19mm. The 9x19mm version has not yet been widely well received and is rarely seen. This is a general duty weapon of very rugged and simple construction.

ASSESSMENT 2.5 in @ 25 yds
WEAPON Ruger GS-32N
AMMO 9x33mmR SWC
DISPERSION ANGLE .160408 degrees, 2.8517 NATO mils.

Range	Group Circle Width (mm)	Probability (0<p<.099) (m)			
		Body	Head	Hand	Bullseye
5.0	13.998	0.990	0.990	0.990	0.990
10.0	27.997	0.990	0.990	0.990	0.900
15.0	41.995	0.990	0.990	0.989	0.785
20.0	55.993	0.990	0.990	0.967	0.684
25.0	69.991	0.990	0.990	0.934	0.602
50.0	139.983	0.990	0.934	0.744	0.369
75.0	209.974	0.973	0.837	0.596	0.264
100.0	279.965	0.934	0.744	0.494	0.206
125.0	349.956	0.887	0.663	0.420	0.168
150.0	419.948	0.837	0.596	0.365	0.142

DAMAGE 20/.55

▼ Smith & Wesson ASP

ASP: Note the translucent grips revealing the loaded magazine

CARTRIDGE 9x19mm
OPERATION Short recoil
TYPE OF FIRE Semiautomatic, Double-action
RATE OF FIRE (SS) 35 rpm
MUZZLE VELOCITY 347 m/s (1138 fps)
MUZZLE ENERGY 480 J (354 ft/lb)
SIGHTS Fixed, non-adjustable "guttersnipe" trough
FEED 7 round removable box magazine

WEIGHTS:
WEAPON (EMPTY) 0.624 kg
WEAPON (LOADED) 0.765 kg
MAGAZINE (EMPTY) 0.057 kg
MAGAZINE (LOADED) 0.141 kg
SERVICE CARTRIDGE 12 g
BULLET 8 g
LENGTHS:
WEAPON OVERALL 17.1 cm
BARREL 8.3 cm
SIGHT RADIUS 5.1 cm
STATUS In production
SERVICE Commercial sales
COST $1,100

The ASP is a highly modified Smith & Wesson M39 series pistol. The operation of the ASP remains unchanged from the M39, but the finished product only bears a slight resemblance to the earlier weapon. The slide of the M39 is shortened and refitted to the frame and barrel to reduce size and weight, and to increase reliability. The barrel has also been shortened and refitted to the weapon so well that it will reliably feed empty brass from the magazine. The frame is also extensively refitted with clear plastic grips installed that show available ammunition at a glance. Magazines are also reworked for the best in functioning. The special "guttersnipe" sight is designed for very fast target acquisition rather than precision sighting. The entire ASP is coated with a Teflon-S finish that protects the weapon from its environment and eliminates the need for lubrication. The final result is a weapon that is very popular among professionals and the intelligence community for whom the ASP was originally designed.

ASSESSMENT 3 in @ 6.4 m Two-hand, standing
WEAPON ASP
AMMO 9x19mm
DISPERSION ANGLE .68038 degrees, 12.0956 NATO mils.

Range	Group Circle Width (mm)	Probability (0<p<.099) (m)			
		Body	Head	Hand	Bullseye
5.0	59.375	0.990	0.990	0.960	0.663
10.0	118.750	0.990	0.960	0.799	0.419
15.0	178.125	0.986	0.882	0.657	0.304
20.0	237.500	0.960	0.799	0.552	0.238
25.0	296.875	0.923	0.723	0.474	0.195
50.0	593.750	0.723	0.474	0.274	0.103
75.0	890.625	0.575	0.348	0.193	0.070
100.0	1187.500	0.474	0.274	0.148	0.053
125.0	1484.375	0.402	0.226	0.120	0.043
150.0	1781.250	0.348	0.193	0.101	0.036

DAMAGE 24/.15

▼ Smith & Wesson Model 645

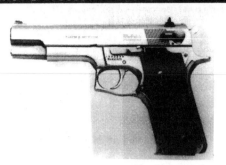

CARTRIDGE	11.43x23mm
OPERATION	Short recoil
TYPE OF FIRE	Semiautomatic, Double-action
RATE OF FIRE (SS)	24 rpm
MUZZLE VELOCITY	259 m/s (850 fps)
MUZZLE ENERGY	500 J (369 ft/lbs)
SIGHTS	Fixed, non-adjustable iron
FEED	8 round removable box magazine
WEIGHTS:	
WEAPON (EMPTY)	0.974 kg
WEAPON (LOADED)	1.238 kg
MAGAZINE (EMPTY)	0.092 kg
MAGAZINE (LOADED)	0.264 kg
SERVICE CARTRIDGE	21.5 kg
BULLET	15 g
LENGTHS:	
WEAPON OVERALL	22.1 cm
BARREL	12.7 cm
SIGHT RADIUS	17 cm
STATUS	In production
SERVICE	Commercial sales
COST	$550.00

This is Smith & Wesson's first offer to the large bore autoloader market and it is being well received by the American public. In many ways an enlarged Model 59, the 645 is made entirely of stainless steel to avoid corrosion and it has the extensive safety system found in other S&W designs. Many of the features found on the 645 such as the beveled magazine well, checkered forestrap and trigger guard, and the fixed barrel bushing, are adopted from the more popular custom weapons found on the market, adding to the weapon's overall appeal.

WEAPON	Model 645
AMMO	11.43x23
DISPERSION ANGLE	.16596 degrees, 2.9504 NATO mils.

Range	Group Circle Width (mm)	Probability (0<p<.099) (m)			
		Body	Head	Hand	Bullseye
5.0	14.483	0.990	0.990	0.990	0.988
10.0	28.966	0.990	0.990	0.990	0.892
15.0	43.448	0.990	0.990	0.988	0.773
20.0	57.931	0.990	0.990	0.963	0.672
25.0	72.414	0.990	0.990	0.928	0.590
50.0	144.828	0.990	0.928	0.732	0.359
75.0	217.241	0.970	0.827	0.584	0.257
100.0	289.655	0.928	0.732	0.482	0.200
125.0	362.069	0.878	0.651	0.409	0.163
150.0	434.483	0.827	0.584	0.355	0.138

DAMAGE 23/.26

▼ Smith & Wesson Model 469

CARTRIDGE	9x19mm
OPERATION	Short recoil
TYPE OF FIRE	Semiautomatic, Double-action
RATE OF FIRE (SS)	36 rpm
MUZZLE VELOCITY	360 m/s (1181 fps)
MUZZLE ENERGY	517 J (381 ft/lb)
SIGHTS	Fixed, non-adjustable iron
FEED	12 or 14 round box magazine
WEIGHTS:	
WEAPON (EMPTY)	0.666 kg
WEAPON (LOADED)	0.881 kg
MAGAZINE (EMPTY)	0.071 kg (12 rd)
MAGAZINE (LOADED)	0.215 kg (12 rd)
SERVICE CARTRIDGE	12 g
BULLET	8 g
LENGTHS:	
WEAPON OVERALL	14.9 cm
BARREL	8.9 cm
SIGHT RADIUS	13 cm
STATUS	In production
SERVICE	Commercial sales

COST $400.00

This is Smith & Wesson's commercial answer to the custom variations of the M39 and M59 series pistols (see ASP). The 469 is a shortened and lightened M59 which was originally developed to meet a U.S. Air Force specification. Very comfortable to hold and easy to conceal, the 469 satisfies a need for undercover pistols of reasonable cost and availability. The lightened hammer has no spur for single action cocking but does have a sharply serrated top that can be grasped with the thumb when the trigger is slightly pulled. The 469 can use the 14 round magazines of the M459 but these magazines will extend from the bottom of the grip. The M469 is also available as a stainless steel weapon called the M669.

ASSESSMENT	2.25 in @ 20 yd
WEAPON	S&W M469
AMMO	9x19mm
DISPERSION ANGLE	.178658 degrees, 3.17613 NATO mils.

Range	Group Circle Width (mm)	Probability (0<p<.099) (m)			
		Body	Head	Hand	Bullseye
5.0	15.591	0.990	0.990	0.990	0.984
10.0	31.182	0.990	0.990	0.990	0.874
15.0	46.772	0.990	0.990	0.983	0.748
20.0	62.363	0.990	0.990	0.953	0.645
25.0	77.954	0.990	0.990	0.913	0.563
50.0	155.908	0.990	0.913	0.705	0.339
75.0	233.862	0.962	0.804	0.557	0.241
100.0	311.816	0.913	0.705	0.457	0.187
125.0	389.770	0.858	0.624	0.387	0.153
150.0	467.724	0.804	0.557	0.335	0.129

DAMAGE 25/.15

▼ Smith & Wesson Model 10

CARTRIDGE	9x29mmR
OPERATION	Manual
TYPE OF FIRE	Double action revolver
RATE OF FIRE (SS)	24 rpm
MUZZLE VELOCITY	(A) 232 m/s (762 fps), (B) 253 m/s (829 fps), (C) 257 m/s (844 fps), (D) 261 m/s (855 fps)
MUZZLE ENERGY	(A) 277 J (204 ft/lb), (B) 327 J (241 ft/lb), (C) 339 J (250 ft/lb), (D) 347 J (256 ft/lb)
SIGHTS	Fixed, non-adjustable iron
FEED	6 round cylinder
WEIGHTS:	
WEAPON (EMPTY)	(A) 0.822 kg, (B) 0.865 kg, (C) 0.887 kg, (D) 0.907 kg
WEAPON (LOADED)	(A) 0.912 kg, (B) 0.955 kg, (C) 0.977 kg, (D) 0.997 kg
MAGAZINE (LOADED)	0.090 kg (6 rds)
SERVICE CARTRIDGE	15 g
BULLET	10.3 g
LENGTHS:	
WEAPON OVERALL	(A) 18.8 cm, (B) 23.5 cm, (C) 26 cm, (D) 28.5 cm
BARREL	(A) 5.1 cm, (B) 10.2 cm, (C) 12.7 cm, (D) 15.2 cm
SIGHT RADIUS	(A) 10 cm, (B) 15.1 cm, (C) 17.6 cm, (D) 20.1 cm
STATUS	In production
SERVICE	Many U.S. police agencies, extensive commercial sales
COST	$300.00

This is the workhorse of the Smith & Wesson revolver line. More Model 10's have been made in various configurations than any other American made revolver. Including copies, the Model 10 in its 10.2cm barrel is probably the most common revolver in the world. It is also the most common 9x29mmR chambered police weapon in North America. Reliable and versatile, the basic K-frame on which the Model 10 is built has had many custom weapons designed around it.

☞ continued on next page

☞ Smith & Wesson Model 10 continued

WEAPON MODEL 10 w/10.2 cm bbl
AMMO 9x29 SWC
DISPERSION ANGLE .173863 degrees, 3.0909 NATO mils.

Range	Group Circle Width (mm)	Probability (0<p<.099) (m)			
		Body	Head	Hand	Bullseye
5.0	15.172	0.990	0.990	0.990	0.986
10.0	30.345	0.990	0.990	0.990	0.881
15.0	45.517	0.990	0.990	0.985	0.758
20.0	60.690	0.990	0.990	0.957	0.655
25.0	75.862	0.990	0.990	0.919	0.573
50.0	151.724	0.990	0.919	0.715	0.346
75.0	227.586	0.965	0.813	0.567	0.247
100.0	303.448	0.919	0.715	0.466	0.191
125.0	379.310	0.866	0.634	0.395	0.156
150.0	455.172	0.813	0.567	0.342	0.132

DAMAGE (A) w/5.1 cm bbl 12/.33, (B) w/10.2 cm bbl 13/.36, (C) w/12.7 cm bbl 14/.37, (D) w/15.2 cm bbl 14/.37

▼ Smith & Wesson Model 19

CARTRIDGE 9x33mmR
OPERATION Manual
TYPE OF FIRE Double-action revolver
RATE OF FIRE (SS) 24 rpm
MUZZLE VELOCITY (A) 331 m/s (1086 fps), (B) 368 m/s (1206 fps), (C) 387 m/s (1270 fps)
MUZZLE ENERGY (A) 579 J (427 ft/lb), (B) 713 J (526 ft/lb), (C) 792 J (584 ft/lb)
SIGHTS Adjustable, open iron

FEED 6 round cylinder
WEIGHTS:
WEAPON (EMPTY) (A) 0.879 kg, (B) 0.992 kg, (C) 1.152 kg
WEAPON (LOADED) (A) 0.975 kg, (B) 1.088 kg, (C) 1.248 kg
MAGAZINE (LOADED) 0.096 kg (6 rds)
SERVICE CARTRIDGE 16 g
BULLET 10.6 g
LENGTHS:
WEAPON OVERALL (A) 19 cm, (B) 24.1 cm, (C) 29.2 cm
BARREL (A) 6.6 cm, (B) 10.2 cm, (C) 15.3 cm
SIGHT RADIUS (A) 11.3 cm, (B) 14.9 cm, (C) 20 cm
STATUS In production
SERVICE Police issue and commercial sales
COST $350.00

Originally developed in 1956 as a more powerful police duty weapon, the Model 19 is made on the proven K-frame but is chambered for the more powerful 9x33mmR round. The Model 19 and its variants are very popular and are the most common type of 9x33mmR revolver to be found in use by U.S. police agencies as well as being found throughout the world's law enforcement community.

ASSESSMENT (C) 125 gr JHP, 2.4 in @ 25 yd
WEAPON S&W M19 w/10.2 cm bbl
AMMO 9x33mmR SWC
DISPERSION ANGLE .152889 degrees, 2.71803 NATO mils.

Range	Group Circle Width (mm)	Probability (0<p<.099) (m)			
		Body	Head	Hand	Bullseye
5.0	13.342	0.990	0.990	0.990	0.990
10.0	26.684	0.990	0.990	0.990	0.911
15.0	40.026	0.990	0.990	0.990	0.800
20.0	53.368	0.990	0.990	0.972	0.701
25.0	66.710	0.990	0.990	0.942	0.620
50.0	133.421	0.990	0.942	0.760	0.383
75.0	200.131	0.978	0.851	0.614	0.276
100.0	266.842	0.942	0.760	0.510	0.215
125.0	333.552	0.898	0.681	0.435	0.176
150.0	400.262	0.851	0.614	0.379	0.149

DAMAGE (A) w/6.6 cm bbl 18/.49, (B) w/10.2 cm bbl 20/.54, (C) w/15.3 cm bbl 21/.57

▼ Smith & Wesson Model 439

CARTRIDGE 9x19mm
OPERATION Short recoil
TYPE OF FIRE Semiautomatic
RATE OF FIRE (SS) 24 rpm
MUZZLE VELOCITY 356 m/s (1169 fps)

MUZZLE ENERGY 506 J (373 ft/lb)
SIGHTS Adjustable, open iron
FEED 8 round removable box magazine
WEIGHTS:
WEAPON (EMPTY) 0.779 kg
WEAPON (LOADED) 0.946 kg
MAGAZINE (EMPTY) 0.071 kg
MAGAZINE (LOADED) 0.167 kg
SERVICE CARTRIDGE 12 g
BULLET 8 g
LENGTHS:
WEAPON OVERALL 19.4 cm
BARREL 10.2 cm
SIGHT RADIUS 14.1 cm
STATUS In production
SERVICE Commercial sales
COST $450.00

The Model 439 is the improved, current production model of the Model 39 autoloader. The new sights, safety system, and extractor have gone far in improving an already worthwhile design. This same weapon, originally designed as a possible U.S. service pistol, is also made in a slightly modified form as the Model 639 which is constructed from stainless steel.

WEAPON Model 439
AMMO 9x19
DISPERSION ANGLE .162009 degrees, 2.88016 NATO mils.

Range	Group Circle Width (mm)	Probability (0<p<.099) (m)			
		Body	**Head**	**Hand**	**Bullseye**
5.0	14.138	0.990	0.990	0.990	0.990
10.0	28.276	0.990	0.990	0.990	0.898
15.0	42.414	0.990	0.990	0.989	0.781
20.0	56.552	0.990	0.990	0.966	0.680
25.0	70.690	0.990	0.990	0.932	0.598
50.0	141.379	0.990	0.932	0.740	0.366
75.0	212.069	0.972	0.834	0.593	0.262
100.0	282.759	0.932	0.740	0.490	0.204
125.0	353.448	0.884	0.660	0.417	0.167
150.0	424.138	0.834	0.593	0.362	0.141

DAMAGE 24/.15

▼ Smith & Wesson Model 459

CARTRIDGE 9x19mm
OPERATION Short recoil
TYPE OF FIRE Semiautomatic, Double-action
RATE OF FIRE (SS) 45 rpm

MUZZLE VELOCITY 355 m/s (1165 fps)
MUZZLE ENERGY 502 J (370 ft/lb)
SIGHTS Adjustable, open iron
FEED 14 round removable box magazine
WEIGHTS:
WEAPON (EMPTY) 0.947 kg
WEAPON (LOADED) 1.021 kg
MAGAZINE (EMPTY) 0.083 kg
MAGAZINE (LOADED) 0.263 kg
SERVICE CARTRIDGE 12 g
BULLET 8 g
LENGTHS:
WEAPON OVERALL 19.4 cm
BARREL 10.2 cm
SIGHT RADIUS 14.1 cm
STATUS In production
SERVICE Commercial sales
COST $500.00

Developed from an earlier experimental U.S. Navy pistol, the M459 is the latest improved version of the Smith & Wesson Model 59 pistol. A rugged, proven design, the M459 is an enlarged version of the earlier Model 39 weapon. A slight drawback of the M459 is the width of the grip which is made necessary by the 14 round magazine. People with small hands who are uncomfortable with the M459 should find the M439 more to their liking. The two weapons are virtually identical except for the magazine capacity. The M459 is also available in a stainless steel version known as the M659.

WEAPON Model 459
AMMO 9x19
DISPERSION ANGLE .162009 degrees, 2.88016 NATO mils.

Range	Group Circle Width (mm)	Probability (0<p<.099) (m)			
		Body	**Head**	**Hand**	**Bullseye**
5.0	14.138	0.990	0.990	0.990	0.990
10.0	28.276	0.990	0.990	0.990	0.898
15.0	42.414	0.990	0.990	0.989	0.781
20.0	56.552	0.990	0.990	0.966	0.680
25.0	70.690	0.990	0.990	0.932	0.598
50.0	141.379	0.990	0.932	0.740	0.366
75.0	212.069	0.972	0.834	0.593	0.262
100.0	282.759	0.932	0.740	0.490	0.204
125.0	353.448	0.884	0.660	0.417	0.167
150.0	424.138	0.834	0.593	0.362	0.141

DAMAGE 24/.15

▼ Smith & Wesson Model 29

Smith & Wesson M29 with 16.5cm barrel

M29 .44 Magnum with 29cm barrel

CARTRIDGE	10.97x33mmR
OPERATION	Manual
TYPE OF FIRE	Double-action revolver
RATE OF FIRE (SS)	24 rpm
MUZZLE VELOCITY	(A) 425 m/s (1395 fps), (B) 448 m/s (1470 fps), (C) 459 m/s (1505 fps), (D) 475 m/s (1560 fps)
MUZZLE ENERGY	(A) 1406 J (1037 ft/lb), (B) 1561 J (1151 ft/lb), (C) 1637 J (1207 ft/lb), (D) 1759 J (1297 ft/lb)
SIGHTS	Adjustable, open iron
FEED	6 round cylinder
WEIGHTS:	
WEAPON (EMPTY)	(A) 1.219 kg, (B) 1.332 kg, (C) 1.460 kg, (D) 1.644 kg
WEAPON (LOADED)	(A) 1.365 kg, (B) 1.478 kg, (C) 1.606 kg, (D)1.790 kg
MAGAZINE (LOADED)	0.146 kg (6 rds)
SERVICE CARTRIDGE	24.4 g
BULLET	15.6 g
LENGTHS:	
WEAPON OVERALL	(A) 23.9 cm, (B) 30.2 cm, (C) 34.9 cm, (D) 41 cm
BARREL	(A) 10.2 cm, (B) 16.5 cm, (C) 21.3 cm, (D) 29 cm
SIGHT RADIUS	(A) 11.7 cm, (B) 18 cm, (C) 22.8 cm, (D) 30.5 cm
STATUS	In production
SERVICE	Commercial sales
COST	$450.00

This is one of the most powerful commercially available revolvers and the first one to be chambered for the 10.97x33mmR round. A very large weapon, the M29 is a difficult weapon to master, especially in the 10.2cm barrel length, because of the muzzle blast and noise. For those who can use the weapon capably, the M29 is effective at controlling almost any situation. When used with the proper ammunition, the M29 is very accurate and has been used by hunters instead of a rifle.

WEAPON Model 29 w/16.5 cm bbl
AMMO 10.97x33 SWC
DISPERSION ANGLE .158057 degrees, 2.80991 NATO mils.

Range	Group Circle Width (mm)	Probability (0<p<.099) (m)			
		Body	**Head**	**Hand**	**Bullseye**
5.0	13.793	0.990	0.990	0.990	0.990
10.0	27.586	0.990	0.990	0.990	0.903
15.0	41.379	0.990	0.990	0.990	0.790
20.0	55.172	0.990	0.990	0.968	0.689
25.0	68.966	0.990	0.990	0.937	0.608
50.0	137.931	0.990	0.937	0.749	0.374
75.0	206.897	0.975	0.841	0.602	0.268
100.0	275.862	0.937	0.749	0.499	0.208
125.0	344.828	0.890	0.669	0.424	0.171
150.0	413.793	0.841	0.602	0.369	0.144

WEAPON Model 29 w/29 cm bbl
AMMO 10.97x33 SWC
DISPERSION ANGLE .122494 degrees, 2.17768 NATO mils.

Range	Group Circle Width (mm)	Probability (0<p<.099) (m)			
		Body	**Head**	**Hand**	**Bullseye**
5.0	10.690	0.990	0.990	0.990	0.990
10.0	21.379	0.990	0.990	0.990	0.951
15.0	32.069	0.990	0.990	0.990	0.866
20.0	42.759	0.990	0.990	0.988	0.779
25.0	53.448	0.990	0.990	0.972	0.701
50.0	106.897	0.990	0.972	0.832	0.453
75.0	160.345	0.990	0.907	0.695	0.331
100.0	213.793	0.972	0.832	0.590	0.260
125.0	267.241	0.942	0.760	0.510	0.214
150.0	320.690	0.907	0.695	0.448	0.182
175.0	374.138	0.870	0.639	0.399	0.158
200.0	427.586	0.832	0.590	0.360	0.140

DAMAGE (A) w/10.2 cm bbl 27/1.10,
(B) w/16.5 cm bbl 29/1.16,
(C) w/21.3 cm bbl 29/1.19,
(D) w/29 cm bbl 31/1.24

▼ MAC Ruger Mark I Standard Suppressed

CARTRIDGE	5.7x17mmR
OPERATION	Blowback
TYPE OF FIRE	Semiautomatic
RATE OF FIRE (SS)	40 rpm
MUZZLE VELOCITY	300 m/s (984 fps)
MUZZLE ENERGY	117 J (86 ft/lb)
SIGHTS	Fixed, non-adjustable iron
FEED	9 round removable box magazine
WEIGHTS:	
WEAPON (EMPTY)	1.153 kg
WEAPON (LOADED)	1.307 kg
MAGAZINE (EMPTY)	0.130 kg
MAGAZINE (LOADED)	0.154 kg
SERVICE CARTRIDGE	3.5 g
BULLET	2.6 g
LENGTHS:	
WEAPON OVERALL	29.5 cm
BARREL	15.7 cm
SIGHT RADIUS	24.7 cm
STATUS	Out of production
SERVICE	U.S. military and intelligence agencies
COST	$500.00

This is representative of a suppressed 5.7mm semiautomatic pistol. The Ruger design is a very popular one with the weapon being found throughout the world because of its good commercial sales. The suppressed version is popular with clandestine operators since the weapon is quiet, accurate, and has readily available ammunition. Intended for close-in quiet work, the 5.7mm chambering is commonly used by professionals who know their business.

WEAPON	MAC Ruger
AMMO	5.7x17 RNL
DISPERSION ANGLE	.134349 degrees, 2.38842 NATO mils.

Range	Group Circle Width (mm)	Probability (0<p<.099) (m)			
		Body	**Head**	**Hand**	**Bullseye**
5.0	11.724	0.990	0.990	0.990	0.990
10.0	23.448	0.990	0.990	0.990	0.936
15.0	35.172	0.990	0.990	0.990	0.840
20.0	46.897	0.990	0.990	0.983	0.747
25.0	58.621	0.990	0.990	0.961	0.667
30.0	70.345	0.990	0.990	0.933	0.600
35.0	82.069	0.990	0.990	0.902	0.544
40.0	93.793	0.990	0.983	0.869	0.497
45.0	105.517	0.990	0.973	0.836	0.457
50.0	117.241	0.990	0.961	0.803	0.423

DAMAGE 8/.04

▼ Mark 22 Model 0 "Hush Puppy"

CARTRIDGE	9x19mm
OPERATION	Short recoil or manual
TYPE OF FIRE	Semiautomatic or single shot repeater
RATE OF FIRE (SS)	24 rpm
MUZZLE VELOCITY	274 m/s (900 fps)
MUZZLE ENERGY	385 J (284 ft/lbs)
SIGHTS	Adjustable, open iron
FEED	8 round removable box magazine
WEIGHTS:	
WEAPON (EMPTY)	0.737 kg, 0.964 kg w/suppressor
WEAPON (LOADED)	0.954 kg, 1.181 kg w/suppressor
MAGAZINE (EMPTY)	0.103 kg
MAGAZINE (LOADED)	0.217 kg
SERVICE CARTRIDGE	14.3 g
BULLET	10.3 g
LENGTHS:	
WEAPON OVERALL	21.6 cm (pistol), 12.7 cm (suppressor), 32.4 cm (pistol w/suppressor mounted)
BARREL	12.7 cm
SIGHT RADIUS	13.4 cm
STATUS	Out of production
SERVICE	U.S. Navy SEAL teams

This is presently the standard issue U.S. Navy suppressed pistol for use by the SEAL teams. Developed from the commercial Smith & Wesson M39 pistol, the Mark 22 Model 0 weapon has a longer barrel which is threaded to accept the Mark 3 Model 0 silencer and a special slide latch for locking the slide shut, eliminating mechanical noise when the weapon is fired. Special plugs and a long holster were made so that the Mark 22 can be carried underwater without damage. Only the front plug need be removed and the slide operated to allow the weapon to be fired. The Mark 3 silencer has a special polycarbonate insert that suppresses the sound of firing. This insert is good for about 30 rounds of the special subsonic Mark 144 ammunition or 6 rounds of standard NATO 9x19mm. The accessory kit Mark 26 Model 0 is issued for the weapon and it contains a new silencer insert with 22 Mark 144 rounds. The name "Hush Puppy" was coined from the weapon's original use, quietly eliminating enemy guard dogs.

WEAPON	Mark 22 Mod 0
AMMO	9x19mm Mark 144

☞ continued on next page

☛ Mark 22 Model 0 "Hush Puppy" continued

DISPERSION ANGLE .185717 degrees, 3.30164 NATO mils.

Range	Group Circle Width (mm)	Probability (0<p<.099) (m)			
		Body	Head	Hand	Bullseye
5.0	16.207	0.990	0.990	0.990	0.981
10.0	32.414	0.990	0.990	0.990	0.863
15.0	48.621	0.990	0.990	0.980	0.735
20.0	64.828	0.990	0.990	0.947	0.630
25.0	81.034	0.990	0.990	0.905	0.549
50.0	162.069	0.990	0.905	0.691	0.328
75.0	243.103	0.956	0.791	0.543	0.233
100.0	324.138	0.905	0.691	0.444	0.180
125.0	405.172	0.848	0.610	0.375	0.147
150.0	486.207	0.791	0.543	0.324	0.124

DAMAGE 19/.15

▼ MAC Stinger

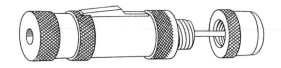

CARTRIDGE	5.7x17mmR
OPERATION	Manual
TYPE OF FIRE	Single shot
MUZZLE VELOCITY	213 m/s (700 fps)
MUZZLE ENERGY	60 J (44 ft/lbs)
SIGHTS	None
FEED	Single round
WEIGHTS:	
WEAPON (EMPTY)	0.057 kg (0.411 kg w/suppressor)
WEAPON (LOADED)	0.061 kg (0.415 kg w/suppressor)
SERVICE CARTRIDGE	3.5 g
BULLET	2.6 g
LENGTHS:	
WEAPON OVERALL	8.9 cm (32 cm w/suppressor)
BARREL	0.6 cm
STATUS	Out of production
SERVICE	U.S. intelligence agencies and clandestine services
COST	$45

This is a very small weapon developed from an earlier OSS design and intended for close-in defense. Relatively few Stingers were made during the Vietnam War and even fewer suppressors were specially designed for the weapon. The very short barrel of the Stinger was unscrewed for loading and it took a single round. The rounded end cap would be extended until it was caught by the sear mechanism to prepare it for firing. Pressure on the sear would fire the Stinger. The lack of sights and extremely short barrel prevent the Stinger from being usable at more than the closest ranges, 1 meter at the most. The relatively large suppressor allowed the Stinger to be used as a close-in assassination weapon.

WEAPON	MAC STINGER
AMMO	5.7x17 RNL
DISPERSION ANGLE	3.43672 degrees, 61.0972 NATO mils.

Range	Group Circle Width (mm)	Probability (0<p<.099) (m)			
		Body	Head	Hand	Bullseye
1.0*	60.000	0.990	0.990	0.958	0.659
2.0	120.000	0.990	0.958	0.796	0.416
3.0	180.000	0.985	0.880	0.653	0.301
4.0	240.000	0.958	0.796	0.548	0.236
5.0	300.000	0.921	0.719	0.470	0.193
6.0	360.000	0.880	0.653	0.411	0.164
7.0	420.000	0.837	0.596	0.365	0.142
8.0	480.000	0.796	0.548	0.328	0.126
9.0	540.000	0.756	0.506	0.297	0.113
10.0	600.000	0.719	0.470	0.272	0.102

* indicates range for which data was supplied

DAMAGE 6/.03

▼ CIA Cigarette

CARTRIDGE	5.7x17mmR
OPERATION	manual
TYPE OF FIRE	Single shot disposable
MUZZLE VELOCITY	231 m/s (759 fps)
MUZZLE ENERGY	(51 ft/lbs)
WEIGHTS:	
WEAPON (LOADED)	0.018 kg
SERVICE CARTRIDGE	3.2 g
BULLET	2.6 g
LENGTHS:	
WEAPON OVERALL	7 cm
BARREL	3.2 cm
STATUS	out of production
SERVICE	Clandestine services

This is a single shot non-reloadable weapon whose chief advantage is its appearance as a popular brand of filtered cigarette. To fire the "cigarette," the tobacco end would be held and the filter pulled with either the fingers or the teeth of the firer. The round would be fired when a string between the filter and the rest of the cigarette would break, at a predetermined pressure. The fired bullet would blow out the tobacco plug at the end of the cigarette. Obviously, the accuracy would be very limited with the cartridge being specially loaded to get the maximum power from such a small weapon.

WEAPON CIA CIGARETTE
AMMO 5.7x17 Special RNL
DISPERSION ANGLE 4.58122 degrees, 81.444 NATO mils.

Range	Group Circle Width (mm)	Probability (0<p<.099) (m)			
		Body	Head	Hand	Bullseye
1.0*	80.000	0.990	0.990	0.908	0.553
2.0	160.000	0.990	0.908	0.696	0.332
3.0	240.000	0.958	0.796	0.548	0.236
4.0	320.000	0.908	0.696	0.449	0.183
5.0	400.000	0.851	0.614	0.379	0.149
6.0	480.000	0.796	0.548	0.328	0.126
7.0	560.000	0.744	0.494	0.288	0.109
8.0	640.000	0.696	0.449	0.257	0.096
9.0	720.000	0.653	0.411	0.232	0.086
10.0	800.000	0.614	0.379	0.212	0.077

* indicates range for which data was supplied

DAMAGE 6/.03

CHAPTER 2

SUBMACHINEGUNS

Gradually seeing a decrease in use in the world's armies, submachineguns appeared to be obsolescent and soon to disappear by the mid-1970's. The advent of modern terrorism appears to have created a new demand for the submachinegun and its compact firepower. The specific definition for a submachinegun is a hand held or shoulder fired weapon capable of fully automatic fire and using a pistol caliber cartridge. The requirement of pistol caliber has become less distinct in recent years with the proliferation of short barreled assault rifles, but, as will be explained, there is a sufficient difference between the pistol and assault rifle rounds to be noticeable. For the purposes of the word, the definition of pistol caliber is what will define the submachinegun from the assault carbine.

Almost none of the first generation of submachineguns is still in use, though occasionally a 1928 Thompson is still found in police armories. The first generation weapons are characterized by being large, carbine-like weapons, mechanically complex and manufactured almost totally by machining. Most first generation weapons were made during the time between World Wars One and Two. Second generation submachineguns were developed just prior to World War II and during the war reached their most popular time with many millions of various designs being made. Characterized by being intended for mass production, second generation guns were made primarily of stampings and simple metal working. The actions were simplified and reliability increased. The M3A1 submachinegun is an example of a second generation weapon and is still issued in the U.S. military.

Third generation submachineguns are by far the most prevalent form of the weapon found today. The third generation system has perfected the mass production aspect of the design with precision stampings, forgings, and plastic moldings being the primary manufacturing methods. Bolts are telescoped in third generation designs with much of the mass of the bolt surrounding the barrel ahead of the chamber. This telescoping allows the bolt to have sufficient mass and travel to operate as a blowback weapon but with a significantly reduced overall length. The UZI is the first true third generation weapon to see popular use. The Ingram is an example of a very compact third generation system. Machine pistols are also very compact as they are true pistols intended for one or two handed fire. The major drawback with the machine pistol is its very high rate of fire and recoil, resulting in an uncontrollable weapon. Few true machine pistols are presently made.

The Beretta 93R is an example, and it cuts down on the controllability problem by only being able to fire three round bursts.

Fourth generation submachineguns are so few as to make a definition of them difficult. The Spectre M4 and JATI are examples of new systems but they have not yet seen enough use to establish their designs. The MP-5 family is considered by some to be an example of a fourth generation system with the weapon firing from closed bolt for accuracy and obtainable with a controlled burst option. With their use of pistol ammunition, submachineguns give an excellent compromise between size and firepower. Rifle caliber rounds would have too much chance of overpenetration in many situations to be usable. The compact size of submachineguns also makes them maneuverable in crowded conditions such as in a vehicle, aircraft, or building hallway. The submachinegun is particularly adapted to close-in, rapid confrontations with multiple targets where only light cover is available. Used in short two and three round bursts, the submachinegun is able to quickly neutralize a target with precise bullet placement. ●

▼ AUG 9mm

CARTRIDGE	9x19 mm
OPERATION	Blowback
TYPE OF FIRE	Selective
RATE OF FIRE (SS)	40 rpm (A) 128 rpm (CYCLIC) 700 rpm
MUZZLE VELOCITY	400 m/s (1097 fps)
MUZZLE ENERGY	445 J (328 ft/lb)
SIGHTS	1.5x optical sight built into handle w/ fixed non adjustable backup iron sights
FEED	25 or 32 round removable box magazines
WEIGHTS:	
WEAPON (EMPTY)	3.300 kg
WEAPON (LOADED)	3.921 kg w/32 rds
MAGAZINE (EMPTY)	0.199 kg (25 rd), 0.237 kg (32 rd)
MAGAZINE (LOADED)	0.499 kg (20 rd), 0.621 kg (32 rd)
SERVICE CARTRIDGE	12 g
BULLET	8 g
LENGTHS:	
WEAPON OVERALL	66.5 cm
BARREL	42 cm
STATUS	In production

This is a conversion of the AUG system. The conversion can be obtained in either a kit form or as a complete weapon. The kit consists of a barrel, bolt group, magazine adaptor, and magazine. The magazine used in the system is the same one used in the Steyr MPi 69. Firing from a closed bolt gives the AUG 9mm excellent accuracy on the first shot while the bullpup design allows for a relatively long barrel in a compact package. The use of the 9mm conversion now allows the AUG to be employed in situations where the penetration of the 5.56 x45mm round would be excessive.

ASSESSMENT	12.5cm @ 100m
WEAPON	AUG 9mm
AMMO	9x19
DISPERSION ANGLE	.0716198 degrees, 1.27324 NATO mils.

Range	Group Circle Width (mm)	Probability (0<p<.099) (m)			
		Body	**Head**	**Hand**	**Bullseye**
5.0	6.250	0.990	0.990	0.990	0.990
10.0	12.500	0.990	0.990	0.990	0.990
15.0	18.750	0.990	0.990	0.990	0.968
20.0	25.000	0.990	0.990	0.990	0.924
25.0	31.250	0.990	0.990	0.990	0.873
50.0	62.500	0.990	0.990	0.953	0.644
75.0	93.750	0.990	0.983	0.869	0.497
100.0*	125.000	0.990	0.953	0.782	0.403
125.0	156.250	0.990	0.913	0.705	0.338
150.0	187.500	0.983	0.869	0.638	0.291
175.0	218.750	0.969	0.825	0.581	0.255
200.0	250.000	0.953	0.782	0.533	0.227

* indicates range for which data was supplied

DAMAGE 23/.14

▼ Beretta 93R

Beretta 93R with separate folding shoulder stock

Beretta 93R with front grip folded

Beretta 93R with stock attached and extended

☞ continued on next page

☞ *Beretta 93R continued*

Beretta 93R being held for firing without stock

CARTRIDGE	9x19 mm
OPERATION	Short recoil, fires from closed bolt.
TYPE OF FIRE	Selective, three round burst, single action
RATE OF FIRE (SS)	35 rpm (A) 110 rpm (CYCLIC) 750 rpm
MUZZLE VELOCITY	375 m/s (1230 fps)
MUZZLE ENERGY	560 J (413 ft/lb)
SIGHTS	Fixed, non-adjustable iron
FEED	15 or 20 round removable box magazine
WEIGHTS:	
WEAPON (EMPTY)	1.160 kg (Stock wt. 0.270 kg)
WEAPON (LOADED)	1.556 w/20 rds (1.826 kg w/stock)
MAGAZINE (EMPTY)	0.106 kg (15 rd), 0.156 kg (20 rd) "3
MAGAZINE (LOADED)	0.286 kg (15 rd), 0.396 kg (20 rd)
SERVICE CARTRIDGE	12 g
BULLET	8 g
LENGTHS:	
WEAPON OVERALL	24 cm (43.5/60.8 cm w/stock)
BARREL	15.6 cm w/muzzle brake
SIGHT RADIUS	16 cm
STATUS	In production.
SERVICE	In use by Italian Special Forces and some foreign sales.

This is a true machine pistol variant of the Beretta 92 family of pistols. Though only capable of 3 round bursts and not full automatic fire, the Model 93R is about as controllable as a weapon of this class and caliber can be. The folding forward handgrip is held by the non-firing hand with the thumb through the oversized trigger guard. With the hands separated, the leverage created allows for good control when firing bursts. The 93R can be used as a normal, larger sized, 9mm handgun if desired and is comfortably fired with one hand.

WEAPON	Beretta 93R
AMMO	9x19
DISPERSION ANGLE	.162009 degrees, 2.88016 NATO mils.

Range	Group Circle Width (mm)	Probability (0<p<.099) (m)			
		Body	**Head**	**Hand**	**Bullseye**
5.0	14.138	0.990	0.990	0.990	0.990
10.0	28.276	0.990	0.990	0.990	0.898
15.0	42.414	0.990	0.990	0.989	0.781
20.0	56.552	0.990	0.990	0.966	0.680
25.0	70.690	0.990	0.990	0.932	0.598
50.0	141.379	0.990	0.932	0.740	0.366
75.0	212.069	0.972	0.834	0.593	0.262
100.0	282.759	0.932	0.740	0.490	0.204
125.0	353.448	0.884	0.660	0.417	0.167
150.0	424.138	0.834	0.593	0.362	0.141
175.0	494.828	0.786	0.537	0.320	0.122
200.0	565.517	0.740	0.490	0.286	0.108

* indicates range for which data was supplied

DAMAGE 26/.16

▼ MPi 69 • Mpi 81

MPi 69 with bolt forward (fired)

MPi 81 with stock folded

CARTRIDGE	9x19mm
OPERATION	Blowback, fires from open bolt.
TYPE OF FIRE	Selective
RATE OF FIRE (SS)	50 rpm (A) 100 rpm (CYCLIC) 550 rpm (700 rpm)

	MUZZLE VELOCITY	381 m/s (1250 fps)
	MUZZLE ENERGY	579 J (427 ft/lb)
	SIGHTS	Fixed, non-adjustable iron
	FEED	25 or 32 round removable box magazine

WEIGHTS:

	WEAPON (EMPTY)	2.930 kg
	WEAPON (LOADED)	3.551 kg w/32 rds
	MAGAZINE (EMPTY)	0.199 kg (25 rd), 0.237 kg (32 rd)
	MAGAZINE (LOADED)	0.499 kg (25 rd), 0.621 kg (32 rd)
	SERVICE CARTRIDGE	12 g
	BULLET	8 g

LENGTHS:

	WEAPON OVERALL	46.5/67 cm
	BARREL	26 cm
	SIGHT RADIUS	32.6 cm
	STATUS	In production
	SERVICE	Military and police forces

Range	Group Circle Width (mm)	Probability (0<p<.099) (m)			
		Body	Head	Hand	Bullseye
5.0	10.000	0.990	0.990	0.990	0.990
10.0	20.000	0.990	0.990	0.990	0.960
15.0	30.000	0.990	0.990	0.990	0.884
20.0	40.000	0.990	0.990	0.990	0.801
25.0	50.000	0.990	0.990	0.978	0.725
50.0	100.000	0.990	0.978	0.851	0.475
75.0	150.000	0.990	0.921	0.719	0.349
100.0	200.000	0.978	0.851	0.614	0.276
125.0	250.000	0.953	0.782	0.533	0.227
150.0	300.000	0.921	0.719	0.470	0.193
175.0	350.000	0.887	0.663	0.420	0.168
200.0	400.000	0.851	0.614	0.379	0.149

* indicates range for which data was supplied

DAMAGE 26/.16

The MPi 69 is a very easy to handle, strong, and simply designed submachinegun. Having the same general lines as an UZI, the MPi is even simpler to operate. The trigger is of the progressive type with a half-pull to the rear giving semiautomatic fire and pulling the trigger all of the way back giving full automatic fire. Although it sounds complex, this manner of selecting the type of fire is quickly mastered and is the fastest for switching from one type to the other. The safety is a standard push through type located in front of the trigger guard with an additional series of safeties preventing accidental bolt movement in the event that the weapon is dropped or jarred. By pushing the safety to the halfway position, the trigger is locked into allowing only semiautomatic fire. The cocking method of the MPi 69 is unusual in that the weapon has no recognizable cocking knob. Instead of the regular knob, the front sling swivel is attached to the bolt. It is first drawn out from the gun to unlock it and then drawn to the rear to cock the gun.

In the MPi 81, the sling-cocking feature has been replaced with a conventional cocking knob and there is also an increase in the cyclic rate of fire. Other than these differences, the MPi 69 and 81 operate in the same manner.

	WEAPON	MPi 69
	AMMO	9x19
	DISPERSION ANGLE	.114592 degrees, 2.03718 NATO mils.

▼ JATI MATIC

JATI MATIC with front handygrip/safety unfolded

	CARTRIDGE	9x19mm
	OPERATION	Blowback, fires from open bolt.
	TYPE OF FIRE	Selective
	RATE OF FIRE (SS)	40 rpm (A) 120 rpm (CYCLIC) 600-650 rpm
	MUZZLE VELOCITY	411 m/s (1347 fps)
	MUZZLE ENERGY	671 J (495 ft/lbs)
	SIGHTS	Fixed, non-adjustable iron
	FEED	20 or 40 round removable box magazine

WEIGHTS:

	WEAPON (EMPTY)	1.650 kg
	WEAPON (LOADED)	2.280 kg w/40 rds
	MAGAZINE (EMPTY)	0.099 kg (20 rd), 0.150 kg

☞ continued on next page

☞ *JATI MATIC continued*

MAGAZINE (LOADED)	0.339 kg (20 rd), 0.630 kg
SERVICE CARTRIDGE	12 g
BULLET	8 g
LENGTHS:	
WEAPON OVERALL	37.5 cm
BARREL	20.3 cm
SIGHT RADIUS	29 cm
STATUS	In production

This very unusual weapon is a new design from Finland and has some very unique features. The outline and alignment of the pistol grip and barrel are the external indications of the JATI's patented inclined bolt. Instead of sliding straight back, the bolt of the JATI slides up an incline away from the barrel, forcing the weapon down and retarding the bolt's travel. An advantage of this is the ability to place the rear grip higher, in line with the barrel and the weapon's recoil. With the higher grip, the recoil does not force the weapon to pivot upwards in the firer's hand. The JATI also has a progressive trigger, allowing fast and simple access to semi or full automatic fire. The forward folding foregrip does double duty. With the handle folded underneath the weapon, it streamlines the JATI's outline as well as locking the bolt in place, preventing its movement. Unfolding the foregrip unlocks the bolt, allowing the weapon to fire. It can also be drawn to the rear, cocking the weapon. The bolt of the JATI is of the usual telescoping type but has a single cutout in its right side as well as the words FIRE and SAFE inscribed in its right side to the front and rear respectively. With the weapon cocked, the word FIRE can be read through the ejection port. With the bolt in the forward position, the word SAFE is showing. Only while the bolt is moving is the ejection port open to eject casings; this helps seal the weapon from dirt. All these design innovations make the JATI one of the most controllable submachineguns to fire. This controllability is demonstrated in the JATI's lack of a buttstock while it still retains a high accuracy in full automatic fire.

WEAPON	JATI MATIC
AMMO	9x19
DISPERSION ANGLE	.126446 degrees, 2.24793 NATO mils.

Range	Group Circle Width (mm)	Probability (0<p<.099) (m)			
		Body	Head	Hand	Bullseye
5.0	11.034	0.990	0.990	0.990	0.990
10.0	22.069	0.990	0.990	0.990	0.946
15.0	33.103	0.990	0.990	0.990	0.858
20.0	44.138	0.990	0.990	0.987	0.768
25.0	55.172	0.990	0.990	0.968	0.689
50.0	110.345	0.990	0.968	0.822	0.443
75.0	165.517	0.990	0.900	0.684	0.323

☞ *continued*

Range	Group Circle Width (mm)	Probability (0<p<.099) (m)			
		Body	Head	Hand	Bullseye
100.0	220.690	0.968	0.822	0.578	0.253
125.0	275.862	0.937	0.749	0.499	0.208
150.0	331.034	0.900	0.684	0.438	0.177
175.0	386.207	0.861	0.627	0.389	0.154
200.0	441.379	0.822	0.578	0.351	0.136

* indicates range for which data was supplied

DAMAGE 28/.17

▼ MAT 49

MAT 49 without magazine and with stock folded

MAT 49 with magazine folded and with stock extended

CARTRIDGE	9x19mm
OPERATION	Blowback, fires from open bolt
TYPE OF FIRE	Full automatic
RATE OF FIRE (A)	128 rpm (CYCLIC) 600 rpm
MUZZLE VELOCITY	354 m/s (1161 fps)
MUZZLE ENERGY	499 J (368 ft/lb)
SIGHTS	Fixed, non-adjustable iron
FEED	32 round removable box magazine
WEIGHTS:	
WEAPON (EMPTY)	3.640 kg
WEAPON (LOADED)	4.760 kg
MAGAZINE (EMPTY)	0.256 kg
MAGAZINE (LOADED)	0.640 kg
SERVICE CARTRIDGE	12 g
BULLET	8 g
LENGTHS:	
WEAPON OVERALL	46/72 cm
BARREL	22.8 cm
SIGHT RADIUS	37.8 cm
STATUS	Out of production

SERVICE In use with French forces and French affiliates

This is the most successful of the post-World War II French designs. The square cross section receiver has a spring loaded cover over the ejection port that flies open when the bolt moves. An unusual feature of the MAT 49 is the folding magazine housing. With or without a magazine in place, the magazine housing will fold forward underneath the barrel and can be locked in place. With the bolt forward, the magazine folded and the ejection cover closed, the MAT 49 is effectively sealed from dirt entering the action. There is a grip safety built into the rear pistol grip that locks the bolt either in the open or closed position. The sliding stock and folding magazine allow the MAT 49 to be closed into a compact package. The design and construction of the MAT 49 make it a very rugged and reliable weapon that is often seen in the hands of the French police.

WEAPON MAT 49
AMMO 9x19
DISPERSION ANGLE .596662 degrees, 10.6073 NATO mils.

Range	Group Circle Width (mm)	Probability (0<p<.099) (m)			
		Body	Head	Hand	Bullseye
5.0	52.069	0.990	0.990	0.974	0.710
10.0	104.138	0.990	0.974	0.839	0.462
15.0	156.207	0.990	0.913	0.705	0.338
20.0	208.276	0.974	0.839	0.599	0.266
25.0	260.345	0.946	0.769	0.519	0.219
50.0	520.690	0.769	0.519	0.306	0.117
75.0	781.034	0.623	0.386	0.216	0.079
100.0	1041.379	0.519	0.306	0.167	0.060
125.0	1301.724	0.443	0.254	0.136	0.048
150.0	1562.069	0.386	0.216	0.115	0.040
175.0	1822.414	0.342	0.189	0.099	0.035
200.0	2082.759	0.306	0.167	0.087	0.030

DAMAGE 24/.15

▼ Walther MP-K • MP-L

Walther MP-L with stock extended

Walther MP-K with stock folded

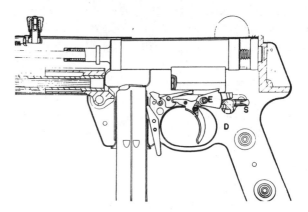

CARTRIDGE 9x19mm
OPERATION Blowback, fires from open bolt.
TYPE OF FIRE Selective
RATE OF FIRE (SS) 40 rpm (A) 96 rpm (CYCLIC) 550 rpm
MUZZLE VELOCITY 356 m/s (1168 fps),(396 m/s, <1299 fps>)
MUZZLE ENERGY 506 J (373 ft/lb), (625 J <461 ft/lb>)
SIGHTS Fixed, non-adjustable iron
FEED 32 round removable box magazine
WEIGHTS:
WEAPON (EMPTY) 2.800 kg (3.000 kg, MP-L)
WEAPON (LOADED) 3.384 kg (3.584 kg, MP-L)
MAGAZINE (EMPTY) 0.200 kg
MAGAZINE (LOADED) 0.584 kg
SERVICE CARTRIDGE 12 g
BULLET 8 g
LENGTHS:
WEAPON OVERALL 36.8/65.3 cm (45.5/73.7 cm, MP-L)
BARREL 17.1 cm (25.7 cm, MP-L)
SIGHT RADIUS 27 cm (35.7 cm, MP-L)
STATUS In production
SERVICE Commercial sales and police depts.

☞ *continued on next page*

☞ *Walther MP-K • MP-L continued*

This is one of the first commercially successful submachineguns to use the "L" shaped telescoping bolt. The bolt extends over the barrel, the long arm of the "L" thereby reducing the overall length of the weapon's receiver and moving the center of gravity over the magazine. With the center of gravity over the magazine, the balance of the weapon does not change as the magazine empties. This weapon is often seen in the hands of the German police, especially at airports. The MP-K and L are virtually identical with the L model having a longer barrel and forward receiver than the K (for Kurz - short) model.

WEAPON MP-K
AMMO 9x19
DISPERSION ANGLE .205474 degrees, 3.65288 NATO mils.

Range	Group Circle Width (mm)	Probability (0<p<.099) (m)			
		Body	**Head**	**Hand**	**Bullseye**
5.0	17.931	0.990	0.990	0.990	0.973
10.0	35.862	0.990	0.990	0.990	0.834
15.0	53.793	0.990	0.990	0.971	0.699
20.0	71.724	0.990	0.990	0.930	0.593
25.0	89.655	0.990	0.986	0.881	0.513
50.0	179.310	0.986	0.881	0.654	0.302
75.0	268.966	0.941	0.757	0.508	0.213
100.0	358.621	0.881	0.654	0.412	0.165
125.0	448.276	0.817	0.573	0.346	0.134
150.0	537.931	0.757	0.508	0.298	0.113
175.0	627.586	0.703	0.455	0.262	0.098
200.0	717.241	0.654	0.412	0.233	0.086

* indicates range for which data was supplied

DAMAGE 24/.15

WEAPON MP-L
AMMO 9x19
DISPERSION ANGLE .173863 degrees, 3.0909 NATO mils.

Range	Group Circle Width (mm)	Probability (0<p<.099) (m)			
		Body	**Head**	**Hand**	**Bullseye**
5.0	15.172	0.990	0.990	0.990	0.986
10.0	30.345	0.990	0.990	0.990	0.881
15.0	45.517	0.990	0.990	0.985	0.758
20.0	60.690	0.990	0.990	0.957	0.655
25.0	75.862	0.990	0.990	0.919	0.573
50.0	151.724	0.990	0.919	0.715	0.346
75.0	227.586	0.965	0.813	0.567	0.247
100.0	303.448	0.919	0.715	0.466	0.191

☞ *continued*

Range	Group Circle Width (mm)	Probability (0<p<.099) (m)			
		Body	**Head**	**Hand**	**Bullseye**
125.0	379.310	0.866	0.634	0.395	0.156
150.0	455.172	0.813	0.567	0.342	0.132
175.0	531.034	0.762	0.512	0.301	0.114
200.0	606.897	0.715	0.466	0.269	0.101

* indicates range for which data was supplied
DAMAGE 27/.17

THE HECKLER & KOCH MP5 WEAPONS SYSTEM

Of all the weapons to be found in the hands of counterterrorist forces throughout the world, by far the most common is the Heckler and Koch MP5 submachinegun and its variants. Due to such widespread use and popularity, the MP5 system and its operational concepts will be gone into in some detail here.

In the closing months of World War 2 the German military was developing a new assault rifle, the Stg 45, with the Mauser developed Gerat 06H being the most likely contender. After the war and the fall of Nazi Germany the designers of the Gerat 06 went to the CETME arms works in Spain where the design was perfected. The Stg 45(m) utilized much the same roller locking system of the battle proved MG-42 light machinegun but was chambered for the 7.92x33mm Kurz assault rifle cartridge. The first weapon produced by CETME was chambered for a special 7.9x40mm cartridge firing an exotic bullet but the cartridge was never widely accepted and soon died out. The basic CETME design was modified and perfected for use with the new NATO 7.62x51mm round and was submitted for trials with the new German army. The rechambering and redesign of the CETME was accomplished in Germany by the new Heckler and Koch company as their first major weapons development. The new rifle passed all tests and was adopted by the German military as the G3.

The roller-locking system is in effect a form of delayed blowback that carries with it some substantial problems. The lack of a rotating bolt limits primary extraction and fired cases sticking in the chamber pose a real difficulty. The sticking case problem is solved in the H&K system by the chamber being cut with a series of longitudinal flutes along two/thirds of its length. The flutes allow the hot propellant gases to flow along the body of the cartridge along the area of most expansion "floating" the casing on a layer of gas and easing extraction. The fluted chamber/gas flotation system eliminates much of the sticking case problem but still allows the roller locking system to have a very violent case ejection and the cases, often dented, have a series of distinguishing marks on them indicating the weapon they were fired from.

Expended 7.62mm casing fired from a G3 rifle

The complete roller locking system works via two rollers in the bolt that are driven into locking recesses in the barrel extension by the forward movement of the wedge shaped firing pin. The rearward pressure of the cartridge being fired bears against the bolt and drives the rollers against the rear of the recesses in the barrel extension. The rear surfaces of the barrel extension recesses allow the rollers to force themselves inward against the firing pin, driving the pin backwards but at a great mechanical disadvantage to the force of the rollers. This disadvantage the rollers work against slows the opening of the breech until the bullet has left the barrel and pressures have dropped to safe levels.

The roller locking, delayed blowback system has been applied by Heckler and Koch to a large family of weapons including light machineguns, rifles, submachineguns, and pistols. With the roller locking system eliminating the need for the heavy bolt found in most of its contemporaries, the MP5 is lighter than many weapons of its class as well as being able to fire from the closed bolt position. This firing from the closed bolt gives the MP5 excellent accuracy for its first round and this accuracy is what makes the weapon so popular among the world's HRUs. Though not adopted in quantity by any major military force, the MP5 series is also very popular among the various military elite units of the free world including the U. S. Seals and Special Forces.

To meet this high demand, the MP5 weapon is offered in over a dozen variations all using the same basic action and operating system. This commonality of operation allows quick familiarity with different members of the weapons family by anyone trained in one weapon's operation. At the time of this writing, the following models of the MP5 are, or have been offered by, Heckler & Koch.

HK-54: This was the original designation for the first submachinegun made by H&K and was later modified to the MP5 configuration.

MP5A1: This model has a receiver cap and no buttstock giving it the shortest overall length of the standard MP5s.

MP5A2: The standard MP5 with a fixed buttstock.

MP5A3: The standard model fitted with a retractable sliding metal buttstock.

☛ continued on next page

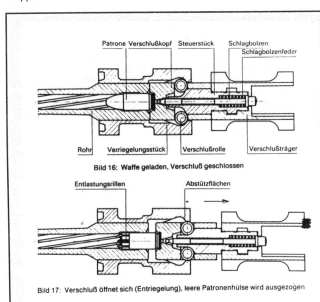

Bild 16: Waffe geladen, Verschluß geschlossen

Bild 17: Verschluß öffnet sich (Entriegelung), leere Patronenhülse wird ausgezogen

The Heckler & Koch Roller Locking System

Bild 16 (upper schematic)	Rifle loaded, bolt locked
Bild 17 (lower schematic)	Lock cams inward (unlocks) empty cartridge case extracting
Patrone	Cartridge
Verschlusskopf	Bolthead
Steuerstück	Cam piece
Schlagbolzen	Firing pin
Schlagbolzenfeder	Firing pin spring
Rohr	Barrel
Verriegolungsstück	Locking piece
Verschlussrolle	Locking rollers
Verschlussträgen	Bolt carrier
Entlastungsrillen	Gas relief flutes (grooves)
Abstützflächen	Locking flat

☞ *Heckler & Koch MP5 Weapons System continued*

MP5A4 : The newer model MP5 with a fixed buttstock and a group allows semiautomatic fire, 3-round controlled bursts, or full automatic fire to be selected.

MP5A5: The newer model MP5 with a retractable sliding metal buttstock and controlled burst trigger group.

MP5SD1: The suppressed version of the MP5 with an integral suppressor and receiver cap.

MP5SD2: The suppressed version with a fixed buttstock.

MP5SD3: The suppressed version with a retractable metal stock.

MP5SD4: The suppressed version with a receiver cap and controlled burst trigger group.

MP5SD5: The suppressed version with a controlled burst trigger group and fixed buttstock.

MP5SD6 : Suppressed version with a controlled burst trigger group and retractable buttstock.

MP5K: The shortest MP5 with no buttstock and a vertical front grip as well as adjustable sights.

MP5KA1: Shortened MP5 with nonadjustable, lowered sights for maximum concealability.

MP5KA4: Shortened MP5 with adjustable sights and controlled burst trigger group.

MP5KA5: Shortened MP5 with the small nonadjustable sights and controlled burst trigger group.

MP5A4 PT: Standard fixed stock MP5 with the controlled burst trigger group but designed to fire plastic bulleted training ammunition only.

MP5A5 PT: The training MP5 for plastic bullets with the controlled burst trigger group and retracting metal stock.

In addition to the weapons listed, Heckler and Koch make a very comprehensive line of accessories for the MP5 weapon to which they are continually adding. At present the list includes the following:

Magazine clips for holding two magazines together parallel to each other
Blank firing adaptors
Tear gas canister launchers

Rifle grenade launchers
Removable aiming point projectors
Removable telescopic sights
Two types of briefcases that can carry an MP5K and fire it while concealed
Removable starlight scopes
A subcaliber device firing .22 long rifle ammunition that can be fitted to any standard MP5 and allow it to fire .22s instead of 9x19mm ammunition
An infrared sighting scope
A replacement front grip with a built in flashlight for aiming or illumination
A miniature laser sight for use with night vision goggles that is built into the weapon.

The result of this wide range of weapons and accessories is to make the MP5 weapons system one of the most versatile available. During the early 1970s it was found that curving the magazines slightly allows the MP5 to have more positive feeding. New curved magazines became available around 1978 and are now the only ones used. These magazines are completely interchangeable with the earlier straight type and all MP5 weapons can use both magazines. ●

▼ Heckler & Koch
MP5A1 • MP5A2 • MP5A3 • MP5A4 • MP5A5

Heckler & Koch MP5A2 with early magazine

MP5A5 without magazine and with stock retracted

CARTRIDGE	9x19mm
OPERATION	Retarded blowback
TYPE OF FIRE	Selective, Three round burst and full (A4, A5)
RATE OF FIRE (SS)	45 rpm (A) 100 rpm (CYCLIC) 650 rpm
MUZZLE VELOCITY	400 m/s (1312 fps)
MUZZLE ENERGY	637 J (470 ft/lb)

SIGHTS Adjustable, open iron
FEED 15, 30, or 60 (2x30) round removable box magazines
WEIGHTS:
WEAPON (EMPTY) 2.540 kg (A2, A4), 2.880 kg (A3, A5)
WEAPON (LOADED) 2.710 kg w/30 rds (A2, A4), 4.104 kg w/60 rds (A3, A5)
MAGAZINE (EMPTY) 0.120 kg (15 rd), 0.170 kg (30 rd), 0.504 kg (2x30 rd)
MAGAZINE (LOADED) 0.300 kg (15 rd), 0.530 kg (30 rd), 1.224 kg (2x30 rd)
SERVICE CARTRIDGE 12 g
BULLET 8 g
LENGTHS:
WEAPON OVERALL 49 cm (A1), 68 cm (A2, A4), 49/68 cm (A3, A5)
BARREL 22.5 cm
SIGHT RADIUS 34 cm
STATUS In production
SERVICE In service with many police and military agencies.

Range	Group Circle Width (mm)	Probability (0<p<.099) (m)			
		Body	Head	Hand	Bullseye
5.0	7.586	0.990	0.990	0.990	0.990
10.0	15.172	0.990	0.990	0.990	0.986
15.0	22.759	0.990	0.990	0.990	0.941
20.0	30.345	0.990	0.990	0.990	0.881
25.0	37.931	0.990	0.990	0.990	0.817
50.0	75.862	0.990	0.990	0.919	0.573
75.0	113.793	0.990	0.965	0.813	0.433
100.0	151.724	0.990	0.919	0.715	0.346
125.0	189.655	0.982	0.866	0.634	0.288
150.0	227.586	0.965	0.813	0.567	0.247
175.0	265.517	0.943	0.762	0.512	0.216
200.0	303.448	0.919	0.715	0.466	0.191

DAMAGE 27/.17

▼ Heckler & Koch MP5A4 PT • MP5A5 PT

5A4PT Sub-machine gun

Heckler & Koch MP5A4 PT

CARTRIDGE 9x19mm Plastic Training
OPERATION Blowback w/gas assist, fires from closed bolt.
TYPE OF FIRE Selective, three round burst and full auto
RATE OF FIRE (SS) 45 rpm (A) 100 rpm (CYCLIC) 700 rpm
MUZZLE VELOCITY 700 m/s (2297 fps)
MUZZLE ENERGY 103 J (76 ft/lb)
SIGHTS Adjustable, open iron
FEED 15, 30, or 60 (2x30) round removable box magazines
WEIGHTS:
WEAPON (EMPTY) 2.540 kg (MP5A4 PT), 2.880 kg (MP5A5 PT)
WEAPON (LOADED) 2.818 kg (MP5A4 PT), 3.158 kg (MP5A5 PT)
MAGAZINE (EMPTY) 0.120 kg (15 rds), 0.170 kg (30 rds), 0.504 kg (2x30 rds)
MAGAZINE (LOADED) 0.174 kg (15 rd), 0.278 kg (30 rd), 0.720 kg (2x30 rd)

These are the standard weapons from which all of the other variants are derived. The earlier version, the HK 54, has been improved to what is now the MP5. The MP5A1 version with the receiver cap and no stock is no longer listed in the company's literature but can still be made available. The retractable stock model, the MP5A3, is probably the most common version of the MP5. With the stocks and trigger housings being interchangeable, the model number of a specific MP5 can easily change. The A4 and A5 models utilize the newest trigger housing that is capable of semiautomatic, full automatic, or three round controlled burst firing. Rather than the normal letter or number symbols to indicate the type of fire selected, the new trigger housings use a more universal symbol system. When the selector is pointing at the white symbol of a bullet that is crossed out, the weapon is on safe. The red single bullet in a box is the symbol for semiautomatic fire. Three red bullets in a box indicates three round controlled bursts and seven bullets in an open ended box indicates full automatic fire. The symbols can be seen from either side of the weapon and the new trigger housing can be retrofitted to earlier weapons.

WEAPON MP5A2
AMMO 9x19
DISPERSION ANGLE .0869316 degrees, 1.54545 NATO mils.

☞ continued on next page

☞ *Heckler & Koch MP5A4 • MP5A5 PT continued*

SERVICE CARTRIDGE	3.6 g
BULLET	0.42 g
LENGTHS:	
WEAPON OVERALL	68 cm (MP5A4 PT),
	49/66 cm (MP5A5 PT)
BARREL	22.5 cm
SIGHT RADIUS	34 cm
STATUS	In production

This variant of the MP5 system is designed expressly to fire plastic bulleted training ammunition. The plastic training bullet quickly loses energy and as a result, has a very limited danger area. The roller locking system has been removed and the weapon works on straight blowback. Because the pressure is low on the plastic rounds, there is a floating chamber system in the PT weapons that increase the velocity of the bolt, insuring positive functioning. The blowback and floating chamber system prevent the PT from using standard ammunition. If ball ammo is fired in the PT, the bolt will fly violently to the rear, severely damaging the weapon but not injuring the firer. The A4 PT has a fixed stock and the A5 has a sliding metal stock. The plastic bullets give the PT weapons an effective lethal range of eight meters with a maximum range of 125 meters. Although the plastic bullets can be lethal within eight meters, they will not penetrate the aluminum wall of an aircraft.

WEAPON	MP5A4 PT
AMMO	9x19 PT
DISPERSION ANGLE	.371434 degrees, 6.60327 NATO mils.

Range	Group Circle Width (mm)	Probability (0<p<.099) (m)			
		Body	**Head**	**Hand**	**Bullseye**
2.0	12.966	0.990	0.990	0.990	0.990
4.0	25.931	0.990	0.990	0.990	0.917
6.0	38.897	0.990	0.990	0.990	0.810
8.0	51.862	0.990	0.990	0.975	0.712
10.0	64.828	0.990	0.990	0.947	0.630
12.0	77.793	0.990	0.990	0.914	0.564
14.0	90.759	0.990	0.985	0.877	0.509
16.0	103.724	0.990	0.975	0.841	0.463
18.0	116.690	0.990	0.962	0.805	0.425
20.0	129.655	0.990	0.947	0.770	0.392

* indicates range for which data was supplied
DAMAGE 4/.1

**▼ Heckler & Koch
MP5 SD1• MP5 SD2 • MP5 SD3
MP5 SD4 • MP5 SD5 • MP5 SD6**

MP5 SD3 with buttstock folded, twin (stacked) 30 rd magazines, and telescopic sight on a quick removal mount

MP5 SD5 with LS-45 laser sight, suppressor body, and hand guard is removed showing the perforated barrel

MP5 SD2

MP5 SD3

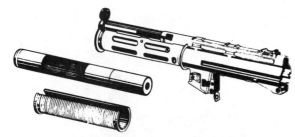

MP5 SD upper receiver and barrel showing the special handguard and unmounted suppressor

CARTRIDGE	9x19mm
OPERATION	Retarded blowback, fires from closed bolt.
TYPE OF FIRE	Selective, Three round burst and full auto (SD4, SD5)
RATE OF FIRE (SS)	45 rpm (A) 100 rpm (CYCLIC) 800 rpm
MUZZLE VELOCITY	285 m/s (935 fps)
MUZZLE ENERGY	380 J (239 ft/lbs)
SIGHTS	Adjustable, open iron
FEED	15, 30, or 60 (2x30) round removable box magazines
WEIGHTS:	
WEAPON (EMPTY)	2.800 kg (SD1)
	3.100 kg (SD2, SD4)
	3.400 kg (SD3, SD5)
WEAPON (LOADED)	3.33 kg w/30 rds (SD1)
	3.63 kg w/30 rds (SD2, SD4)
	3.93 kg w/30 rds (SD3, SD5)
MAGAZINE (EMPTY)	0.120 kg (15 rd), 0.170 kg (30 rd), 0.504 kg (2x30 rd)
MAGAZINE (LOADED)	0.300 kg (15 rd), 0.530 kg (30 rd), 1.224 kg (2x30 rd)
SERVICE CARTRIDGE	12 g
BULLET	8 g
LENGTHS:	
WEAPON OVERALL	55 cm (SD1)
	78 cm (SD2, SD4)
	61/78 cm (SD3, SD5)
BARREL	14.6 cm
SIGHT RADIUS	34 cm
STATUS	In production

This variant of the MP5 has an integral noise suppression system built into the weapon. The SD in the weapon's name stands for Scholldamper, German for silencer. The barrel in the SD has been drilled with a series of thirty 3mm holes so that some propellant gases are bled away before the bullet has left the barrel, slowing the projectile below the speed of sound. The slowing of the bullet eliminates the supersonic crack that would otherwise be heard and allows the SD to operate effectively with normal NATO ammunition. The drawback to slowing standard ammunition to below normal velocity is the lowering of the penetration and wounding potential of the round but this is considered of secondary importance to the SD being able to use NATO ammo and still have the maximum sound suppression. The increased weight of the MP5SD in the forward section has been found to increase the stability of the weapon, especially when fired on full automatic. The sound suppression and accuracy of the MP5SD is so good that it is often used, with a telescopic sight, as a close in (under 100 meters) sniper system. The suppressor is built onto the MP5 with the main tube being removable for cleaning of the barrel and ports. The suppressor itself is not designed to be broken down for cleaning and is considered to have a service life of 10,000 rounds or more.

WEAPON	MP5SD2
AMMO	9x19
DISPERSION ANGLE	.0869316 degrees, 1.54545 NATO mils.

Range	Group Circle Width (mm)	Probability (0<p<.099) (m)			
		Body	**Head**	**Hand**	**Bullseye**
5.0	7.586	0.990	0.990	0.990	0.990
10.0	15.172	0.990	0.990	0.990	0.986
15.0	22.759	0.990	0.990	0.990	0.941
20.0	30.345	0.990	0.990	0.990	0.881
25.0	37.931	0.990	0.990	0.990	0.817
50.0	75.862	0.990	0.990	0.919	0.573
75.0	113.793	0.990	0.965	0.813	0.433
100.0	151.724	0.990	0.919	0.715	0.346
125.0	189.655	0.982	0.866	0.634	0.288
150.0	227.586	0.965	0.813	0.567	0.247
175.0	265.517	0.943	0.762	0.512	0.216
200.0	303.448	0.919	0.715	0.466	0.191

DAMAGE 20/.12

▼ Heckler & Koch
MP5K • MP5KA1 • MP5KA4 • MP5KA5

Attache case with MP5K

MP5KA4

Briefcase with MP5K with 30rd magazine

CARTRIDGE	9x19 mm
OPERATION	Retarded blowback, fires from closed bolt.
TYPE OF FIRE	Selective, Three round burst and full auto (KA4, KA5)
RATE OF FIRE (SS)	45 rpm (A) 100 rpm (CYCLIC) 900 rpm
MUZZLE VELOCITY	375 m/s (1230 fps)
MUZZLE ENERGY	570 J (412 ft/lbs)
SIGHTS	Adjustable, open iron (K, KA4), Non-adjustable (KA1, KA5)
FEED	15, 30, and 60 (2x30) round removable box magazines
WEIGHTS:	
WEAPON (EMPTY)	2.000 kg
WEAPON (LOADED)	2.300 kg w/15 rds
MAGAZINE (EMPTY)	0.120 kg (15 rd), 0.170 kg (30 rd), 0.504 kg (2x30 rd)
MAGAZINE (LOADED)	0.300 kg (15 rd), 0.530 kg (30 rd), 1.224 kg, (2x30 rd)
SERVICE CARTRIDGE	12 g
BULLET	8 g
LENGTHS:	
WEAPON OVERALL	32.5 cm
BARREL	11.5 cm
SIGHT RADIUS	26 cm (K, KA4), 19 cm (KA1, KA5)

STATUS In production

This is the shortest version of the MP5 and was designed for concealed carry. The basic receiver was somewhat shortened with the barrel and front portion being severely shortened. The modification to the receiver prevents any of the buttstocks from being mounted on the MP5K and the weapon is issued with a modified receiver cap. The MP5K and KA4 have the same adjustable iron sights as are found on the other weapons in the MP5 series with a large ringed front sight and an adjustable aperture rear sight. To increase the concealability when carried under clothes, the MP5KA1 and KA5 have only a small front sight with a rectangular rear notch much like a normal pistol sight to eliminate any snagging on clothes when the weapon is drawn. Since the front of the weapon is so short, a special front grip is made with a guard to prevent the firer's hand from slipping into the muzzle blast. The K and KA1 models are fitted with the older trigger housing with the KA4 and KA5 models having the trigger housing with the three round burst option.

Two of the most unusual accessories for a weapon are specifically made for the MPK series by Heckler and Koch. The accessories, a hard sided brief case and a soft sided attache case, are designed to hold an MP5K or KA, a spare magazine, and cleaning kit and allow the weapon to be fired while inside the case. The hard brief case has a trigger mechanism and safety built into the handle with the weapon firing through a small port in the end of the case. While the handle safety prevents the weapon from being accidentally fired, the trigger mechanism has to be set to the type of fire desired while the case is open. The soft sided leather bag has a vertical slit in the end that allows the weapon inside to be held and fired while inside the case. The normal safety selector and trigger are used in the leather case. The upper section of the soft bag is removable by releasing four snap connectors and the weapon comes with it when the top is released. Both cases hold the weapons in place with a quick release clamp and can retain a loaded (thirty rounds) weapon, spare thirty round magazine, and cleaning kit securely.

Dimensions:
Briefcase 43.8 x 10.8 x 32.2 cm
Weight (empty) 3.50 kg

Attache case (leather bag) 40 x 31 x 14.3 cm
Weight (empty) 2.90 kg

ASSESSMENT 3.4 cm @ 25 yd.
WEAPON MP5K
AMMO 9x19
DISPERSION ANGLE .0852169 degrees, 1.51497 NATO mils.

Range	Group Circle Width (mm)	Probability (0<p<.099) (m)			
		Body	Head	Hand	Bullseye
5.0	7.437	0.990	0.990	0.990	0.990
10.0	14.873	0.990	0.990	0.990	0.987
15.0	22.310	0.990	0.990	0.990	0.944
20.0	29.746	0.990	0.990	0.990	0.886
25.0	37.183	0.990	0.990	0.990	0.824
50.0	74.366	0.990	0.990	0.923	0.580
75.0	111.549	0.990	0.967	0.819	0.439
100.0	148.731	0.990	0.923	0.722	0.352
125.0	185.914	0.983	0.871	0.641	0.293
150.0	223.097	0.967	0.819	0.574	0.251
175.0	260.280	0.946	0.769	0.519	0.219
200.0	297.463	0.923	0.722	0.473	0.195

DAMAGE 26/.16

▼ MP 2000

MP-2000 with suppressor unmounted, selector set to 0 (safe) and gas selector set to high pressure. Retracting stock is slightly extended

MP-2000 with stock extended and suppressor attached, bolt is locked to the rear on an empty magazine, selector switch on 0, gas selector on high (H)

CARTRIDGE 9x19mm
OPERATION Blowback, fires from closed bolt

☞ continued on next page

☞ *MP-2000 continued*

TYPE OF FIRE	Selective w/3 rd burst or full automatic, manual repeater using optional bolt lock
RATE OF FIRE (SS)	40 rpm (A) 120 rpm (CYCLIC) 875 rpm
MUZZLE VELOCITY	366 m/s (1200 fps), 285 m/s (935 fps) w/ gas lever set to low velocity
MUZZLE ENERGY	533 J (393 ft/lb), 327 J (241 ft/lb) w/ gas lever set to low velocity
SIGHTS	Adjustable, aperture/post w/luminous inserts, adjusts for low or high velocity firing
FEED	30 round removable polycarbonate box magazine
WEIGHTS:	
WEAPON (EMPTY)	2.781 kg (3.570 kg w/suppressor)
WEAPON (LOADED)	3.221 kg (4.010 kg w/suppressor)
MAGAZINE (EMPTY)	0.080 kg
MAGAZINE (LOADED)	0.440 kg
SUPPRESSOR	0.789 kg
SERVICE CARTRIDGE	12 g
BULLET	8 g
LENGTHS:	
WEAPON OVERALL	38.7/56.6 cm (65.7/83.5cm w/suppressor)
BARREL	14.9 cm
SUPPRESSOR LENGTH	27.3 cm
SUPPRESSOR DIA.	4.1 cm
SIGHT RADIUS	29.2 cm
STATUS	Prototype
SERVICE	Under evaluation

The MP 2000 was developed, in part according to specifications put out by the U.S. Navy SEAL Team Six, and various other counterterrorist and police forces. A primary intent in the design of the MP 2000 was to combine the best aspects of the MP5 weapons family in a single flexible package. The retractable stock lies flush with the receiver when folded, eliminating any projections. The general layout and size of the MP 2000 allows it to be carried concealed in much the same manner as the MP5 K series. The vertical forward grip also allows for quick point-and-shoot techniques to be effectively used with the stock collapsed. The barrel is completely enclosed by the square front portion of the receiver with cutouts along the sides to allow for cooling air circulation. The most unusual points of the MP-2000 center around the removable suppressor. A long extension on the rear of the suppressor threads onto the barrel and gives a very rigid mount which when tightened, enhances accuracy. There is a gas valve lever just in front of the magazine well that accounts for either normal or subsonic ammunition to be used. When being used without the suppressor in normal firing or when using subsonic ammunition with the suppressor, the gas lever is set to the high pressure (H) position. With the lever set to the low pressure (L) position, ports are opened in the barrel just in front of the chamber leading into an expansion chamber below the barrel. Propellant gasses are bled off into the expansion

chamber, lowering the muzzle velocity of normal NATO ammunition to below the speed of sound, eliminating the supersonic "crack" of the fired bullet. To further limit the sound of firing, the cocking handle can rotate 90 degrees, locking the bolt closed but still allowing the weapon to be fired. With the bolt locked, most of the mechanical sound of firing is eliminated and the MP 2000 is turned into a suppressed manual repeater. To account for different ballistics at supersonic and subsonic ammunition fired in the same weapon, the sights can be switched by the operator to easily match either ammunition. Luminous inserts are also available to increase accuracy in low light situations. The MP 2000 fires from the closed bolt position, retaining the accuracy of the MP 5 series but the new weapon has eliminated the roller-delayed locking system in favor of the mechanically simpler system of recoil operation. To increase the reliability and service life of the MP 2000, all components are completely interchangeable between weapons and the system is made of corrosion resistant materials. The magazines are polycarbonate plastic for light weight and strength. They are not interchangeable with MP 5 magazines. There is a bolt hold open device that locks the bolt to the rear when the last round is fired. The bolt and magazine release buttons are located just ahead and above the trigger on either side of the weapon, allowing for comfortable use by either right or left-handed firers. A standard sight mounting bracket is integral with the receiver of the MP 2000 and allows the weapon to accept any sight system with a NATO standard base. A forward bolt assist is found on the right side of the receiver to aid in closing the bolt in dirty conditions.

ASSESSMENT	10.2 cm @ 100 m w/NATO ball
WEAPON	MP 2000
AMMO	9x19
DISPERSION ANGLE	.0584417 degrees, 1.03896 NATO mils.

Range	Group Circle Width (mm)	Probability (0<p<.099) (m)			
		Body	**Head**	**Hand**	**Bullseye**
5.0	5.100	0.990	0.990	0.990	0.990
10.0	10.200	0.990	0.990	0.990	0.990
15.0	15.300	0.990	0.990	0.990	0.985
20.0	20.400	0.990	0.990	0.990	0.958
25.0	25.500	0.990	0.990	0.990	0.920
50.0	51.000	0.990	0.990	0.976	0.718
75.0	76.500	0.990	0.990	0.917	0.570
100.0*	102.000	0.990	0.976	0.846	0.469
125.0	127.500	0.990	0.950	0.776	0.397
150.0	153.000	0.990	0.917	0.712	0.344
175.0	178.500	0.986	0.882	0.656	0.303
200.0	204.000	0.976	0.846	0.607	0.271

* indicates range for which data was supplied

DAMAGE	25/0.16
DAMAGE (SUPPRESSED)	20/0.12

▼ UZI

UZI with Hebrew markings, fitted with a 25 rd magazine and metal stock (folded)

UZI with M16 flash suppressor on the muzzle

CARTRIDGE	9x19 mm (11.43x23 mm)
OPERATION	Blowback, fires from open bolt.
TYPE OF FIRE	Selective
RATE OF FIRE (SS)	64 rpm (32 rpm) (A) 128 rpm (64 rpm) (CYCLIC) 600 rpm (500 rpm)
MUZZLE VELOCITY	400 m/s (1312 fps), (280 m/s <920 fps>)
MUZZLE ENERGY	637 J (470 ft/lb), (586 J <432 ft/lb>)
SIGHTS	Adjustable, open iron
FEED	20, 25, or 32 round removable box magazine (16 rd in 11.43 mm)
WEIGHTS:	
WEAPON (EMPTY)	3.5 kg
WEAPON (LOADED)	4.104 kg w/32 rds (4.064 kg w/16 rds)
MAGAZINE (EMPTY)	0.160 kg (20 rd), 0.200 kg (25 rd), 0.220 kg (32 rd), (0.220 kg <16 rd>)
MAGAZINE (LOADED)	0.400 kg (20 rd), 0.500 kg (25 rd), 0.604 kg (32 rd), (0.564 kg <16 rd>)
SERVICE CARTRIDGE	12 g (21.5 g)
BULLET	8 g (15 g)
LENGTHS:	
WEAPON OVERALL	47/65 cm
BARREL	26 cm
SIGHT RADIUS	30.9 cm
STATUS	In production
SERVICE	In service with Israel, Belgium, West Germany, Iran, Ireland, the Netherlands, Thailand, Venezuela, and

others with extensive police agency sales throughout the world.

Next to the MP5, the UZI is the most widely seen submachinegun in the hands of HRUs and special police forces. Considered the first of the third generation submachineguns, the UZI is easily recognized by the public to the point where the name UZI is something of a "buzz" word and is applied to almost any weapon by some members of the media. Developed in Israel during the early 1950's, the UZI is manufactured in several countries and is the primary submachinegun of several of the world's militaries. The telescoping bolt of the UZI surrounds the barrel, putting much of the weapon's weight forward as well as allowing a shorter receiver length. Seen most commonly with a folding metal buttstock, the UZI originally had an easily removable wooden buttstock and this is still available today. The overall ruggedness and relative simplicity of the UZI has given it a reputation as a very reliable weapon, capable of operating under the severest conditions. Safety is also paramount in the design of the UZI and the weapon has three safeties. The fire selector on the left of the weapon is a locking safety that can be operated with thumb pressure. There is a grip safety that locks the sear, preventing the bolt from moving unless the handle is properly held. Lastly, there is a ratchet safety in the cocking knob that prevents the bolt from going forward if the knob should slip from the operator's hand while the weapon is being cocked.

Two conversion kits have been developed for the UZI that allows the weapon to fire either .45 ACP (11.43x23mm) or .22 long rifle (5.7x17mmR) ammunition. The .45 ACP adaption is considered for field use though it is somewhat restricted by its limited magazine capacity. The .22 LR version was primarily developed for training purposes. There is a carbine version of the UZI with a long barrel that fires semiautomatically from a closed bolt. Many of the carbines are seen by the public in films where they have been extensively modified to fire on full automatic from a closed bolt and with their barrels cut back.

WEAPON	UZI
AMMO	9x19
DISPERSION ANGLE	.19362 degrees, 3.44214 NATO mils.

Range	Group Circle Width (mm)	Probability (0<p<.099) (m)			
		Body	**Head**	**Hand**	**Bullseye**
5.0	16.897	0.990	0.990	0.990	0.978
10.0	33.793	0.990	0.990	0.990	0.852
15.0	50.690	0.990	0.990	0.977	0.720
20.0	67.586	0.990	0.990	0.940	0.615
25.0	84.483	0.990	0.989	0.895	0.534
50.0	168.966	0.989	0.895	0.676	0.317
75.0	253.448	0.951	0.778	0.528	0.225
100.0	337.931	0.895	0.676	0.431	0.174

☛ continued on next page

☞ UZI continued

Range	Group Circle Width (mm)	Probability (0<p<.099) (m)			
		Body	Head	Hand	Bullseye
125.0	422.414	0.835	0.594	0.363	0.142
150.0	506.897	0.778	0.528	0.313	0.119
175.0	591.379	0.724	0.475	0.275	0.103
200.0	675.862	0.676	0.431	0.246	0.091

DAMAGE (9MM) 27/.17, (45) 24/.28

▼ Mini UZI

Mini UZI fitted with the Armson OEG sight, with 20 rd magazine

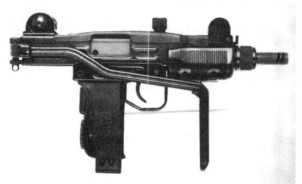

Mini UZI with 20 rd magazine and stock folded

CARTRIDGE 9x19mm
OPERATION Blowback, fires from open (closed) bolt.
TYPE OF FIRE Selective
RATE OF FIRE (SS) 64 rpm (A) 128 rpm (CYCLIC) 950 rpm, 900 rpm (closed bolt variant), 750 rpm (heavy bolt variant)
MUZZLE VELOCITY 350 m/s (1148 fps)
MUZZLE ENERGY 488 J (360 ft/lbs)
SIGHTS Adjustable, open iron
FEED 20, 25, or 32 round removable box magazine
WEIGHTS:
WEAPON (EMPTY) 2.700 kg
WEAPON (LOADED) 3.100 kg w/20 rds
MAGAZINE (EMPTY) 0.160 kg (20 rd), 0.200 kg (25 rd), 0.220 kg (32 rd)

MAGAZINE (LOADED) 0.400 kg (20 rd), 0.500 kg (25 rd), 0.604 kg (32 rd)
SERVICE CARTRIDGE 12 g
BULLET 8 g
LENGTHS:
WEAPON OVERALL 36/60 cm
BARREL 19.7 cm
SIGHT RADIUS 23.5 cm
STATUS In production

This is a shortened, lighter version of the standard UZI submachinegun with all of the basic operating principles remaining the same. The shorter length of travel and lighter breechblock result in the Mini UZI having a cyclic rate of fire which is 50% higher than the full sized weapon. The stock on the Mini UZI is vastly different from the full sized model. The stock is a single strut covered with a padding material and folding to the right side of the weapon. When the stock is folded, the buttplate, which protrudes down slightly further than the pistol grip, can be held with the non-firing hand, resulting in a very secure grip. The stock can be unfolded quickly in a much simpler manner than the more complex folding metal stock of the full sized UZI. There are several subvariants of the Mini UZI besides the standard model. There is also a heavy bolt available with tungsten inserts that reduces the cyclic rate of fire of the standard Mini UZI to 750 rounds per minute.

WEAPON MINI-UZI
AMMO 9x19
DISPERSION ANGLE .217329 degrees, 3.86362 NATO mils.

Range	Group Circle Width (mm)	Probability (0<p<.099) (m)			
		Body	Head	Hand	Bullseye
5.0	18.966	0.990	0.990	0.990	0.967
10.0	37.931	0.990	0.990	0.990	0.817
15.0	56.897	0.990	0.990	0.965	0.678
20.0	75.862	0.990	0.990	0.919	0.573
25.0	94.828	0.990	0.982	0.866	0.493
50.0	189.655	0.982	0.866	0.634	0.288
75.0	284.483	0.931	0.738	0.488	0.203
100.0	379.310	0.866	0.634	0.395	0.156
125.0	474.138	0.800	0.552	0.331	0.127
150.0	568.966	0.738	0.488	0.285	0.107
175.0	663.793	0.683	0.437	0.249	0.093
200.0	758.621	0.634	0.395	0.222	0.082

DAMAGE 24/.15

▼ Micro UZI

Prototype Micro UZI with extended stock

CARTRIDGE	9x19 mm
OPERATION	Blowback, fires from open bolt.
TYPE OF FIRE	Selective
RATE OF FIRE (SS)	40 rpm (A) 80 rpm (CYCLIC) 1250 rpm
MUZZLE VELOCITY	350 m/s (1148 fps)
MUZZLE ENERGY	488 J (360 ft/lbs)
SIGHTS	Adjustable, open iron
FEED	20, 25, or 32 round removable box magazine
WEIGHTS:	
WEAPON (EMPTY)	1.950 kg
WEAPON (LOADED)	2.350 kg w/20 rds
MAGAZINE (EMPTY)	0.160 kg (20 rd), 0.200 kg (25 rd), 0.220 kg (32 rd)
MAGAZINE (LOADED)	0.400 kg (20 rd), 0.500 kg (25 rd), 0.604 kg (32 rd)
SERVICE CARTRIDGE	12 g
BULLET	8 g
LENGTHS:	
WEAPON OVERALL	26.7/47 cm
BARREL	11.4 cm
SIGHT RADIUS	17.5 cm
STATUS	In production

Micro UZI

This is the smallest version of the UZI available and is very much a selective fire version of the UZI pistol. The Micro UZI also has a simple folding metal stock much like the larger Mini UZI and early production weapons were made from an UZI pistol converted to selective fire. In fact, many of the pistols were converted before the Micro UZI became available and these are what appear most often on television and in the movies. Able to use all of the standard UZI magazines, the Micro UZI is a very concealable, potent firepower package.

ASSESSMENT	S/A - 5 in @ 25 yd, standing
WEAPON	MICRO UZI
AMMO	9x19
DISPERSION ANGLE	.318309 degrees, 5.65883 NATO mils.

Micro UZI with stock extended

☞ continued on next page

☞ *Micro UZI continued*

Range	Group Circle Width (mm)	Probability (0<p<.099) (m)			
		Body	Head	Hand	Bullseye
5.0	27.778	0.990	0.990	0.990	0.902
10.0	55.556	0.990	0.990	0.968	0.687
15.0	83.333	0.990	0.990	0.898	0.539
20.0	111.111	0.990	0.968	0.820	0.440
25.0	138.889	0.990	0.936	0.746	0.371
50.0	277.778	0.936	0.746	0.496	0.207
75.0	416.667	0.839	0.599	0.367	0.143
100.0	555.556	0.746	0.496	0.290	0.110
125.0	694.444	0.666	0.422	0.240	0.089
150.0	833.333	0.599	0.367	0.204	0.074
175.0	972.222	0.543	0.324	0.178	0.064
200.0	1111.111	0.496	0.290	0.158	0.056

DAMAGE 24/.15

▼ PM-12S

PM-12S with stock extended and bolt forward

CARTRIDGE	9x19mm
OPERATION	Blowback, fires from open bolt.
TYPE OF FIRE	Selective
RATE OF FIRE (SS)	40 rpm (A) 120 rpm (CYCLIC) 550 rpm
MUZZLE VELOCITY	381 m/s (1250 fps)
MUZZLE ENERGY	579 J (427 ft/lb)
SIGHTS	Adjustable, open iron
FEED	20, 32, or 40 round removable box magazine
WEIGHTS:	
WEAPON (EMPTY)	3.240 kg
WEAPON (LOADED)	3.850 kg w/32 rds
MAGAZINE (EMPTY)	0.190 kg (20 rd), 0.226 kg (32 rd), 0.250 kg (40 rd)
MAGAZINE (LOADED)	0.430 kg (20 rd), 0.610 kg (32 rd), 0.730 kg (40 rd)
SERVICE CARTRIDGE	12 g

BULLET	8 g
LENGTHS:	
WEAPON OVERALL	41.8/66 cm
BARREL	20 cm
SIGHT RADIUS	28.5 cm
STATUS	In production

This S model of the PM-12 series is the latest and most popular of the post World War Two Italian designs. The telescoping bolt gives the PM-12S a reasonably short overall length and this, combined with the two vertical grips, make the weapon very fast handling. An unusual grip safety is found on this Beretta with the safety being in the form of a trigger-like projection on the front of the rear grip, below the trigger guard. The location of the safety allows the weapon to be firmly held and the safety unlocked only when the operator pulls in the lock with the middle finger of his firing hand. The tubular receiver has longitudinal recesses built into it to allow the bolt to operate in very dirty conditions as well as to add to the overall strength of the weapon. The 32 round magazine is now standard in the Beretta PM-12S but earlier 20 or 40 round magazines may still be used.

WEAPON	PM-12S
AMMO	9x19
DISPERSION ANGLE	.197572 degrees, 3.51238 NATO mils.

Range	Group Circle Width (mm)	Probability (0<p<.099) (m)			
		Body	Head	Hand	Bullseye
5.0	17.241	0.990	0.990	0.990	0.976
10.0	34.483	0.990	0.990	0.990	0.846
15.0	51.724	0.990	0.990	0.975	0.713
20.0	68.966	0.990	0.990	0.937	0.608
25.0	86.207	0.990	0.988	0.890	0.527
50.0	172.414	0.988	0.890	0.669	0.312
75.0	258.621	0.947	0.771	0.521	0.221
100.0	344.828	0.890	0.669	0.424	0.171
125.0	431.034	0.829	0.587	0.357	0.139
150.0	517.241	0.771	0.521	0.308	0.117
175.0	603.448	0.717	0.468	0.271	0.101
200.0	689.655	0.669	0.424	0.241	0.089

DAMAGE 27/.16

▼ Spectre M-4

Spectre M-4

Spectre M-4, left side cutaway view

Spectre M-4 with stock extended

Spectre M-4 with stock folded and 30 rd magazine

CARTRIDGE	9x19 mm
OPERATION	Blowback, fires from closed bolt.
TYPE OF FIRE	Selective, double action.
RATE OF FIRE (SS)	40 rpm (A) 120 rpm (CYCLIC) 850 rpm
MUZZLE VELOCITY	399 m/s (1310 fps)
MUZZLE ENERGY	636 J (469 ft/lb)
SIGHTS	Fixed, non-adjustable iron
FEED	30 or 50 round removable box magazines
WEIGHTS:	
WEAPON (EMPTY)	2.903 kg
WEAPON (LOADED)	3.793 kg w/50 rds
MAGAZINE (EMPTY)	0.204 kg (30 rd), 0.290 kg (50 rd)
MAGAZINE (LOADED)	0.564 kg (30 rd), 0.890 kg (50 rd)
SERVICE CARTRIDGE	12 g
BULLET	8 g
LENGTHS:	
WEAPON OVERALL	35/58 cm
BARREL	13 cm
SIGHT RADIUS	30.9 cm
STATUS	In production

The Spectre is a very new design with several unique features. The most innovative feature of the Spectre is its system of double action firing from a closed bolt. The bolt of the weapon is drawn to the rear by the cocking knob and returns to battery to chamber a round. When the bolt closes a striker block is held to the rear and can be released to fire the weapon by simply pulling the trigger. If the weapon is to be held in the loaded condition, the smaller lever above the rear grip is used to decock the weapon, lowering the striker safely without firing the round in the chamber. With the striker lowered, the weapon is completely safe to handle and will not fire until the trigger is pulled to cock and release the striker. This double action feature eliminates the need for a separate safety and there is no manual safety on the weapon. The double action feature and lack of a separate safety combine to make the Spectre one of the fastest weapons of its class to get into action as only the trigger has to be pulled to fire the weapon from the safe condition. A four column magazine system, referred to as a 4-file system by the parent company, is used in the Spectre to greatly increase magazine capacity without increasing size by a large amount. The compact magazines are only 3.5cm thick with the 30 round magazine being 16cm long and the 50 round 21cm long, an average double column 32 round standard magazine is 2.5cm thick and 28cm in length. To help eliminate the cook-off problems raised by the closed bolt system and large magazine capacity, a forced-air cooling system has been developed. In the Spectre system, air is forced through and around the barrel by the movement of the bolt to help cool the weapon with the system working well enough to give the Spectre a practical rate of fire equal to or greater than comparative open bolt weapons. Sinusoidal rifling is used in the Spectre's barrel

☞ continued on next page

☛ *Spectre M-4 continued*

to also help in cooling and increase the useful life of the barrel. In sinusoidal rifling, the lands of the barrel have rounded and not sharp edges so that the bullet may pass through more easily and cut down on heating of the barrel through friction. The selector and decocking lever are duplicated on both sides of the weapon with the cocking knob being on the top and sides of the receiver and the magazine release being at the front of the trigger guard. The location of the controls make the Spectre completely ambidextrous with the ejection of spent cartridges being to the right side. Designed for quick use in close-in reaction situations, the Spectre M4 is considered by some to be the first example of a fourth generation submachinegun.

	WEAPON	Spectre M-4
	AMMO	9x19
	DISPERSION ANGLE	.0948345 degrees, 1.68595 NATO mils.

Range	Group Circle Width (mm)	Probability (0<p<.099) (m)			
		Body	Head	Hand	Bullseye
5.0	8.276	0.990	0.990	0.990	0.990
10.0	16.552	0.990	0.990	0.990	0.980
15.0	24.828	0.990	0.990	0.990	0.926
20.0	33.103	0.990	0.990	0.990	0.858
25.0	41.379	0.990	0.990	0.990	0.790
50.0	82.759	0.990	0.990	0.900	0.541
75.0	124.138	0.990	0.954	0.784	0.405
100.0	165.517	0.990	0.900	0.684	0.323
125.0	206.897	0.975	0.841	0.602	0.268
150.0	248.276	0.954	0.784	0.536	0.229
175.0	289.655	0.928	0.732	0.482	0.200
200.0	331.034	0.900	0.684	0.438	0.177

DAMAGE 27/.17

▼ Z-62 • Z-70/B

Z-70 with stock folded and no magazine

Z-70 with stock extended

CARTRIDGE	9x19 mm
OPERATION	Blowback, fires from open bolt
TYPE OF FIRE	Selective
RATE OF FIRE (SS)	40 rpm (A) 120 rpm (CYCLIC) 550 rpm
MUZZLE VELOCITY	381 m/s (1250 fps)
MUZZLE ENERGY	579 J (427 ft/lbs)
SIGHTS	Fixed, non-adjustable iron
FEED	20 or 30 round removable box magazine
WEIGHTS:	
WEAPON (EMPTY)	2.870 kg
WEAPON (LOADED)	3.430 kg w/30 rds
MAGAZINE (EMPTY)	0.100 kg (20 rd), 0.200 kg (200 rd)
MAGAZINE (LOADED)	0.340 kg (20 rd), 0.560 kg (30 rd)
SERVICE CARTRIDGE	12 g
BULLET	8 g
LENGTHS:	
WEAPON OVERALL	48/70 cm
BARREL	20 cm
SIGHT RADIUS	37 cm
STATUS	In production (as the Z-70)
SERVICE	Spanish forces

This Z-62 is a Spanish made weapon that has seen good commercial sales as well as use by the Spanish military. There are several unusual features in the Z-62 with the most obvious being the long trigger with the double inset curve. The lower notch of the trigger is pulled for semiautomatic fire while pulling by the upper notch results in full automatic fire. There is also an unusual bolt locking safety that engages when the bolt is closed, on an empty chamber. When the cocking handle is pulled, the safety automatically unlocks. An updated and improved Z-62 has been put on the market as the Z-70/B replaced by a standard type trigger and thumb actuated selector lever. The automatic bolt lock of the Z-62 is replaced in the Z-70/B by a bolt blocking sear that prevents the bolt from being closed without the trigger being pulled.

	WEAPON	Z-62
	AMMO	9x19
	DISPERSION ANGLE	.16596 degrees, 2.9504 NATO mils.

Range	Group Circle Width (mm)	Probability (0<p<.099) (m)			
		Body	Head	Hand	Bullseye
5.0	14.483	0.990	0.990	0.990	0.988
10.0	28.966	0.990	0.990	0.990	0.892
15.0	43.448	0.990	0.990	0.988	0.773
20.0	57.931	0.990	0.990	0.963	0.672
25.0	72.414	0.990	0.990	0.928	0.590
50.0	144.828	0.990	0.928	0.732	0.359
75.0	217.241	0.970	0.827	0.584	0.257
100.0	289.655	0.928	0.732	0.482	0.200
125.0	362.069	0.878	0.651	0.409	0.163
150.0	434.483	0.827	0.584	0.355	0.138
175.0	506.897	0.778	0.528	0.313	0.119
200.0	579.310	0.732	0.482	0.280	0.105

DAMAGE 26/.16

▼ Z-84 Short • Long

Z-84 with stock folded and no magazine

Z-84 with stock extended, no magazine, and short barrel

CARTRIDGE	9x19mm
OPERATION	Blowback, fires from open bolt.
TYPE OF FIRE	Selective
RATE OF FIRE (SS)	40 rpm (A) 100 rpm (CYCLIC) 600 rpm
MUZZLE VELOCITY	362 m/s (1187 fps), (365 m/s <1198 fps>)
MUZZLE ENERGY	522 J (385 ft/lb), 532 J (392 ft/lb)
SIGHTS	Fixed, non-adjustable iron
FEED	25 or 30 round removable box magazine
WEIGHTS:	
WEAPON (EMPTY)	3.100 kg (3.150 kg)
WEAPON (LOADED)	3.700 kg w/30 rds (3.750 kg w/30 rds)

MAGAZINE (EMPTY)	0.220 kg (25 rd), 0.240 kg (30 rd)
MAGAZINE (LOADED)	0.520 kg (25 rd), 0.600 kg (30 rd)
SERVICE CARTRIDGE	12 g
BULLET	8 g
LENGTHS:	
WEAPON OVERALL	41/61.5 cm (46.5/67 cm)
BARREL	21.5 cm (27 cm)
SIGHT RADIUS	33 cm
STATUS	In production

This is the newest submachinegun design to come out of Spain. Following modern tactical requirements, the Z-84 is a balanced, light weight, and simple weapon, rugged enough to work under hard usage. The pistol grip/magazine well follows the "hand-finds-hand" principal coming into common usage. There is a manual sliding safety/selector above the trigger on the left side of the weapon. In addition to the manual safety there is an automatic bolt lock that will lock the bolt in the forward position until opened by the cocking handle. Should the cocking handle slip from the firer's grasp, there are additional notches in the bolt that prevent its forward movement unless it is fully cocked. A simple barrel nut is removable, allowing an exchange of barrels. Both a long and short barrel are available for the Z-84.

WEAPON	Z-84
AMMO	9x19
DISPERSION ANGLE	.177815 degrees, 3.16115 NATO mils.

Range	Group Circle Width (mm)	Probability (0<p<.099) (m)			
		Body	Head	Hand	Bullseye
5.0	15.517	0.990	0.990	0.990	0.984
10.0	31.034	0.990	0.990	0.990	0.875
15.0	46.552	0.990	0.990	0.983	0.750
20.0	62.069	0.990	0.990	0.954	0.646
25.0	77.586	0.990	0.990	0.914	0.565
50.0	155.172	0.990	0.914	0.707	0.340
75.0	232.759	0.962	0.805	0.559	0.242
100.0	310.345	0.914	0.707	0.459	0.188
125.0	387.931	0.860	0.625	0.388	0.153
150.0	465.517	0.805	0.559	0.336	0.129
175.0	543.103	0.754	0.504	0.296	0.112
200.0	620.690	0.707	0.459	0.264	0.099

DAMAGE 25/.15 (25/.16)

▼ M45B (US Suppressed version)

M45

M45B with U.S. issued suppressor

CARTRIDGE 9x19 mm
OPERATION Blowback, fires from open bolt.
TYPE OF FIRE Full automatic
RATE OF FIRE (A) 144 rpm (60 rpm)
(CYCLIC) 600 rpm (550 rpm)
MUZZLE VELOCITY 370 m/s (1213 fps)
(298 m/s <980 fps>)
MUZZLE ENERGY 545 J (402 ft/lb), (355 J <262 ft/lb>)
SIGHTS Fixed, non-adjustable iron
FEED 36 round removable box magazine
WEIGHTS:
WEAPON (EMPTY) 3.900 kg (4.564 kg)
WEAPON (LOADED) 4.559 kg (5.223 kg)
MAGAZINE (EMPTY) 0.227 kg
MAGAZINE (LOADED) 0.659 kg
SERVICE CARTRIDGE 12 g
BULLET 8 g
LENGTHS:
WEAPON OVERALL 55.2 cm
BARREL 21.3 cm
SIGHT RADIUS 35.9 cm (51.9 cm)
STATUS Out of production (Obsolescent)
SERVICE Swedish forces, also sold to Egypt, Indonesia, and Ireland, also extensive commercial sales (used by American Special Forces and Intelligence agencies in South East Asia).

This version of the M45 submachinegun was developed to give the U.S. forces in Indochina a suppressed weapon that could not be directly traced to the U.S. The suppressor is heavy by today's standards and not as efficient as a modern design. Due to the widespread sales of the M45, it can be found in many places throughout the world and the suppressed version is still available.

ASSESSMENT 12 3/4 in @ 75 yd.
WEAPON M45B
AMMO 9x19
DISPERSION ANGLE .19132 degrees, 3.40125 NATO mils.

Range	Group Circle Width (mm)	Probability (0<p<.099) (m)			
		Body	Head	Hand	Bullseye
5.0	16.696	0.990	0.990	0.990	0.979
10.0	33.392	0.990	0.990	0.990	0.855
15.0	50.087	0.990	0.990	0.978	0.724
20.0	66.783	0.990	0.990	0.942	0.619
25.0	83.479	0.990	0.990	0.898	0.538
50.0	167.153	0.990	0.898	0.680	0.320
75.0	250.730	0.952	0.781	0.532	0.227
100.0	334.307	0.898	0.680	0.434	0.175
125.0	417.883	0.839	0.598	0.366	0.143
150.0	501.460	0.781	0.532	0.316	0.121
175.0	585.036	0.728	0.479	0.278	0.104
200.0	668.613	0.680	0.434	0.248	0.092

DAMAGE 25/.16

WEAPON M45B Suppressed
AMMO 9x19
DISPERSION ANGLE .270688 degrees, 4.81224 NATO mils.

Range	Group Circle Width (mm)	Probability (0<p<.099) (m)			
		Body	Head	Hand	Bullseye
5.0	23.622	0.990	0.990	0.990	0.935
10.0	47.244	0.990	0.990	0.982	0.745
15.0	70.866	0.990	0.990	0.932	0.598
20.0	94.488	0.990	0.982	0.867	0.495
25.0	118.110	0.990	0.960	0.801	0.421
50.0	236.220	0.960	0.801	0.554	0.239
75.0	354.331	0.884	0.659	0.416	0.166
100.0	472.441	0.801	0.554	0.332	0.128
125.0	590.551	0.725	0.475	0.276	0.103
150.0	708.661	0.659	0.416	0.236	0.087
175.0	826.772	0.602	0.369	0.206	0.075
200.0	944.882	0.554	0.332	0.183	0.066

DAMAGE 20/.13

▼ Sterling L2A3
(Mark IV, commercial designation)

SERVICE CARTRIDGE	12 g
BULLET	8 g
LENGTHS:	
WEAPON OVERALL	48.3/69 cm
BARREL	19.8 cm
SIGHT RADIUS	41 cm
STATUS	In production
SERVICE	In service with the British military, extensive foreign sales, as the Mark 4, to over 90 countries.

Sterling L2A3 with bolt forward, stock folded, and 34 rd magazine

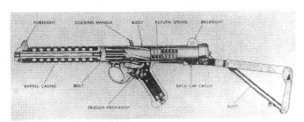

Sterling L2A3 cutaway view

CARTRIDGE	9x19 mm
OPERATION	Blowback, fires from open bolt.
TYPE OF FIRE	Selective
RATE OF FIRE (SS)	40 rpm (A) 102 rpm (CYCLIC) 550 rpm
MUZZLE VELOCITY	390 m/s (1280 fps)
MUZZLE ENERGY	606 J (447 ft/lb)
SIGHTS	Fixed, non-adjustable iron
FEED	10, 15, 34, 2x10, 2x15, or 2x34 round removable box magazines
WEIGHTS:	
WEAPON (EMPTY)	2.720 kg
WEAPON (LOADED)	3.440 kg w/34 rds
MAGAZINE (EMPTY)	0.134 kg (10 rd), 0.191 kg (15 rd), 0.312 kg (34 rd), 0.276 kg (2x10 rd), 0.390 kg (2x15 rd), 0.638 kg (2x34 rd)
MAGAZINE (LOADED)	0.254 kg (10 rd), 0.371 kg (15 rd), 0.720 kg (34 rd), 0.516 kg (2x10), 0.750 kg (2x15 rd), 1.454 kg (2x34 rd)

The Sterling, as it is more popularly known, is the British post war replacement for the STEN series of weapons. Extremely robust and easy to operate, the Sterling has achieved good commercial success with over 2 million being produced and some 90 countries having purchased it. Light and handy with its folding buttstock, the Sterling continues the left side horizontal magazine mounting established in the Sten. Though unusual to most who are not familiar with it, the side mounted magazine allows a very low profile to be shown when firing from the prone position. The magazines were designed to be very reliable with several short models available for use in areas of limited space, such as a truck cab. Cleaning surfaces on the bolt help scrape the receiver while being fired, and the Sterling has a wide reputation for reliability. There is a semiautomatic only version of the Sterling made which is called the Sterling Police Carbine. It is identical to the normal weapon but fires from a closed bolt. A long barreled version of the carbine is marketed for the U.S. Civilian market. The Police Carbine was widely sold in Kenya to farmers during the Mau Mau uprising.

WEAPON	Sterling L2A3
AMMO	9x19
DISPERSION ANGLE	.150154 degrees, 2.66941 NATO mils.

Range	Group Circle Width (mm)	Probability (0<p<.099) (m)			
		Body	**Head**	**Hand**	**Bullseye**
5.0	13.103	0.990	0.990	0.990	0.990
10.0	26.207	0.990	0.990	0.990	0.915
15.0	39.310	0.990	0.990	0.990	0.806
20.0	52.414	0.990	0.990	0.974	0.708
25.0	65.517	0.990	0.990	0.945	0.626
50.0	131.034	0.990	0.945	0.766	0.389
75.0	196.552	0.979	0.856	0.621	0.280
100.0	262.069	0.945	0.766	0.517	0.218
125.0	327.586	0.902	0.687	0.441	0.179
150.0	393.103	0.856	0.621	0.384	0.151
175.0	458.621	0.810	0.564	0.340	0.131
200.0	524.138	0.766	0.517	0.305	0.116

DAMAGE 27/.17

▼ Sterling L34A1

Sterling L34A1 with bolt forward and stock folded

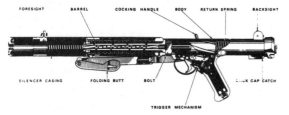

Sterling L34A1 cutaway view showing suppressor

CARTRIDGE 9x19 mm
OPERATION Blowback, fires from open bolt.
TYPE OF FIRE Selective
RATE OF FIRE (SS) 40 rpm (A) 102 rpm (CYCLIC) 550 rpm
MUZZLE VELOCITY 307 m/s (1010 fps)
MUZZLE ENERGY 378 J (279 ft/lb)
SIGHTS Fixed, non-adjustable iron
FEED 10, 15, 34, 2x10, 2x15, or
2x34 round removable box magazine

WEIGHTS:
WEAPON (EMPTY) 3.600 kg
WEAPON (LOADED) 4.320 kg w/34 rds
MAGAZINE (EMPTY) 0.134 kg (10 rd), 0.191 kg (15 rd),
0.312 kg (34 rd), 0.276 kg (2x10 rd),
0.390 kg (2x15 rd), 0.638 kg (2x34 rd)
MAGAZINE (LOADED) 0.254 kg (10 rd), 0.371 kg (15 rd),
0.720 kg (34 rd), 0.516 kg (2x10 rd),
0.750 kg (2x15 rd), 1.454 kg (2x34 rd)
SERVICE CARTRIDGE 12 g
BULLET 8 g
LENGTHS:
WEAPON OVERALL 66/86.4 cm
BARREL 19.8 cm
SIGHT RADIUS 50.2 cm
STATUS In production
SERVICE In service with the British military,
commercial sales, as the Mark 5, to
over 90 countries.

This weapon is a silenced version of the L2A3 Sterling. Available commercially as the Mark 5 Sterling, the L34A1 is the standard suppressed weapon found in the British forces. The wide commercial sales also sees the L34A1 in a great range of hands. The Mark 5 is popular among Argentinean commandos where it faced the L34A1 in the hands of the SAS during the Falklands conflict. The standard stated by the British military was for a weapon whose "mechanical noise is to be unheard at

30 meters and not to be recognized as a firearm at 50 meters". The L34A1 achieves these requirements well and fires the NATO standard ball round while achieving them. The long sleeve of the barrel contains the silencer and it is an integral part of the design. The barrel is perforated with 72 holes along a good deal of its length to lower the standard NATO ball projectile to below the speed of sound. The overall soundness of the design shows, as the L34A1 is considered the most quiet production open bolt weapon on today's market.

ASSESSMENT 5 rd group 50.8 mm dia. @ 25 m
WEAPON Sterling L34A1
AMMO 9x19
DISPERSION ANGLE .116425 degrees, 2.06978 NATO mils.

Range	Group Circle Width (mm)	Probability (0<p<.099) (m)			
		Body	**Head**	**Hand**	**Bullseye**
5.0	10.160	0.990	0.990	0.990	0.990
10.0	20.320	0.990	0.990	0.990	0.958
15.0	30.480	0.990	0.990	0.990	0.880
20.0	40.640	0.990	0.990	0.990	0.795
25.0*	50.800	0.990	0.990	0.976	0.719
50.0	101.600	0.990	0.976	0.847	0.470
75.0	152.400	0.990	0.918	0.713	0.345
100.0	203.200	0.976	0.847	0.608	0.272
125.0	254.000	0.950	0.777	0.528	0.224
150.0	304.800	0.918	0.713	0.465	0.191
175.0	355.600	0.883	0.657	0.415	0.166
200.0	406.400	0.847	0.608	0.374	0.147

* indicates range for which data was supplied
DAMAGE 21/.13

▼ Sterling Mark 7 A4 • Mark 7 A8

Sterling Mark 7A4 with bolt forward and 15 rd magazine

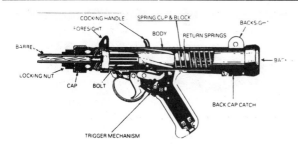

Sterling Mark 7A4 cutaway view

CARTRIDGE | 9x19 mm
OPERATION | Blowback, fires from open bolt
TYPE OF FIRE | Selective
RATE OF FIRE (SS) | 40 rpm (A) 102 rpm (CYCLIC) 560 rpm
MUZZLE VELOCITY | 356m/s (1169 fps), (382 m/s <1254 fps>)
MUZZLE ENERGY | 506 J (373 ft/lb), (582 J <429 ft/lb>)
SIGHTS | Fixed, non-adjustable, iron
FEED | 10, 15, 34, 2x10, 2x15, or 2x34 round removable box magazine

WEIGHTS:

WEAPON (EMPTY) | 2.200 kg (2.300 kg <A8>)
WEAPON (LOADED) | 2.454 kg w/10 rds (2.554 kg w/10 rds <A8>)
MAGAZINE (EMPTY) | 0.134 kg (10 rd), 0.191 kg (15 rd), 0.312 kg (34 rd), 0.276 kg (2x10 rd), 0.390 kg (2x15 rd), 0.638 kg (2x34 rd)
MAGAZINE (LOADED) | 0.254 kg (10 rd), 0.371 kg (15 rd), 0.720 kg (34 rd), 0.516 kg (2x10 rd), 0.750 kg (2x15 rd), 1.454 kg (2x34 rd)
SERVICE CARTRIDGE | 12 g
BULLET | 8 g

LENGTHS:

WEAPON OVERALL | 35.5 cm (47 cm <A8>)
BARREL | 10.8 cm (19.8 cm <A8>)
SIGHT RADIUS | 24.1 cm
STATUS | In production
SERVICE | Commercial sales

This is a specialized compact version of the standard L2A3 submachinegun. Designed for use by vehicle crews, pilots, and special units, the Mark 7 has all the firepower and characteristics of the full length weapon in a much smaller size. The A4 and A8 in the Mark 7's designation indicates the barrel length with all other features being identical. Use of the 10 or 15 round magazines allow the Mark 7 to be carried in a holster. there is also a specialized shoulder holster available to carry the Mark 7 as well as two extra 34 round magazines. A silencer is available for the A4 version but no details are yet available.

ASSESSMENT | 2 3/4 in @ 25 yds w/4 in bbl S/A
WEAPON | Sterling Mark 7 A4
AMMO | 9x19

DISPERSION ANGLE .175446 degrees, 3.11905 NATO mils.

Range	Group Circle Width (mm)	Probability (0<p<.099) (m)			
		Body	Head	Hand	Bullseye
5.0	15.311	0.990	0.990	0.990	0.985
10.0	30.621	0.990	0.990	0.990	0.878
15.0	45.932	0.990	0.990	0.984	0.754
20.0	61.242	0.990	0.990	0.955	0.651
25.0	76.553	0.990	0.990	0.917	0.569
50.0	153.106	0.990	0.917	0.712	0.344
75.0	229.659	0.964	0.810	0.564	0.245
100.0	306.212	0.917	0.712	0.463	0.190
125.0	382.765	0.863	0.630	0.392	0.155
150.0	459.318	0.810	0.564	0.339	0.131
175.0	535.871	0.759	0.509	0.299	0.113
200.0	612.423	0.712	0.463	0.267	0.100

DAMAGE 24/.15 (26/.16)

▼ Ingram M10

CARTRIDGE | 9x19 mm (11.43x23 mm)
OPERATION | Blowback, fires from open bolt.
TYPE OF FIRE | Selective
RATE OF FIRE (SS) | 40 rpm (A) 96 rpm (90 rpm) (CYCLIC) 1090 rpm (1145 rpm)
MUZZLE VELOCITY | 366 m/s (1200 fps) (280 m/s <918 fps>)
MUZZLE ENERGY | 533 J (393 ft/lb) (583 J <430 ft/lb>)
SIGHTS | Fixed, non-adjustable iron
FEED | 32 round (30 round) removable box magazine

WEIGHTS:

WEAPON (EMPTY) | 2.840 kg, 3.385 kg w/suppressor
WEAPON (LOADED) | 3.424 kg, 3.969 kg w/suppressor (3.825 kg, 4.370 w/suppressor)
MAGAZINE (EMPTY) | 0.200 kg (32 rd), (.340 kg <30 rd>)
MAGAZINE (LOADED) | 0.584 kg (32 rd), (0.985 kg <30 rd>)
SERVICE CARTRIDGE | 12 g (21.5 g)

☞ continued on next page

☞ *Ingram M10 continued*

BULLET	8 g (15 g)
LENGTHS:	
WEAPON OVERALL	26.9/54.8 cm, 54.5/79.8 cm w/suppressor
BARREL	14.6 cm
SIGHT RADIUS	21 cm
STATUS	Still in limited production
SERVICE	In service with Bolivia, Columbia, Guatemala, Honduras, Israel, Portugal, Britain, the U.S., and Venezuela with the 9mm version being the most common.
COST	$300 ($400 w/suppressor)

Probably one of the most publicly recognizable submachineguns, the Ingram is seen far more often in popular movies and in criminal hands than in official use. Developed as a possible replacement sidearm for the U.S. military, the Ingram is a very compact weapon, while still firing a powerful round. The M10 was made in either 9 x 19mm, using the Walther MPL magazine, or in 11.43 x 23mm, using a slightly modified M3A1 magazine. Both weapons were dimensionally and functionally identical. The sliding buttstock is too short for really comfortable use by most firers and the front strap, hanging under the barrel, is a useful but not very satisfactory front handgrip. The very high cyclic rate of fire makes the Ingram a difficult weapon to master, but it can be fired in controlled bursts, contrary to some beliefs. A muzzle suppressor was designed for use with the Ingram and this makes the weapon much more manageable to use. The Ingram is most successful when used as a close-in weapon where its high rate of fire can quickly put a number of rounds on target.

WEAPON	Ingram M10
AMMO	9x19
DISPERSION ANGLE	.229183 degrees, 4.07437 NATO mils.

Range	Group Circle Width (mm)	Probability (0<p<.099) (m)			
		Body	**Head**	**Hand**	**Bullseye**
5.0	20.000	0.990	0.990	0.990	0.960
10.0	40.000	0.990	0.990	0.990	0.801
15.0	60.000	0.990	0.990	0.958	0.659
20.0	80.000	0.990	0.990	0.908	0.553
25.0	100.000	0.990	0.978	0.851	0.475
50.0	200.000	0.978	0.851	0.614	0.276
75.0	300.000	0.921	0.719	0.470	0.193
100.0	400.000	0.851	0.614	0.379	0.149
125.0	500.000	0.782	0.533	0.317	0.121
150.0	600.000	0.719	0.470	0.272	0.102
175.0	700.000	0.663	0.420	0.238	0.088
200.0	800.000	0.614	0.379	0.212	0.077

DAMAGE 25/.16 (24/.28)

▼ Ingram M11

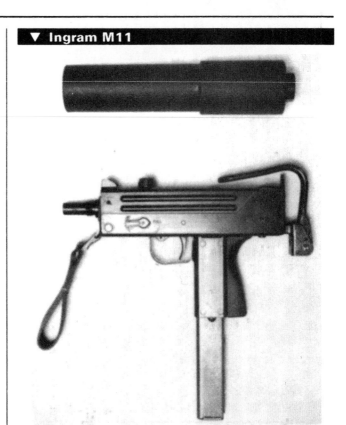

Ingram M11 with MAC suppressor separate and 32 rd magazine

Ingram M11 with MAC suppressor mounted and 32 rd magazine, selector set to full automatic and bolt in forward position

CARTRIDGE	9x17 mm
OPERATION	Blowback, fires from open bolt.
TYPE OF FIRE	Selective
RATE OF FIRE (SS)	40 rpm (A) 96 rpm (CYCLIC) 1200 rpm
MUZZLE VELOCITY	293 m/s (960 fps)
MUZZLE ENERGY	263 J (194 ft/lb)
SIGHTS	Fixed, non-adjustable iron
FEED	16 or 32 round removable box magazine
WEIGHTS:	
WEAPON (EMPTY)	1.59 kg, 2.045 kg
WEAPON (LOADED)	2.100 kg w/32 rds, 2.555 kg w/ 32 rds & suppressor

MAGAZINE (EMPTY)	0.127 kg (16 rd), 0.200 kg
MAGAZINE (LOADED)	0.282 kg (16 rd), 0.510 kg (32 rd)
SERVICE CARTRIDGE	9.7 g
BULLET	6.18 g
LENGTHS:	
WEAPON OVERALL	24.8/46 cm, 44/65 cm w/suppressor
BARREL	12.9 cm
SIGHT RADIUS	17.6 cm
STATUS	In limited production

This is the smallest of the Ingram series of weapons. The M11 is not much larger than most military handguns and there is a smaller magazine available for it to take advantage of this size. A suppressor is also available for this weapon and it is much more comfortable to fire with the suppressor fitted. There are two safeties to be found on the Ingram submachineguns, the first is a sliding safety just in front of the trigger on the right side. This safety is placed so that it can be pushed off with the trigger finger. The second safety is the cocking knob which can be rotated 90 degrees to lock the bolt in either the forward or cocked position.

WEAPON	Ingram M11
AMMO	9x17
DISPERSION ANGLE	.241037 degrees, 4.28511 NATO mils.

Range	Group Circle Width (mm)	Probability (0<p<.099) (m)			
		Body	**Head**	**Hand**	**Bullseye**
5.0	21.034	0.990	0.990	0.990	0.953
10.0	42.069	0.990	0.990	0.989	0.784
15.0	63.103	0.990	0.990	0.951	0.640
20.0	84.138	0.990	0.989	0.896	0.535
25.0	105.172	0.990	0.973	0.837	0.458
50.0	210.345	0.973	0.837	0.596	0.264
75.0	315.517	0.911	0.701	0.453	0.185
100.0	420.690	0.837	0.596	0.364	0.142
125.0	525.862	0.765	0.515	0.304	0.115
150.0	631.034	0.701	0.453	0.261	0.097
175.0	736.207	0.645	0.404	0.228	0.084
200.0	841.379	0.596	0.364	0.203	0.074

DAMAGE 20/.10

▼ Ingram M11/9mm

Ingram M11/9mm with Interand suppressor showing both 15 and 30 rd magazines

M11/9mm with stock folded, no magazine, bolt forward, safety off

CARTRIDGE	9x19 mm
OPERATION	Blowback, fires from open bolt.
TYPE OF FIRE	Selective
RATE OF FIRE (SS)	40 rpm (A) 96 rpm (CYCLIC) 1200 rpr
MUZZLE VELOCITY	366 m/s (1200 fps)
MUZZLE ENERGY	533 J (393 ft/lb)
SIGHTS	Fixed, non-adjustable iron
FEED	15 or 32 round plastic removable b(magazine
WEIGHTS:	
WEAPON (EMPTY)	1.701 kg (2.033 kg w/larand suppressor)
WEAPON (LOADED)	2.179 kg w/32 rds (2.511 kg w/ 32 rds & larand suppressor)
MAGAZINE (EMPTY)	0.056 kg (15 rd), 0.094 kg (32 rd)
MAGAZINE (LOADED)	0.180 kg (15 rd), 0.478 kg (32 rd)
SERVICE CARTRIDGE	12 g
BULLET	8 g
LENGTHS:	
WEAPON OVERALL	33/58.4 cm (54.9/77 cm w/larand suppressor)
BARREL	13.3 cm
SIGHT RADIUS	23 cm

☞ *continued on next page*

THE EDGE OF THE SWORD

☞ *Ingram M11/9mm continued*

STATUS In production
SERVICE Commercial sales
COST $300

This is the most recent version of the Ingram submachinegun series. The M11/9mm, also known as the M11 long, has the same cross section as the M11 in 9x17mm but has a much longer receiver, redesigned shoulder stock, and other slight design changes that make the weapon much better to use. The magazine has been changed from a sheet metal fabrication to a cast Zytel plastic model that saves a good deal of weight. Dimensional changes in the magazine prevent the M11/9mm from using magazines from the earlier Ingrams. Very much a special purpose weapon, the M11/9mm has a very high rate of fire and will empty its 32 round magazine in one and one half seconds. A trained individual can easily engage multiple targets using the high rate of fire and this is what the weapon is most intended for, engaging multiple targets at close range, such as a room. An attached suppressor makes the M11/9mm much more controllable with the Larand model being particularly effective.

ASSESSMENT 89mm group @ 22.9m S/A, Standing, 147mm 3 rd group @ 9.2m, F/A, Rest, 91mm 3 rd group @ 9.2m, F/A, rest w/suppressor

WEAPON Ingram M11/9mm
AMMO 9x19
DISPERSION ANGLE .222678 degrees, 3.95872 NATO mils.

Range	Group Circle Width (mm)	Probability (0<p<.099) (m)			
		Body	Head	Hand	Bullseye
5.0	19.432	0.990	0.990	0.990	0.964
10.0	38.865	0.990	0.990	0.990	0.810
15.0	58.297	0.990	0.990	0.962	0.669
20.0	77.729	0.990	0.990	0.914	0.564
25.0	97.162	0.990	0.980	0.859	0.485
50.0	194.323	0.980	0.859	0.625	0.282
75.0	291.485	0.927	0.729	0.480	0.199
100.0	388.646	0.859	0.625	0.387	0.153
125.0	485.808	0.792	0.544	0.324	0.124
150.0	582.969	0.729	0.480	0.279	0.105
175.0	680.131	0.674	0.429	0.244	0.090
200.0	777.293	0.625	0.387	0.217	0.080

DAMAGE 25/.16

▼ Smith & Wesson Model 76

Smith & Wesson M76 with stock extended, bolt forward in the fired position and selector set to safe

CARTRIDGE 9x19 mm
OPERATION Blowback, fires from open bolt
TYPE OF FIRE Selective
RATE OF FIRE (SS) 72 rpm (A) 144 rpm (CYCLIC) 750 rpm
MUZZLE VELOCITY 381 m/s (1250 fps)
MUZZLE ENERGY 583 J (430 ft/lb)
SIGHTS Fixed, non-adjustable iron
FEED 36 round removable box magazine
WEIGHTS:
WEAPON (EMPTY) 3.289 kg
WEAPON (LOADED) 3.969 kg
MAGAZINE (EMPTY) 0.248 kg
MAGAZINE (LOADED) 0.680 kg
SERVICE CARTRIDGE 12 g
BULLET 8 g
LENGTHS:
WEAPON OVERALL 51.4/77.2 cm
BARREL 20.3 cm
SIGHT RADIUS 28.7 cm
STATUS Out of production, copy presently being manufactured as the Model 760
SERVICE U. S. Navy, commercial sales

The Model 76 was developed by Smith and Wesson as a commercial venture during the late 1960's. Intended for use by both the military and law enforcement agencies, the weapon was not a great commercial success. The U. S. Navy SEALS, who were impressed by the performance and availability of the Model 76, purchased a number of them which they continue to use to the present day.

Closely resembling the Swedish Carl Gustav (M45b) submachinegun in both layout and operation, the Model 76 is a simple and reliable weapon that is relatively light in weight. The placement of the safety/selector switch is poor, requiring one of the hands to release its grip on the weapon to operate the switch. The perforated guard around the barrel is removable and the weapon can be properly operated without it.

WEAPON S&W M76
AMMO 9x19 mm
DISPERSION ANGLE .733377 degrees, 13.0378 NATO mils.

Range	Group Circle Width (mm)	Probability (0<p<.099) (m)			
		Body	Head	Hand	Bullseye
5.0	64.000	0.990	0.990	0.949	0.635
10.0	128.000	0.990	0.949	0.774	0.396
15.0	192.000	0.981	0.863	0.629	0.285
20.0	256.000	0.949	0.774	0.525	0.223
25.0	320.000	0.908	0.696	0.449	0.183
50.0	640.000	0.696	0.449	0.257	0.096
75.0	960.000	0.548	0.328	0.180	0.065
100.0	1280.000	0.449	0.257	0.138	0.049
125.0	1600.000	0.379	0.212	0.112	0.040
150.0	1920.000	0.328	0.180	0.094	0.033
175.0	2240.000	0.288	0.156	0.082	0.028
200.0	2560.000	0.257	0.138	0.072	0.025

DAMAGE 26/.16

▼ Viking

Viking with stock folded and bolt in forward position

Viking with stock extended

CARTRIDGE	9x19 mm
OPERATION	Blowback, fires from open bolt.
TYPE OF FIRE	Selective
RATE OF FIRE (SS)	40 rpm (A) 144 rpm (CYCLIC) 650 rpm
MUZZLE VELOCITY	400 m/s (1312 fps)
MUZZLE ENERGY	637 J (470 ft/lb)

SIGHTS	Fixed, non-adjustable iron
FEED	36 round removable box magazine
WEIGHTS:	
WEAPON (EMPTY)	2.722 kg
WEAPON (LOADED)	3.352 kg
MAGAZINE (EMPTY)	0.198 kg
MAGAZINE (LOADED)	0.630 kg
SERVICE CARTRIDGE	12 g
BULLET	8 g
LENGTHS:	
WEAPON OVERALL	38.7/59 cm
BARREL	24.1 cm
SIGHT RADIUS	25.8 cm
STATUS	Limited number produced, design ready for production
SERVICE	Some commercial sales

The Viking is a fully developed weapon that has seen very few commercial sales. Due to a reorganization of the parent company, production has ceased with only a few hundred weapons being made. A rugged, simple design, the Viking is straightforward to operate and maintain while remaining compact and controllable when fired. The Ingram M10 9mm suppressor can be fitted to the Viking as well as a full line of optical sights.

WEAPON	Viking
AMMO	9x19
DISPERSION ANGLE	.209426 degrees, 3.72313 NATO mils.

Range	Group Circle Width (mm)	Probability (0<p<.099) (m)			
		Body	Head	Hand	Bullseye
5.0	18.276	0.990	0.990	0.990	0.971
10.0	36.552	0.990	0.990	0.990	0.829
15.0	54.828	0.990	0.990	0.969	0.692
20.0	73.103	0.990	0.990	0.926	0.586
25.0	91.379	0.990	0.985	0.876	0.506
50.0	182.759	0.985	0.876	0.647	0.297
75.0	274.138	0.938	0.751	0.501	0.210
100.0	365.517	0.876	0.647	0.406	0.162
125.0	456.897	0.811	0.566	0.341	0.132
150.0	548.276	0.751	0.501	0.294	0.111
175.0	639.655	0.696	0.449	0.258	0.096
200.0	731.034	0.647	0.406	0.229	0.084

DAMAGE 27/.17

▼ M3A1

M3A1 with stock folded and barrel fitted with a removable flash hider

M3A1 with stock extended, no magazine, and the dust cover/safety in the closed/safe position

CARTRIDGE	11.43x23 mm
OPERATION	Blowback, fires from open bolt.
TYPE OF FIRE	Full automatic
RATE OF FIRE (A)	120 rpm (CYCLIC) 450 rpm
MUZZLE VELOCITY	280 m/s (918 fps)
MUZZLE ENERGY	583 J (430 ft/lb)
SIGHTS	Fixed, non-adjustable iron
FEED	30 round removable box magazine
WEIGHTS:	
WEAPON (EMPTY)	3.470 kg
WEAPON (LOADED)	4.455 kg
MAGAZINE (EMPTY)	0.340 kg
MAGAZINE (LOADED)	0.985 kg
SERVICE CARTRIDGE	21.5 g
BULLET	15 g
LENGTHS:	
WEAPON OVERALL	57.9/75.7 cm
BARREL	20.3 cm
SIGHT RADIUS	27.6 cm
STATUS	Out of production
SERVICE	In service with the U.S. military and several other countries

The U.S. military has had very few officially adopted submachineguns with the M3A1 being the last one of these. Developed from the earlier M3, the M3A1 was first used in 1944 and still continues in use as a secondary weapon for armored vehicle crewmen. Though over 40 years old, the M3A1 is still capable of good service and, due to its using the .45 ACP round, has excellent stopping power. Much of the longevity of the M3 design is attributable to the extreme simplicity of the weapon. This simplicity is demonstrated by examination of the weapon, especially the cocking and safety arrangements. Where in other weapons there is some form of external cocking handle, in the

M3A1 there is simply a hole in the bolt so that a finger can pull it back to full cock. The safety is a protrusion in the ejection port cover. When the cover is closed, the bolt is locked in either the forward or cocked position. The sliding metal stock was intentionally made so that the length from the butt to the trigger was the same as that of the issue rifle. In 1944, the OSS had 1,000 silencers made for the M3 which consisted of a replacement barrel assembly with the silencer built as a part of it. The silencer assembly will easily replace the barrel of the M3A1 and can be used on either weapon. The silencer adds 16.2cm in length, and 0.626kg to the weight of an M3A1. The muzzle velocity with the silenced barrel is reduced to 234 m/s (768 fps).

WEAPON M3A1
AMMO 11.43x23
DISPERSION ANGLE .754714 degrees, 13.4171 NATO mils.

Range	Group Circle Width (mm)	Probability (0<p<.099) (m)			
		Body	**Head**	**Hand**	**Bullseye**
5.0	65.862	0.990	0.990	0.945	0.624
10.0	131.724	0.990	0.945	0.765	0.387
15.0	197.586	0.979	0.855	0.619	0.279
20.0	263.448	0.945	0.765	0.515	0.217
25.0	329.310	0.901	0.686	0.439	0.178
50.0	658.621	0.686	0.439	0.251	0.093
75.0	987.931	0.538	0.320	0.175	0.063
100.0	1317.241	0.439	0.251	0.135	0.048
125.0	1646.552	0.370	0.207	0.109	0.038
150.0	1975.862	0.320	0.175	0.092	0.032
175.0	2305.172	0.281	0.152	0.079	0.028
200.0	2634.483	0.251	0.135	0.070	0.024

DAMAGE 24/.28

▼ ARES Folding

FMG partially field stripped showing the bolt/barrel assembly separate from the weapon, the hinged trigger guard and magazine well are unlocked and partially folded

SUBMACHINEGUNS ■

FMG Prototype

FMG with bolt in the forward, uncocked position

FMG in the folded (collapsed) position

This is a very new design idea from ARES Inc. From a rectangular box 26.2 x 8.4 x 3.5 cm in size with no protruding controls, the ARES FMG can be unfolded, cocked, and fired in under two seconds. The interest shown in this design is due in no small part to its great concealability. When folded the FMG could be carried in a large transceiver case and not draw any comment. This aspect of the FMG makes it especially valuable for undercover or VIP escort duties.

WEAPON ARES Folding
AMMO 9x19
DISPERSION ANGLE .347725 degrees, 6.18178 NATO mils.

Range	Group Circle Width (mm)	Probability (0<p<.099) (m)			
		Body	Head	Hand	Bullseye
5.0	30.345	0.990	0.990	0.990	0.881
10.0	60.690	0.990	0.990	0.957	0.655
15.0	91.034	0.990	0.985	0.877	0.508
20.0	121.379	0.990	0.957	0.792	0.412
25.0	151.724	0.990	0.919	0.715	0.346
50.0	303.448	0.919	0.715	0.466	0.191
75.0	455.172	0.813	0.567	0.342	0.132
100.0	606.897	0.715	0.466	0.269	0.101
125.0	758.621	0.634	0.395	0.222	0.082
150.0	910.345	0.567	0.342	0.189	0.068
175.0	1062.069	0.512	0.301	0.164	0.059
200.0	1213.793	0.466	0.269	0.145	0.052

DAMAGE 26/.16

▼ Colt 9mm

Colt 9mm with stock folded and 32 rd magazine inserted

CARTRIDGE 9x19 mm
OPERATION Blowback, fires from open bolt.
TYPE OF FIRE Selective
RATE OF FIRE (SS) 40 rpm (A) 128 rpm (CYCLIC) 650 rpm
MUZZLE VELOCITY 378 m/s (1240 fps)
MUZZLE ENERGY 570 J (420 ft/lb)
SIGHTS none
FEED 20, 25, or 32 round removable box magazine
WEIGHTS:
WEAPON (EMPTY) 2.250 kg
WEAPON (LOADED) 2.854 kg w/32 rds
MAGAZINE (EMPTY) .160 kg (20 rd), .200 kg (25 rd), .220 kg (32 rd)
MAGAZINE (LOADED) 0.400 kg (20 rd), 0.500 kg (25 rd), 0.604 kg (32 rd)
SERVICE CARTRIDGE 12 g
BULLET 8g
LENGTHS:
WEAPON OVERALL 26.2 cm (folded), 50.3 cm (extended)
BARREL 18.7 cm
STATUS Prototype

CARTRIDGE 9x19 mm
OPERATION Blowback, fires from closed bolt.
TYPE OF FIRE Selective
RATE OF FIRE (SS) 40 rpm (A) 128 rpm (CYCLIC) 900 rpm
MUZZLE VELOCITY 397 m/s (1300 fps)
MUZZLE ENERGY 625 J (461 ft/lbs)
SIGHTS Adjustable, open iron
FEED 20 or 32 round removable box magazine

☞ continued on next page

☞ *Colt 9mm continued*

WEIGHTS:
WEAPON (EMPTY) 2.608 kg
WEAPON (LOADED) 3.219 kg w/32 rds
MAGAZINE (EMPTY) 0.181 kg (20 rd), 0.227 kg (32 rd)
MAGAZINE (LOADED) 0.421 kg (20 rd), 0.611 kg (32 rd)
SERVICE CARTRIDGE 12 g
BULLET 8 g
LENGTHS:
WEAPON OVERALL 65.1/73.4 cm
BARREL 26.7 cm
SIGHT RADIUS 36.8 cm
STATUS In production

As a converted M16, the Colt 9mm and its operation would be very familiar to anyone trained on the former. The rifle-like outline of the Colt 9mm also adds a good deal to the weapon's accuracy as does its firing on closed bolt. The feed ramp was designed in such a way that the Colt 9mm is able to use any hollowpoint or softnose 9mm round available. Though its size is something of a handicap, the Colt 9mm with its excellent accuracy is expected to see good sales.

ASSESSMENT 2.5 inch group @ 25 yds S/A
WEAPON Colt 9mm
AMMO 9x19
DISPERSION ANGLE .159155 degrees, 2.82942 NATO mils.

Range	Group Circle Width (mm)	Probability (0<p<.099) (m)			
		Body	Head	Hand	Bullseye
5.0	13.889	0.990	0.990	0.990	0.990
10.0	27.778	0.990	0.990	0.990	0.902
15.0	41.667	0.990	0.990	0.990	0.787
20.0	55.556	0.990	0.990	0.968	0.687
25.0	69.444	0.990	0.990	0.936	0.605
50.0	138.889	0.990	0.936	0.746	0.371
75.0	208.333	0.974	0.839	0.599	0.266
100.0	277.778	0.936	0.746	0.496	0.207
125.0	347.222	0.889	0.666	0.422	0.170
150.0	416.667	0.839	0.599	0.367	0.143
175.0	486.111	0.791	0.543	0.324	0.124
200.0	555.556	0.746	0.496	0.290	0.110

DAMAGE 27/.17

▼ Colt 9mm Suppressed

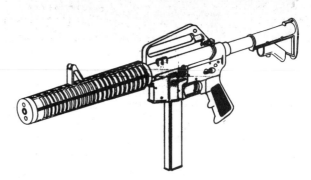

Colt 9mm Suppressed with stock extended

CARTRIDGE 9x19 mm
OPERATION Blowback, fires from closed bolt.
TYPE OF FIRE Selective
RATE OF FIRE (SS) 40 rpm (A) 128 rpm (CYCLIC) 700 rpm
MUZZLE VELOCITY 285 m/s (934 fps)
MUZZLE ENERGY 298 J (220 ft/lb)
SIGHTS Adjustable, open iron
FEED 20 or 32 round removable box magazine
WEIGHTS:
WEAPON (EMPTY) 3.062 kg
WEAPON (LOADED) 3.628 kg w/32 rds
MAGAZINE (EMPTY) 0.181 kg (20 rd), 0.227 kg (32 rd)
MAGAZINE (LOADED) 0.393 kg (20 rd), 0.566 kg (32 rd)
SERVICE CARTRIDGE 10.6 g
BULLET 7.45 g (115 grains)
LENGTHS:
WEAPON OVERALL 69.7/77.2 cm
BARREL 15.2 cm
SIGHT RADIUS 36.8 cm
STATUS In production

The unusual outline of this weapon results from its using the long handguards of the M16A2 to cover the built in suppressor. The front sight rising from the handguard is anchored to the barrel which ends at that point with the continuation of the guard covering the remainder of the suppressor,. The barrel has ports cut into it that allow the weapon to use standard 9mm ball ammunition while reducing the muzzle velocity to subsonic, enhancing the noise suppression. The great similarity between this weapon and the M16 series allows for easy use by anyone familiar with the M16 rifles.

ASSESSMENT 3 inch groups @ 15 yds offhand, 120 decibels at firing
WEAPON Colt 9mm Suppressed
AMMO 9x19
DISPERSION ANGLE .190986 degrees, 3.39531 NATO mils.

Range	Group Circle Width (mm)	Probability (0<p<.099) (m)			
		Body	Head	Hand	Bullseye
5.0	16.667	0.990	0.990	0.990	0.979
10.0	33.333	0.990	0.990	0.990	0.856
15.0	50.000	0.990	0.990	0.978	0.725
20.0	66.667	0.990	0.990	0.943	0.620
25.0	83.333	0.990	0.990	0.898	0.539
50.0	166.667	0.990	0.898	0.681	0.321
75.0	250.000	0.953	0.782	0.533	0.227
100.0	333.333	0.898	0.681	0.435	0.176
125.0	416.667	0.839	0.599	0.367	0.143
150.0	500.000	0.782	0.533	0.317	0.121
175.0	583.333	0.729	0.480	0.279	0.105
200.0	666.667	0.681	0.435	0.249	0.092

DAMAGE 20/.11

CHAPTER 3

ASSAULT & BATTLE RIFLES

The assault rifle is quickly becoming the most common military weapon. Developed during World War II by the Germans, the weapons class is characterized by being light, short range (400m), capable of automatic fire, having a large magazine capacity, and firing an intermediate sized cartridge. The ammunition has progressed from the shortened military round firing a full-caliber, but lighter, bullet such as the 7.62 x 39mm round, to the modern small caliber, high velocity rounds such as the 5.56 x 45mm round. The lower weight rounds are necessary to give the weapon controllability when fired on full automatic. The light and handy nature of this class of weapon is further increased with the shortened carbine designs such as the XM177E2 or AKR.

Battle rifles are a larger, heavier class of weapon chambered for a long range, full sized round such as the 7.62 x 51mm. Most modern battle rifles are semiautomatic with full automatic capability, shoulder fired, long range (600m+), and have a 20 round maximum capacity. Examples of this type are the FN-FAL and G3 rifle series. ●

▼ FN FAL

FN FAL with folding carrying handle raised

CARTRIDGE	7.62x51mm
OPERATION	Gas
TYPE OF FIRE	Selective
RATE OF FIRE	(SS) 60 rpm (A) 120 rpm (CYCLIC) 700 rpm
MUZZLE VELOCITY	823 m/s (2700 fps)
MUZZLE ENERGY	3313 J (2443 ft/lb)
SIGHTS	Adjustable, aperture/post, 600m range
FEED	20 round removable box magazine
WEIGHTS:	
WEAPON (EMPTY)	4.310 kg
WEAPON (LOADED)	5.01 kg
MAGAZINE (EMPTY)	0.249 kg
MAGAZINE (LOADED)	0.761 kg
SERVICE CARTRIDGE	25.6 g
BULLET	9.8 g
LENGTHS:	
WEAPON OVERALL	110 cm
BARREL	53.3 cm
SIGHT RADIUS	55.4 cm
STATUS	In production
SERVICE	In service in Belgium, Argentina,

Australia, Canada, India, Israel, Mexico, Nigeria, South Africa, The UK, and Venezuela. Other users of the FAL include Austria, Barbados, Brazil, Burundi, Chile, Cuba, Dominican Republic, Ecuador, Gambia, Federal Germany, Ghana, Guyana, Indonesia, Ireland, Kampuchea, Kuwait, Liberia, Libya, Luxembourg, Malawi, Malaysia, Morocco, Mozambique, Oman, New Zealand, Norway, Paraguay, Peru, Portugal, Singapore, and the United Arab Emirates.

COST $600

This very popular rifle was, at one time, under very strong consideration as the new military weapon for the United States after World War II. Originally intended for a smaller cartridge, the FAL is made in 7.62mm NATO and is used, in several configurations, by over forty countries with several million weapons produced. Made in both selective fire and semiautomatic versions, the in-line stock configuration makes the FAL more controllable on full automatic fire than many other rifles of the same caliber. The FAL is very robust and will continue to operate for extended periods in very bad conditions. Very accurate and reliable, the FN FAL is considered to be a prime example of a main battle rifle.

ASSESSMENT 3.1 in @ 100 yds
WEAPON FN FAL

AMMO 7.62x51
DISPERSION ANGLE .0493381 degrees, .877121 NATO mils.

Range	Group Circle Width (mm)	Probability (0<p<.099) (m)			
		Body	**Head**	**Hand**	**Bullseye**
25.0	21.528	0.990	0.990	0.990	0.950
50.0	43.056	0.990	0.990	0.988	0.776
75.0	64.583	0.990	0.990	0.948	0.632
100.0	86.111	0.990	0.988	0.891	0.527
125.0	107.639	0.990	0.971	0.830	0.451
150.0	129.167	0.990	0.948	0.771	0.393
175.0	150.694	0.990	0.920	0.718	0.348
200.0	172.222	0.988	0.891	0.669	0.312
300.0	258.333	0.948	0.771	0.522	0.221
400.0	344.444	0.891	0.669	0.425	0.171
500.0	430.556	0.830	0.587	0.358	0.139
600.0	516.667	0.771	0.522	0.308	0.117
700.0	602.778	0.718	0.469	0.271	0.101
800.0	688.889	0.669	0.425	0.242	0.089
900.0	775.000	0.626	0.388	0.218	0.080
1000.0	861.111	0.587	0.358	0.198	0.072

DAMAGE 49/.37

▼ Heckler & Koch G3A3 • G3A4

CARTRIDGE	7.62x51mm
OPERATION	Retarded blowback
TYPE OF FIRE	Selective
RATE OF FIRE	(SS) 40 rpm (A) 100 rpm (CYCLIC) 600 rpm
MUZZLE VELOCITY	800 m/s (2624 fps)
MUZZLE ENERGY	3130 J (2308 ft/lb)
SIGHTS	Adjustable, U-notch/post
FEED	20 round removable box magazine
WEIGHTS:	
WEAPON (EMPTY)	4.400 kg (4.717 kg)
WEAPON (LOADED)	5.192 kg (5.509 kg)
MAGAZINE (EMPTY)	0.280 kg
MAGAZINE (LOADED)	0.792 kg
SERVICE CARTRIDGE	25.6 g
BULLET	9.8 g
LENGTHS:	
WEAPON OVERALL	102.6 cm (84.1/102 cm)
BARREL	45 cm
SIGHT RADIUS	57.2 cm
STATUS	In production
SERVICE	In service with the military or police

agencies of, or produced by, the following countries: (Europe) Denmark, France, Federal Germany, Greece, Italy, Netherlands, Norway,

☞ continued on next page

☞ *G3A3 • G3A4 continued*

Portugal, Sweden, Switzerland, Turkey, (Africa) Burkina Faso, Chad, Ghana, Ivory Coast, Kenya, Malawi, Morocco, Niger, Nigeria, Senegal, Sudan, Tanzania, Togo, Uganda, Zambia, (South America) Bolivia, Brazil, Chile, Colombia, Dominican Republic, El Salvador, Guyana, Haiti, Mexico, Peru, (Middle East) Iran, Jordan, Qatar, Saudi Arabia, United Arab Emirates, (Far East) Bangladesh, Brunei, Burma, Indonesia, Malaysia, Pakistan, Philippines, Thailand.

COST $600

This is the most recent version of the G3 rifle that has reached full issue with the German military. The weapon in general has been the German army's standard issue since 1959. The G3 was the first commercially successful rifle to utilize the roller-locked system of delayed blowback. The roller locking system is described in detail in the submachinegun section under the MP5. As roller locking is a form of delayed blowback, the G3 is one of the ten rifle caliber weapons to successfully employ such a system. The heart of the system is the two rollers that resist the opening of the bolt when they are driven outwards into locking recesses by the wedge shaped firing pin carrier. To insure the positive extraction of the fired case, the chamber is fluted for two-thirds of its length.

The same basic roller system is used in almost all of the Heckler and Koch weapons, demonstrating the system's versatility. As the G3 was the first of the HK weapons, it has undergone several changes through the last two decades. The relatively few variations of the G3 are as follows:

G3: The original issue rifle to the German military. The buttstock was made of wood, the handguard was perforated metal, and the rear sight, a flipped over L-shaped type, was very similar to the sight on the FN FAL.

G3A1: Few of this model were made. The stock is a metal foldover style, similar to the type found on the MP-40 submachinegun. Other details are the same as the G3.

G3A2: This weapon has the same stock and handguard as the G3, but with the rotary drum type adjustable sight which has become the standard H & K rear sight.

G3A3: This is the currently manufactured version with a solid plastic buttstock, perforated plastic handguard, a modified front sight protector, and a closed prong-type, flash suppressor.

G3A4: This is the same as the G3A3 but with a retractable sliding metal buttstock.

G3AZF: This is the G3A3 with a removable four power telescoped sight for sniping or observation.

HK91A2: This is a semiautomatic only model of the G3 that cannot be easily modified to selective fire and is intended for the civilian and police market. The HK91A2 has the same stock and sights as the G3A3 and can use the same accessories, but has a solid handguard instead of a perforated one.

HK91A3: This weapon is the same semiautomatic fire only model as the HK91A2 but with the retractable metal stock.

The G3 weapon series is a very rugged and reliable design that has had a long service life. Because of this long life, many third world countries and various rebel/guerrilla groups are obtaining G3's as other countries sell off their stocks because they are switching to 5.56 NATO designs.

ASSESSMENT	2.4 in @ 100 yds
WEAPON	G3A3
AMMO	7.61x51
DISPERSION ANGLE	.0382223 degrees, .679507 NATO mils.

Range	Group Circle Width (mm)	Probability (0<p<.099) (m)			
		Body	**Head**	**Hand**	**Bullseye**
25.0	16.678	0.990	0.990	0.990	0.979
50.0	33.355	0.990	0.990	0.990	0.855
75.0	50.033	0.990	0.990	0.978	0.724
100.0	66.710	0.990	0.990	0.942	0.620
125.0	83.388	0.990	0.990	0.898	0.539
150.0	100.066	0.990	0.978	0.851	0.475
175.0	116.743	0.990	0.962	0.804	0.424
200.0	133.421	0.990	0.942	0.760	0.383
300.0	200.131	0.978	0.851	0.614	0.276
400.0	266.842	0.942	0.760	0.510	0.215
500.0	333.552	0.898	0.681	0.435	0.176
600.0	400.262	0.851	0.614	0.379	0.149
700.0	466.973	0.804	0.558	0.335	0.129
800.0	533.683	0.760	0.510	0.300	0.114
900.0	600.394	0.719	0.470	0.272	0.102
1000.0	667.104	0.681	0.435	0.248	0.092

DAMAGE 48/.36

▼ Heckler & Koch G3K

G3K with stock extended and optional folding bipod fitted

CARTRIDGE	7.62x51mm
OPERATION	Retarded blowback
TYPE OF FIRE	Selective
RATE OF FIRE	(SS)40 rpm (A) 100 rpm (CYCLIC) 600 rpm

MUZZLE VELOCITY	740 m/s (2450 fps)
MUZZLE ENERGY	2728 J (2012 ft/lb)
SIGHTS	Adjustable, U-notch/post, range 400m
FEED	20 round removable box magazine
WEIGHTS:	
WEAPON (EMPTY)	4.400 kg
WEAPON (LOADED)	5.192 kg
MAGAZINE (EMPTY)	0.280 kg
MAGAZINE (LOADED)	0.792 kg
SERVICE CARTRIDGE	25.6 g
BULLET	9.8
LENGTHS:	
WEAPON OVERALL	72/90 cm
BARREL	32.2 cm
SIGHT RADIUS	51 cm
STATUS	In production
SERVICE	Commercial sales

This is the latest variant of the G3 rifle to reach production. the barrel and forearm have been shortened with the front sight moved back and the flash suppressor mounted just in front of the sight. The shortness of the exposed barrel prevents rifle grenades from being launched. The sliding metal stock is normally fitted though the G3K can accept the standard fixed stock. The G3K is a compact carbine version of the G3 series with a barrel as short as is practical while still keeping muzzle flash and report at a reasonable level.

WEAPON	G3K
AMMO	7.62x51
DISPERSION ANGLE	.0276601 degrees, .491734 NATO mils.

Range	Group Circle Width (mm)	Probability (0<p<.099) (m)			
		Body	**Head**	**Hand**	**Bullseye**
25.0	12.069	0.990	0.990	0.990	0.990
50.0	24.138	0.990	0.990	0.990	0.931
75.0	36.207	0.990	0.990	0.990	0.832
100.0	48.276	0.990	0.990	0.981	0.737
125.0	60.345	0.990	0.990	0.957	0.657
150.0	72.414	0.990	0.990	0.928	0.590
175.0	84.483	0.990	0.989	0.895	0.534
200.0	96.552	0.990	0.981	0.861	0.487
300.0	144.828	0.990	0.928	0.732	0.359
400.0	193.103	0.981	0.861	0.627	0.284
500.0	241.379	0.957	0.794	0.546	0.234
600.0	289.655	0.928	0.732	0.482	0.200
700.0	337.931	0.895	0.676	0.431	0.174
800.0	386.207	0.861	0.627	0.389	0.154
900.0	434.483	0.827	0.584	0.355	0.138
1000.0	482.759	0.794	0.546	0.326	0.125

DAMAGE 44/.34

▼ G8A1

CARTRIDGE	7.62x51mm
OPERATION	Retarded blowback
TYPE OF FIRE	Selective w/three round burst and full auto
RATE OF FIRE	(SS)40 rpm (A) 100 rpm (CYCLIC) 800 rpm
MUZZLE VELOCITY	800 m/s (2625 fps)
MUZZLE ENERGY	3132 J (2310 ft/lb)
SIGHTS	ZF 4 power telescopic sight, range 600 m
FEED	20 round removable box magazine or 50 round removable drum
WEIGHTS:	
WEAPON (EMPTY)	9.148 kg w/scope
WEAPON (LOADED)	9.940 kg w/scope & 20 rds
MAGAZINE (EMPTY)	0.280 kg (20 rd), 0.690 kg (50 rd)
MAGAZINE (LOADED)	0.792 kg (20 rd), 1.97 kg (50 rd)
SERVICE CARTRIDGE	25.6 g
BULLET	9.8 g
LENGTHS:	
WEAPON OVERALL	103 cm
BARREL	45 cm
SIGHT RADIUS	68.5 cm
STATUS	In production
SERVICE	Commercial sales

This is a very unusual rifle developed especially for the German antiterrorist police forces but also available for commercial sale. The G8A1 is unusual in that it was developed from the HK11E light machinegun, but is intended to be used as a rifle rather than in the sustained fire role of a machinegun. The quick change barrel of the HK11E was retained but increased in weight and carefully rifled for maximum accuracy. The G8A1 also has a folding bipod and is fitted with the drum type sights associated with Heckler and Koch weapons although the weapon is intended to be used with the available 4 power telescopic sight. The feed mechanism of the G8A1 will only accept magazines and there is a special 50 round drum available. The trigger mechanism has a three round controlled burst facility as well as being capable of either semi or full automatic fire.

WEAPON	G8A1
AMMO	7.62x51
	4 x power scope installed.
DISPERSION ANGLE	.0118543 degrees, .210743 NATO mils.

☞ *continued on next page*

☞ *G8A1 continued*

Range	Group Circle Width (mm)	Probability (0<p<.099) (m)			
		Body	Head	Hand	Bullseye
25.0	5.172	0.990	0.990	0.990	0.990
50.0	10.345	0.990	0.990	0.990	0.990
75.0	15.517	0.990	0.990	0.990	0.984
100.0	20.690	0.990	0.990	0.990	0.956
125.0	25.862	0.990	0.990	0.990	0.917
150.0	31.034	0.990	0.990	0.990	0.875
175.0	36.207	0.990	0.990	0.990	0.832
200.0	41.379	0.990	0.990	0.990	0.790
300.0	62.069	0.990	0.990	0.954	0.646
400.0	82.759	0.990	0.990	0.900	0.541
500.0	103.448	0.990	0.975	0.841	0.464
600.0	124.138	0.990	0.954	0.784	0.405
700.0	144.828	0.990	0.928	0.732	0.359
800.0	165.517	0.990	0.900	0.684	0.323
900.0	186.207	0.983	0.871	0.641	0.293
1000.0	206.897	0.975	0.841	0.602	0.268

DAMAGE 48/.36

▼ 7.62mm Galil AR (SAR)

CARTRIDGE	7.62x51mm
OPERATION	Gas
TYPE OF FIRE	Selective
RATE OF FIRE	(SS)40 rpm (A) 100 rpm (CYCLIC) 650 rpm
MUZZLE VELOCITY	850 m/s (2789 fps) (800 m/s <2625 fps>)
MUZZLE ENERGY	3536 J (2608 ft/lb), (3132 J <2310 ft/lb>)
SIGHTS	Adjustable, aperture/post, range 500m, flip-up 3-dot night sights.
FEED	25 round removable box magazine
WEIGHTS:	
WEAPON (EMPTY)	4.300 kg w/bipod & handle (3.750 kg)
WEAPON (LOADED)	5.230 kg w/bipod & handle (4.680 kg)
MAGAZINE (EMPTY)	0.290 kg
MAGAZINE (LOADED)	0.930 kg
SERVICE CARTRIDGE	25.6 g
BULLET	9.8 g
BIPOD WEIGHT	0.250 kg
LENGTHS:	
WEAPON OVERALL	81/105 cm (67.5/91.5 cm)
BARREL	53.3 cm (40 cm)
SIGHT RADIUS	47.5 cm (44.5 cm)
STATUS	In production
SERVICE	Israeli forces

This is a larger version of the earlier Galil and is chambered for the 7.62 x 51mm NATO cartridge. The general characteristics of the 5.56mm Galil are reflected in the 7.62mm model with it also having the same variations. The 7.62 ARM has the same bipod and handle as the 5.56 ARM but does not have an enlarged magazine. The 7.62 Galil may also launch rifle grenades, except for the SAR model.

ASSESSMENT	8.25 in group @ 300 yds
WEAPON	Galil ARM
AMMO	7.62x51
DISPERSION ANGLE	.0437677 degrees, .778092 NATO mils.

Range	Group Circle Width (mm)	Probability (0<p<.099) (m)			
		Body	Head	Hand	Bullseye
25.0	19.097	0.990	0.990	0.990	0.966
50.0	38.194	0.990	0.990	0.990	0.815
75.0	57.292	0.990	0.990	0.964	0.676
100.0	76.389	0.990	0.990	0.917	0.570
125.0	95.486	0.990	0.982	0.864	0.491
150.0	114.583	0.990	0.964	0.810	0.430
175.0	133.681	0.990	0.942	0.760	0.383
200.0	152.778	0.990	0.917	0.713	0.344
300.0	229.167	0.964	0.810	0.565	0.245
400.0	305.556	0.917	0.713	0.464	0.190
500.0	381.944	0.864	0.631	0.393	0.155
600.0	458.333	0.810	0.565	0.340	0.131
700.0	534.722	0.760	0.510	0.300	0.114
800.0	611.111	0.713	0.464	0.268	0.100
900.0	687.500	0.670	0.425	0.242	0.090
1000.0	763.889	0.631	0.393	0.221	0.081

DAMAGE (AR) 51/0.38, (SAR) 48/0.36

▼ CETME C

CARTRIDGE	7.62x51mm
OPERATION	Retarded blowback
TYPE OF FIRE	Selective
RATE OF FIRE	(SS)40 rpm (A) 100 rpm (CYCLIC) 600 rpm
MUZZLE VELOCITY	780 m/s (2559 fps)
MUZZLE ENERGY	2976 J (2195 ft/lb)
SIGHTS	Adjustable, aperture/post, range 400 m
FEED	20 round removable box magazine
WEIGHTS:	
WEAPON (EMPTY)	4.200 kg
WEAPON (LOADED)	4.987 kg
MAGAZINE (EMPTY)	0.275 kg
MAGAZINE (LOADED)	0.787 kg
SERVICE CARTRIDGE	25.6 g

BULLET 9.8 g
LENGTHS:
WEAPON OVERALL 101.5 cm
BARREL 45 cm
SIGHT RADIUS 58 cm
STATUS In production
SERVICE Spanish forces and commercial sales

This is the present production standard military rifle for Spain and is a direct descendant of the earlier CETME designs that resulted in the Heckler and Koch G3. The Model C is chambered for the standard 7.62mm NATO round and is effectively identical to the G3. The stock and fore-end of the Model C are made of wood with the rear sight being the folding leaf type. The leaves for 100 meters have a V-notch and those for 200, 300, and 400 meters have apertures.

WEAPON CETME C
AMMO 7.62x51
DISPERSION ANGLE .0197572 degrees, .351239 NATO mils.

Range	Group Circle Width (mm)	Probability (0<p<.099) (m)			
		Body	Head	Hand	Bullseye
25.0	8.621	0.990	0.990	0.990	0.990
50.0	17.241	0.990	0.990	0.990	0.976
75.0	25.862	0.990	0.990	0.990	0.917
100.0	34.483	0.990	0.990	0.990	0.846
125.0	43.103	0.990	0.990	0.988	0.776
150.0	51.724	0.990	0.990	0.975	0.713
175.0	60.345	0.990	0.990	0.957	0.657
200.0	68.966	0.990	0.990	0.937	0.608
300.0	103.448	0.990	0.975	0.841	0.464
400.0	137.931	0.990	0.937	0.749	0.374
500.0	172.414	0.988	0.890	0.669	0.312
600.0	206.897	0.975	0.841	0.602	0.268
700.0	241.379	0.957	0.794	0.546	0.234
800.0	275.862	0.937	0.749	0.499	0.208
900.0	310.345	0.914	0.707	0.459	0.188
1000.0	344.828	0.890	0.669	0.424	0.171

DAMAGE 46/0.35

▼ SIG 510-4

Stg 57, Swiss military issue version of the 510-4 except for being chambered for 7.5 Swiss and having a 24 round magazine, the Stg 57 is identical to the 510-4

CARTRIDGE 7.62x51mm
OPERATION Gas
TYPE OF FIRE Selective
RATE OF FIRE (SS)40 rpm (A) 80 rpm (CYCLIC) 600 rpm
MUZZLE VELOCITY 790 m/s (2600 fps)
MUZZLE ENERGY 3073 J (2266 ft/lb)
SIGHTS Adjustable, aperture/post, range 600m
FEED 20 round removable box magazine
WEIGHTS:
WEAPON (EMPTY) 4.463 kg w/bipod
WEAPON (LOADED) 5.273 kg w/bipod
MAGAZINE (EMPTY) 0.298 kg
MAGAZINE (LOADED) 0.810 kg
SERVICE CARTRIDGE 25.6 g
BULLET 9.8 g
LENGTHS:
WEAPON OVERALL 101.6 cm
BARREL 50.5 cm
SIGHT RADIUS 59.3 cm
STATUS Out of production
SERVICE Swiss army (as Stgw 57 in 7.5x55mm Swiss), Chile, Bolivia, and commercial sales.

The SG 510-4 is a development of the Swiss Stgw 57 that was intended for export sales. The operating system has its roots in the German Stg 45(M) and as such, is roller locked in the same manner as the Heckler and Koch G3. The locking system is actually a form of delayed blowback and the Swiss system utilizes a round "rocker" rather than the rollers found in the Heckler and Koch system. The rocker seatings are designed to be replaceable and since the hammer forged barrel has a very long accurate life, the replacement feature greatly extends the service life of the weapon. The hammer forged barrel also helps give the SG 510-4 the outstanding reputation for accuracy which it receives. As Switzerland depends on a citizen militia rather than a standing army, the population takes its shooting sports very seriously. The Stgw 57 is very similar to the 510-4 except for being chambered for the 7.5 x 55mm round and is commonly used in competitive shooting in Switzerland. A folding bipod is part of the SG 510-4 as well as a folding carrying handle. The flash hider can be used to launch rifle grenades. Altogether, the SG 510-4 is one of the most accurate production assault rifles available today. It is also one of the most expensive.

WEAPON SIG 510-4
AMMO 7.62x51
DISPERSION ANGLE .0158058 degrees, .280991 NATO mils.

☞ continued on next page

☞ SIG 510-4 continued

Range	Group Circle Width (mm)	Probability (0<p<.099) (m)			
		Body	Head	Hand	Bullseye
25.0	6.897	0.990	0.990	0.990	0.990
50.0	13.793	0.990	0.990	0.990	0.990
75.0	20.690	0.990	0.990	0.990	0.956
100.0	27.586	0.990	0.990	0.990	0.903
125.0	34.483	0.990	0.990	0.990	0.846
150.0	41.379	0.990	0.990	0.990	0.790
175.0	48.276	0.990	0.990	0.981	0.737
200.0	55.172	0.990	0.990	0.968	0.689
300.0	82.759	0.990	0.990	0.900	0.541
400.0	110.345	0.990	0.968	0.822	0.443
500.0	137.931	0.990	0.937	0.749	0.374
600.0	165.517	0.990	0.900	0.684	0.323
700.0	193.103	0.981	0.861	0.627	0.284
800.0	220.690	0.968	0.822	0.578	0.253
900.0	248.276	0.954	0.784	0.536	0.229
1000.0	275.862	0.937	0.749	0.499	0.208

DAMAGE 47/0.36

▼ SIG 542

CARTRIDGE 7.62x51mm
OPERATION Gas
TYPE OF FIRE Selective, w/three round burst and full auto
RATE OF FIRE (SS)40 rpm (A) 80 rpm (CYCLIC) 725 rpm
MUZZLE VELOCITY 820 m/s (2675 fps)
MUZZLE ENERGY 3253 J (2399 ft/lb)
SIGHTS Adjustable, aperture/post, Range 600m
FEED 20 round removable box magazine
WEIGHTS:
WEAPON (EMPTY) 3.357 kg w/ fixed or folding stock w/o bipod
WEAPON (LOADED) 4.109 kg
MAGAZINE (EMPTY) 0.240 kg
MAGAZINE (LOADED) 0.752 kg
SERVICE CARTRIDGE 25.6 g
BULLET 9.8 g
BIPOD WEIGHT 0.280 kg
LENGTHS:
WEAPON OVERALL 101.9 cm w/ fixed stock, 75.4/100 cm w/folding stock
BARREL 49.5 cm
SIGHT RADIUS 51.8 cm

STATUS In production
SERVICE See SIG 540

This is the 7.62 x 51mm member of the SIG 540 series. Operationally the same as the SIG 540 or 543 weapons, the 542 is physically the largest of the series. There is both a folding and fixed stock available for the 542 as well as a folding bipod. All operational characteristics are the same for the 542 model as well as other members of the 540 series.

WEAPON SIG 542
AMMO 5.56x45
DISPERSION ANGLE .0276601 degrees, .491734 NATO mils.

Range	Group Circle Width (mm)	Probability (0<p<.099) (m)			
		Body	Head	Hand	Bullseye
25.0	12.069	0.990	0.990	0.990	0.990
50.0	24.138	0.990	0.990	0.990	0.931
75.0	36.207	0.990	0.990	0.990	0.832
100.0	48.276	0.990	0.990	0.981	0.737
125.0	60.345	0.990	0.990	0.957	0.657
150.0	72.414	0.990	0.990	0.928	0.590
175.0	84.483	0.990	0.989	0.895	0.534
200.0	96.552	0.990	0.981	0.861	0.487
300.0	144.828	0.990	0.928	0.732	0.359
400.0	193.103	0.981	0.861	0.627	0.284
500.0	241.379	0.957	0.794	0.546	0.234
600.0	289.655	0.928	0.732	0.482	0.200
700.0	337.931	0.895	0.676	0.431	0.174
800.0	386.207	0.861	0.627	0.389	0.154
900.0	434.483	0.827	0.584	0.355	0.138
1000.0	482.759	0.794	0.546	0.326	0.125

DAMAGE 48/0.37

▼ FNC Long • Short

FNC Short version with 30 rd magazine and selector set to full automatic

CARTRIDGE	5.56x45mm
OPERATION	Gas
TYPE OF FIRE	Selective w/three round burst and full auto
RATE OF FIRE	(SS) 60 rpm (A) 120 rpm (CYCLIC) 700 rpm
MUZZLE VELOCITY	915 m/s (3002 fps)
MUZZLE ENERGY	1410 J (1040 ft/lb)
SIGHTS	Adjustable, aperture/post, range 400 m
FEED	20 or 30 round removable box magazine (M16)
WEIGHTS:	
WEAPON (EMPTY)	3.800 kg (3.700 kg)
WEAPON (LOADED)	4.412 kg w/30 rds, (4.312 kg w/30 rds)
MAGAZINE (EMPTY)	0.091 kg (20 rd), 0.117 kg (30 rd), 0.210 kg (FN manufacture 30 rd)
MAGAZINE (LOADED)	0.421 kg (20 rd), 0.612 kg (30 rd)
SERVICE CARTRIDGE	16.5 g
BULLET	3.4 kg
LENGTHS:	
WEAPON OVERALL	76.6/99.7 cm (66.6/91.1 cm)
BARREL	44.9 cm (36.6 cm)
SIGHT RADIUS	51.3 cm
STATUS	In production
SERVICE	Undergoing trials, commercial sales
COST	$1,250 ($1,450)

After the Vietnam War, many countries have been considering a change from 7.62mm NATO weapons to the U.S. 5.56x45mm round. Not to be left out on possible sales, FN developed what was effectively a 5.56mm version of the FAL rifle, the CAL. Sales of the CAL were poor and in the mid-1970's, the FNC weapon was developed to replace the CAL. The FNC has all of the rugged characteristics of the earlier FAL, but is much lighter in weight. One FNC with 300 rounds of ammunition contained in ten 30 round magazines weighs the same as an FAL with five 20 round magazines (100 rounds). The short FNC has a shorter barrel and cannot be fitted with a bayonet but is otherwise identical to the standard FNC. There is also a "law enforcement" version of the FNC that is only capable of semiautomatic fire. The fact that the FNC uses standard M16 magazines increases its value and makes it an excellent companion weapon to the MINIMI light machinegun.

ASSESSMENT	54mm group @ 100 yds
WEAPON	FNC

AMMO 5.56x45

DISPERSION ANGLE .0338361 degrees, .601531 NATO mils.

Range	Group Circle Width (mm)	Probability (0<p<.099) (m)			
		Body	**Head**	**Hand**	**Bullseye**
25.0	14.764	0.990	0.990	0.990	0.987
50.0	29.528	0.990	0.990	0.990	0.887
75.0	44.291	0.990	0.990	0.986	0.767
100.0	59.055	0.990	0.990	0.960	0.665
125.0	73.819	0.990	0.990	0.924	0.583
150.0	88.583	0.990	0.986	0.884	0.517
175.0	103.346	0.990	0.975	0.842	0.464
200.0	118.110	0.990	0.960	0.801	0.421
250.0	147.638	0.990	0.924	0.725	0.354
300.0	177.165	0.986	0.884	0.659	0.305
350.0	206.693	0.975	0.842	0.602	0.268
400.0	236.220	0.960	0.801	0.554	0.239
450.0	265.748	0.943	0.762	0.512	0.216
500.0	295.276	0.924	0.725	0.475	0.196

DAMAGE 35/.52

▼ AUG

AUG, rifle version with 79cm barrel and bayonet lug

AUG, carbine version with 40.7cm barrel

CARTRIDGE	5.56x45mm
OPERATION	Gas
TYPE OF FIRE	Selective
RATE OF FIRE	(SS) 40 rpm (A) 120 rpm (CYCLIC) 700 rpm
MUZZLE VELOCITY	(A) 882 m/s (2893 fps), (B) 894 m/s (2933 fps), (C) 921 m/s (3023 fps)
MUZZLE ENERGY	(A) 1536 J (1133 ft/lb), (B) 1580 J (1165 ft/lb), (C) 1679 J (1238 ft/lb)

☛ continued on next page

☞ AUG continued

SIGHTS	1.5 power optical scope built into handle w/ fixed V notch/blade iron sights built into handle for emergency use
FEED	30 or 42 round removable box magazine
WEIGHTS:	
WEAPON (EMPTY)	(A) 3.175 kg, (B) 3.266 kg, (C) 3.583 kg
WEAPON (LOADED)	(A) 3.683 kg w/30 rds, (B) 3.774 kg w/ 30 rds, (C) 4.091 kg w/30 rds
MAGAZINE (EMPTY)	0.142 kg (30 rd), 0.159 kg (42 rd)
MAGAZINE (LOADED)	0.508 kg (30 rd), 0.671 kg (42 rd)
SERVICE CARTRIDGE	12.2 g
BULLET	4 g
LENGTHS:	
WEAPON OVERALL	(A) 63.5 cm, (B) 68.6 cm, (C) 78.7 cm
BARREL	(A) 35.6 cm, (B) 40.6 cm, (C) 50.8 cm
SIGHT RADIUS	19.2 cm (iron backup sights)
STATUS	In production
SERVICE	Austrian army and commercial sales

The AUG weapon system is probably one of the most exotic appearing weapons to have found military acceptance. With its bullpup layout and wide versatility with the range of options available, the AUG is seeing good sales with both the Austrian and Australian armies adopting it. The stock and a large portion of the weapon is made of special plastics with the receiver being an aluminum die casting. This gives the AUG a very light overall weight. The barrels of the AUG are easily removable and each has a folding handle which aids in barrel removal as well as acting as a front grip. The normal sighting arrangement for the AUG is a low power telescopic sight built into the handle. The sight has a ring retical that surrounds a 1.8 meter diameter, the height of an average man, at 300 meters and can act as a range finder. The telescopic sight on the AUG is the first such sight rugged enough to find acceptance with the military.

WEAPON	AUG
AMMO	5.56x45

1.5 x power scope installed.

DISPERSION ANGLE .0671744 degrees, 1.19421 NATO mils.

Range	Group Circle Width (mm)	Probability (0<p<.099) (m)			
		Body	Head	Hand	Bullseye
25.0	29.310	0.990	0.990	0.990	0.889
50.0	58.621	0.990	0.990	0.961	0.667
75.0	87.931	0.990	0.987	0.885	0.520
100.0	117.241	0.990	0.961	0.803	0.423
125.0	146.552	0.990	0.926	0.727	0.356
150.0	175.862	0.987	0.885	0.662	0.307

☞ continued

Range	Group Circle Width (mm)	Probability (0<p<.099) (m)			
		Body	Head	Hand	Bullseye
175.0	205.172	0.976	0.844	0.605	0.270
200.0	234.483	0.961	0.803	0.556	0.240
250.0	293.103	0.926	0.727	0.478	0.198
300.0	351.724	0.885	0.662	0.418	0.168
350.0	410.345	0.844	0.605	0.371	0.145
400.0	468.966	0.803	0.556	0.334	0.128
450.0	527.586	0.764	0.514	0.303	0.115
500.0	586.207	0.727	0.478	0.277	0.104

DAMAGE	(A) w/35.6 cm bbl 34/.59, (B) w/40.6cm bbl 34/.59, (C) w/50.8cm bbl 35/.61

▼ FA MAS

CARTRIDGE	5.56x45mm
OPERATION	Gas
TYPE OF FIRE	Selective w/three round burst and full auto
RATE OF FIRE	(SS) 50 rpm (A) 125 rpm (CYCLIC) 1000 rpm
MUZZLE VELOCITY	960 m/s (3150 fps)
MUZZLE ENERGY	1822 J (1344 ft/lb)
SIGHTS	Adjustable, aperture/blade, range 300m
FEED	25 round removable box magazine
WEIGHTS:	
WEAPON (EMPTY)	3.780 kg w/bipod
WEAPON (LOADED)	4.235 kg
MAGAZINE (EMPTY)	0.150 kg
MAGAZINE (LOADED)	0.455 kg
SERVICE CARTRIDGE	12.2 g
BULLET	4 g
LENGTHS:	
WEAPON OVERALL	75.7 cm
BARREL	48.8 cm
SIGHT RADIUS	33 cm
STATUS	In production
SERVICE	French military also Gabon, Djibuti, Senegal, the United Arab Emirates, and commercial sales.

This French design has the distinction of being the first bullpup design to find acceptance with a major military force. Perfected over a period between 1973 and 1979, the FA MAS is now the standard issue rifle of the French forces and is seeing good commercial sales. One of the main reasons for the success of the FA MAS is the elimination of several major drawbacks of the bullpup design. The largest of these, the need to fire them right handed only because of the ejection of the fired casing, is eliminated in the FA MAS, with it being almost completely ambidextrous. Removal of the cheek rest on the stock and switching it to the other side exposes the left side ejection port as well as accommodating the stock to a left handed firer. The bolt is also easily changed by the operator for right or left ejection. The cocking handle is placed in the upper center of the receiver so that it may be reached from either side. The safety/selector is placed inside the trigger guard in front of the trigger where it can easily be reached by the operator's finger. With the selector pushed to the left, on R, the weapon fires on full automatic. Pushing the selector to the right, on 1, the weapon will fire semiautomatically. The burst fire mechanism is behind the magazine and with it set on 3, putting the selector on R allows the weapon to fire three round controlled bursts. Separating the standard firing mechanism from the burst fire controller prevents operating failure of one system from affecting the operation of the other. NATO standard rifle grenades are easily fired by the FA MAS and it has an integral folding bipod to assist firing.

ASSESSMENT	200 mm group @ 200 m
WEAPON	FA MAS
AMMO	5.56x45
DISPERSION ANGLE	.0572958 degrees, 1.01859 NATO mils.

Range	Group Circle Width (mm)	Probability (0<p<.099) (m)			
		Body	Head	Hand	Bullseye
25.0	25.000	0.990	0.990	0.990	0.924
50.0	50.000	0.990	0.990	0.978	0.725
75.0	75.000	0.990	0.990	0.921	0.577
100.0	100.000	0.990	0.978	0.851	0.475
125.0	125.000	0.990	0.953	0.782	0.403
150.0	150.000	0.990	0.921	0.719	0.349
175.0	175.000	0.987	0.887	0.663	0.308
200.0*	200.000	0.978	0.851	0.614	0.276
250.0	250.000	0.953	0.782	0.533	0.227
300.0	300.000	0.921	0.719	0.470	0.193
350.0	350.000	0.887	0.663	0.420	0.168
400.0	400.000	0.851	0.614	0.379	0.149
450.0	450.000	0.816	0.571	0.345	0.134
500.0	500.000	0.782	0.533	0.317	0.121

DAMAGE 36/.64

▼ Heckler & Koch HK33A2 • HK33A3

CARTRIDGE	5.56x45mm
OPERATION	Retarded blowback
TYPE OF FIRE	Selective (E models also have three round burst and full auto)
RATE OF FIRE	(SS) 40 rpm (A) 100 rpm (CYCLIC) 750 rpm
MUZZLE VELOCITY	920 m/s (3020 fps)
MUZZLE ENERGY	1675 J (1235 ft/lb)
SIGHTS	Adjustable, U-notch/post, range 400m
FEED	25 round removable box magazine
WEIGHTS:	
WEAPON (EMPTY)	3.651 kg (3.969 kg)
WEAPON (LOADED)	4.206 kg (4.524 kg)
MAGAZINE (EMPTY)	0.250 kg
MAGAZINE (LOADED)	0.555 kg
SERVICE CARTRIDGE	12.2 g
BULLET	4 g
LENGTHS:	
WEAPON OVERALL	92 cm (73.5/94 cm)
BARREL	39 cm
SIGHT RADIUS	48 cm
STATUS	In production
SERVICE	Malaysia, Chile, Brazil (air force), and Thailand, commercial sales

This is a reduced scale version of the G3 rifle and is chambered for the 5.56 x 45mm cartridge. Originally there was a 40 round as well as a 25 round magazine available, but the 40 round magazine is no longer manufactured. The HK33A2 has a fixed plastic stock with the HK33A3 having a sliding metal collapsible stock. Today, both the A2 and A3 versions are referred to as the HK33E (E for Export) with the differences in type being referred to as the fixed or sliding butt models. An optional trigger group is now available that allows single shots, controlled three round bursts, or continuous full automatic fire to be selected.

ASSESSMENT	2 inch group @ 100 yds
WEAPON	HK33A2
AMMO	5.56x45
DISPERSION ANGLE	.031831 degrees, .565885 NATO mils.

Range	Group Circle Width (mm)	Probability (0<p<.099) (m)			
		Body	Head	Hand	Bullseye
25.0	13.889	0.990	0.990	0.990	0.990
50.0	27.778	0.990	0.990	0.990	0.902
75.0	41.667	0.990	0.990	0.990	0.787
100.0	55.556	0.990	0.990	0.968	0.687
125.0	69.444	0.990	0.990	0.936	0.605
150.0	83.333	0.990	0.990	0.898	0.539
175.0	97.222	0.990	0.980	0.859	0.485
200.0	111.111	0.990	0.968	0.820	0.440
250.0	138.889	0.990	0.936	0.746	0.371
300.0	166.667	0.990	0.898	0.681	0.321

☞ continued on next page

☛ *HK33A2 • HK33A3 continued*

Range	Group Circle Width (mm)	Probability (0<p<.099) (m)			
		Body	Head	Hand	Bullseye
350.0	194.444	0.980	0.859	0.625	0.282
400.0	222.222	0.968	0.820	0.576	0.252
450.0	250.000	0.953	0.782	0.533	0.227
500.0	277.778	0.936	0.746	0.496	0.207

DAMAGE 35/.61

▼ Heckler & Koch HK33KA1

CARTRIDGE 5.56x45mm
OPERATION Retarded blowback
TYPE OF FIRE Selective (E model has three round burst and full auto)
RATE OF FIRE (SS) 40 rpm (A) 100 rpm (CYCLIC) 700 rpm
MUZZLE VELOCITY 880 m/s (2880 fps)
MUZZLE ENERGY 1523 J (1123 ft/lb)
SIGHTS Adjustable, U-notch/post, range 400m
FEED 25 round removable box magazine
WEIGHTS:
WEAPON (EMPTY) 3.969 kg
WEAPON (LOADED) 4.524 kg
MAGAZINE (EMPTY) 0.250 kg
MAGAZINE (LOADED) 0.555 kg
SERVICE CARTRIDGE 12.2 g
BULLET 4 g
LENGTHS:
WEAPON OVERALL 67.5/86.5 cm
BARREL 32.2 cm
SIGHT RADIUS 48 cm
STATUS In production
SERVICE Commercial sales

This shortened version of the HK33 has the barrel cut off and flash suppressor refitted to just in front of the front sight. The weapon cannot be used to fire rifle grenades but is otherwise identical to the HK33. The sliding buttstock is standard on the HK33KA1.

WEAPON HK33KA1
AMMO 5.56x45
DISPERSION ANGLE .0316115 degrees, .561982 NATO mils.

Range	Group Circle Width (mm)	Probability (0<p<.099) (m)			
		Body	Head	Hand	Bullseye
25.0	13.793	0.990	0.990	0.990	0.990
50.0	27.586	0.990	0.990	0.990	0.903
75.0	41.379	0.990	0.990	0.990	0.790
100.0	55.172	0.990	0.990	0.968	0.689
125.0	68.966	0.990	0.990	0.937	0.608
150.0	82.759	0.990	0.990	0.900	0.541
175.0	96.552	0.990	0.981	0.861	0.487
200.0	110.345	0.990	0.968	0.822	0.443
250.0	137.931	0.990	0.937	0.749	0.374
300.0	165.517	0.990	0.900	0.684	0.323
350.0	193.103	0.981	0.861	0.627	0.284
400.0	220.690	0.968	0.822	0.578	0.253
450.0	248.276	0.954	0.784	0.536	0.229
500.0	275.862	0.937	0.749	0.499	0.208

DAMAGE 34/.58

▼ Heckler & Koch HK53

HK 53 with stock extended and 25 rd magazine, with optional flashlight forend

HK 53 with selector set on safe and stock collapsed, optional forend with integral flashlight

CARTRIDGE 5.56x45mm
OPERATION Retarded blowback
TYPE OF FIRE Selective three round burst and full auto
RATE OF FIRE (SS) 40 rpm (A) 100 rpm (CYCLIC) 700 rpm
MUZZLE VELOCITY 750 m/s (2460 fps)
MUZZLE ENERGY 1112 J (820 ft/lb)
SIGHTS Adjustable, U-notch/post, range 400m

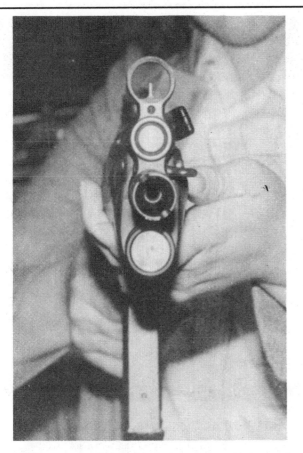

HK53 showing optional flashlight front grip with light control below muzzle. Pressure switch for light is just visible as the rectangular strip on the upper left side just above fingertips

in use with the HK53. The muzzle blast and report are large with the short barrel of the HK53, making its firing, especially in enclosed areas, particularly uncomfortable.

WEAPON	HK53	
AMMO	5.56x45	
DISPERSION ANGLE	.0790287 degrees, 1.40496 NATO mils.	

Range	Group Circle Width (mm)	Probability (0<p<.099) (m)			
		Body	Head	Hand	Bullseye
25.0	34.483	0.990	0.990	0.990	0.846
50.0	68.966	0.990	0.990	0.937	0.608
75.0	103.448	0.990	0.975	0.841	0.464
100.0	137.931	0.990	0.937	0.749	0.374
125.0	172.414	0.988	0.890	0.669	0.312
150.0	206.897	0.975	0.841	0.602	0.268
175.0	241.379	0.957	0.794	0.546	0.234
200.0	275.862	0.937	0.749	0.499	0.208
250.0	344.828	0.890	0.669	0.424	0.171
300.0	413.793	0.841	0.602	0.369	0.144
350.0	482.759	0.794	0.546	0.326	0.125
400.0	551.724	0.749	0.499	0.292	0.110
450.0	620.690	0.707	0.459	0.264	0.099
500.0	689.655	0.669	0.424	0.241	0.089

DAMAGE 29/.50

▼ Heckler & Koch G41 • G41A2

H&K G41

CARTRIDGE	5.56x45mm
OPERATION	Retarded blowback
TYPE OF FIRE	Selective w/three round burst and full auto
RATE OF FIRE	(SS) 40 rpm (A) 100 rpm (CYCLIC) 900 rpm
MUZZLE VELOCITY	910 m/s (2985 fps)
MUZZLE ENERGY	1637 J (1207 ft/lb)
SIGHTS	Adjustable, aperture/post, range 400 m
FEED	20, 30 or 30/45 round removable box magazine (M16)
WEIGHTS:	
WEAPON (EMPTY)	4.100 kg (4.400 kg)
WEAPON (LOADED)	4.583 kg w/30 rds (4.883 kg w/30 rds)

FEED	25 or 40 round removable box magazine
WEIGHTS:	
WEAPON (EMPTY)	3.048 kg
WEAPON (LOADED)	3.603 kg w/25 rds
MAGAZINE (EMPTY)	0.250 kg (25 rd), 0.157 kg (40 rd)
MAGAZINE (LOADED)	0.555 kg (25 rd), 0.157 kg (40 rd)
SERVICE CARTRIDGE	12.2 g
BULLET	4 g
LENGTHS:	
WEAPON OVERALL	56.3/75.5 cm
BARREL	21.1 cm
SIGHT RADIUS	39 cm
STATUS	In production
SERVICE	Commercial sales

Referred to as a submachinegun by Heckler and Koch, this weapon is a very short carbine version of the HK33 and it fits our definition of assault carbine with its firing of a rifle caliber cartridge. The HK53 has a very short overall length and is very handy to use. There is an alternate trigger group assembly that can be fitted to the weapon, giving it the capacity to fire three round controlled bursts as well as semi and full automatic fire. The earlier 40 round magazine can most often be found

☞ *continued on next page*

☛ *continued*

MAGAZINE (EMPTY)	0.091 kg (20 rd), 0.117 kg (30 rd), 0.149 kg (30/45 rd)
MAGAZINE (LOADED)	0.335 kg (20 rd), 0.483 kg (30 rd), 0.698kg (30/45 rd w/45 rds)
SERVICE CARTRIDGE	12.2 g
BULLET	4 g
LENGTHS:	
WEAPON OVERALL	99.7 cm (80.6/99.6 cm)
BARREL	45 cm
SIGHT RADIUS	56.6 cm
STATUS	In production
SERVICE	Undergoing trials and commercial sales

This is the most recent development by Heckler and Koch and is designed to compete with other 5.56 x 45mm chambered for future NATO trials. The G41 was intended to fit more closely into existing NATO supply systems and for this reason, can use both the magazine and the bipod of the M16. Also found on the G41 is a folding carrying handle, a dust cover that will close over the ejection port, a positive bolt closure device, and a last shot hold open for the bolt. The top of the G41 receiver will accept all standard NATO sighting devices and the weapon can fire all NATO standard rifle grenades. The trigger mechanism is of the newest Heckler and Koch type, incorporating a three round controlled burst option. A cleaning kit is mounted inside the grip and there is a slide-on winter trigger available to allow the G41 to be fired with mittens on. There are four models of the G41 available, differing only in their rifling pitch and type of stock, they are as follows:

G41: rifling pitch 178mm (1 turn in 7 inches), fixed buttstock.

G41A1: rifling pitch 305mm (1 turn in 12 inches), fixed butt stock.

G41A2: rifling pitch 178mm (1 turn in 7 inches), retractable metal stock.

G41A3: rifling pitch 305mm (1 turn in 12 inches), retractable metal stock.

WEAPON	G41
AMMO	5.56x45
DISPERSION ANGLE	.0237086 degrees, .421487 NATO mils.

Range	Group Circle Width (mm)	Probability (0<p<.099) (m)			
		Body	Head	Hand	Bullseye
25.0	10.345	0.990	0.990	0.990	0.990
50.0	20.690	0.990	0.990	0.990	0.956
75.0	31.034	0.990	0.990	0.990	0.875
100.0	41.379	0.990	0.990	0.990	0.790
125.0	51.724	0.990	0.990	0.975	0.713
150.0	62.069	0.990	0.990	0.954	0.646
175.0	72.414	0.990	0.990	0.928	0.590
200.0	82.759	0.990	0.990	0.900	0.541
250.0	103.448	0.990	0.975	0.841	0.464
300.0	124.138	0.990	0.954	0.784	0.405
350.0	144.828	0.990	0.928	0.732	0.359
400.0	165.517	0.990	0.900	0.684	0.323
450.0	186.207	0.983	0.871	0.641	0.293
500.0	206.897	0.975	0.841	0.602	0.268

DAMAGE 35/.61

▼ Heckler & Koch G41K

CARTRIDGE	5.56x45mm
OPERATION	Retarded blowback
TYPE OF FIRE	Selective w/three round burst and full auto
RATE OF FIRE	(SS) 40 rpm (A) 100 rpm (CYCLIC) 850 rpm
MUZZLE VELOCITY	870 m/s (2870 fps)
MUZZLE ENERGY	1512 J (1115 ft/lb)
SIGHTS	Adjustable, aperture/post, range 400m
FEED	20, 30, or 30/45 round removable box magazine (M16)
WEIGHTS:	
WEAPON (EMPTY)	4.309 kg
WEAPON (LOADED)	4.792 kg w/30 rds
MAGAZINE (EMPTY)	0.091 kg (20 rd), 0.117 kg (30 rd), 0.149 kg (30/45 rd)
MAGAZINE (LOADED)	0.335 kg (20 rd), 0.483 kg (30 rd), 0.698 kg (30/45 rd w/45 rds)
SERVICE CARTRIDGE	12.2 g
BULLET	4 g
LENGTHS:	
WEAPON OVERALL	74/93 cm
BARREL	38.4 cm
SIGHT RADIUS	56.6 cm
STATUS	In production
SERVICE	Undergoing trials and commercial sales

This is a shortened, K for Kurz (short), version of the standard G41 with a retractable metal stock. The barrel is shortened with the flash suppressor mounted just ahead of the front sight. The only major differences between the G41K and the standard G41's is that the K model cannot fire rifle grenades or use the M16 bipod.

WEAPON	G41K
AMMO	5.56x45
DISPERSION ANGLE	.0237086 degrees, .421487 NATO mils.

Range	Group Circle Width (mm)	Probability (0<p<.099) (m)			
		Body	Head	Hand	Bullseye
25.0	10.345	0.990	0.990	0.990	0.990
50.0	20.690	0.990	0.990	0.990	0.956
75.0	31.034	0.990	0.990	0.990	0.875
100.0	41.379	0.990	0.990	0.990	0.790
125.0	51.724	0.990	0.990	0.975	0.713
150.0	62.069	0.990	0.990	0.954	0.646
175.0	72.414	0.990	0.990	0.928	0.590
200.0	82.759	0.990	0.990	0.900	0.541
250.0	103.448	0.990	0.975	0.841	0.464
300.0	124.138	0.990	0.954	0.784	0.405
350.0	144.828	0.990	0.928	0.732	0.359
400.0	165.517	0.990	0.900	0.684	0.323
450.0	186.207	0.983	0.871	0.641	0.293
500.0	206.897	0.975	0.841	0.602	0.268

DAMAGE 34/.58

▼ Heckler & Koch G11

CARTRIDGE	4.73X33MM DM11
OPERATION	Gas
TYPE OF FIRE	Selective w/three shot burst and full auto
RATE OF FIRE	(SS) 40 rpm (A) 200 rpm (CYCLIC) 600 (2000 rpm on 3 rd burst)
MUZZLE VELOCITY	930 m/s (3051 fps)
MUZZLE ENERGY	1374 J(1013 Ft/lb)
SIGHTS	1 power telescopic sight built into the handle
FEED	50 round removable box magazine

WEIGHTS:	
WEAPON (EMPTY)	3.666 kg
WEAPON (LOADED)	4.180 kg
MAGAZINE (EMPTY)	0.254 kg
MAGAZINE (LOADED)	0.514 kg
SERVICE CARTRIDGE	5.2 g
BULLET	3.2 g
LENGTHS:	
WEAPON OVERALL	75 cm
BARREL	54 cm
STATUS	Under development
SERVICE	Undergoing trials

This is presently a developmental weapon using several innovations in its operation. The most obvious innovation is the use of caseless ammunition where the propellant acts as the binder for the bullet and primer. The main advantage of caseless ammunition is the elimination of the metallic cartridge casing. Elimination of the casing saves the use of materials to make it, removes its weight from the weapon system and ends the need for fired casing extraction or ejection. The development of the G11 started with the finding of a suitable material to make up the round's body. The final round is made up of a modified form of the explosive RDX that works as a propellant rather than explosive. Use of modified RDX helps eliminate the problem of cook-off, where the residual heat in the chamber will fire a round. The normal metallic cartridge case removes some of the heat of firing and protects normal propellants. The development of the solid heat resistant propellant opens the door for the weapon's development to commence. The present design of the round is a square cross-section rectangle with the bullet seated fully into the block. The firing mechanism was next developed with the design centering around a cylindrical breech block that rotates to align the round with the barrel. The square crosssection allows the rounds to be closely packed with no wasted space into the G11's 50 round in-line magazine. The magazine is set along the barrel in line with the weapon making for a very streamlined outline. the cartridges are fed downward, nose first into the rotating breechblock. The breechblock is externally operated by the folding knob behind the left side of the pistol grip. The knob can be rotated to load the weapon as well as unload the chambered round through a port in the bottom of the weapon. The unloading port is the only opening, besides the barrel muzzle, to be found in the weapon. This effectively seals out dirt and debris from the action. The action of the G11 is able to move within the stock while operating. The length of movement combined with the action's design and 2000 rpm rate of fire allows a three round controlled burst to be fired with the last round leaving the barrel before the firer can react to the recoil. The 600 rpm rate of fire is automatically set when the weapon is set to full automatic fire. The high rate of fire used on three round burst combined with the effective lack of recoil and muzzle climb greatly increases the probability of a first round hit. On the physical side, the G11 uses

☞ continued on next page

☞ *Heckler & Koch G11 continued*

a bullpup layout giving an excellent barrel length while retaining a short overall length for handiness. The upper handle contains a 1 power telescopic sight with a circular reticle, useful for range finding. Still under development, the G11 has been field tested by troops both US and German. Though well received, the weapon is not expected to be adopted in the imediate future by any major military force.

ASSESSMENT	3.6 cm @ 300m, three shot burst
WEAPON	G11
AMMO	4.73x33
	1 x power scope installed.
DISPERSION ANGLE	.0068755 degrees, .122231 NATO mils.

Range	Group Circle Width (mm)	Probability (0<p<.099) (m)			
		Body	Head	Hand	Bullseye
25.0	3.000	0.990	0.990	0.990	0.990
50.0	6.000	0.990	0.990	0.990	0.990
75.0	9.000	0.990	0.990	0.990	0.990
100.0	12.000	0.990	0.990	0.990	0.990
125.0	15.000	0.990	0.990	0.990	0.986
150.0	18.000	0.990	0.990	0.990	0.972
175.0	21.000	0.990	0.990	0.990	0.954
200.0	24.000	0.990	0.990	0.990	0.932
250.0	30.000	0.990	0.990	0.990	0.884
300.0*	36.000	0.990	0.990	0.990	0.833
350.0	42.000	0.990	0.990	0.989	0.785
400.0	48.000	0.990	0.990	0.981	0.739
450.0	54.000	0.990	0.990	0.971	0.697
500.0	60.000	0.990	0.990	0.958	0.659

DAMAGE 30/0.41

▼ 5.56mm Galil AR • SAR

CARTRIDGE	5.56x45mm
OPERATION	Gas
TYPE OF FIRE	Selective
RATE OF FIRE	(SS) 40 rpm (A) 105 rpm
	(CYCLIC) 650 rpm
MUZZLE VELOCITY	980 m/s (3215 fps) (920 m/s <3018 fps>)
MUZZLE ENERGY	1898 J (1400 ft/lb), (1672 J <1233 ft/lb>)
SIGHTS	Adjustable, aperture/post, range 500m, flip-up 3-dot night sights
FEED	35 or 50 round removable box magazine
WEIGHTS:	
WEAPON (EMPTY)	4.300 kg w/bipod & handle (3.65 kg)
WEAPON (LOADED)	5.117 kg w/35 rds (4.467 kg w/35 rds)
MAGAZINE (EMPTY)	0.390 kg (35 rd), 0.440 kg (50 rd)
MAGAZINE (LOADED)	0.817 kg (35 rd), 1.050 kg (50 rd)
SERVICE CARTRIDGE	12.2 g
BULLET	4 g
LENGTHS:	
WEAPON OVERALL	74.2/97.9 cm (61.4/85.1 cm)
BARREL	46 cm (33.2 cm)
SIGHT RADIUS	47.5 cm
STATUS	In production
SERVICE	Israeli forces and commercial sales

The Galil is a native development of Israel that owes most of its basic design to the AKM-47. The original receivers used for the Galil were from Valmet in Finland's M-62 rifles and so, the Galil can be considered presently to be the most sophisticated of the many AK-47 copies. The three models of the Galil are the ARM (assault rifle machinegun), the AR (assault rifle), and the SAR (shortened assault rifle). The ARM can be used as a light machinegun, and for this role it is normally fitted with the fifty round magazine. The fulcrum of the bipod has a notch cut into it that allows it to be used as a wire cutter by moving the bipod legs. The bipod legs fold under and into the foregrip and the retaining hooks have been modified so that they can act as a bottle opener, probably the most unusual accessory found on any modern rifle today. Without the folding carrying handle and bipod the Galil is referred to as the AR model. The flash suppressor on the Galil can be used to launch rifle grenades. The SAR has a shortened barrel reducing the overall length and cannot accept the bipod or launch rifle grenades but is otherwise identical to the other models. Normally equipped with a folding buttstock, the Galil can be fitted with either a wood or plastic fixed stock. It has folding tritium filled night sights that glow and are zeroed for 100 meters. The cocking handle is raised at a 90 degree angle to the bolt so that the weapon may be cocked from either side, and the selector switch is also arranged so that it can be manipulated from either side. The Galil has developed a reputation for accuracy and reliability, contained in a rugged package which is usable in any environment.

ASSESSMENT	0.9 inch @ 100 yds ARM
WEAPON	Galil ARM
AMMO	5.56x45
DISPERSION ANGLE	.014324 degrees, .254648 NATO mils.

Range	Group Circle Width (mm)	Probability (0<p<.099) (m)			
		Body	Head	Hand	Bullseye
25.0	6.250	0.990	0.990	0.990	0.990
50.0	12.500	0.990	0.990	0.990	0.990
75.0	18.750	0.990	0.990	0.990	0.968
100.0	25.000	0.990	0.990	0.990	0.924
125.0	31.250	0.990	0.990	0.990	0.873
150.0	37.500	0.990	0.990	0.990	0.821

☞ *continued*

Range	Group Circle Width (mm)	Probability (0<p<.099) (m)			
		Body	Head	Hand	Bullseye
175.0	43.750	0.990	0.990	0.987	0.771
200.0	50.000	0.990	0.990	0.978	0.725
250.0	62.500	0.990	0.990	0.953	0.644
300.0	75.000	0.990	0.990	0.921	0.577
350.0	87.500	0.990	0.987	0.887	0.522
400.0	100.000	0.990	0.978	0.851	0.475
450.0	112.500	0.990	0.966	0.816	0.436
500.0	125.000	0.990	0.953	0.782	0.403

DAMAGE (A) 38/.65 (AR), (B) 35/.61 (SAR)

▼ Beretta AR 70 • SC 70

SC 70

AR 70

CARTRIDGE	5.56x45mm
OPERATION	Gas
TYPE OF FIRE	Selective
RATE OF FIRE	(SS) 40 rpm (A) 100 rpm (CYCLIC) 650 rpm
MUZZLE VELOCITY	950 m/s (3117 fps)
MUZZLE ENERGY	1784 J (1316 ft/lb)
SIGHTS	Adjustable, aperture/post, range 300m
FEED	30 round removable box magazine
WEIGHTS:	
WEAPON (EMPTY)	3.545 kg (3.595 kg)
WEAPON (LOADED)	4.166 kg (4.216 kg)
MAGAZINE (EMPTY)	0.255 kg
MAGAZINE (LOADED)	0.621 kg
SERVICE CARTRIDGE	12.2 g
BULLET	4 g
LENGTHS:	
WEAPON OVERALL	99.5 cm (73.6/96 cm)
BARREL	45 cm
SIGHT RADIUS	50.7 cm
STATUS	In production

SERVICE Italian special forces, Jordan, Malaysia, and commercial sales

The AR-70 was Beretta's first design in 5.56 x 45 and has met with some success. The number of parts have been held to a minimum, 85 in the AR-70, with as little machining as possible needed to manufacture the weapon. The fixed buttstock of the AR70 is removable and can be replaced with a wire frame folding stock. When fitted with the folding stock, the weapon is referred to as the SC-70. Both models are fitted with front and rear folding sights for use when firing rifle grenades. When the front rifle grenade sight is raised, it automatically cuts off the gas system turning the weapon into a manually operated repeater and allows all the gas from the cartridge to be used propelling the grenade. There is a spring loaded cover that snaps into place behind the bolt effectively sealing out dirt that springs out of the way when the weapon is fired.

WEAPON AR 70
AMMO 5.56x45
DISPERSION ANGLE .0276601 degrees, .491734 NATO mils.

Range	Group Circle Width (mm)	Probability (0<p<.099) (m)			
		Body	Head	Hand	Bullseye
25.0	12.069	0.990	0.990	0.990	0.990
50.0	24.138	0.990	0.990	0.990	0.931
75.0	36.207	0.990	0.990	0.990	0.832
100.0	48.276	0.990	0.990	0.981	0.737
125.0	60.345	0.990	0.990	0.957	0.657
150.0	72.414	0.990	0.990	0.928	0.590
175.0	84.483	0.990	0.989	0.895	0.534
200.0	96.552	0.990	0.981	0.861	0.487
250.0	120.690	0.990	0.957	0.794	0.414
300.0	144.828	0.990	0.928	0.732	0.359
350.0	168.966	0.989	0.895	0.676	0.317
400.0	193.103	0.981	0.861	0.627	0.284
450.0	217.241	0.970	0.827	0.584	0.257
500.0	241.379	0.957	0.794	0.546	0.234

DAMAGE 37/0.63

▼ Beretta SC 70 Short

CARTRIDGE	5.56x45mm
OPERATION	Gas
TYPE OF FIRE	Selective
RATE OF FIRE	(SS) 40 rpm (A) 100 rpm (CYCLIC) 600 rpm
MUZZLE VELOCITY	885 m/s (2904 fps)

☞ *continued on next page*

☞ *Beretta SC 70 Short continued*

MUZZLE ENERGY	1549 J (1142 ft/lb)
SIGHTS	Adjustable, aperture/post, range 300m
FEED	30 round removable box magazine
WEIGHTS:	
WEAPON (EMPTY)	3.445 kg
WEAPON (LOADED)	4.066 kg
MAGAZINE (EMPTY)	0.255 kg
MAGAZINE (LOADED)	0.621 kg
SERVICE CARTRIDGE	12.2 g
BULLET	4 g
LENGTHS:	
WEAPON OVERALL	59.6/82 cm
BARREL	32 cm
SIGHT RADIUS	45.5 cm
STATUS	In production
SERVICE	Commercial sales

This is a shortened version of the SC-70. The weapon is fitted with the wire frame folding stock. The shortened barrel also results in a shorter sight radius. Since the SC-70 Short cannot launch rifle grenades, the folding grenade launcher sights and gas cutoff system are not fitted.

WEAPON	SC 70
AMMO	5.56x45
DISPERSION ANGLE	.0355629 degrees, .63223 NATO mils.

Range	Group Circle Width (mm)	Probability (0<p<.099) (m)			
		Body	**Head**	**Hand**	**Bullseye**
25.0	15.517	0.990	0.990	0.990	0.984
50.0	31.034	0.990	0.990	0.990	0.875
75.0	46.552	0.990	0.990	0.983	0.750
100.0	62.069	0.990	0.990	0.954	0.646
125.0	77.586	0.990	0.990	0.914	0.565
150.0	93.103	0.990	0.983	0.871	0.500
175.0	108.621	0.990	0.970	0.827	0.448
200.0	124.138	0.990	0.954	0.784	0.405
250.0	155.172	0.990	0.914	0.707	0.340
300.0	186.207	0.983	0.871	0.641	0.293
350.0	217.241	0.970	0.827	0.584	0.257
400.0	248.276	0.954	0.784	0.536	0.229
450.0	279.310	0.935	0.744	0.494	0.206
500.0	310.345	0.914	0.707	0.459	0.188

DAMAGE 34/0.59

▼ AR 70/90 • SC 70/90

CARTRIDGE	5.56x45mm
OPERATION	Gas
TYPE OF FIRE	Selective w/3 rd burst and full automatic
RATE OF FIRE	(SS) 40 rpm (A) 120 rpm (CYCLIC) 680 rpm
MUZZLE VELOCITY	945 m/s (3100 fps)
MUZZLE ENERGY	1794 J (1323 ft/lb)
SIGHTS	Adjustable aperture/post, range 400m, fixed, nonadjustable u-notch/post battle sights w/3 dot luminous inserts
FEED	20, 30, or 30/45 round removable box magazine
WEIGHTS:	
WEAPON (EMPTY)	3.990 kg (bipod wt 0.365 kg)
WEAPON (LOADED)	4.473 kg w/30 rds (4.838 w/30 rds and bipod)
MAGAZINE (EMPTY)	0.091 kg (20 rd), 0.117 kg (30 rd), 0.145 kg (30/45 rd)
MAGAZINE (LOADED)	0.335 kg (20 rd), 0.483 kg (30 rd), 0.698 kg (30/45 rd)
SERVICE CARTRIDGE	12.2 g
BULLET	4 g
LENGTHS:	
WEAPON OVERALL	99.8 cm (75.1/98.6 cm)
BARREL	45 cm
SIGHT RADIUS	55.5 cm (handle battle sight) 20 cm
STATUS	In production
COST	$1250

The AR 70/90 weapons system is based on the AR-70 rifle with improvements indicated by field experience with the earlier weapon. The receiver of the AR 70/90 is made from a metal stamping with steel bolt guides welded in place. The construction methods result in a lower production cost as well as a stronger and more durable design. The most noticeable new feature is the addition of a removable carrying handle which is attached to mounts at the top of the receiver. With the handle removed, the receiver mounts will accept any NATO standard (STANAG 2324) based sighting device. The handle has a complete set of front and rear sights along its top with luminous inserts for use in low light situations. A set of adjustable iron sights are mounted on the weapon proper and they are used for more precision shooting. The gas system operating the 70/90 has three positions: the first for normal firing, the second for firing under adverse conditions, and the third is a system shutoff for launching rifle grenades. To shut off the gas system for grenade launching, an arched lever is raised which blocks the normal sight line. With the shutoff lever lowered to the normal (open) position, it prevents rifle grenades from being seated over the muzzle launcher. The firing mechanism is designed to allow single-shots, controlled three-round bursts, or full automatic fire to be selected. The selector is also able to be easily changed for ones allowing only single shots, single shots with three round bursts, or single shots and full automatic fire. The trigger guard can be folded down against the pistol grip, allowing the trigger to be reached by an operator wearing heavy gloves. Both the firing selector as well as the magazine release are duplicated on both sides of the receiver, allowing easy use by right or left-handed firers. The magazine well is designed to accept any M16 type magazines according to NATO standard (STANAG 4179). The AR 70/90 is the standard rifle version of the 70/90 weapons family with the SC 70/90 being a carbine version of the system. The SC 70/90 is identical to the rifle version except for the folding stock. Both weapons will accept a removable bipod which can fold up under the front grip.

WEAPON	AR 70/90
AMMO	5.56x45
DISPERSION ANGLE	.0237086 degrees, .421487 NATO mils.

Range	Group Circle Width (mm)	Probability (0<p<.099) (m)			
		Body	**Head**	**Hand**	**Bullseye**
25.0	10.345	0.990	0.990	0.990	0.990
50.0	20.690	0.990	0.990	0.990	0.956
75.0	31.034	0.990	0.990	0.990	0.875
100.0	41.379	0.990	0.990	0.990	0.790
125.0	51.724	0.990	0.990	0.975	0.713
150.0	62.069	0.990	0.990	0.954	0.646
175.0	72.414	0.990	0.990	0.928	0.590
200.0	82.759	0.990	0.990	0.900	0.541
250.0	103.448	0.990	0.975	0.841	0.464
300.0	124.138	0.990	0.954	0.784	0.405
350.0	144.828	0.990	0.928	0.732	0.359
400.0	165.517	0.990	0.900	0.684	0.323
450.0	186.207	0.983	0.871	0.641	0.293
500.0	206.897	0.975	0.841	0.602	0.268

DAMAGE 36/0.64

▼ SCS 70/90

CARTRIDGE	5.56x45mm
OPERATION	Gas
TYPE OF FIRE	Selective w/3 rd burst and full automatic
RATE OF FIRE	(SS) 40 rpm (A) 120 rpm (CYCLIC) 680 rpm
MUZZLE VELOCITY	841 m/s (2760 fps)
MUZZLE ENERGY	1399 J (1032 ft/lb)
SIGHTS	Adjustable aperture/post, range 400m, fixed, nonadjustable u-notch/post battle sights w/3 dot luminous inserts

FEED	20, 30, or 30/45 round removable box magazine (STANAG 4179)
WEIGHTS:	
WEAPON (EMPTY)	3.790 kg
WEAPON (LOADED)	4.273 kg w/30 rds
MAGAZINE (EMPTY)	0.091 kg (20 rd), 0.117 kg (30 rd), 0.145 kg (30/45 rd)
MAGAZINE (LOADED)	0.335 kg (20 rd), 0.483 kg (30 rd), 0.698 kg (30/45 rd)
SERVICE CARTRIDGE	12.2 g
BULLET	4 g
LENGTHS:	
WEAPON OVERALL	64.7/87.6 cm
BARREL	35.2 cm
SIGHT RADIUS	51.4 cm (handle battle sight 20 cm)
STATUS	In production

The shortened special carbine version of the 70/90 weapons system has the same receiver and folding stock as the standard weapon but with a shortened barrel. The shortened barrel prevents the SCS 70/90 from accepting a bayonet or launching rifle grenades. Since grenades are not fired, the gas valve does not have the arched shutoff lever of the standard barrels. The folding bipod will not attach to the barrel of the SCS 70/90.

WEAPON	SCS 70/90
AMMO	5.56x45
DISPERSION ANGLE	.0276601 degrees, .491734 NATO mils.

Range	Group Circle Width (mm)	Probability (0<p<.099) (m)			
		Body	**Head**	**Hand**	**Bullseye**
25.0	12.069	0.990	0.990	0.990	0.990
50.0	24.138	0.990	0.990	0.990	0.931
75.0	36.207	0.990	0.990	0.990	0.832
100.0	48.276	0.990	0.990	0.981	0.737
125.0	60.345	0.990	0.990	0.957	0.657
150.0	72.414	0.990	0.990	0.928	0.590
175.0	84.483	0.990	0.989	0.895	0.534
200.0	96.552	0.990	0.981	0.861	0.487
250.0	120.690	0.990	0.957	0.794	0.414
300.0	144.828	0.990	0.928	0.732	0.359
350.0	168.966	0.989	0.895	0.676	0.317
400.0	193.103	0.981	0.861	0.627	0.284
450.0	217.241	0.970	0.827	0.584	0.257
500.0	241.379	0.957	0.794	0.546	0.234

DAMAGE 32/0.56

▼ SAR 80

CARTRIDGE	5.56x45mm
OPERATION	Gas
TYPE OF FIRE	Selective
RATE OF FIRE	(SS) 40 rpm (A) 90 rpm (CYCLIC) 700 rpm
MUZZLE VELOCITY	970 m/s (3182 fps)
MUZZLE ENERGY	1859 J (1371 ft/lb)
SIGHTS	Adjustable, aperture/post
FEED	20, 30, or 30/45 round removable box magazine (M16)
WEIGHTS:	
WEAPON (EMPTY)	3.400 kg
WEAPON (LOADED)	3.883 kg w/30 rds
MAGAZINE (EMPTY)	0.091 kg (20 rd), 0.117 kg (30 rd), 0.149 kg (30/45 rd
MAGAZINE (LOADED)	0.335 kg (20 rd), 0.483 kg (30 rd), 0.698 kg (30/45 rd w/45 rds)
SERVICE CARTRIDGE	12.2 g
BULLET	4 g
LENGTHS:	
WEAPON OVERALL	97 cm
BARREL	45.9 cm
SIGHT RADIUS	51.7 cm
STATUS	In production
SERVICE	Singapore armed forces and commercial sales

The SAR 80 is a development of a design originally from Sterling in England, finalized and improved in Singapore. The SAR, Singapore Assault Rifle, is very much an improved AR-18 and as such, is particularly easy to manufacture. The use of the M16 magazine as well as M16 accessories allows the SAR-80 to quickly interface with units that have already trained with the M16. The firing and operating mechanism is very similar to the AR-18 with most of the improvements being in the outer layout of the weapon. One option available on the SAR-80 is that the weapon is made with either a right or left side magazine release, though the release cannot be changed by the operator. The simplification of the mechanism has resulted in the SAR 80 having an excellent reliability with the weapon commonly passing a 6,000 round firing test without a malfunction.

ASSESSMENT	12.2 cm group @ 91.4 m
WEAPON	SAR 80
AMMO	5.56x45
DISPERSION ANGLE	.0764446 degrees, 1.35901 NATO mils.

Range	Group Circle Width (mm)	Probability (0<p<.099) (m)			
		Body	**Head**	**Hand**	**Bullseye**
25.0	33.355	0.990	0.990	0.990	0.855
50.0	66.710	0.990	0.990	0.942	0.620
75.0	100.066	0.990	0.978	0.851	0.475
100.0	133.421	0.990	0.942	0.760	0.383
125.0	166.776	0.990	0.898	0.681	0.321
150.0	200.131	0.978	0.851	0.614	0.276
175.0	233.486	0.962	0.804	0.558	0.241
200.0	266.842	0.942	0.760	0.510	0.215
250.0	333.552	0.898	0.681	0.435	0.176
300.0	400.262	0.851	0.614	0.379	0.149
350.0	466.973	0.804	0.558	0.335	0.129
400.0	533.683	0.760	0.510	0.300	0.114
450.0	600.394	0.719	0.470	0.272	0.102
500.0	667.104	0.681	0.435	0.248	0.092

DAMAGE 37/0.65

▼ CETME L

CETMI Model L with bipod

CARTRIDGE	5.56x45mm
OPERATION	Retarded blowback
TYPE OF FIRE	Selective
RATE OF FIRE	(SS) 40 rpm (A) 100 rpm (CYCLIC) 600–750 rpm
MUZZLE VELOCITY	875 m/s (2871 fps)
MUZZLE ENERGY	1513 J (1116 ft/lb)
SIGHTS	Adjustable, aperture/post, range 400m
FEED	20, 30, or 30/45 round removable box magazine (M16)
WEIGHTS:	
WEAPON (EMPTY)	3.400 kg
WEAPON (LOADED)	3.883 kg w/30 rds
MAGAZINE (EMPTY)	0.091 kg (20 rd), 0.117 kg (30 rd), 0.149 kg (30/45 rd)
MAGAZINE (LOADED)	0.335 kg (20 rd), 0.483 kg (30 rd), 0.698 kg (30/45 rd w/45 rds)
SERVICE CARTRIDGE	12.2 g
BULLET	4 g
LENGTHS:	
WEAPON OVERALL	92.5 cm

BARREL	40 cm
SIGHT RADIUS	44 cm
STATUS	In production
SERVICE	Commercial sales

The CETME Model L is Spain's entry into the 5.56 x 45mm rifle market. Very similar to the Heckler and Koch 33 series, both the H&K and Spanish weapons come from the same roots. The Model L uses the M16 magazine, allowing logistic interoperability with NATO. The rear sight is a flip-over leaf with apertures for 200 and 400 meters. The stock and grips are of plastic and there is a manual bolt hold open underneath the rear sight on the right side. The selector switch allows for safety, semiautomatic, or full automatic fire with an option for a three round burst fourth position offered by the manufacturer.

WEAPON	CETME L
AMMO	5.56x45
DISPERSION ANGLE	.0355629 degrees, .63223 NATO mils.

Range	Group Circle Width (mm)	Probability (0<p<.099) (m)			
		Body	**Head**	**Hand**	**Bullseye**
25.0	15.517	0.990	0.990	0.990	0.984
50.0	31.034	0.990	0.990	0.990	0.875
75.0	46.552	0.990	0.990	0.983	0.750
100.0	62.069	0.990	0.990	0.954	0.646
125.0	77.586	0.990	0.990	0.914	0.565
150.0	93.103	0.990	0.983	0.871	0.500
175.0	108.621	0.990	0.970	0.827	0.448
200.0	124.138	0.990	0.954	0.784	0.405
250.0	155.172	0.990	0.914	0.707	0.340
300.0	186.207	0.983	0.871	0.641	0.293
350.0	217.241	0.970	0.827	0.584	0.257
400.0	248.276	0.954	0.784	0.536	0.229
450.0	279.310	0.935	0.744	0.494	0.206
500.0	310.345	0.914	0.707	0.459	0.188

DAMAGE 34/0.58

▼ CETME LC

CETMl Model LC with bipod

CARTRIDGE	5.56x45mm
OPERATION	Retarded blowback

TYPE OF FIRE	Selective
RATE OF FIRE	(SS) 40 rpm (A) 100 rpm (CYCLIC) 650–800 rpm
MUZZLE VELOCITY	832 m/s (2730 fps)
MUZZLE ENERGY	1368 J (1009 ft/lb)
SIGHTS	Adjustable, aperture/post, range 400m
FEED	20, 30, or 30/45 round removable box magazine (M16)
WEIGHTS:	
WEAPON (EMPTY)	3.400 kg
WEAPON (LOADED)	3.883 kg w/30 rds
MAGAZINE (EMPTY)	0.091 kg (20 rd), 0.117 kg (30 rd), 0.149 kg (30/45 rd)
MAGAZINE (LOADED)	0.335 kg (20 rd), 0.483 kg (30 rd), 0.698 kg (30/45 rd w/45 rds)
SERVICE CARTRIDGE	12.2 g
BULLET	4 g
LENGTHS:	
WEAPON OVERALL	66.5/86 cm
BARREL	32 cm
SIGHT RADIUS	44 cm
STATUS	In production
SERVICE	Commercial sales

A compact version of the Model L, the Model LC has a shortened barrel and collapsible sliding metal stock. The short barrel prevents the Model LC from being able to launch rifle grenades but it is otherwise identical to the CETME Model L.

WEAPON	CETME LC
AMMO	5.56x45
DISPERSION ANGLE	.0355629 degrees, .63223 NATO mils.

Range	Group Circle Width (mm)	Probability (0<p<.099) (m)			
		Body	**Head**	**Hand**	**Bullseye**
25.0	15.517	0.990	0.990	0.990	0.984
50.0	31.034	0.990	0.990	0.990	0.875
75.0	46.552	0.990	0.990	0.983	0.750
100.0	62.069	0.990	0.990	0.954	0.646
125.0	77.586	0.990	0.990	0.914	0.565
150.0	93.103	0.990	0.983	0.871	0.500
175.0	108.621	0.990	0.970	0.827	0.448
200.0	124.138	0.990	0.954	0.784	0.405
250.0	155.172	0.990	0.914	0.707	0.340
300.0	186.207	0.983	0.871	0.641	0.293
350.0	217.241	0.970	0.827	0.584	0.257
400.0	248.276	0.954	0.784	0.536	0.229

☞ continued on next page

☞ *CETME LC continued*

Range	Group Circle Width (mm)	Probability (0<p<.099) (m)			
		Body	**Head**	**Hand**	**Bullseye**
450.0	279.310	0.935	0.744	0.494	0.206
500.0	310.345	0.914	0.707	0.459	0.188

DAMAGE 32/0.55

▼ SIG 540

CARTRIDGE	5.56x45mm
OPERATION	Gas
TYPE OF FIRE	Selective, w/three round burst and full auto
RATE OF FIRE	(SS) 40 rpm (A) 90 rpm (CYCLIC) 800 rpm
MUZZLE VELOCITY	980 m/s (3215 fps)
MUZZLE ENERGY	1894 J (1400 ft/lb)
SIGHTS	Adjustable, aperture/post, range 500m
FEED	20 or 30 round removable box magazine
WEIGHTS:	
WEAPON (EMPTY)	3.540 kg w/bipod & fixed stock, 3.590 kg w/bipod & folding stock.
WEAPON (LOADED)	4.146 kg w/bipod, fixed stock & 30 rds, 4.196 kg w/bipod & folding stock.
MAGAZINE (EMPTY)	0.200 kg (20 rd), 0.240 kg (30 rd)
MAGAZINE (LOADED)	0.444 kg (20 rd), 0.606 kg (30 rd)
SERVICE CARTRIDGE	12.2 g
BULLET	4 g
BIPOD WEIGHT	0.280 kg
LENGTHS:	
WEAPON OVERALL	95 cm w/fixed stock, 72/95 cm w/ folding stock
BARREL	46 cm
SIGHT RADIUS	49.5 cm
STATUS	In production
SERVICE	Bolivia, Burkina Faso, Chad, Djibouti,

Ecuador, France, Gabon, Indonesia, Ivory Coast, Lebanon, Mauritus, Nicaragua, Nigeria, Oman, Paraguay, Senegal, Swaziland, Upper Volta, and commercial sales.

Designed and developed in Switzerland the SIG 540 series is made in France by Manurhin for export sales to avoid the very strict Swiss export laws. The 540 model is the standard infantry version chambered for the 5.56 x 45mm round. There is both an optional bipod which can fold up under the barrel and folding stock that can be fitted. There is a gas regulator under the front sight that can be rotated to increase the gas to operate the weapon in very dirty conditions as well as rotating to cut off the gas to the operating system when launching rifle grenades. The firing mechanism allows for semi or full automatic fire to be selected with an optional 3 round controlled burst feature that can be fitted at the factory or in the field. The SIG designs are noted for both accuracy as well as reliability. The 540 series upholds this reputation and is seeing good commercial sales.

WEAPON	SIG 540
AMMO	5.56x45
DISPERSION ANGLE	.0276601 degrees, .491734 NATO mils.

Range	Group Circle Width (mm)	Probability (0<p<.099) (m)			
		Body	**Head**	**Hand**	**Bullseye**
25.0	12.069	0.990	0.990	0.990	0.990
50.0	24.138	0.990	0.990	0.990	0.931
75.0	36.207	0.990	0.990	0.990	0.832
100.0	48.276	0.990	0.990	0.981	0.737
125.0	60.345	0.990	0.990	0.957	0.657
150.0	72.414	0.990	0.990	0.928	0.590
175.0	84.483	0.990	0.989	0.895	0.534
200.0	96.552	0.990	0.981	0.861	0.487
300.0	144.828	0.990	0.928	0.732	0.359
400.0	193.103	0.981	0.861	0.627	0.284
500.0	241.379	0.957	0.794	0.546	0.234
600.0	289.655	0.928	0.732	0.482	0.200
700.0	337.931	0.895	0.676	0.431	0.174
800.0	386.207	0.861	0.627	0.389	0.154
900.0	434.483	0.827	0.584	0.355	0.138
1000.0	482.759	0.794	0.546	0.326	0.125

DAMAGE 38/0.65

▼ SIG 543

CARTRIDGE	5.56x45mm
OPERATION	Gas
TYPE OF FIRE	Selective, w/three round burst and full auto
RATE OF FIRE	(SS) 40 rpm (A) 90 rpm (CYCLIC) 725 rpm
MUZZLE VELOCITY	875 m/s (2871 fps)
MUZZLE ENERGY	1513 J (1116 ft/lb)
SIGHTS	Adjustable, aperture/post, range 500m
FEED	20 or 30 round removable box magazine
WEIGHTS:	
WEAPON (EMPTY)	3.000 kg
WEAPON (LOADED)	3.606 kg w/30 rds

MAGAZINE (EMPTY)	0.200 kg (20 rd), 0.240 kg (30 rd)
MAGAZINE (LOADED)	0.444 kg (20 rd), 0.606 kg (30 rd)
SERVICE CARTRIDGE	12.2 g
BULLET	4 g
LENGTHS:	
WEAPON OVERALL	56.9/80.5 cm
BARREL	30 cm
SIGHT RADIUS	
STATUS	In production
SERVICE	See SIG 540

This is a shortened version of the SIG 540 and is also chambered for the 5.56 x 45mm round. The folding buttstock is normally fitted and the 543 model cannot take the optional bipod. The 543 also cannot effectively launch rifle grenades but is operationally identical to the SIG 540.

WEAPON	SIG 543
AMMO	5.56x45
DISPERSION ANGLE	.0355629 degrees, .63223 NATO mils.

Range	Group Circle Width (mm)	Probability (0<p<.099) (m)			
		Body	Head	Hand	Bullseye
25.0	15.517	0.990	0.990	0.990	0.984
50.0	31.034	0.990	0.990	0.990	0.875
75.0	46.552	0.990	0.990	0.983	0.750
100.0	62.069	0.990	0.990	0.954	0.646
125.0	77.586	0.990	0.990	0.914	0.565
150.0	93.103	0.990	0.983	0.871	0.500
175.0	108.621	0.990	0.970	0.827	0.448
200.0	124.138	0.990	0.954	0.784	0.405
250.0	155.172	0.990	0.914	0.707	0.340
300.0	186.207	0.983	0.871	0.641	0.293
350.0	217.241	0.970	0.827	0.584	0.257
400.0	248.276	0.954	0.784	0.536	0.229
450.0	279.310	0.935	0.744	0.494	0.206
500.0	310.345	0.914	0.707	0.459	0.188

DAMAGE 34/0.58

▼ SIG 550

SG 550 Standard version

SG 551 Short version

CARTRIDGE	5.56x45mm
OPERATION	Gas
TYPE OF FIRE	Selective, w/three round burst and full auto
RATE OF FIRE	(SS) 40 rpm (A) 120 rpm (CYCLIC) 800 rpm
MUZZLE VELOCITY	931 m/s (3053 fps)
MUZZLE ENERGY	1711 J (1262 ft/lb)
SIGHTS	Adjustable, aperture/blade
FEED	20 or 30 round removable box magazine
WEIGHTS:	
WEAPON (EMPTY)	4.005 kg w/bipod
WEAPON (LOADED)	4.481 kg w/bipod & 30 rds
MAGAZINE (EMPTY)	0.095 kg (20 rd), 0.110 kg (30 rd)
MAGAZINE (LOADED)	0.339 kg (20 rd), 0.476 kg (30 rd)
SERVICE CARTRIDGE	12.2 g
BULLET	4 g
LENGTHS:	
WEAPON OVERALL	77/100 cm
BARREL	52.8 cm
SIGHT RADIUS	54 cm
STATUS	In production
SERVICE	Swiss forces

This SIG design has been accepted as the new Swiss issue assault rifle for their change to 5.56 as their standard military round. Plastic is used for the stocks, grips, and magazines and results in a significant weight saving. The magazine being made of plastic allows for a transparent body and remaining rounds can be seen at a glance. One of the more unusual aspects of the 550 is also found in the magazines as clips are cast into the magazine's body, allowing two or more magazines to be attached together. The firing mechanism allows for semiautomatic, full automatic, or three round controlled bursts to be fired. Luminous inserts are found in the sights to act as an aid when firing at night. The trigger guard can be folded to the side to allow clear access to the trigger when firing with gloves on. The bipod folds up closely to the handguard out of the way with a no snag outline. The 550 can also launch all of the standard NATO style rifle grenades.

WEAPON	SIG 550
AMMO	5.56x45
DISPERSION ANGLE	.0237086 degrees, .421487 NATO mils.

Range	Group Circle Width (mm)	Probability (0<p<.099) (m)			
		Body	Head	Hand	Bullseye
25.0	10.345	0.990	0.990	0.990	0.990
50.0	20.690	0.990	0.990	0.990	0.956
75.0	31.034	0.990	0.990	0.990	0.875

☞ continued on next page

☞ *SIG 550 continued*

Range	Group Circle Width (mm)	Probability (0<p<.099) (m)			
		Body	Head	Hand	Bullseye
100.0	41.379	0.990	0.990	0.990	0.790
125.0	51.724	0.990	0.990	0.975	0.713
150.0	62.069	0.990	0.990	0.954	0.646
175.0	72.414	0.990	0.990	0.928	0.590
200.0	82.759	0.990	0.990	0.900	0.541
250.0	103.448	0.990	0.975	0.841	0.464
300.0	124.138	0.990	0.954	0.784	0.405
350.0	144.828	0.990	0.928	0.732	0.359
400.0	165.517	0.990	0.900	0.684	0.323
450.0	186.207	0.983	0.871	0.641	0.293
500.0	206.897	0.975	0.841	0.602	0.268

DAMAGE 36/0.62

▼ SIG 551

<see SIG 550 for photo>

CARTRIDGE	5.56x45mm
OPERATION	Gas
TYPE OF FIRE	Selective w/three round burst and full auto
RATE OF FIRE	(SS) 40 rpm (A) 120 rpm (CYCLIC) 800 rpm
MUZZLE VELOCITY	882 m/s (2893 fps)
MUZZLE ENERGY	1536 J (1133 ft/lb)
SIGHTS	Adjustable, aperture/blade
FEED	20 or 30 round removable box magazine
WEIGHTS:	
WEAPON (EMPTY)	3.405 kg w/bipod
WEAPON (LOADED)	3.881 kg w/bipod & 30 rds
MAGAZINE (EMPTY)	0.095 kg (20 rd), 0.110 kg (30 rd)
MAGAZINE (LOADED)	0.339 kg (20 rd), 0.476 kg (30 rd)
SERVICE CARTRIDGE	12.2 g
BULLET	4 g
LENGTHS:	
WEAPON OVERALL	60/82.3 cm
BARREL	35.7 cm
SIGHT RADIUS	46.6 cm
STATUS	In production
SERVICE	Swiss forces

This is a shortened carbine version of the 550 and is intended for use by headquarters staff. The barrel and foregrip are shortened from the SG 550 model and the bipod is not fitted.

WEAPON	SIG 551
AMMO	5.56x45
DISPERSION ANGLE	.0316115 degrees, .561982 NATO mils.

Range	Group Circle Width (mm)	Probability (0<p<.099) (m)			
		Body	Head	Hand	Bullseye
25.0	13.793	0.990	0.990	0.990	0.990
50.0	27.586	0.990	0.990	0.990	0.903
75.0	41.379	0.990	0.990	0.990	0.790
100.0	55.172	0.990	0.990	0.968	0.689
125.0	68.966	0.990	0.990	0.937	0.608
150.0	82.759	0.990	0.990	0.900	0.541
175.0	96.552	0.990	0.981	0.861	0.487
200.0	110.345	0.990	0.968	0.822	0.443
250.0	137.931	0.990	0.937	0.749	0.374
300.0	165.517	0.990	0.900	0.684	0.323
350.0	193.103	0.981	0.861	0.627	0.284
400.0	220.690	0.968	0.822	0.578	0.253
450.0	248.276	0.954	0.784	0.536	0.229
500.0	275.862	0.937	0.749	0.499	0.208

DAMAGE 34/0.59

▼ AKM • AKMS

AKM-S with stock folded

AKM-47 with selector set to safe

CARTRIDGE	7.62x39mm
OPERATION	Gas
TYPE OF FIRE	Selective
RATE OF FIRE	(SS) 40 rpm (A) 100 rpm (CYCLIC) 600 rpm
MUZZLE VELOCITY	715 m/s (2346 fps)
MUZZLE ENERGY	2004 J (1478 ft/lb)
SIGHTS	Non-adjustable, U-notch/post,

FEED	30 round removable box magazine
WEIGHTS:	
WEAPON (EMPTY)	3.150 kg (3.460 kg)
WEAPON (LOADED)	3.967 kg (4.277 kg)
MAGAZINE (EMPTY)	0.322 kg (steel)
MAGAZINE (LOADED)	0.817 kg
SERVICE CARTRIDGE	16.5 g
BULLET	7.9 g
LENGTHS:	
WEAPON OVERALL	87.6 cm (69.9/86.9 cm)
BARREL	41.4 cm
SIGHT RADIUS	39.4 cm
STATUS	In production
SERVICE	All Warsaw Pact countries, extensively manufactured and shipped throughout the world.
COST	$250

This is the mostly widely distributed and easily recognized weapon manufactured since World War II. Including variants, there have been from 30 to 50 million Kalashnikovs built since the original AK-47 was issued in the Soviet Union. Between 3.0 and 8.7 million AK-47's were manufactured before the design was changed in 1959 to what is called the AKM-47. The earlier AK-47 was made from a milled steel receiver that was extremely strong, but much heavier than the AKM which used a stamped steel receiver: 3.14 kg for the AKM against 4.30 kg for the AK. The AKM, Automat Kalashnikova Modernizirovanniyi, is the model of AK most people have seen and is the most copied version. Having probably the best reputation for reliability of any military weapon, the AKM is also very easy to operate and maintain which makes it especially valuable to undeveloped countries. The sights are unsophisticated and have a short sight radius but the AK series is intended for use on full automatic area, rather than single-shot aimed, fire. The safety/selector on the AKM is on the right hand side and also acts as a cover for the bolt slot when set on safe. The safety clicks down first into full automatic and down further to semiautomatic fire. The setup of the safety indicates the intended role for the AKM, as it is quickest to set to full automatic. There is a loud click heard when the selector is set to any of the three positions. The click was referred to as "AK-CLACK" by U.S. troops in Vietnam and would be a warning before an ambush. The widespread use of the AKM has resulted in it being found in many hands throughout the world with large numbers having been captured by the Western countries. In many covert operations, AK's would be used by troops to help disguise themselves. The folding stock version of the AKM, the AKMS, was issued to mechanized troops with limited space in their armored personnel carriers.

ASSESSMENT	6.2 in @ 100 yds
WEAPON	AKM-47
AMMO	7.62x39

DISPERSION ANGLE .0983754 degrees, 1.7489 NATO mils.

Range	Group Circle Width (mm)	Probability (0<p<.099) (m)			
		Body	**Head**	**Hand**	**Bullseye**
25.0	42.924	0.990	0.990	0.988	0.777
50.0	85.849	0.990	0.988	0.891	0.528
75.0	128.773	0.990	0.948	0.772	0.394
100.0	171.697	0.988	0.891	0.670	0.313
125.0	214.622	0.971	0.831	0.588	0.260
150.0	257.546	0.948	0.772	0.523	0.222
175.0	300.470	0.921	0.719	0.470	0.193
200.0	343.395	0.891	0.670	0.426	0.171
250.0	429.243	0.831	0.588	0.358	0.140
300.0	515.092	0.772	0.523	0.309	0.118
350.0	600.941	0.719	0.470	0.272	0.102
400.0	686.789	0.670	0.426	0.242	0.090
450.0	772.638	0.627	0.389	0.219	0.080
500.0	858.486	0.588	0.358	0.199	0.072

DAMAGE 43/0.26

▼ **AK-74 • AKS-74**

AK-74 with selector set to safe

CARTRIDGE	5.45x39mm
OPERATION	Gas
TYPE OF FIRE	Selective
RATE OF FIRE	(SS) 50 rpm (A) 120 rpm (CYCLIC) 650 rpm
MUZZLE VELOCITY	900 m/s (2953 fps)
MUZZLE ENERGY	1365 J (1007 ft/lb)
SIGHTS	Non-adjustable, U-notch/post
FEED	30 round removable box magazine
WEIGHTS:	
WEAPON (EMPTY)	3.600 kg
WEAPON (LOADED)	4.151 kg
MAGAZINE (EMPTY)	0.227 kg
MAGAZINE (LOADED)	0.551 kg
SERVICE CARTRIDGE	10.8 g
BULLET	3.4 g
LENGTHS:	
WEAPON OVERALL	93 cm (69/93 cm)
BARREL	40 cm
SIGHT RADIUS	39.4 cm

☞ *continued on next page*

☛ *AK-74 • AKS-74 continued*

STATUS In production
SERVICE Soviet Union and some
Warsaw Pact units

In the early 1970's, the Soviets completed the development of a new small caliber round to be used in a modified AKM-47. The Soviets had been developing a new round of ammunition since the 1960's and have settled on a 5.45 caliber bullet in a 39mm case. The 52 grain bullet of the 5.45 x 39mm moves out at around 900 meters per second and has a relatively low muzzle energy. The construction of the 5.45 bullet allows for maximum destruction to tissue to help make up for its low energy. The bullet has a steel penetrator for about two thirds of its length with a lead plug at the front, behind a 5mm long airspace at the tip. All of this is contained in a very long (25mm) body for its caliber. The effect of this complicated construction is a bullet with excellent penetration for its size and greater wounding power than the original 7.62 x 39mm. At the time of adoption of the 5.45 x 39mm round, the standard AKM was slightly modified to accept the new round. Besides the barrel, few parts needed to be changed. A new bolt was designed to accept the smaller head of the 5.45 round along with a new and improved extractor. Much of the noted reliability of the AK design comes from the bolt carrier and bolt assembly weight ratio which in the AK47 series is 5 to 1 and in the AK74 series is 6 to 1, giving even greater reliability. The new magazine for the AK74 series is a composite of steel and fiberglass of great strength but heavy weight. The most externally visible change is the addition of a large muzzle brake. The brake is very efficient in reducing recoil and keeping the muzzle down on automatic fire, but greatly increases the muzzle blast and noise for anyone on either side of the firer. The brake is also designed primarily for the right handed shooter as is the general AK design. A horizontal finger groove is seen on both sides of the buttstock to aid in identification of the AK-74 series. As in the AK-47, there is a folding stock version of the AK-74 and this model is identified by the S for Skladyvayushchimsya in the designation AKS-74. The folding stock of the AKS-74 is of a triangular shape and folds to the left side rather than underneath as the AKS-47 stock does.

WEAPON AK-74
AMMO 5.45x39
DISPERSION ANGLE .0395144 degrees, .702478 NATO mils.

Range	Group Circle Width (mm)	Probability (0<p<.099) (m)			
		Body	Head	Hand	Bullseye
25.0	17.241	0.990	0.990	0.990	0.976
50.0	34.483	0.990	0.990	0.990	0.846
75.0	51.724	0.990	0.990	0.975	0.713
100.0	68.966	0.990	0.990	0.937	0.608
125.0	86.207	0.990	0.988	0.890	0.527
150.0	103.448	0.990	0.975	0.841	0.464

☛ *continued*

Range	Group Circle Width (mm)	Probability (0<p<.099) (m)			
		Body	Head	Hand	Bullseye
175.0	120.690	0.990	0.957	0.794	0.414
200.0	137.931	0.990	0.937	0.749	0.374
250.0	172.414	0.988	0.890	0.669	0.312
300.0	206.897	0.975	0.841	0.602	0.268
350.0	241.379	0.957	0.794	0.546	0.234
400.0	275.862	0.937	0.749	0.499	0.208
450.0	310.345	0.914	0.707	0.459	0.188
500.0	344.828	0.890	0.669	0.424	0.171

DAMAGE 35/0.51

▼ AKR

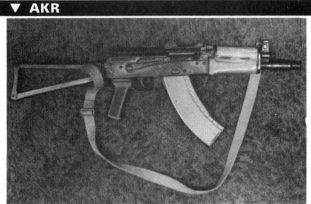

AKR with stock extended

CARTRIDGE 5.45x39mm
OPERATION Gas
TYPE OF FIRE Selective
RATE OF FIRE (SS) 40 rpm (A) 90 rpm (CYCLIC) 800 rpm
MUZZLE VELOCITY 800 m/s (2625 fps)
MUZZLE ENERGY 1078 J (795 ft/lb)
SIGHTS Non-adjustable, U-notch/post, range 400m
FEED 30 round removable box magazine
WEIGHTS:
WEAPON (EMPTY) 2.500 kg
WEAPON (LOADED) 3.051 kg
MAGAZINE (EMPTY) 0.227 kg
MAGAZINE (LOADED) 0.551 kg
SERVICE CARTRIDGE 10.8 g
BULLET 3.4 g
LENGTHS:
WEAPON OVERALL 42/67.5 cm
BARREL 20 cm
SIGHT RADIUS 24 cm
STATUS In production
SERVICE Soviet Union

This is an unusual development for the Soviets, being a carbine version of the AK-74 series. The barrel of an AKS-74 was shortened considerably in the AKR as was the gas tube and piston. There is a large cylindrical muzzle attachment that allows the shortened gas system to safely operate using the standard fullpower rifle cartridge. A second feature of the muzzle attachment would be to limit the large muzzle flash that would be found in such a weapon. The muzzle attachment does not act as the normal muzzle brake found on the AK-74 and the AKR would have a greater recoil and muzzle climb than the parent weapon. The action cover is hinged at the front unlike the cover on the AK-74. The rear sight of the AKR is considerably simplified consisting of a nonadjustable, flip-over, L-shaped, notched leaf for two different ranges. The Automat Kalashnikov Ruzhya (AKR) is primarily issued to armored vehicle crews to give them a compact personal weapon of considerable power, making the AKR the closest return to a submachinegun that the Soviets have fielded since the 1950's.

WEAPON	AKR
AMMO	5.45x39
DISPERSION ANGLE	.0553201 degrees, .983469 NATO mils.

Range	Group Circle Width (mm)	Probability (0<p<.099) (m)			
		Body	**Head**	**Hand**	**Bullseye**
25.0	24.138	0.990	0.990	0.990	0.931
50.0	48.276	0.990	0.990	0.981	0.737
75.0	72.414	0.990	0.990	0.928	0.590
100.0	96.552	0.990	0.981	0.861	0.487
125.0	120.690	0.990	0.957	0.794	0.414
150.0	144.828	0.990	0.928	0.732	0.359
175.0	168.966	0.989	0.895	0.676	0.317
200.0	193.103	0.981	0.861	0.627	0.284
250.0	241.379	0.957	0.794	0.546	0.234
300.0	289.655	0.928	0.732	0.482	0.200
350.0	337.931	0.895	0.676	0.431	0.174
400.0	386.207	0.861	0.627	0.389	0.154
450.0	434.483	0.827	0.584	0.355	0.138
500.0	482.759	0.794	0.546	0.326	0.125

DAMAGE 31/0.46

▼ L85A1

L85A1 with SUSAT sight fitted

CARTRIDGE	5.56x45mm
OPERATION	Gas
TYPE OF FIRE	Selective
RATE OF FIRE	(SS) 40 rpm (A) 100 rpm (CYCLIC) 800 rpm
MUZZLE VELOCITY	940 m/s (3084 fps)
MUZZLE ENERGY	1747 J (1288 ft/lb)
SIGHTS	SUSAT 4 power telescopic sight (standard) (WT. 0.800 kg) or adjustable, aperture/blade iron sights (WT. 0.300 kg)
FEED	20, 30, or 30/45 round removable box magazine (M16)
WEIGHTS:	
WEAPON (EMPTY)	4.600 kg w/SUSAT sight
WEAPON (LOADED)	5.083 kg w/SUSAT sight & 30 rds
MAGAZINE (EMPTY)	0.091 kg (20 rd), 0.117 kg (30 rd), 0.149 kg (30/45 rd)
MAGAZINE (LOADED)	0.335 kg (20 rd), 0.483 kg (30 rd), 0.698 kg (30/45 rd w/45 rds)
SERVICE CARTRIDGE	12.2 g
BULLET	4 g
LENGTHS:	
WEAPON OVERALL	78.5 cm
BARREL	51.8 cm
SIGHT RADIUS	33.5 cm
STATUS	In production
SERVICE	British military

This is the rifle version of the new Enfield weapon system that is reaching general issue to the British military. The L85A1 is a development of an earlier design, the XL64E5, that was chambered for a 4.85 x 49mm round, specially designed for it. The changes that resulted in the L85A1 were primarily a rechambering to 5.56 x 45mm to allow a greater interoperability with NATO as well as modifications to utilize the M16 magazine which is now NATO standard. The bullpup design is one that Great Britain has been championing since the early 1950's. There are a variety of sights that can be fitted to the L85A1 with the standard sight being a four power telescopic sight known as the SUSAT (Sight Unit Small Arms Trilux). The SUSAT is a very rugged optical sight with an illuminated retical system for low light use. The top of the SUSAT has a simple open sight for emergency use and the mounting bracket will accept standard sighting devices such as starlight or infrared sights. An aperture type iron sight is available on an attachable carrying handle that can use the SUSAT sight mounts. The iron sight/handle with the corresponding attachable front sight is intended for all other troops but the front line infantry who are issued the SUSAT sight. There is also a complete bayonet assembly available for the L85A1 that incorporates an insulated wirecutter, serrated rope-cutting edge, and folding metal-cutting hacksaw blade as well as a stainless steel knife blade.

☞ continued on next page

☞ *L85A1 continued*

WEAPON	L85A1				
AMMO	5.56x45				
DISPERSION ANGLE	.0474172 degrees, .842973 NATO mils.				

Range	Group Circle Width (mm)	Probability (0<p<.099) (m)			
		Body	**Head**	**Hand**	**Bullseye**
25.0	20.690	0.990	0.990	0.990	0.956
50.0	41.379	0.990	0.990	0.990	0.790
75.0	62.069	0.990	0.990	0.954	0.646
100.0	82.759	0.990	0.990	0.900	0.541
125.0	103.448	0.990	0.975	0.841	0.464
150.0	124.138	0.990	0.954	0.784	0.405
175.0	144.828	0.990	0.928	0.732	0.359
200.0	165.517	0.990	0.900	0.684	0.323
250.0	206.897	0.975	0.841	0.602	0.268
300.0	248.276	0.954	0.784	0.536	0.229
350.0	289.655	0.928	0.732	0.482	0.200
400.0	331.034	0.900	0.684	0.438	0.177
450.0	372.414	0.871	0.641	0.400	0.159
500.0	413.793	0.841	0.602	0.369	0.144

DAMAGE 36/0.63

▼ AR-18

CARTRIDGE	5.56x45mm
OPERATION	Gas
TYPE OF FIRE	Selective
RATE OF FIRE	(SS) 40 rpm (A) 80 rpm (CYCLIC) 800 rpm
MUZZLE VELOCITY	1000 m/s (3281 fps)
MUZZLE ENERGY	1977 J (1458 ft/lb)
SIGHTS	Adjustable, aperture/post, range 400m, removable 3 power telescopic sight, (WT. 0.420 kg).
FEED	20, 30, or 40 round removable box magazine
WEIGHTS:	
WEAPON (EMPTY)	3.170 kg
WEAPON (LOADED)	4.078 kg w/40 rds
MAGAZINE (EMPTY)	0.091 kg (20 rd), 0.117 kg (30 rd), 0.266 kg (40 rd)
MAGAZINE (LOADED)	0.335 kg (20 rd), o.483 kg (30 rd), 0.908 kg (40 rd)
SERVICE CARTRIDGE	12.2 g
BULLET	4 g
LENGTHS:	
WEAPON OVERALL	73.6/94 cm
BARREL	46.4 cm

SIGHT RADIUS	50.8 cm
STATUS	Out of production
SERVICE	Commercial sales
COST	$500

This weapon was developed in the mid-1960's as a more inexpensive alternative to the M16. Utilizing metal stampings for much of its construction the AR-18 can be made with much simpler machinery than its M16 predecessor. The gas system of the AR-18 is a straightforward piston type that eliminates many of the complications of other operating systems. Using a double guide rod mainspring system that telescopes somewhat into the bolt carrier eliminates the need for a rear extended mainspring and the AR-18 has a side folding buttstock as a result. A slightly modified M16 type magazine is used in the AR-18. Though not adopted in any large quantity, the AR-18 and its semiautomatic-only counterpart, the AR-180, has seen good commercial sales, especially in the U.S. for police issue. The AR-18 has been made in the U.S. by Armalite, in Japan by the HOWA Machinery Co., and in England by the Sterling Armament Company. Being manufactured by Armalite resulted in all AR-18's or AR180's used by the IRA terrorists in Ireland, who prefer them for their compactness and accuracy, being referred to as "Armalites".

ASSESSMENT	3.75 in @ 100 yds
WEAPON	AR-18
AMMO	5.56x45
DISPERSION ANGLE	.0595265 degrees, 1.05825 NATO mils.

Range	Group Circle Width (mm)	Probability (0<p<.099) (m)			
		Body	**Head**	**Hand**	**Bullseye**
25.0	25.973	0.990	0.990	0.990	0.917
50.0	51.947	0.990	0.990	0.974	0.711
75.0	77.920	0.990	0.990	0.913	0.563
100.0	103.893	0.990	0.974	0.840	0.463
125.0	129.867	0.990	0.947	0.769	0.391
150.0	155.840	0.990	0.913	0.705	0.339
175.0	181.813	0.985	0.877	0.649	0.299
200.0	207.787	0.974	0.840	0.600	0.267
250.0	259.733	0.947	0.769	0.520	0.220
300.0	311.680	0.913	0.705	0.457	0.187
350.0	363.626	0.877	0.649	0.408	0.163
400.0	415.573	0.840	0.600	0.368	0.144
450.0	467.520	0.804	0.557	0.335	0.129
500.0	519.466	0.769	0.520	0.307	0.117

DAMAGE 39/0.67

▼ M16A1

CARTRIDGE	5.56x45mm
OPERATION	Gas, direct action
TYPE OF FIRE	Selective
RATE OF FIRE	(SS) 45 rpm (A) 150 rpm (CYCLIC) 800 rpm
MUZZLE VELOCITY	1000 m/s (3281 fps)
MUZZLE ENERGY	1847 J (1362 ft/lb)
SIGHTS	Adjustable, aperture/post, range 500m
FEED	20, 30, or 30/45 round removable box magazine

WEIGHTS:

WEAPON (EMPTY)	3.175 kg
WEAPON (LOADED)	3.649 kg w/30 rds
MAGAZINE (EMPTY)	0.091 kg (20 rd), 0.117 kg (30 rd), 0.698 kg (30/45 rd)
MAGAZINE (LOADED)	0.329 kg (20 rd), 0.474 kg (30 rd), 0.685 kg (30/45 rd w/45 rds)
SERVICE CARTRIDGE	11.9 g
BULLET	3.7 g

LENGTHS:

WEAPON OVERALL	99.1 cm
BARREL	50.8 cm
SIGHT RADIUS	50.2 cm
STATUS	In production
SERVICE	U.S. Military, Chile, Dominican Republic, Haiti, Italy, Jordan, Republic of Korea, Mexico, Nicaragua, Panama, the Philippines, United Kingdom, Vietnam, and commercial sales.
COST	$550

The M16 series were the first small caliber weapons to be accepted by any major military and also the weapon for which the 5.56 x 45mm round was developed. The original AR-15 rifle was developed in the late 1950's and was first adopted by the U.S. Air Force in 1961 and in 1962, designated the M16. By 1963 the U.S. Army was purchasing the M16 for use in South East Asia and by its various elite forces. The M16 uses a direct gas system to operate the weapon and is one of the very few designs to do so. In the direct gas system, gas from the fired round is tapped from the barrel and guided back into the action of the weapon to directly operate the bolt. To operate the bolt, gas presses back on the bolt carrier, driving it rearward. As the carrier moves back, a cam pin attached to the bolt moves along a camming track, rotating the bolt to unlock it from the barrel. The 5.56 caliber bullet has to leave the muzzle of the M16 at a very high, over 3,000 feet per second, velocity to be effective and this velocity results in a chamber pressure over 50,000 psi. To safely control this high chamber pressure. The M16 uses a multiple lug bolt that locks into an extension screwed onto the rear of the barrel giving a very large effective locking area to the bolt while only requiring a small rotation to unlock it from the

barrel. The receiver and major parts of the M16 are either made from aluminum alloy forgings or cast plastic/fiberglass with high strength steel being used for the barrel and stressed parts of the weapon. Drawbacks were discovered during field use in Vietnam and these resulted in modifications to the ammunition and the weapon. The weapon was changed so that there was a positive forward assist to help close the bolt when dirty, the chamber and bore were chromium plated to resist corrosion, the gas system improved and a new bolt buffer designed to control the rate of fire on full automatic. In 1967 the new modified weapon, the M16A1 was adopted by the U.S. Army as its Standard A issue infantry weapon. Over 6 million M16A1's and variants have been produced to date with production still ongoing in the United States and elsewhere. There is a semiautomatic-only version of the M16 sold in the United States as the AR-15. Many versions of the civilian AR-15 are found but most are like the original M16 and do not have the forward bolt assist.

ASSESSMENT	2.0 in @ 100 yds
WEAPON	M16A1
AMMO	5.56x45
DISPERSION ANGLE	.031831 degrees, .565885 NATO mils.

Range	Group Circle Width (mm)	Probability (0<p<.099) (m)			
		Body	Head	Hand	Bullseye
25.0	13.889	0.990	0.990	0.990	0.990
50.0	27.778	0.990	0.990	0.990	0.902
75.0	41.667	0.990	0.990	0.990	0.787
100.0	55.556	0.990	0.990	0.968	0.687
125.0	69.444	0.990	0.990	0.936	0.605
150.0	83.333	0.990	0.990	0.898	0.539
175.0	97.222	0.990	0.980	0.859	0.485
200.0	111.111	0.990	0.968	0.820	0.440
250.0	138.889	0.990	0.936	0.746	0.371
300.0	166.667	0.990	0.898	0.681	0.321
350.0	194.444	0.980	0.859	0.625	0.282
400.0	222.222	0.968	0.820	0.576	0.252
450.0	250.000	0.953	0.782	0.533	0.227
500.0	277.778	0.936	0.746	0.496	0.207

DAMAGE 39/0.62

▼ M16A1 Carbine

CARTRIDGE	5.56x45mm
OPERATION	Gas direct action
TYPE OF FIRE	Selective
RATE OF FIRE	(SS) 45 rpm (A) 150 rpm (CYCLIC) 750 rpm
MUZZLE VELOCITY	922 m/s (3024 fps)
MUZZLE ENERGY	1569 J (1157 ft/lb)
SIGHTS	Adjustable, aperture/post, range 500 m
FEED	20, 30, or 30/45 round removable box magazine
WEIGHTS:	
WEAPON (EMPTY)	2.631 kg
WEAPON (LOADED)	3.105 kg
MAGAZINE (EMPTY)	0.091 kg (20 rd), 0.117 kg (30 rd), 0.149 kg (30/45 rd)
MAGAZINE (LOADED)	0.329 kg (20 rd), 0.474 kg (30 rd), 0.685 kg (30/45 rd w/45 rds)
SERVICE CARTRIDGE	11.9 g
BULLET	3.7 g
LENGTHS:	
WEAPON OVERALL	80.6/88.9 cm
BARREL	40.6 cm
SIGHT RADIUS	37.4 cm
STATUS	In production
SERVICE	Commercial sales

This carbine version of the M16 is derived from the M177E3 and was originally intended for civilian sale as a semiautomatic only rifle. The carbine has the collapsing buttstock and short, round handguard of the M177E3, combined with a 16 inch barrel to meet U.S. civilian gun law requirements. An interesting point about this weapon is that a military demand for a selective fire version of it developed. In the early 1960's, Colt offered a version of the M16 that had the barrel cut off just in front of the sight, but retained the standard M16 buttstock and handguards. That version did not do well on the market. Today, Colt offers a selective fire version of the carbine with either the 16 inch or a 14.5 inch barrel. The handiness of the carbine combined with its lethality make this a very popular weapon among units where size or weight is at a premium.

ASSESSMENT	2 in @ 100 yds
WEAPON	M16A1 Carbine
AMMO	5.56x45
DISPERSION ANGLE	.031831 degrees, .565885 NATO mils.

Range	Group Circle Width (mm)	Probability (0<p<.099) (m)			
		Body	Head	Hand	Bullseye
25.0	13.889	0.990	0.990	0.990	0.990
50.0	27.778	0.990	0.990	0.990	0.902
75.0	41.667	0.990	0.990	0.990	0.787
100.0	55.556	0.990	0.990	0.968	0.687
125.0	69.444	0.990	0.990	0.936	0.605
150.0	83.333	0.990	0.990	0.898	0.539
175.0	97.222	0.990	0.980	0.859	0.485
200.0	111.111	0.990	0.968	0.820	0.440
250.0	138.889	0.990	0.936	0.746	0.371
300.0	166.667	0.990	0.898	0.681	0.321
350.0	194.444	0.980	0.859	0.625	0.282
400.0	222.222	0.968	0.820	0.576	0.252
450.0	250.000	0.953	0.782	0.533	0.227
500.0	277.778	0.936	0.746	0.496	0.207

DAMAGE 35/0.57

▼ CAR-15

CAR-15 with stock extended

CARTRIDGE	5.56x45mm
OPERATION	Gas direct action
TYPE OF FIRE	Selective
RATE OF FIRE	(SS) 45 rpm (A) 150 rpm (CYCLIC) 750 rpm
MUZZLE VELOCITY	838 m/s (2750 fps)
MUZZLE ENERGY	1298 J (957 ft/lb)
SIGHTS	Adjustable, aperture/post, range 500m
FEED	20, 30, or 30/45 round removable box magazine
WEIGHTS:	
WEAPON (EMPTY)	2.780 kg
WEAPON (LOADED)	3.254 kg w/30 rds
MAGAZINE (EMPTY)	0.091 kg (20 rd), 0.117 kg (30 rd), 0.149 kg (30/45 rd)
MAGAZINE (LOADED)	0.329 kg (20 rd), 0.474 kg (30 rd), 0.685 kg (30/45 rd w/45 rds)
SERVICE CARTRIDGE	11.9 g

BULLET 3.7 g
LENGTHS:
WEAPON OVERALL 71.1/78.7 cm
BARREL 25.4 cm
SIGHT RADIUS 37.4 cm
STATUS In production
SERVICE U.S. military (as XM177E2), commercial sales

This weapon is referred to by a variety of names, XM177E2, CAR-15 (Colt Automatic Rifle), and Commando submachinegun, but all the names describe the short version of the M16 we shall call here the CAR-15. The CAR-15 went through a variety of changes, most referring to a slight, one or two inch, change in barrel length but the most common version was accepted by the U.S. Army in small numbers as the XM177E2. This weapon has a very short barrel and still utilizes the normal rifle cartridge. The firing of a cartridge designed for a 20 inch barrel from one half that length results in a massive muzzle blast and flame. To limit the large muzzle blast, the XM177E2 had a special noise and flash suppressor made for it that helped alleviate the problem. A special mainspring, buffer, and spring housing allowed for a sliding metal buttstock to be fitted that can collapse about one third of its length to help give a short overall length. The short barrel results in the bullet being not as stable as the same round fired from a normal length barrel. This instability gives the CAR-15 a much shorter effective range than other weapons of this caliber. In spite of the shortcomings, the CAR15 is a very popular design for its small size and light weight. Originally intended for Tank and A.P.C. or helicopter crews, the CAR-15 is often carried by officers and NCO's as it gives them good firepower, while not encumbering them as a full sized weapon would.

ASSESSMENT 2.75 in @ 100 yds
WEAPON CAR-15
AMMO 5.56x45
DISPERSION ANGLE .0437677 degrees, .778092 NATO mils.

Range	Group Circle Width (mm)	Probability (0<p<.099) (m)			
		Body	Head	Hand	Bullseye
25.0	19.097	0.990	0.990	0.990	0.966
50.0	38.194	0.990	0.990	0.990	0.815
75.0	57.292	0.990	0.990	0.964	0.676
100.0	76.389	0.990	0.990	0.917	0.570
125.0	95.486	0.990	0.982	0.864	0.491
150.0	114.583	0.990	0.964	0.810	0.430
175.0	133.681	0.990	0.942	0.760	0.383
200.0	152.778	0.990	0.917	0.713	0.344
250.0	190.972	0.982	0.864	0.631	0.287

☞ continued

Range	Group Circle Width (mm)	Probability (0<p<.099) (m)			
		Body	Head	Hand	Bullseye
300.0	229.167	0.964	0.810	0.565	0.245
350.0	267.361	0.942	0.760	0.510	0.214
400.0	305.556	0.917	0.713	0.464	0.190
450.0	343.750	0.891	0.670	0.425	0.171
500.0	381.944	0.864	0.631	0.393	0.155

DAMAGE 32/0.52

▼ M16A2

CARTRIDGE 5.56x45mm M855
OPERATION Gas direct action
TYPE OF FIRE Selective w/three round burst
RATE OF FIRE (SS) 45 rpm (A) 150 rpm (CYCLIC) 600–940 rpm
MUZZLE VELOCITY 945 m/s (3100 fps)
MUZZLE ENERGY 1764 J (2392 ft/lb)
SIGHTS Adjustable, aperture/post, range 800 m
FEED 20, 30, or 30/45 rd removable box magazine
WEIGHTS:
WEAPON (EMPTY) 3.583 kg
WEAPON (LOADED) 4.066 kg
MAGAZINE (EMPTY) 0.091 kg (20 rd), 0.117 kg (30 rd), 0.149 kg (30/45 rd)
MAGAZINE (LOADED) 0.335 kg (20 rd), 0.483 kg (30 rd), 0.698 kg (30/45 rd)
SERVICE CARTRIDGE 12.2 g
BULLET 4 g
LENGTHS:
WEAPON OVERALL 100 cm
BARREL 51 cm
SIGHT RADIUS 50.1 cm
STATUS In production
SERVICE U.S. forces and commercial sales

This is a product upgrade of the original M16A1. The barrel of the A2 version has a rifling turn rate of 1 turn in 7 inches so that it can effectively use the new SS109 (M855) 5.56mm round that is now NATO standard. The new rifling/ammunition combination gives the

☞ continued on next page

☞ *M16A2 continued*

M16A2 an effective range of 800 meters, a great improvement over the original. The M16A2 can also effectively use the original M193 ball round, allowing older ammunition stocks to be consumed efficiently. A new rear sight is found on the M16A2 that is completely adjustable for windage and elevation to make use of the longer effective range. The handguard, buttstock, and pistol grip are redesigned and made of a stronger material than the original. The handguard is of a cylindrical cross-section with both pieces being interchangeable. The pistol grip has a finger groove for a better grip and the buttstock is longer to better fit taller soldiers. The barrel is heavier for part of its length adding to its strength and assisting in obtaining the longer effective range. A new flash hider is fitted that more greatly stabilizes the weapon during full automatic fire. The firing mechanism is modified to give three round controlled bursts rather than true full automatic fire, though full auto is offered as a possible option by the manufacturer. A cartridge case deflector is forged into the upper receiver to guide ejected casings away from the faces of left handed shooters. Altogether, the M16A2 is a good improvement and has been accepted as standard issue by the U.S. military.

ASSESSMENT	17.55 in @ 400 yds
WEAPON	M16A2
AMMO	5.56x45
DISPERSION ANGLE	.0698293 degrees, 1.24141 NATO mils.

Range	Group Circle Width (mm)	Probability (0<p<.099) (m)			
		Body	**Head**	**Hand**	**Bullseye**
25.0	30.469	0.990	0.990	0.990	0.880
50.0	60.938	0.990	0.990	0.956	0.653
75.0	91.406	0.990	0.985	0.876	0.506
100.0	121.875	0.990	0.956	0.791	0.411
125.0	152.344	0.990	0.918	0.714	0.345
150.0	182.813	0.985	0.876	0.647	0.297
175.0	213.281	0.972	0.832	0.591	0.261
200.0	243.750	0.956	0.791	0.542	0.232
250.0	304.688	0.918	0.714	0.465	0.191
300.0	365.625	0.876	0.647	0.406	0.162
350.0	426.563	0.832	0.591	0.360	0.140
400.0	487.500	0.791	0.542	0.323	0.124
450.0	548.438	0.751	0.501	0.293	0.111
500.0	609.375	0.714	0.465	0.268	0.100

DAMAGE 36/0.64

▼ M16A2 HBAR

CARTRIDGE	5.56x45mm
OPERATION	Gas direct action
TYPE OF FIRE	Semiautomatic or selective
RATE OF FIRE	(SS) 45 rpm

MUZZLE VELOCITY	1000 m/s (3281 fps)
MUZZLE ENERGY	1977 J (1458 ft/lb)
SIGHTS	Adjustable, aperture/post, range 800m
FEED	20, 30, or 30/45 round removable box magazine
WEIGHTS:	
WEAPON (EMPTY)	3.583 kg
WEAPON (LOADED)	4.066 kg w/30 rds
MAGAZINE (EMPTY)	0.091 kg (20 rd), 0.117 kg (30 rd), 0.149 kg (30/45 rd)
MAGAZINE (LOADED)	0.335 kg (20 rd), 0.483 kg (30 rd), 0.698 kg (30/45 rd w/45 rds)
SERVICE CARTRIDGE	12.2 g
BULLET	4 g
LENGTHS:	
WEAPON OVERALL	99.1 cm
BARREL	50.8 cm
SIGHT RADIUS	50.1 cm
STATUS	In production
SERVICE	Commercial sales

The HBAR, Heavy Barreled Automatic Rifle, is an interesting development from the M16A2 program. Initially, the M16A2 was to have a full length heavy barrel much thicker than the barrel on the earlier M16A1. It was found that some accessories, most notably the M203 40mm grenade launcher, would not be able to clip onto the heavy barrel without modification. Because of the accessory problem, the full length heavy barrel was dropped from the M16A2. In the HBAR model the full length heavy barrel, 0.96 inch diameter up to the front sight, is returned to the M16A2 model with all of its advantages. The primary advantage is that the HBAR model can group its shots to 1 1/2 Minutes of Angle (MOA) against 2 to 3 MOA for the M16A2. the additional weight of the heavy barrel also adds to the stability and quick second-shot recovery of the weapon. The additional mass of the heavy barrel also acts as a greater heat sink, allowing longer periods of full automatic firing. This heat sink effect is allowing Colt to offer the M16A2 HBAR as a possible squad automatic weapon. As the civilian semiautomatic fire only version, the AR-15A2 HBAR is receiving a good welcome from military match shooters as well as police departments for its excellent accuracy.

ASSESSMENT	1.5 in @ 100 yds
WEAPON	M16A2 HBAR
AMMO	5.56x45
DISPERSION ANGLE	.0238733 degrees, .424414 NATO mils.

☞ *continued*

Range	Group Circle Width (mm)	Probability (0<p<.099) (m)			
		Body	Head	Hand	Bullseye
25.0	10.417	0.990	0.990	0.990	0.990
50.0	20.833	0.990	0.990	0.990	0.955
75.0	31.250	0.990	0.990	0.990	0.873
100.0	41.667	0.990	0.990	0.990	0.787
125.0	52.083	0.990	0.990	0.974	0.710
150.0	62.500	0.990	0.990	0.953	0.644
175.0	72.917	0.990	0.990	0.927	0.587
200.0	83.333	0.990	0.990	0.898	0.539
250.0	104.167	0.990	0.974	0.839	0.462
300.0	125.000	0.990	0.953	0.782	0.403
350.0	145.833	0.990	0.927	0.729	0.357
400.0	166.667	0.990	0.898	0.681	0.321
450.0	187.500	0.983	0.869	0.638	0.291
500.0	208.333	0.974	0.839	0.599	0.266

DAMAGE 38/0.66

▼ M16A2 Carbine

CARTRIDGE	5.56x45mm M855
OPERATION	Gas direct action
TYPE OF FIRE	Selective w/three round burst
RATE OF FIRE	(SS) 45 rpm (A) 150 rpm (CYCLIC) 600–940 rpm
MUZZLE VELOCITY	841 m/s (2760 fps)
MUZZLE ENERGY	1399 J (1032 ft/lb)
SIGHTS	Adjustable, aperture/post, range 300m
FEED	20, 30, or 40 round removable box magazine
WEIGHTS:	
WEAPON (EMPTY)	2.676 kg
WEAPON (LOADED)	3.159 kg
MAGAZINE (EMPTY)	0.091 kg (20 rd), 0.117 kg (30 rd), 0.149 kg (30/45 rd)
MAGAZINE (LOADED)	0.335 kg (20 rd), 0.483 kg (30 rd), 0.698 kg (30/45 rd w/45 rds)
SERVICE CARTRIDGE	12.2 g
BULLET	4 g

LENGTHS:

WEAPON OVERALL	75.7/83.8 cm
BARREL	36.8 cm
SIGHT RADIUS	36.8 cm
STATUS	In production
SERVICE	Commercial sales

This weapon is referred to as the Model 723 Carbine by its manufacturer, Colt Industries. The carbine has a shorter barrel than its civilian counterpart, and is somewhat shorter overall, with very quick handling as a result. The same style of handguard is found on the carbine as is on the M16A2 with the guard on the carbine being only half as long as the rifles. The barrel is of the thinner diameter of the M16A1 for lightness but is fitted with the new model flash hider/compensator at the muzzle. The pistol grip is of the new reinforced plastic for additional weight savings. The upper receiver retains the original sights of the M16A1, but has the new, round, forward bolt assist of the A2 model. The brass deflector for left handed firing is not found on the carbine. The firing mechanism can be had with the three round controlled burst option installed but most are made selective fire with a full automatic option.

WEAPON	M16A2 Carbine
AMMO	5.56x45
DISPERSION ANGLE	.0695453 degrees, 1.23636 NATO mils.

Range	Group Circle Width (mm)	Probability (0<p<.099) (m)			
		Body	Head	Hand	Bullseye
25.0	10.417	0.990	0.990	0.990	0.990
50.0	20.833	0.990	0.990	0.990	0.955
75.0	31.250	0.990	0.990	0.990	0.873
100.0	41.667	0.990	0.990	0.990	0.787
125.0	52.083	0.990	0.990	0.974	0.710
150.0	62.500	0.990	0.990	0.953	0.644
175.0	72.917	0.990	0.990	0.927	0.587
200.0	83.333	0.990	0.990	0.898	0.539
250.0	104.167	0.990	0.974	0.839	0.462
300.0	125.000	0.990	0.953	0.782	0.403
350.0	145.833	0.990	0.927	0.729	0.357
400.0	166.667	0.990	0.898	0.681	0.321
450.0	187.500	0.983	0.869	0.638	0.291
500.0	208.333	0.974	0.839	0.599	0.266

DAMAGE 38/0.66

THE EDGE OF THE SWORD

▼ M16A2 Commando

CARTRIDGE	5.56x45mm M855
OPERATION	Gas direct action
TYPE OF FIRE	Selective
RATE OF FIRE	(SS) 45 rpm (A) 150 rpm (CYCLIC) 700–900 rpm
MUZZLE VELOCITY	796 m/s (2610 fps)
MUZZLE ENERGY	1252 J (923 ft/lb)
SIGHTS	Adjustable, aperture/post, range 300m
FEED	20, 30, or 30/45 round removable box magazine
WEIGHTS:	
WEAPON (EMPTY)	2.608 kg
WEAPON (LOADED)	3.091 kg w/30 rds
MAGAZINE (EMPTY)	0.091 kg (20 rd), 0.117 kg (30 rd), 0.149 kg (30/45 rd)
MAGAZINE (LOADED)	0.335 kg (20 rd), 0.483 kg (30 rd), 0.698 kg (30/45 rd w/45 rds)
SERVICE CARTRIDGE	12.2 g
BULLET	4 g
LENGTHS:	
WEAPON OVERALL	68.1/76.2 cm
BARREL	29.2 cm
SIGHT RADIUS	36.8 cm
STATUS	In production

Also referred to as the Model 733 Commando, this weapon is effectively the A2 version of the XM177E2. Essentially exactly the same as the Carbine Model 723, the Commando has the barrel shortened to the minimum length for positive functioning. The result is a rifle caliber weapon of submachinegun size and portability. The shortened barrel is fitted with the A2 model flash hider/compensator which helps control muzzle climb on full automatic but does little to limit the large muzzle blast.

WEAPON	M16A2 Commando
AMMO	5.56x45
DISPERSION ANGLE	.0695453 degrees, 1.23636 NATO mils.

Range	Group Circle Width (mm)	Probability (0<p<.099) (m)			
		Body	Head	Hand	Bullseye
25.0	30.345	0.990	0.990	0.990	0.881
50.0	60.690	0.990	0.990	0.957	0.655
75.0	91.034	0.990	0.985	0.877	0.508
100.0	121.379	0.990	0.957	0.792	0.412
125.0	151.724	0.990	0.919	0.715	0.346
150.0	182.069	0.985	0.877	0.649	0.298

☞ continued

Range	Group Circle Width (mm)	Probability (0<p<.099) (m)			
		Body	Head	Hand	Bullseye
175.0	212.414	0.972	0.834	0.592	0.262
200.0	242.759	0.957	0.792	0.544	0.233
250.0	303.448	0.919	0.715	0.466	0.191
300.0	364.138	0.877	0.649	0.407	0.162
350.0	424.828	0.834	0.592	0.361	0.141
400.0	485.517	0.792	0.544	0.325	0.124
450.0	546.207	0.752	0.502	0.294	0.111
500.0	606.897	0.715	0.466	0.269	0.101

DAMAGE 31/0.53

▼ Ruger Mini-14

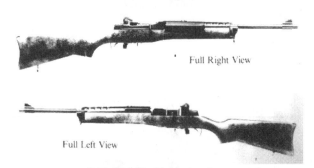

Full Right View

Full Left View

Ruger Mini-14 without magazine

CARTRIDGE	5.56x45mm
OPERATION	Gas
TYPE OF FIRE	Semiautomatic
RATE OF FIRE	(SS) 40 rpm
MUZZLE VELOCITY	1005 m/s (3297 fps)
MUZZLE ENERGY	1866 J (1376 ft/lb)
SIGHTS	Adjustable, aperture/post,
FEED	5, 20, or 30 round removable box magazine
WEIGHTS:	
WEAPON (EMPTY)	2.900 kg
WEAPON (LOADED)	3.484 kg w/30 rds
MAGAZINE (EMPTY)	0. (5 rd), 0.170 kg (20 rd), 0.227 kg (30 rd)
MAGAZINE (LOADED)	0. (5 rd), 0.408 kg (20 rd), 0.584 kg (30 rd)
SERVICE CARTRIDGE	11.9 g
BULLET	3.7 g
LENGTHS:	
WEAPON OVERALL	94.6 cm
BARREL	47 cm
SIGHT RADIUS	56.1 cm
STATUS	In production
SERVICE	Commercial sales

Introduced in 1973, the Mini-14 is very much a simplified, scaled down M1 Garand chambered for the 5.56 x 45mm round. Built along the lines of a standard rifle , the Mini-14 was originally intended for the military and police markets but the expected military sales never appeared. The popularity of the Mini-14 for the police and civilian markets has soared, with it quickly becoming one of the most popular semiautomatic 5.56mm rifles available. The action is very similar to that used on the M1 and M14 rifles, but has been strengthened and improved for greater reliability. Early difficulties were addressed by the manufacturer in 1977 and an improved model made available. The improved model is recognizable by its having a "181" or greater serial number prefix. Though only made in a semiautomatic version for the public, the Mini-14 is available in a wide number of variations made of stainless or blued steel and having a selection of sights as well as an available folding stock. The data given above is for the blued steel, walnut stocked version which is the most predominant model.

ASSESSMENT	4.4 in @ 100 yds
WEAPON	MINI-14
AMMO	5.56x45
DISPERSION ANGLE	.0700282 degrees, 1.24495 NATO mils.

Range	Group Circle Width (mm)	Probability (0<p<.099) (m)			
		Body	**Head**	**Hand**	**Bullseye**
25.0	30.556	0.990	0.990	0.990	0.879
50.0	61.111	0.990	0.990	0.956	0.652
75.0	91.667	0.990	0.984	0.875	0.505
100.0	122.222	0.990	0.956	0.790	0.410
125.0	152.778	0.990	0.917	0.713	0.344
150.0	183.333	0.984	0.875	0.646	0.297
175.0	213.889	0.972	0.832	0.590	0.260
200.0	244.444	0.956	0.790	0.541	0.232
250.0	305.556	0.917	0.713	0.464	0.190
300.0	366.667	0.875	0.646	0.405	0.161
350.0	427.778	0.832	0.590	0.359	0.140
400.0	488.889	0.790	0.541	0.323	0.124
450.0	550.000	0.750	0.500	0.293	0.111
500.0	611.111	0.713	0.464	0.268	0.100

DAMAGE 39/0.62

▼ AC-556

AC-556 with 20 rd magazine

AC-556 with 20 rd magazine and selector, below and behind the rear sight, set to 3 rd burst

CARTRIDGE	5.56mm
OPERATION	Gas
TYPE OF FIRE	Selective w/three round burst and full auto
RATE OF FIRE	(SS) 40 rpm (A) 150 rpm (CYCLIC) 750 rpm
MUZZLE VELOCITY	1005 m/s (3297 fps)
MUZZLE ENERGY	1866 J (1376 ft/lb)
SIGHTS	Adjustable, aperture/post,
FEED	5, 20, or 30 round removable box magazine
WEIGHTS:	
WEAPON (EMPTY)	2.892 kg
WEAPON (LOADED)	3.476 kg w/30 rds
MAGAZINE (EMPTY)	0. (5 rd), 0.170 kg (20 rd), 0.227 kg (30 rd)
MAGAZINE (LOADED)	0. (5 rd), 0.408 kg (20 rd), 0.584 kg (30 rd)
SERVICE CARTRIDGE	11.9 g
BULLET	3.7 g
LENGTHS:	
WEAPON OVERALL	94.6 cm
BARREL	47 cm
SIGHT RADIUS	44.5 cm
STATUS	In production
SERVICE	Commercial sales

This weapon is a development of the Mini-14 rifle and is intended solely for military or police use. The standard inside the trigger guard safety is used on the AC-556 with a selector switch found on the upper part of the receiver on the right side behind the rear sight. The action of the AC-556 is designed to give either semiautomatic, three round controlled burst, or full automatic fire according to the selector setting. The front sight is moved back on the AC-556 to allow for a standard M7 (M16) bayonet to be fixed. The moved-back front sight allows rifle grenades to be launched from the modified flash hider. The stock of the AC-556 is made of walnut with a reinforced plastic ventilated handguard over the barrel. A folding stock is also available, as is a stainless steel model (KAC-556) for use in corrosive environments such as on shipboard . An F suffix indicates a folding stock model.

WEAPON	AC-556
AMMO	5.56x45
DISPERSION ANGLE	.0700282 degrees, 1.24495 NATO mils.

☞ continued on next page

☞ *AC-556 continued*

Range	Group Circle Width (mm)	Probability (0<p<.099) (m)			
		Body	Head	Hand	Bullseye
25.0	30.556	0.990	0.990	0.990	0.879
50.0	61.111	0.990	0.990	0.956	0.652
75.0	91.667	0.990	0.984	0.875	0.505
100.0	122.222	0.990	0.956	0.790	0.410
125.0	152.778	0.990	0.917	0.713	0.344
150.0	183.333	0.984	0.875	0.646	0.297
175.0	213.889	0.972	0.832	0.590	0.260
200.0	244.444	0.956	0.790	0.541	0.232
250.0	305.556	0.917	0.713	0.464	0.190
300.0	366.667	0.875	0.646	0.405	0.161
350.0	427.778	0.832	0.590	0.359	0.140
400.0	488.889	0.790	0.541	0.323	0.124
450.0	550.000	0.750	0.500	0.293	0.111
500.0	611.111	0.713	0.464	0.268	0.100

DAMAGE 39/0.62

▼ AC-556K

AC-556F with 30 rd magazine and extended buttstock

CARTRIDGE	5.56x45mm
OPERATION	Gas
TYPE OF FIRE	Selective w/three round burst and full auto
RATE OF FIRE	(SS) 40 rpm (A) 150 rpm (CYCLIC) 750 rpm
MUZZLE VELOCITY	828 m/s (2715 fps)
MUZZLE ENERGY	1265 J (933 ft/lb)
SIGHTS	Adjustable, aperture/post
FEED	5, 20, or 30 round removable box magazine
WEIGHTS:	
WEAPON (EMPTY)	3.147 kg
WEAPON (LOADED)	3.731 kg w/30 rds
MAGAZINE (EMPTY)	0. (5 rd) 0.170 kg (20 rd), 0.227 kg (30 rd)
MAGAZINE (LOADED)	0. (5 rd), 0.408 kg (20 rd), 0.584 kg (30 rd)
SERVICE CARTRIDGE	11.9 g
BULLET	3.7 g

LENGTHS:	
WEAPON OVERALL	58.4/82.6 cm
BARREL	29.2 cm
SIGHT RADIUS	36.3 cm
STATUS	In production
SERVICE	Commercial sales
COST	$550

This is the shortest version of the Mini-14/AC-556 series made. Intended primarily for undercover use such as VIP protection and as a military weapon for vehicle crews the AC-556K has the barrel shortened to just in front of the stock with the flash hider remounted and the front sight blade attached to the front of the stock. The folding stock is standard with the AC556K and recent product literature lists it as the AC-556F as a result. The folding stock is a very strong design and folds to the right side of the weapon to be fired with the stock folded. The muzzle flash and report are large with the AC-556K as a result of the full power rifle cartridge being fired in such a short barrel.

WEAPON	AC-556K
AMMO	5.56x45
DISPERSION ANGLE	.0790287 degrees, 1.40496 NATO mils.

Range	Group Circle Width (mm)	Probability (0<p<.099) (m)			
		Body	Head	Hand	Bullseye
25.0	34.483	0.990	0.990	0.990	0.846
50.0	68.966	0.990	0.990	0.937	0.608
75.0	103.448	0.990	0.975	0.841	0.464
100.0	137.931	0.990	0.937	0.749	0.374
125.0	172.414	0.988	0.890	0.669	0.312
150.0	206.897	0.975	0.841	0.602	0.268
175.0	241.379	0.957	0.794	0.546	0.234
200.0	275.862	0.937	0.749	0.499	0.208
250.0	344.828	0.890	0.669	0.424	0.171
300.0	413.793	0.841	0.602	0.369	0.144
350.0	482.759	0.794	0.546	0.326	0.125
400.0	551.724	0.749	0.499	0.292	0.110
450.0	620.690	0.707	0.459	0.264	0.099
500.0	689.655	0.669	0.424	0.241	0.089

DAMAGE 32/0.51

▼ AIWS
(Advanced Individual Weapon System)

AIWS with optional sight

CARTRIDGE	5x54mm
OPERATION	Gas
TYPE OF FIRE	Selective
RATE OF FIRE	(SS) 40 rpm (A) 180 rpm (CYCLIC) 550 rpm
MUZZLE VELOCITY	945 m/s (3100 fps)
MUZZLE ENERGY	945 m/s (3100 fps)
SIGHTS	4 power optical sight w/adjustable, aperture/post folding iron sights for backup
FEED	60 rounds removable magazine box holding semi-linked rounds
WEIGHTS:	
WEAPON (EMPTY)	3.136 kg w/o sight (optical sight wt 0.254 kg)
WEAPON (LOADED)	3.992 kg w/optical sight and 60 rds
MAGAZINE (EMPTY)	0.182 kg
MAGAZINE (LOADED)	0.602 kg
SERVICE CARTRIDGE	6.5 g (7 g w/plastic link)
BULLET	2.9 g
LENGTHS:	
WEAPON OVERALL	77.8 cm
BARREL	60.3 cm
SIGHT RADIUS	37.5 cm
STATUS	Prototype

This is the newest candidate for the U.S. Army's Advanced Combat Rifle program and, as of the time of this writing, it has only recently been declassified. The weapon is designed around a telescoped, plastic cased round with a metallic base. In the telescoped round, the bullet is set inside the case and does not protrude from the mouth of the cartridge at all. This results in a shorter, more streamlined cartridge with no protrusions. The body of the round is of plastic and is intended only to support the round through handling. The metallic case head contains the primer and receives the brunt of impact when the round is fired. The smooth, cylindrical appearance of the round allows the AIWS to have a unique method of firing. The round is carried in a plastic link belt contained in the magazine. When the action strips a round forward, the used link is ejected to the right. The cartridge is driven forward into a separate chamber piece where it remains through

the rest of the firing cycle. The chamber piece is cammed upward into line with the barrel where its cartridge is fired by a normal firing pin. During the ejection portion of the cycle, the chamber piece is cammed downward to where a fresh round is chambered from the rear. As the fresh round enters the chamber, the fired casing is driven forward and out of the weapon by the incoming round. The use of a separate chamber piece limits the amount of heat to which the loaded cartridge is subjected because the majority of the firing heat is retained in the barrel. As the chamber is cammed upwards when the weapon is fired, the effect is that of a closed-bolt weapon with little disturbance of the firer's aim, while retaining the positive cooling effects of an open-bolt weapon. The receiver of the AIWS is surrounded by a plastic body which both streamlines and protects the weapon. The bullpup layout of the AIWS also gives the weapon a short overall length while still retaining a long barrel length. The long barrel gives the 5mm projectile the same terminal effects as the new U.S. M855 5.56x45mm round. The optical sight is considered a standard fitting with folding iron sights being available for emergency use.

WEAPON	AIWS
AMMO	5x54
	4 x power scope installed.
DISPERSION ANGLE	.0395144 degrees, .702478 NATO mils.

Range	Group Circle Width (mm)	Probability (0<p<.099) (m)			
		Body	**Head**	**Hand**	**Bullseye**
25.0	17.241	0.990	0.990	0.990	0.976
50.0	34.483	0.990	0.990	0.990	0.846
75.0	51.724	0.990	0.990	0.975	0.713
100.0	68.966	0.990	0.990	0.937	0.608
125.0	86.207	0.990	0.988	0.890	0.527
150.0	103.448	0.990	0.975	0.841	0.464
175.0	120.690	0.990	0.957	0.794	0.414
200.0	137.931	0.990	0.937	0.749	0.374
250.0	172.414	0.988	0.890	0.669	0.312
300.0	206.897	0.975	0.841	0.602	0.268
350.0	241.379	0.957	0.794	0.546	0.234
400.0	275.862	0.937	0.749	0.499	0.208
450.0	310.345	0.914	0.707	0.459	0.188
500.0	344.828	0.890	0.669	0.424	0.171

DAMAGE 32/0.41

CHAPTER 4

SNIPER RIFLES

Specifically designed sniper weapons are a relatively new development. In the past, long range sporting weapons or particularly accurate individual military weapons were outfitted with more precise sights and issued to selected marksmen. With the need for absolute precision of shot placement in hostage situations new, specially-designed rifles, rests, and sighting systems were created. All such weapons share the same purpose of firing relatively few rounds with maximum accuracy. ●

▼ Steyr SSG 69

CARTRIDGE	7.62x51mm
OPERATION	Manual, bolt action
TYPE OF FIRE	Single shot repeater
RATE OF FIRE	(SS) 20 rpm
MUZZLE VELOCITY	860 m/s (2800 fps)
MUZZLE ENERGY	3541 J (2611 ft/lb)
SIGHTS	ZF-69 Kahles 6 power telescopic sight ranged to 800 m, Fixed, non-adjustable iron sights (backup)
FEED	5 or 10 round removable box magazine
WEIGHTS:	
WEAPON (EMPTY)	4.535 kg w/scope
WEAPON (LOADED)	4.728 kg
MAGAZINE (EMPTY)	0.065 kg (5 rd)
MAGAZINE (LOADED)	0.193 kg
SERVICE CARTRIDGE	25.6 g
BULLET	9.8
LENGTHS:	
WEAPON OVERALL	114 cm
BARREL	65 cm
SIGHT RADIUS	50.5 cm
STATUS	In production
SERVICE	Austrian army and several foreign police and military groups, commercial sales
COST	$900 ($1,600 w/scope)

The SSG 69 is considered by many to be one of the most accurate military issue sniper rifles available on today's market. Much of this weapon's accuracy comes from its receiver design and barrel. The receiver of the SSG-69 is of fairly standard outline but of exceptionally long length for the caliber. The long receiver length allows two and a half inches of the barrel to be seated into the receiver giving an outstanding alignment and rigidity between the barrel and receiver. Another point towards the barrel/receiver interface is that the receiver is shrunk fit onto the barrel rather than threaded as in most other rifles. The barrel is made by hammer forging onto a mandrel rather than cutting the rifling into the bore. the forging process allows for very tight tolerances to be held on the bore as well as greatly increasing the barrel's strength. The bolt has the characteristic "butter-knife" Mannlicher handle as well as having six locking lugs. The magazine is of a rotary type long associated with the Mannlicher design, with a 10 round box magazine offered as an accessory. The stock is made of a black Cycolac plastic with earlier models having a green stock of the same material. Removable spacers are found under the buttplate to allow the length of the stock to be changed to fit a variety of firers. A fixed rear sight and adjustable front blade are fitted to the SSG but the weapon is normally fitted with a telescopic sight. The Kahles ZF84 six power scope is offered by the factory as a standard fitting

but any applicable sighting device may be fitted. The result of all this is a rugged military weapon with the accuracy of a fragile custom made target rifle.

ASSESSMENT	0.9 in @ 100 yds (20 cm @ 600m w/ special <190 gr match> ammo
WEAPON	SSG 69
AMMO	7.62x51
	6 x power scope installed.
DISPERSION ANGLE	.0190986 degrees, .339531 NATO mils.

Range	Group Circle Width (mm)	Probability (0<p<.099) (m)			
		Body	**Head**	**Hand**	**Bullseye**
50.0	16.667	0.990	0.990	0.990	0.979
100.0	33.333	0.990	0.990	0.990	0.856
150.0	50.000	0.990	0.990	0.978	0.725
200.0	66.667	0.990	0.990	0.943	0.620
250.0	83.333	0.990	0.990	0.898	0.539
300.0	100.000	0.990	0.978	0.851	0.475
350.0	116.667	0.990	0.962	0.805	0.425
400.0	133.333	0.990	0.943	0.760	0.384
450.0	150.000	0.990	0.921	0.719	0.349
500.0	166.667	0.990	0.898	0.681	0.321
600.0*	200.000	0.978	0.851	0.614	0.276
700.0	233.333	0.962	0.805	0.558	0.242
800.0	266.667	0.943	0.760	0.511	0.215
900.0	300.000	0.921	0.719	0.470	0.193
1000.0	333.333	0.898	0.681	0.435	0.176
1100.0	366.667	0.875	0.646	0.405	0.161
1200.0	400.000	0.851	0.614	0.379	0.149

* indicates range for which data was supplied

DAMAGE 51/.38

▼ Steyr SSG 69 PII

Steyr SSG PII showing the ART IV telescopic sight and its controls

☞ *Steyr SSG 69 PII continued*

SSG PII on custom bipod with bolt open, rifle fitted with Leatherwood ART IV telescopic sight

CARTRIDGE	7.62x51 mm
OPERATION	Manual bolt action
TYPE OF FIRE	Single shot repeater
RATE OF FIRE	(SS) 20 rpm
MUZZLE VELOCITY	860 m/s (2800 fps)
MUZZLE ENERGY	3541 J (2611 ft/lb)
SIGHTS	ZF-69 Kahles 6 power telescopic sight fitted as standard
FEED	5 or 10 round removable box magazine
WEIGHTS:	
WEAPON (EMPTY)	4.200 kg w/scope
WEAPON (LOADED)	4.393 kg w/5 rds & scope
MAGAZINE (EMPTY)	0.065 kg
MAGAZINE (LOADED)	0.193 kg
SERVICE CARTRIDGE	25.6 cm
BULLET	9.8 cm
LENGTHS:	
WEAPON OVERALL	113.5 cm
BARREL	65 cm
STATUS	In production
SERVICE	Extensive sales to police and security forces
COST	$1,800 ($2,500 w/scope)

This is an improved model of the SSG-69 rifle and is presently the most accurate production sniper rifle available on the commercial market. The excellent receiver and bolt design of the SSG-69 rifle was mated to the barrel of the Steyr UIT Olympic class match rifle. The heavy bull barrel increases the weight of the SSG-PII making it more stable to shoot than the lighter SSG69 but also, making it less applicable to a military environment. The traditional butter-knife bolt handle is replaced by a newly designed handle that is faster to use but less streamlined than the earlier model. No iron sights are fitted as the SSG-PII is intended to be fired with a telescopic sight. To assist in changing sights for specialized instances, the scope mounts are of a quick-removable type that retain their alignment with the barrel. The trigger can be either the normal single trigger type or a dual set-trigger can be installed and is the preferred type. In the set trigger, the front trigger has a normal pull adjustable from 2.5 to 4.7 pounds (1.134-2.132kg). When the rear trigger is pulled to the set position, the front trigger has a let-off of from two to eight ounces (57-227 grams) adjustable by the operator. Though the set trigger requires some getting used to by a new operator, it allows the SSG-PII to have its excellent first-round accuracy for long range shots.

ASSESSMENT	70 mm group @ 300m w/match ammo
WEAPON	SSG 69 PII
AMMO	7.62x51
	6 x power scope installed.
DISPERSION ANGLE	.013369 degrees, .237672 NATO mils.

Range	Group Circle Width (mm)	Probability (0<p<.099) (m)			
		Body	**Head**	**Hand**	**Bullseye**
50.0	11.667	0.990	0.990	0.990	0.990
100.0	23.333	0.990	0.990	0.990	0.937
150.0	35.000	0.990	0.990	0.990	0.842
200.0	46.667	0.990	0.990	0.983	0.749
250.0	58.333	0.990	0.990	0.962	0.669
300.0*	70.000	0.990	0.990	0.934	0.602
350.0	81.667	0.990	0.990	0.903	0.546
400.0	93.333	0.990	0.983	0.870	0.499
450.0	105.000	0.990	0.973	0.837	0.459
500.0	116.667	0.990	0.962	0.805	0.425
600.0	140.000	0.990	0.934	0.744	0.369
700.0	163.333	0.990	0.903	0.688	0.326
800.0	186.667	0.983	0.870	0.640	0.292
900.0	210.000	0.973	0.837	0.596	0.264
1000.0	233.333	0.962	0.805	0.558	0.242
1100.0	256.667	0.949	0.773	0.524	0.222
1200.0	280.000	0.934	0.744	0.494	0.206

* indicates range for which data was supplied
DAMAGE 51/.38

▼ FR-F1

FR-F1 with bipod extended

CARTRIDGE	7.5x54mm
OPERATION	Manual bolt action
TYPE OF FIRE	Single shot repeater
RATE OF FIRE	(SS) 15 rpm
MUZZLE VELOCITY	852 m/s (2795 fps)
MUZZLE ENERGY	3292 J (2428 ft/lb)
SIGHTS	M53 bis 4 power telescopic sight w/ backup iron sights
FEED	10 round removable box magazine
WEIGHTS:	
WEAPON (EMPTY)	5.200 kg

WEAPON (LOADED)	5.656 kg
MAGAZINE (EMPTY)	0.220 kg
MAGAZINE (LOADED)	0.456 kg
SERVICE CARTRIDGE	23.6 g
BULLET	9.1 g
LENGTHS:	
WEAPON OVERALL	113.8 cm
BARREL	55.2 cm
SIGHT RADIUS	39.5 cm
STATUS	Out of production
SERVICE	French military and commercial sales

This weapon has been the standard French sniper rifle for the military and GIGN since 1965. Initial problems with native produced 7.62 NATO rounds resulted in the FR-F1 being accepted in the French 7.5 x 54mm Model 29-C chambering with a commercial model offered in 7.62 x 51mm NATO for export sales. The action of the FR-F1 is a manual bolt action modified from the MAS-36 rifle with integral iron sights built on for emergency use should the telescopic sight become damaged. The unusual flash hider on the muzzle is adjustable to help stabilize the barrel and must be adjusted to the specific ammunition being used for maximum accuracy if the factory setting has been changed. The sight normally used with the FR-F1 is the 3.8 power APX L 806 Modele 1953bis telescopic sight that is mounted on a quick release base so that it can be removed or mounted without changing its alignments. With the scope removed, the iron sights may be used. There are colored luminous inserts in the iron sights for use in low-light conditions. To use the iron sights in the dark, the green luminous dot on the front sight is aligned with the two red dots of the rear sight on either side of it. There is an integral folding bipod on the FR-F1 at the rear of the wooden handguard. There are two heights of checkpiece that can be mounted on the buttstock to adjust for different shooters as well as two spacers for the buttplate, also for size adjustment.

WEAPON	FR-F1
AMMO	7.5x54
	4 x power scope installed.
DISPERSION ANGLE	.0276601 degrees, .491734 NATO mils.

Range	Group Circle Width (mm)	Probability (0<p<.099) (m)			
		Body	Head	Hand	Bullseye
50.0	24.138	0.990	0.990	0.990	0.931
100.0	48.276	0.990	0.990	0.981	0.737
150.0	72.414	0.990	0.990	0.928	0.590
200.0	96.552	0.990	0.981	0.861	0.487
250.0	120.690	0.990	0.957	0.794	0.414
300.0	144.828	0.990	0.928	0.732	0.359
350.0	168.966	0.989	0.895	0.676	0.317
400.0	193.103	0.981	0.861	0.627	0.284

☞ continued

Range	Group Circle Width (mm)	Probability (0<p<.099) (m)			
		Body	Head	Hand	Bullseye
450.0	217.241	0.970	0.827	0.584	0.257
500.0	241.379	0.957	0.794	0.546	0.234
600.0	289.655	0.928	0.732	0.482	0.200
700.0	337.931	0.895	0.676	0.431	0.174
800.0	386.207	0.861	0.627	0.389	0.154
900.0	434.483	0.827	0.584	0.355	0.138
1000.0	482.759	0.794	0.546	0.326	0.125
1100.0	531.034	0.762	0.512	0.301	0.114
1200.0	579.310	0.732	0.482	0.280	0.105

DAMAGE 50/.36

▼ FR-F2

CARTRIDGE	7.62x51mm
OPERATION	Manual bolt action
TYPE OF FIRE	Single shot repeater
RATE OF FIRE	(SS) 15 rpm
MUZZLE VELOCITY	820 m/s (2690 fps)
MUZZLE ENERGY	3812 J (2811 ft/lb)
SIGHTS	6 power telescopic sight w/800 m range
FEED	10 round removable box magazine
WEIGHTS:	
WEAPON (EMPTY)	5.340 kg
WEAPON (LOADED)	5.800 kg
MAGAZINE (EMPTY)	0.207 kg
MAGAZINE (LOADED)	0.460 kg
SERVICE CARTRIDGE	25.3 g
BULLET	11.4 g
LENGTHS:	
WEAPON OVERALL	120 cm
BARREL	65 cm
STATUS	In production
SERVICE	In service with the French military and commercial sales

This is the newest version of the FR-F1 rifle and is gradually replacing

☞ continued on next page

☞ *FR-F2 continued*

the earlier weapon in general service. The caliber has been changed to the 7.62x51mm NATO round and this change has considerably increased sales. The barrel is surrounded by a thermal shield that prevents heat haze from interfering with the sights and cuts down on the infrared signature of the weapon. The basic action has not changed but the scope mounting rail is NATO standard and will accept a wide range of sighting devices. The folding bipod has been changed and it now pivots on a bearing so that a target can be tracked without moving the bipod legs. A new front stock is fitted on the FR-F2 that is made of a composite material that supports the bipod while allowing the barrel to be free-floating for accuracy. The FR-F2 is an improvement on an already excellent design and has replaced the FR-F1 as the sniper rifle used by GIGN. It is gradually becoming general issue for the French military.

ASSESSMENT	37mm group @ 200 m
WEAPON	FR-F2
AMMO	7.62x51
	6 x power scope installed.
DISPERSION ANGLE	.0105997 degrees, .18844 NATO mils.

Range	Group Circle Width (mm)	Probability (0<p<.099) (m)			
		Body	**Head**	**Hand**	**Bullseye**
50.0	9.250	0.990	0.990	0.990	0.990
100.0	18.500	0.990	0.990	0.990	0.969
150.0	27.750	0.990	0.990	0.990	0.902
200.0*	37.000	0.990	0.990	0.990	0.825
250.0	46.250	0.990	0.990	0.984	0.752
300.0	55.500	0.990	0.990	0.968	0.687
350.0	64.750	0.990	0.990	0.947	0.631
400.0	74.000	0.990	0.990	0.924	0.582
450.0	83.250	0.990	0.990	0.899	0.539
500.0	92.500	0.990	0.984	0.872	0.502
600.0	111.000	0.990	0.968	0.820	0.441
700.0	129.500	0.990	0.947	0.770	0.392
800.0	148.000	0.990	0.924	0.724	0.353
900.0	166.500	0.990	0.899	0.682	0.321
1000.0	185.000	0.984	0.872	0.643	0.294
1100.0	203.500	0.976	0.846	0.608	0.272
1200.0	222.000	0.968	0.820	0.576	0.252

* indicates range for which data was supplied

DAMAGE	49/.43

▼ Mauser SP-66

CARTRIDGE	7.62x51mm
OPERATION	Manual bolt action
TYPE OF FIRE	Single shot repeater
RATE OF FIRE	(SS) 9 rpm
MUZZLE VELOCITY	762 m/s (2500 fps)
MUZZLE ENERGY	3292 J (2428 ft/lb)
SIGHTS	Zeiss-Diavari ZA 1.5-6 power telescopic sight
FEED	3 round integral box magazine
WEIGHTS:	
WEAPON (EMPTY)	6.123 kg w/scope
WEAPON (LOADED)	6.199 kg
MAGAZINE (LOADED)	0.076 kg (3 rds)
SERVICE CARTRIDGE	25.3 g
BULLET	11.4 g
LENGTHS:	
WEAPON OVERALL	114 cm
BARREL	68 cm
STATUS	In production
SERVICE	Federal German forces and commercial sales

This is the Mauser bolt action Model 66S Super Match version of their Model 66 rifle system and is offered as a military and police sniper weapon. Specially engineered for maximum accuracy as a competition weapon, the SP66 is also rugged enough to serve as a military sniping system, though it still requires more care than a standard issue weapon. The action of the Mauser 66 is unusual in that it has such a short length for the size of cartridge it uses. To obtain this short length the bolt handle is placed at the front of the bolt and the bolt held in a movable carrier. When the bolt is drawn back to the rear of the travel, the bolt carrier then moves back, effectively doubling the length of travel for the bolt. The barrel locks into a lower receiver and the bolt locks into the barrel, resulting in a great rigidity of the weapon when the bolt is closed. The barrel is of the heavy bull type with a combination muzzle brake/flash hider on the muzzle. No iron sights are fitted and the SP 66 is normally used with the Zeiss Diavari ZA 1.5 to 6 power zoom telescopic sight. The stock is of competition lines and is completely adjustable to fit all builds of firers. The thumbhole type stock is regularly seen among competition rifles and results in excellent holding characteristics, but does somewhat slow down the speed with which the bolt can be manipulated.

WEAPON	SP-66
AMMO	7.62x51
	6 x power scope installed.
DISPERSION ANGLE	.0158058 degrees, .280991 NATO mils.

Range	Group Circle Width (mm)	Probability (0<p<.099) (m)			
		Body	**Head**	**Hand**	**Bullseye**
50.0	13.793	0.990	0.990	0.990	0.990
100.0	27.586	0.990	0.990	0.990	0.903
150.0	41.379	0.990	0.990	0.990	0.790
200.0	55.172	0.990	0.990	0.968	0.689

☞ *continued*

Range	Group Circle Width (mm)	Probability (0<p<.099) (m)			
		Body	Head	Hand	Bullseye
250.0	68.966	0.990	0.990	0.937	0.608
300.0	82.759	0.990	0.990	0.900	0.541
350.0	96.552	0.990	0.981	0.861	0.487
400.0	110.345	0.990	0.968	0.822	0.443
450.0	124.138	0.990	0.954	0.784	0.405
500.0	137.931	0.990	0.937	0.749	0.374
600.0	165.517	0.990	0.900	0.684	0.323
700.0	193.103	0.981	0.861	0.627	0.284
800.0	220.690	0.968	0.822	0.578	0.253
900.0	248.276	0.954	0.784	0.536	0.229
1000.0	275.862	0.937	0.749	0.499	0.208
1100.0	303.448	0.919	0.715	0.466	0.191
1200.0	331.034	0.900	0.684	0.438	0.177

DAMAGE 45/.40

▼ WA-2000

WA-2000 with bipod folded

CARTRIDGE	7.62x66mmB
OPERATION	Gas
TYPE OF FIRE	Semiautomatic
RATE OF FIRE	(SS)18 rpm
MUZZLE VELOCITY	980 m/s (3215 fps)
MUZZLE ENERGY	5227 J (3855 ft/lb)
SIGHTS	Schmidt & Bender 2.5-10 power telescopic sight, range 600m
FEED	6 round removable box magazine
WEIGHTS:	
WEAPON (EMPTY)	7.910 kg w/scope
WEAPON (LOADED)	8.310 kg
MAGAZINE (EMPTY)	0.214 kg
MAGAZINE (LOADED)	0.400 kg
SERVICE CARTRIDGE	31 g
BULLET	10.9 g
LENGTHS:	
WEAPON OVERALL	90.5 cm
BARREL	65 cm
STATUS	In production
SERVICE	Commercial sales

The Walther design team developed the WA-2000 expressly for use as a sniper rifle and not as a modified production weapon. The result is a compact bullpup layout rifle of extreme accuracy and very unusual lines. The barrel is considered the heart of the weapon with all the other parts being in support of it. The rifling was carefully matched to the .300 Winchester magnum cartridge as this was considered the best commercially available round for the purpose. There are longitudinal flutes on the barrel, greatly adding to its strength and cutting down on vibration as well as increasing its surface area for cooling between shots. The barrel is set in a frame that transmits the recoil in a straight line to the shooter's shoulder, eliminating muzzle climb. The frame also acts as a support to the rest of the weapon while protecting the barrel. The caliber of the weapon may be changed as the barrel is easily removable and, by changing it and the bolt, another cartridge may be used. The bolt is gas operated and locks directly to the barrel with seven locking lugs for a very strong joint. The bullpup design allows for a long barrel length with a short overall length resulting in a very compact rifle. The action is to the rear of the pistol grip with the bolt release and ejection being able to be changed to the right or left side, resulting in an ambidextrous weapon. The unusual thumbhole grip is so that it may also be used by right or left handed shooters. The stock is adjustable to fit different shooters and the cheekpiece can be switched from one side to the other, exposing the opposite side ejection port. The large muzzle brake reportedly cuts down recoil by fifty percent without affecting accuracy. The folding bipod is unusual in that it can travel along the rail above the barrel to adjust to a given situation. There are no iron sights fitted to the WA-2000 and the Schmidt & Bender 2.5 to 10 power variable telescopic sight is issued as standard with the weapon. The mounting for the sight is of the quick detachable type and will accept many types of sighting devices. So intent on maximum accuracy were the designers that they did not overlook the smallest detail. An example is the magazine with its two sets of formed guide rails to align the round with the chamber, protecting the nose of the projectile from damage while being chambered or undergoing recoil when still in the magazine.

WEAPON	WA-2000
AMMO	7.62x66B
	10 x power scope installed.
DISPERSION ANGLE	.0068755 degrees, .122231 NATO mils.

Range	Group Circle Width (mm)	Probability (0<p<.099) (m)			
		Body	Head	Hand	Bullseye
50.0	6.000	0.990	0.990	0.990	0.990
100.0*	12.000	0.990	0.990	0.990	0.990
150.0	18.000	0.990	0.990	0.990	0.972
200.0	24.000	0.990	0.990	0.990	0.932
250.0	30.000	0.990	0.990	0.990	0.884
300.0	36.000	0.990	0.990	0.990	0.833

☞ continued on next page

THE EDGE OF THE SWORD

☞ WA-2000 continued

Range	Group Circle Width (mm)	Probability (0<p<.099) (m)			
		Body	**Head**	**Hand**	**Bullseye**
350.0	42.000	0.990	0.990	0.989	0.785
400.0	48.000	0.990	0.990	0.981	0.739
450.0	54.000	0.990	0.990	0.971	0.697
500.0	60.000	0.990	0.990	0.958	0.659
600.0	72.000	0.990	0.990	0.929	0.592
700.0	84.000	0.990	0.989	0.896	0.536
800.0	96.000	0.990	0.981	0.863	0.489
900.0	108.000	0.990	0.971	0.829	0.450
1000.0	120.000	0.990	0.958	0.796	0.416
1100.0	132.000	0.990	0.944	0.764	0.387
1200.0	144.000	0.990	0.929	0.734	0.361

* indicates range for which data was supplied
DAMAGE 58/.5

▼ Heckler & Koch HK94 SG1

HK 94 with 15 rd magazine

CARTRIDGE	9x19mm
OPERATION	Retarded blowback
TYPE OF FIRE	Semiautomatic
RATE OF FIRE	(SS) 40 rpm
MUZZLE VELOCITY	396 m/s (1300 fps)
MUZZLE ENERGY	625 J (461 ft/lb)
SIGHTS	LEUPOLD 6 power telescopic sight w/ adjustable, aperture/post backup iron sights
FEED	15, 30, or 60 (2x30) round removable box magazine
WEIGHTS:	
WEAPON (EMPTY)	3.257 kg
WEAPON (LOADED)	3.557 kg w/15 rds
MAGAZINE (EMPTY)	0.120 kg (15 rd), 0.170 kg (30 rd), 0.504 kg (2x30 rd)
MAGAZINE (LOADED)	0.300 kg (15 rd), 0.530 kg (30 rd), 1.224 kg (2x30 rd)
SERVICE CARTRIDGE	12 g
BULLET	8 g
LENGTHS:	
WEAPON OVERALL	102.6 cm

BARREL	42 cm
SIGHT RADIUS	34 cm
STATUS	In production
SERVICE	Commercial sales

The only sniper system available in this caliber, the HK94 SG/1 is a carbine version of the MP5 submachinegun. The use of the 9 x 19mm round in a precision weapon eliminates the problem of overpenetration for relatively short range engagements while still giving sufficient energy to stop the target. The buttstock of the 94 SG/1 has an adjustable cheekpiece to accommodate the shooter and a non-adjustable rubber buttplate that will not slip against the shoulder. A folding adjustable bipod is fitted as standard and the 15 round magazine normally used to give a low profile. Standard H&K iron sights are fitted and the weapon comes issued with a Leupold six power telescopic sight on a quick release mounting.

WEAPON	HK94 SG/1
AMMO	9x19
	6 x power scope installed.
DISPERSION ANGLE	.0316115 degrees, .561982 NATO mils.

Range	Group Circle Width (mm)	Probability (0<p<.099) (m)			
		Body	**Head**	**Hand**	**Bullseye**
25.0	13.793	0.990	0.990	0.990	0.990
50.0	27.586	0.990	0.990	0.990	0.903
75.0	41.379	0.990	0.990	0.990	0.790
100.0	55.172	0.990	0.990	0.968	0.689
125.0	68.966	0.990	0.990	0.937	0.608
150.0	82.759	0.990	0.990	0.900	0.541
175.0	96.552	0.990	0.981	0.861	0.487
200.0	110.345	0.990	0.968	0.822	0.443
250.0	137.931	0.990	0.937	0.749	0.374
300.0	165.517	0.990	0.900	0.684	0.323
350.0	193.103	0.981	0.861	0.627	0.284
400.0	220.690	0.968	0.822	0.578	0.253
450.0	248.276	0.954	0.784	0.536	0.229
500.0	275.862	0.937	0.749	0.499	0.208

DAMAGE 27/.17

▼ Heckler & Koch HK33 SG/1

CARTRIDGE	5.56x45mm
OPERATION	Retarded blowback
TYPE OF FIRE	Selective
RATE OF FIRE	(SS) 40 rpm (A) 100 rpm (CYCLIC) 750 rpm
MUZZLE VELOCITY	920 m/s (3020 fps)
MUZZLE ENERGY	1675 J (1235 ft/lb)

SIGHTS	Zeiss 1.5 - 6 power telescopic sight, range 600m, adjustable U-notch/post backup iron sight, range 400m
FEED	25 round removable box magazine
WEIGHTS:	
WEAPON (EMPTY)	4.445 kg
WEAPON (LOADED)	5.000 kg
MAGAZINE (EMPTY)	0.250 kg
MAGAZINE (LOADED)	0.555 kg
SERVICE CARTRIDGE	12.2 g
BULLET	4 g
LENGTHS:	
WEAPON OVERALL	92 cm
BARREL	39 cm
SIGHT RADIUS	48 cm
STATUS	In production
SERVICE	Commercial sales

Range	Group Circle Width (mm)	Probability (0<p<.099) (m)			
		Body	Head	Hand	Bullseye
100.0	41.379	0.990	0.990	0.990	0.790
125.0	51.724	0.990	0.990	0.975	0.713
150.0	62.069	0.990	0.990	0.954	0.646
175.0	72.414	0.990	0.990	0.928	0.590
200.0	82.759	0.990	0.990	0.900	0.541
250.0	103.448	0.990	0.975	0.841	0.464
300.0	124.138	0.990	0.954	0.784	0.405
350.0	144.828	0.990	0.928	0.732	0.359
400.0	165.517	0.990	0.900	0.684	0.323
450.0	186.207	0.983	0.871	0.641	0.293
500.0	206.897	0.975	0.841	0.602	0.268

DAMAGE 40/.52

▼ Heckler & Koch G3 SG/1

CARTRIDGE	7.62x51mm
OPERATION	Retarded blowback
TYPE OF FIRE	Selective
RATE OF FIRE	(SS) 40 rpm (A) 100 rpm (CYCLIC) 600 rpm
MUZZLE VELOCITY	742 m/s (2433 fps)
MUZZLE ENERGY	3119 J (2300 ft/lb)
SIGHTS	Zeiss 1.5 - 6 power telescopic sight, range 600 m, adjustable U-notch/post backup iron sight, range 400m
FEED	20 round removable box magazine
WEIGHTS:	
WEAPON (EMPTY)	5.488 kg
WEAPON (LOADED)	6.274 kg
MAGAZINE (EMPTY)	0.280 kg
MAGAZINE (LOADED)	0.786 kg
SERVICE CARTRIDGE	25.3 g
BULLET	11.4 g
LENGTHS:	
WEAPON OVERALL	102.5 cm
BARREL	45 cm
SIGHT RADIUS	57.2 cm
STATUS	In production
SERVICE	Federal German police, Italian carabineri, other police forces and commercial sales.

This is the sniper version of the HK 33A2 rifle and is a precision firing weapon of 5.56mm caliber for use in situations where larger calibers could be prone to overpenetration. The SG version is a standard production weapon that is noted for its particular accuracy during testing and put aside to receive the SG type modifications. The primary modification is the addition of a set trigger mechanism to lower trigger pull. In the set trigger system the rectangular protrusion behind the trigger is pulled back to set the trigger to an adjustable pull between 2 and 3.3 pounds (.9 - 1.5kg) with the selector switch set to "E", semiautomatic fire. Setting the selector to "S" or "F", safety or full automatic, unsets the trigger to its normal pull of 5.7 pounds (2.6kg). The standard folding bipod is normally fitted to the weapon. Standard H&K iron sights are on the SG model and it is issued with a Zeiss 1.5 to 6 power variable telescopic sight on a quick release mount. The fixed buttstock has an adjustable height cheekpiece to fit different shooters. The most unusual aspect of the HK33 SG/1 is that it is one of two production sniper weapons capable of full automatic fire. Though full auto fire would quickly degrade the accuracy of the weapon, it would allow a sniper to put down a suppressive field of fire in an emergency.

WEAPON	HK33 SG/1
AMMO	5.56x45
	6 x power scope installed.
DISPERSION ANGLE	.0237086 degrees, .421487 NATO mils.

Range	Group Circle Width (mm)	Probability (0<p<.099) (m)			
		Body	Head	Hand	Bullseye
25.0	10.345	0.990	0.990	0.990	0.990
50.0	20.690	0.990	0.990	0.990	0.956
75.0	31.034	0.990	0.990	0.990	0.875

☞ continued

Like the HK33 weapon this is a sniper version of the standard G3A3 rifle selected for accuracy and suitably modified. The G3 SG/1 was one of the first Western semiautomatic sniper rifles to see

☞ continued on next page

☞ *Heckler & Koch G3 SG/1 continued*

military acceptance. Fitted with a set trigger mechanism, standard folding bipod, and a Zeiss 1.5 to 6 power variable telescopic sight, the G3 SG/1 has seen wide acceptance among police units and elite military units. One of the reasons for this acceptance is that the G3 SG/1 is the only other production sniper weapon that has the capability for full automatic fire as well as exceptional ruggedness and good accuracy.

WEAPON	G3 SG/1
AMMO	7.62x51
	6 x power scope installed.
DISPERSION ANGLE	.0158058 degrees, .280991 NATO mils.

Range	Group Circle Width (mm)	Probability (0<p<.099) (m)			
		Body	Head	Hand	Bullseye
50.0	13.793	0.990	0.990	0.990	0.990
100.0	27.586	0.990	0.990	0.990	0.903
150.0	41.379	0.990	0.990	0.990	0.790
200.0	55.172	0.990	0.990	0.968	0.689
250.0	68.966	0.990	0.990	0.937	0.608
300.0	82.759	0.990	0.990	0.900	0.541
350.0	96.552	0.990	0.981	0.861	0.487
400.0	110.345	0.990	0.968	0.822	0.443
450.0	124.138	0.990	0.954	0.784	0.405
500.0	137.931	0.990	0.937	0.749	0.374
600.0	165.517	0.990	0.900	0.684	0.323
700.0	193.103	0.981	0.861	0.627	0.284
800.0	220.690	0.968	0.822	0.578	0.253
900.0	248.276	0.954	0.784	0.536	0.229
1000.0	275.862	0.937	0.749	0.499	0.208
1100.0	303.448	0.919	0.715	0.466	0.191
1200.0	331.034	0.900	0.684	0.438	0.177

DAMAGE 44/.39

▼ Heckler & Koch PSG 1

CARTRIDGE	7.62x51mm
OPERATION	Retarded blowback
TYPE OF FIRE	Semiautomatic
RATE OF FIRE	(SS) 40 rpm
MUZZLE VELOCITY	788 m/s (2586 fps)
MUZZLE ENERGY	3523 J (2598 ft/lb)
SIGHTS	Heinsoldt 6 power telescopic sight, range 600m

FEED	5 or 20 round removable box magazine
WEIGHTS:	
WEAPON (EMPTY)	8.100 kg (9.130 kg w/tripod)
WEAPON (LOADED)	8.886 kg w/20 rds (9.916 kg w/tripod & 20 rds)
MAGAZINE (EMPTY)	0.190 kg (5 rd), 0.280 kg (20 rd)
MAGAZINE (LOADED)	0.317 kg (5 rd), 0.786 kg (20 rd)
SERVICE CARTRIDGE	25.3 g
BULLET	11.4 cm
LENGTHS:	
WEAPON OVERALL	120.8 cm
BARREL	65 cm
STATUS	In production
SERVICE	Undergoing trials
COST	$6,000

This weapon, the Prazisions schutzen gewehr Eins (PSG-1), was developed specifically as a police and military snipers' weapon and is not a modified production weapon. The barrel is a smooth bull-barrel design with the H&K polygonal rifling for extended life and accuracy. The action is the same roller-locked delayed blowback system used in most HK weapons with the operating tolerances held extremely close. The trigger mechanism is only capable of semiautomatic fire and has a normal trigger with an adjustable trigger shoe and a crisp pull of 3.2 pounds (1.5kg). The forearm has a rail built into its bottom to allow an adjustable sling to be attached. The bottom of the forearm is also flat and broad to give a stable rest when used with the optional precision adjustable tripod or on the hand. The pistol grip is shaped to fit the hand and has an adjustable palm rest to help eliminate fatigue when the weapon is held for long lengths of time. The buttstock is modified from the machinegun style used by H & K with the flat downward portion intended to be held with the left hand with the weapon resting on a tripod. The stock is fully adjustable for length and height to fit any shooter. A silent bolt closure device is fitted to the right side to allow the weapon to be quietly loaded if the situation demands. The sight is a Hensoldt six power telescopic sight with an illuminated reticle for use in low light situations. The sight mount will accept standard sighting devices but is not of the quick release type. A special aluminum carrying case is made for the PSG-1 and it weighs 10.4kg empty. Filled with the weapon, precision tripod, two filled 20 round and two filled 5 round magazines, the case weighs 21.736kg.

ASSESSMENT	40mm @ 100m
WEAPON	PSG 1
AMMO	7.62x51
	6 x power scope installed.
DISPERSION ANGLE	.0229183 degrees, .407437 NATO mils.

Range	Group Circle Width (mm)	Probability (0<p<.099) (m)			
		Body	Head	Hand	Bullseye
50.0	20.000	0.990	0.990	0.990	0.960
100.0*	40.000	0.990	0.990	0.990	0.801
150.0	60.000	0.990	0.990	0.958	0.659
200.0	80.000	0.990	0.990	0.908	0.553
250.0	100.000	0.990	0.978	0.851	0.475
300.0	120.000	0.990	0.958	0.796	0.416
350.0	140.000	0.990	0.934	0.744	0.369
400.0	160.000	0.990	0.908	0.696	0.332
450.0	180.000	0.985	0.880	0.653	0.301
500.0	200.000	0.978	0.851	0.614	0.276
600.0	240.000	0.958	0.796	0.548	0.236
700.0	280.000	0.934	0.744	0.494	0.206
800.0	320.000	0.908	0.696	0.449	0.183
900.0	360.000	0.880	0.653	0.411	0.164
1000.0	400.000	0.851	0.614	0.379	0.149
1100.0	440.000	0.823	0.579	0.351	0.136
1200.0	480.000	0.796	0.548	0.328	0.126

* indicates range for which data was supplied
DAMAGE 47/.42

▼ Galil Sniper

Galil Sniper without magazine, bipod is folded and selector set to safe

CARTRIDGE 7.62x51mm
OPERATION Gas
TYPE OF FIRE Semiautomatic
RATE OF FIRE (SS) 30 rpm
MUZZLE VELOCITY 780 m/s (2559 fps)
MUZZLE ENERGY 3450 J (2544 ft/lb)
SIGHTS Nimrod 6 power telescopic sight, adjustable aperture/post iron sights, range 500m
FEED 20 or 25 round removable box magazine
WEIGHTS:
WEAPON (EMPTY) 6.400 kg w/ bipod & sling (scope 0.900 kg)
WEAPON (LOADED) 8.020 kg w/bipod, sling, scope, & 20 rds
MAGAZINE (EMPTY) 0.214 kg (20 rd), 0.290 kg (25 rd)
MAGAZINE (LOADED) 0.720 kg (20 rd), 0.923 kg (25 rd)

SERVICE CARTRIDGE 25.3 g
BULLET 11.4 g
LENGTHS:
WEAPON OVERALL 84/111.5 cm
BARREL 50.8 cm
SIGHT RADIUS 47.5 cm
STATUS In production
SERVICE Israeli defense forces, commercial sales

This is a modified version of the 7.62 x 51mm Galil rifle and is intended for military sniping operations. The barrel is heavier than standard as an aid to accuracy and is fitted with a flash hider/muzzle brake. The folding buttstock has a fully adjustable cheekpiece and recoil pad to fit individual firers. The iron sights can be used when the telescopic sight is fixed in place. The Nimrod six power telescopic sight used with the Galil was specifically made for use as a military sight and has a ranging reticle that allows ranges from 200 to 1000 meters to be determined. The mount used with the Nimrod scope attaches to the side of the rifle with a quick release attachment that allows the sight to be removed or added at will without changing its zero. The folding bipod is mounted at the rear of the forearm on a swivel mounting that allows the rifle to be traversed or canted to a limited extent without moving the bipod's legs. The action of the sniper Galil only allows for semiautomatic firing.

ASSESSMENT 12 cm group @ 300 m
WEAPON Galil Sniper
AMMO 7.62x51
6 x power scope installed.
DISPERSION ANGLE .0229183 degrees, .407437 NATO mils.

Range	Group Circle Width (mm)	Probability (0<p<.099) (m)			
		Body	Head	Hand	Bullseye
50.0	20.000	0.990	0.990	0.990	0.960
100.0	40.000	0.990	0.990	0.990	0.801
150.0	60.000	0.990	0.990	0.958	0.659
200.0	80.000	0.990	0.990	0.908	0.553
250.0	100.000	0.990	0.978	0.851	0.475
300.0*	120.000	0.990	0.958	0.796	0.416
350.0	140.000	0.990	0.934	0.744	0.369
400.0	160.000	0.990	0.908	0.696	0.332
450.0	180.000	0.985	0.880	0.653	0.301
500.0	200.000	0.978	0.851	0.614	0.276
600.0	240.000	0.958	0.796	0.548	0.236
700.0	280.000	0.934	0.744	0.494	0.206
800.0	320.000	0.908	0.696	0.449	0.183
900.0	360.000	0.880	0.653	0.411	0.164

☞ continued on next page

☞ *Galil Sniper continued*

Range	Group Circle Width (mm)	Probability (0<p<.099) (m)			
		Body	**Head**	**Hand**	**Bullseye**
1000.0	400.000	0.851	0.614	0.379	0.149
1100.0	440.000	0.823	0.579	0.351	0.136
1200.0	480.000	0.796	0.548	0.328	0.126

* indicates range for which data was supplied
DAMAGE 46/.41

▼ SIG 2000

SIG 2000 with precision adjustable tripod

CARTRIDGE	(A) 7.62x51mm, (B) 7.62x72mmB, (C) 5.56x45mm (D) 7.5x55mm
OPERATION	Manual bolt action
TYPE OF FIRE	Single shot repeater
RATE OF FIRE	(SS)12 rpm
MUZZLE VELOCITY	(A) 792 m/s (2600 fps), (B) 990 m/s (3248 fps), (C) 1000 m/s (3281 fps), (D) 770 m/s (2526 fps)
MUZZLE ENERGY	(A) 3561 J (2626 ft/lb), (B) 6987 J (5153 ft/lb), (C) 1977 J (1458 ft/lb), (D) 3343 J (2465 ft/lb)
SIGHTS	Schmidt & Bender 1.5 - 6 power telescopic sight
FEED	4 round removable box magazine
WEIGHTS:	
WEAPON (EMPTY)	(A, C, D) 6.522 kg, (B) 6.622 kg, 1.120 kg (tripod)
WEAPON (LOADED)	(A) 6.701 kg, (B) 6.839 kg, (C) 6.649 kg, (D) 6.705 kg
MAGAZINE (EMPTY)	0.078 kg
MAGAZINE (LOADED)	(A) 0.179 kg, (B) 0.217 kg, (C) 0.127 kg, (D) 0.183 kg
SERVICE CARTRIDGE	(A) 25.3 g, (B) 34.7 g, (C) 12.2 g, (D) 26.2 g
BULLET	(A) 11.4 g, (B) 14.3 g, (C) 4 g (D) 11.3 g
LENGTHS:	
WEAPON OVERALL	(A, C, D) 121 cm, (B) 126 cm
BARREL	(A, C, D) 61 cm, (B) 66 cm
STATUS	In production
SERVICE	Commercial sales

This is a highly refined version of the Sauer 90 short action system intended for high precision fire. The bolt in the Sauer 90 system does not rotate for its entire length but only a short rear section rotates to cam 3 locking lugs outward to lock the bolt. This non-rotating bolt helps give the SIG 2000 its very smooth operation. The barrel is a hammer forged medium weight target (bull) type with an unusual tapered bore. The bore tapers slightly from breech to muzzle to help keep the bullet aligned and improve accuracy. A large combination flash hider/muzzle brake is attached to the barrel cutting down on muzzle rise for a fast second shot. The trigger is of the single set type with a normal trigger pull of 2 1/4 pounds (1.02kg). By pushing the trigger forward, it becomes "set" with a trigger pull of 14 ounces (0.40kg). Lifting the bolt handle or setting the safety removes the trigger from its set position. The standard sight of the SIG 2000 is a Zeiss Dmiata-ZA 8 power telescope sight on a quick release mount. The stock design is taken from competition weapons with a thumbhole pistol grip, adjustable buttplate and cheekpiece, and a rail fitting for accessories under the forend. A Loga Rifle Rest precision tripod is recommended for use with the weapon and can be supplied by the manufacturer. An unusual aspect of the SSG 2000 is the number of calibers in which it is available. Normally used in the 7.62 x 51mm chambering, the SSG 2000 is the only production sniper rifle chambered for the .300 Weatherby magnum round (7.62 x 72mmB).

WEAPON	SIG 2000
AMMO	7.62x51
	6 x power scope installed.
DISPERSION ANGLE	.0197572 degrees, .351239 NATO mils.

Range	Group Circle Width (mm)	Probability (0<p<.099) (m)			
		Body	**Head**	**Hand**	**Bullseye**
50.0	17.241	0.990	0.990	0.990	0.976
100.0	34.483	0.990	0.990	0.990	0.846
150.0	51.724	0.990	0.990	0.975	0.713
200.0	68.966	0.990	0.990	0.937	0.608
250.0	86.207	0.990	0.988	0.890	0.527
300.0	103.448	0.990	0.975	0.841	0.464
350.0	120.690	0.990	0.957	0.794	0.414
400.0	137.931	0.990	0.937	0.749	0.374
450.0	155.172	0.990	0.914	0.707	0.340
500.0	172.414	0.988	0.890	0.669	0.312
600.0	206.897	0.975	0.841	0.602	0.268
700.0	241.379	0.957	0.794	0.546	0.234
800.0	275.862	0.937	0.749	0.499	0.208
900.0	310.345	0.914	0.707	0.459	0.188
1000.0	344.828	0.890	0.669	0.424	0.171
1100.0	379.310	0.866	0.634	0.395	0.156
1200.0	413.793	0.841	0.602	0.369	0.144

DAMAGE (A) 47/.42, (B) 59/.65, (C) 43/.43, (D) 46/.40

▼ SVD

CARTRIDGE	7.62x54mmR
OPERATION	Gas, short stroke piston
TYPE OF FIRE	Semiautomatic
RATE OF FIRE	(SS) 20 rpm
MUZZLE VELOCITY	830 m/s (2723 fps)
MUZZLE ENERGY	3113 J (2996 ft/lb)
SIGHTS	PSO-1 4 power telescopic sight w/ infrared capability, range 1300m, Backup iron sight, non-adjustable, U-notch/post, range 1100m
FEED	10 round removable box magazine
WEIGHTS:	
WEAPON (EMPTY)	4.300 kg
WEAPON (LOADED)	4.611 kg
MAGAZINE (EMPTY)	0.085 kg
MAGAZINE (LOADED)	0.311 kg
SERVICE CARTRIDGE	22.6 g
BULLET	11.8 g
LENGTHS:	
WEAPON OVERALL	122.5 cm
BARREL	54.7 cm
SIGHT RADIUS	58 cm
STATUS	In production
SERVICE	Soviet Union and Warsaw Pact forces

The SVD, Snayperskaya Vinyovka Dragunov, is a heavily modified version of the Kalashnikov weapon system (AKM-47). First seen in 1963, the SVD is chambered for the older 7.62 x 54mm R round that is still used in Soviet machineguns and is known for its excellent ballistics. The basic mechanism was redesigned to handle this much larger round and accept a 10 round magazine. The action was changed for semiautomatic only fire and the trigger pull improved. The long barrel is fitted with a flash suppressor/compensator that assists the firer in keeping the barrel down for a fast second shot. The buttstock is made of laminated wood for strength and has a distinctive hollow shape. There are iron sights for emergency use with the SVD but the weapon is intended to be used with the PSO-1 telescopic sight. The PSO-1 sight is a fairly sophisticated device with an integral infrared detector, illuminated reticle and range finder, good up to 1300 meters. In the early 1970's, the demand for an example of this weapon was so high with Western intelligence agencies that the CIA offered a $25,000 reward to the first person who could deliver one! Several were finally captured during the 1973 Israeli conflict and supplied to the U.S.

ASSESSMENT	1.25 in @ 100 yds
WEAPON	SVD
AMMO	7.62x54R
	4 x power scope installed.
DISPERSION ANGLE	.0198944 degrees, .353678 NATO mils.

Range	Group Circle Width (mm)	Probability (0<p<.099) (m)			
		Body	Head	Hand	Bullseye
50.0	17.361	0.990	0.990	0.990	0.976
100.0	34.722	0.990	0.990	0.990	0.844
150.0	52.083	0.990	0.990	0.974	0.710
200.0	69.444	0.990	0.990	0.936	0.605
250.0	86.806	0.990	0.988	0.889	0.524
300.0	104.167	0.990	0.974	0.839	0.462
350.0	121.528	0.990	0.957	0.791	0.412
400.0	138.889	0.990	0.936	0.746	0.371
450.0	156.250	0.990	0.913	0.705	0.338
500.0	173.611	0.988	0.889	0.666	0.310
600.0	208.333	0.974	0.839	0.599	0.266
700.0	243.056	0.957	0.791	0.543	0.233
800.0	277.778	0.936	0.746	0.496	0.207
900.0	312.500	0.913	0.705	0.456	0.186
1000.0	347.222	0.889	0.666	0.422	0.170
1100.0	381.944	0.864	0.631	0.393	0.155
1200.0	416.667	0.839	0.599	0.367	0.143

DAMAGE 50/.46

▼ L42A1

CARTRIDGE	7.62x51mm
OPERATION	Manual bolt action
TYPE OF FIRE	single shot repeater
RATE OF FIRE	(SS) 30 rpm
MUZZLE VELOCITY	838 m/s (2749 fps)
MUZZLE ENERGY	3981 J (2936 ft/lb)
SIGHTS	L1A1 4 power telescopic w/ adjustable aperture/blade iron backup sights
FEED	10 round removable box magazine
WEIGHTS:	
WEAPON (EMPTY)	4.430 kg w/scope
WEAPON (LOADED)	4.892 kg w/scope
MAGAZINE (EMPTY)	0.209 kg
MAGAZINE (LOADED)	0.462 kg
SERVICE CARTRIDGE	25.3 g
BULLET	11.4 g
LENGTHS:	
WEAPON OVERALL	118.1 cm

☛ continued on next page

☞ *L42A1 continued*

BARREL	69.9 cm
SIGHT RADIUS	83 cm
STATUS	In production
SERVICE	British forces

This is the last member of the Lee Enfield weapons line to still be in active service with a major military. The World War II Number 4 Mark One or Mark 1*(T) Enfield has been modified into a lighter and more accurate sniper rifle. The major modification was a rebarreling and action adaptions to accept the 7.62 x 51mm NATO round. The stock was shortened at the forearm and a cheekpiece added. The original iron sights have been recalibrated to fit the caliber change and a four power L1A1 telescopic sight fitted. Though being replaced by newer designs, the L42A1 has seen extensive service with the British military and specialized police agencies and still commands a loyal following.

WEAPON	L42A1
AMMO	7.62x51
	4 x power scope installed.
DISPERSION ANGLE	.0355629 degrees, .63223 NATO mils.

Range	Group Circle Width (mm)	Probability (0<p<.099) (m)			
		Body	Head	Hand	Bullseye
50.0	31.034	0.990	0.990	0.990	0.875
100.0	62.069	0.990	0.990	0.954	0.646
150.0	93.103	0.990	0.983	0.871	0.500
200.0	124.138	0.990	0.954	0.784	0.405
250.0	155.172	0.990	0.914	0.707	0.340
300.0	186.207	0.983	0.871	0.641	0.293
350.0	217.241	0.970	0.827	0.584	0.257
400.0	248.276	0.954	0.784	0.536	0.229
450.0	279.310	0.935	0.744	0.494	0.206
500.0	310.345	0.914	0.707	0.459	0.188
600.0	372.414	0.871	0.641	0.400	0.159
700.0	434.483	0.827	0.584	0.355	0.138
800.0	496.552	0.784	0.536	0.319	0.122
900.0	558.621	0.744	0.494	0.289	0.109
1000.0	620.690	0.707	0.459	0.264	0.099
1100.0	682.759	0.672	0.428	0.243	0.090
1200.0	744.828	0.641	0.400	0.226	0.083

DAMAGE 50/.44

▼ PM • L96A1

PM with bolt open and bipod extended, this particular weapon has been fitted with a custom suppresor

CARTRIDGE	7.62x51mm
OPERATION	Manual bolt action
TYPE OF FIRE	Single shot repeater
RATE OF FIRE	(SS) 30 rpm
MUZZLE VELOCITY	782 m/s (2567 fps)
MUZZLE ENERGY	3471 J (2560 ft/lb)
SIGHTS	Schmidt & Bender 6 power telescopic sight
FEED	10 round removable box magazine
WEIGHTS:	
WEAPON (EMPTY)	6.000 kg
WEAPON (LOADED)	6.453 kg
MAGAZINE (EMPTY)	0.200 kg
MAGAZINE (LOADED)	0.453 kg
SERVICE CARTRIDGE	25.3 g
BULLET	11.4 g
LENGTHS:	
WEAPON OVERALL	117.5 cm
BARREL	60.3 cm
STATUS	In production
SERVICE	British military and commercial sales

This rifle was developed from scratch as a military issue sniper rifle and has been accepted by the British military as their new issue sniper weapon, the L96A1. The receiver of the L96A1 is assembled to an aluminum "chassis" on which all of the other parts of the weapon are mounted. Using this chassis approach prevents any change in accuracy from weather or environmental changes to the stock and greatly adds to the overall strength of the design. The trigger is a two stage type that can be set by the operator for a pull between 1 and 2 kg. The barrel is designed to be easily removable so that other ammunition may be used in the rifle with the barrel optimized to fit the rounds being used. The buttstock is adjustable for length and there is a folding bipod attached to the forend by a ball joint to allow for easy movement of the weapon. There are adjustable iron sights built into the weapon and it comes equipped with a Schmidt and Bender PM six power telescopic sight that was specifically designed for it. A collapsible support spike is available that fits into the buttstock. With the spike extended, the weapon is supported on an effective tripod that would prevent fatigue in an operator holding a position for an extended length of time.

WEAPON PM (L96A1)
AMMO 7.62x51
6 x power scope installed.
DISPERSION ANGLE .0237086 degrees, .421487 NATO mils.

Range	Group Circle Width (mm)	Probability (0<p<.099) (m)			
		Body	Head	Hand	Bullseye
50.0	20.690	0.990	0.990	0.990	0.956
100.0	41.379	0.990	0.990	0.990	0.790
150.0	62.069	0.990	0.990	0.954	0.646
200.0	82.759	0.990	0.990	0.900	0.541
250.0	103.448	0.990	0.975	0.841	0.464
300.0	124.138	0.990	0.954	0.784	0.405
350.0	144.828	0.990	0.928	0.732	0.359
400.0	165.517	0.990	0.900	0.684	0.323
450.0	186.207	0.983	0.871	0.641	0.293
500.0	206.897	0.975	0.841	0.602	0.268
600.0	248.276	0.954	0.784	0.536	0.229
700.0	289.655	0.928	0.732	0.482	0.200
800.0	331.034	0.900	0.684	0.438	0.177
900.0	372.414	0.871	0.641	0.400	0.159
1000.0	413.793	0.841	0.602	0.369	0.144
1100.0	455.172	0.813	0.567	0.342	0.132
1200.0	496.552	0.784	0.536	0.319	0.122

DAMAGE 47/.41

▼ M21

CARTRIDGE 7.62x51mm
OPERATION Gas
TYPE OF FIRE Semiautomatic
RATE OF FIRE (SS) 20 rpm
MUZZLE VELOCITY 792 m/s (2600 fps)
MUZZLE ENERGY 3561 J (2626 ft/lb)
SIGHTS Leatherwood ART I 3 - 9 power telescopic sight, autoranging to 900m, Adjustable, aperture/blade, iron sights, range 1100 m
FEED 20 round removable box magazine
WEIGHTS:
WEAPON (EMPTY) 5.045 kg w/scope
WEAPON (LOADED) 5.777 kg
MAGAZINE (EMPTY) 0.226 kg
MAGAZINE (LOADED) 0.732 kg
SERVICE CARTRIDGE 25.3 g
BULLET 11.4 g
LENGTHS:
WEAPON OVERALL 112 cm
BARREL 55.9 cm

SIGHT RADIUS 67.8 cm
STATUS In production
SERVICE U.S. forces, commercial sales
COST $1200

This is presently the standard issue sniper weapon in the U.S. Army. Developed during the Vietnam war, the M21 is a National Match target grade M14 rifle fitted with the ART-I telescopic sight. The standard M14 rifle is fitted with a precision, gauged barrel, the flash suppressor reamed and carefully aligned to the barrel, the barreled action glassbedded to a select epoxy-impregnated walnut stock, and the trigger mechanism tuned and polished for a crisp release. All this work results in a very accurate, rugged rifle with a high level of dependability. The iron sights found on the M14 are replaced with the improved national match sights that are capable of finer adjustment. The sight designed for use with the M21 is the 3 to 9 power variable Leatherwood ART-I telescopic sight. The sight, designed by Captain James Leatherwood, is an automatic adjusting ranging telescope specifically intended for use with the M118 Match 7.62 x 51mm round. The reticle of the scope has a set of stadia lines intended to cover a space of 76cm, the distance from the average soldier's belt to the top of his helmet. With the target set in the sight, the magnification ring is rotated until the stadia lines measure the proper space, that is, mark the space from the belt to the top of the helmet (76cm). As the magnification ring is rotated, a ballistic cam rotates adjusting the aiming point of the sight to match the ballistic arc of the M118 projectile at the distance indicated. The design of the ART-I scope is such that the power setting of the scope is equal to the range in hundreds of meters, i.e. 3x equals 300 meters, 9x equals 900 meters. Though the M21 is a satisfactory weapon, the outstanding feature of the system is the ART scope and this has since been adapted to other weapons.

ASSESSMENT 15 cm @ 300m
WEAPON M21
AMMO 7.62x51
9 x power scope installed.
DISPERSION ANGLE .0286479 degrees, .509296 NATO mils.

Range	Group Circle Width (mm)	Probability (0<p<.099) (m)			
		Body	Head	Hand	Bullseye
50.0	25.000	0.990	0.990	0.990	0.924
100.0	50.000	0.990	0.990	0.978	0.725
150.0	75.000	0.990	0.990	0.921	0.577
200.0	100.000	0.990	0.978	0.851	0.475
250.0	125.000	0.990	0.953	0.782	0.403
300.0*	150.000	0.990	0.921	0.719	0.349
350.0	175.000	0.987	0.887	0.663	0.308
400.0	200.000	0.978	0.851	0.614	0.276
450.0	225.000	0.966	0.816	0.571	0.249

☞ continued on next page

☞ *continued*

Range	Group Circle Width (mm)	Probability (0<p<.099) (m)			
		Body	Head	Hand	Bullseye
500.0	250.000	0.953	0.782	0.533	0.227
600.0	300.000	0.921	0.719	0.470	0.193
700.0	350.000	0.887	0.663	0.420	0.168
800.0	400.000	0.851	0.614	0.379	0.149
900.0	450.000	0.816	0.571	0.345	0.134
1000.0	500.000	0.782	0.533	0.317	0.121
1100.0	550.000	0.750	0.500	0.293	0.111
1200.0	600.000	0.719	0.470	0.272	0.102

* indicates range for which data was supplied

DAMAGE 47/.42

▼ M40A1

CARTRIDGE	7.62x51mm
OPERATION	Manual bolt action
TYPE OF FIRE	Single shot repeater
RATE OF FIRE	(SS)10 rpm
MUZZLE VELOCITY	777 m/s (2549 fps)
MUZZLE ENERGY	3423 J (2524 ft/lb)
SIGHTS	USMC Sniper 10 power telescopic sight
FEED	5 round integral box magazine
WEIGHTS:	
WEAPON (EMPTY)	6.570 kg w/scope
WEAPON (LOADED)	6.697 kg w/scope
MAGAZINE (LOADED)	0.127 kg (5 rds)
SERVICE CARTRIDGE	25.3 g
BULLET	11.4 g
LENGTHS:	
WEAPON OVERALL	111.7 cm
BARREL	61 cm
STATUS	In production
SERVICE	U.S. forces and commercial sales

The U.S. Marine Corps prefers using a bolt action rifle to the Army's semiautomatic M21, and adopted the militarized version of a civilian target rifle during the Vietnam war. The basic rifle is a Remington Model 700 BDL Heavy Barrel Varmint rifle in 7.62 x 51mm NATO. The barrel is of stainless steel darkened with a matte black finish. The stock is of dark camouflage fiberglass that will not swell or warp from moisture. The sight was originally a Redfield three to nine power variable telescopic sight but that has now been replaced by a special Unertl ten power sight specially built for the USMC with an elevation drum ballistically matched to the M118 Match round. The magazine capacity of the Remington action is five rounds and these must be loaded through the top of the magazine singly. The slowness of reloading is not considered a drawback as the USMC sniper will only fire a few rounds before moving his position.

ASSESSMENT	1.25 in @ 400 yds
WEAPON	M40A1
AMMO	7.62x51
	10 x power scope installed.
DISPERSION ANGLE	5.00947 degrees, .0890573 NATO mils.

Range	Group Circle Width (mm)	Probability (0<p<.099) (m)			
		Body	Head	Hand	Bullseye
50.0	4.372	0.990	0.990	0.990	0.990
100.0	8.743	0.990	0.990	0.990	0.990
150.0	13.115	0.990	0.990	0.990	0.990
200.0	17.486	0.990	0.990	0.990	0.975
250.0	21.858	0.990	0.990	0.990	0.948
300.0	26.230	0.990	0.990	0.990	0.914
350.0	30.601	0.990	0.990	0.990	0.878
400.0	34.973	0.990	0.990	0.990	0.842
450.0	39.344	0.990	0.990	0.990	0.806
500.0	43.716	0.990	0.990	0.987	0.771
600.0	52.459	0.990	0.990	0.974	0.708
700.0	61.202	0.990	0.990	0.956	0.651
800.0	69.945	0.990	0.990	0.934	0.602
900.0	78.689	0.990	0.990	0.911	0.559
1000.0	87.432	0.990	0.987	0.887	0.522
1100.0	96.175	0.990	0.981	0.862	0.489
1200.0	104.918	0.990	0.974	0.837	0.459

DAMAGE 46/.41

▼ M24 SWS

CARTRIDGE	7.62x51 mm
OPERATION	Manual bolt action
TYPE OF FIRE	Single shot repeater
RATE OF FIRE	(SS) 20 rpm
MUZZLE VELOCITY	792 m/s (2600 fps)
MUZZLE ENERGY	3561 J (2626 ft/lb)
SIGHTS	M3 Ultra 10 power telescopic sight w/backup adjustable aperture/blade, iron sights
FEED	5 round internal magazine

WEIGHTS:
WEAPON (EMPTY) 5.947 kg w/bipod
WEAPON (LOADED) 6.074 kg w/bipod and 5 rounds
MAGAZINE (LOADED) 0.127 kg (5 rounds)
SERVICE CARTRIDGE 25.3 g
BULLET 11.4 g
LENGTHS:
WEAPON OVERALL 109 cm
BARREL 61 cm
SIGHT RADIUS 69 cm (iron sights)
STATUS In production
SERVICE U.S. Army
COST $5,000

Range	Group Circle Width (mm)	Probability (0<p<.099) (m)			
		Body	Head	Hand	Bullseye
500.0	55.556	0.990	0.990	0.968	0.687
600.0	66.667	0.990	0.990	0.943	0.620
700.0	77.778	0.990	0.990	0.914	0.564
800.0	88.889	0.990	0.986	0.883	0.516
900.0	100.000	0.990	0.978	0.851	0.475
1000.0	111.111	0.990	0.968	0.820	0.440
1100.0	122.222	0.990	0.956	0.790	0.410
1200.0	133.333	0.990	0.943	0.760	0.384

DAMAGE 47/.42

▼ RAI Model 300

CARTRIDGE 7.62x51mm (8.58x71mm)
OPERATION Manual bolt action
TYPE OF FIRE Single shot repeater
RATE OF FIRE (SS)16 rpm (12 rpm)
MUZZLE VELOCITY 800 m/s (2625 fps)
(915 m/s <3002 fps>)
MUZZLE ENERGY 3630 J (2677 ft/lb),
(6783 J <5002 ft/lb>)
SIGHTS Telescopic (Leupold M8 12
power target)
FEED 5 (4) round removable box magazine
WEIGHTS:
WEAPON (EMPTY) 6.442 kg w/scope & base
WEAPON (LOADED) 6.776 w/5 rds (6.823 kg w/4 rds)
MAGAZINE (EMPTY) 0.207 kg
MAGAZINE (LOADED) 0.334 kg (0.381 kg)
SERVICE CARTRIDGE 25.3 g (43.6 kg)
BULLET 11.4 g (16.2 g)
LENGTHS:
WEAPON OVERALL 139 cm
BARREL 61 cm
STATUS Limited production
SERVICE Some U.S. military service
COST $8000

The M24 Sniper Weapon System has been accepted as the new U.S. Army sniper rifle and will be replacing the M21 system starting in 1988. The M24 weapon is basically a Remington M700 with a heavy barrel fitted into a fiberglass stock. The entire assembly receives a black, non-reflective coating. The telescopic sight is a fixed power scope with a graduated reticle, allowing it to be used for limited range determination. A removable micrometer style set of iron sights are supplied with each weapon to be used in the event of the primary telescopic sight being damaged. A commercially produced Harris bipod, protective transit case, and assortment of spare parts completes the weapon system. A specific intent behind using the long action of the Remington 700 is the possibility of rechambering the weapon to fire the .300 Winchester Magnum cartridge (7.62x 66mmB). As the Army is considering the use of the Magnum round for its additional long range capabilities in the sniper role, the bolt-action system allows for this change economically while other systems, especially semiautomatic weapons, have prohibitive difficulties accepting a major caliber change.

WEAPON M24 SWS
AMMO 7.62x51
10 x power scope installed.
DISPERSION ANGLE .0063662 degrees, .113177 NATO mils.

Range	Group Circle Width (mm)	Probability (0<p<.099) (m)			
		Body	Head	Hand	Bullseye
50.0	5.556	0.990	0.990	0.990	0.990
100.0	11.111	0.990	0.990	0.990	0.990
150.0	16.667	0.990	0.990	0.990	0.979
200.0	22.222	0.990	0.990	0.990	0.945
250.0	27.778	0.990	0.990	0.990	0.902
300.0	33.333	0.990	0.990	0.990	0.856
350.0	38.889	0.990	0.990	0.990	0.810
400.0	44.444	0.990	0.990	0.986	0.766
450.0	50.000	0.990	0.990	0.978	0.725

☞ continued

This unusual appearing weapon is designed specifically as a long range sniper weapon and has been tested by the U.S. Government. The barrel is deeply fluted for strength and heat radiating surface area and is full floating, that is, unsupported for its entire length. Changing calibers is simply removing the barrel and bolt head and replacing them with one of another caliber. A specific round developed with this rifle is the 8.58 x 71mm. The 8.58 mm round is a .416 Rigby rifle round necked down to accept a .338 bullet. The result of this is a high velocity round firing

☞ continued on next page

☞ *RAI Model 300 continued*

a heavy bullet with an overall length short enough to fit in a standard length rifle action. The receiver of the RAI 300 is made from a solid bar of steel with openings only for ejection and the magazine, giving a very rigid receiver. The long bar underneath the barrel contains an adjustable tuning rod that dampens barrel vibration, greatly adding to accuracy. The adjustable bipod is placed on the end of the tuner housing so that it can support the weapon without interfering with the barrel. The buttstock is fully adjustable for length and height to fit a variety of shooters. The scope mounting is interesting in that it can be ballistically matched to the round being used and by adjusting the range wheel, graduated from 300 to 1500 meters in 100 meter increments, the point of aim will center to the point of impact. Any standard sighting device can be fitted to the adjustable mount with a telescopic sight of 12 power or greater being the normal fixture.

WEAPON RAI Model 300
AMMO 8.58x71
12 x power scope installed.
DISPERSION ANGLE .0068755 degrees, .122231 NATO mils.

Range	Group Circle Width (mm)	Probability (0<p<.099) (m)			
		Body	Head	Hand	Bullseye
50.0	6.000	0.990	0.990	0.990	0.990
100.0*	12.000	0.990	0.990	0.990	0.990
150.0	18.000	0.990	0.990	0.990	0.972
200.0	24.000	0.990	0.990	0.990	0.932
250.0	30.000	0.990	0.990	0.990	0.884
300.0	36.000	0.990	0.990	0.990	0.833
350.0	42.000	0.990	0.990	0.989	0.785
400.0	48.000	0.990	0.990	0.981	0.739
450.0	54.000	0.990	0.990	0.971	0.697
500.0	60.000	0.990	0.990	0.958	0.659
600.0	72.000	0.990	0.990	0.929	0.592
700.0	84.000	0.990	0.989	0.896	0.536
800.0	96.000	0.990	0.981	0.863	0.489
900.0	108.000	0.990	0.971	0.829	0.450
1000.0	120.000	0.990	0.958	0.796	0.416
1100.0	132.000	0.990	0.944	0.764	0.387
1200.0	144.000	0.990	0.929	0.734	0.361
1300.0	156.000	0.990	0.913	0.705	0.339
1400.0	168.000	0.989	0.896	0.678	0.319
1500.0	180.000	0.985	0.880	0.653	0.301
1600.0	192.000	0.981	0.863	0.629	0.285
1700.0	204.000	0.976	0.846	0.607	0.271
1800.0	216.000	0.971	0.829	0.586	0.258
1900.0	228.000	0.965	0.812	0.566	0.246
2000.0	240.000	0.958	0.796	0.548	0.236

DAMAGE 61/.78 (48/.42 7.62x51)

▼ RAI Model 500

CARTRIDGE 12.7x99mm
OPERATION Manual bolt action
TYPE OF FIRE Single shot
RATE OF FIRE (SS) 6 rpm
MUZZLE VELOCITY 888 m/s (2913 fps)
MUZZLE ENERGY 18137 J (13375 ft/lb) M33, 16093 J (11868 ft/lb) Match
SIGHTS Telescopic sight fitted (Leupold M8-24 power)
FEED Single round
WEIGHTS:
WEAPON (EMPTY) 15.153 w/scope & base
WEAPON (LOADED) 15.271 kg
SERVICE CARTRIDGE (M33) (113 g Match)
BULLET 46.2 g (M33) (40.8 gr Match)
LENGTHS:
WEAPON OVERALL 139 cm
BARREL 84 cm
STATUS Limited production
SERVICE Some U.S. military service
COST $9000

This is a companion weapon to the RAI 300 and greatly follows it in design. Chambered for the .50 Browning round, the RAI 500 has both a rearward angled muzzle brake as well as a combination flash hider/muzzle brake mounted on its heavy, fluted barrel. The action is a multi-lug bolt that acts much like the breech plug on an artillery piece. The bolt is removed by rotating it, and a single cartridge is placed under the extractor. The bolt is reinserted to load the weapon. This unusual system of loading results in a very short action and a slow, but very accurate, rate of fire. The Ranging Scope base described in the RAI 300 is used in the 500 model, usually with a very powerful telescopic sight, 24 power or greater. There is a harmonic balancer tuning fork contained in the bipod support underneath the barrel. The RAI 500 has reportedly been used by the U.S. Navy SEALS but little information has been released. The standard .50 caliber M2 and M33 ball will only give an 18 or 24 inch group respectively at 600 yards (45.7cm or 61cm at 549 meters) and will not reach the maximum accuracy available from the RA1 500. A specialized "match" grade of .50 caliber round is available and should be fired from the RA1 500 when used in the field. Accuracy with the standard military ammunition is acceptable in military sniping missions where the targets for a weapon of this power would normally be vehicles and aircraft.

ASSESSMENT 61 cm @ 549 m w/M33 ball, 16.5 cm @ 457 m w/Match ammo
WEAPON RAI Model 500

AMMO 12.7x99 M33

24 x power scope installed.

DISPERSION ANGLE .063662 degrees, 1.13177 NATO mils.

Range	Group Circle Width (mm)	Probability (0<p<.099) (m)			
		Body	Head	Hand	Bullseye
50.0	55.556	0.990	0.990	0.968	0.687
100.0	111.111	0.990	0.968	0.820	0.440
150.0	166.667	0.990	0.898	0.681	0.321
200.0	222.222	0.968	0.820	0.576	0.252
250.0	277.778	0.936	0.746	0.496	0.207
300.0	333.333	0.898	0.681	0.435	0.176
350.0	388.889	0.859	0.625	0.387	0.153
400.0	444.444	0.820	0.576	0.349	0.135
450.0	500.000	0.782	0.533	0.317	0.121
500.0	555.556	0.746	0.496	0.290	0.110
600.0	666.667	0.681	0.435	0.249	0.092
700.0	777.778	0.625	0.387	0.217	0.080
800.0	888.889	0.576	0.349	0.193	0.070
900.0	1000.000	0.533	0.317	0.173	0.062
1000.0	1111.111	0.496	0.290	0.158	0.056
1100.0	1222.222	0.464	0.268	0.144	0.051
1200.0	1333.333	0.435	0.249	0.133	0.047
1300.0	1444.444	0.410	0.232	0.124	0.044
1400.0	1555.556	0.387	0.217	0.115	0.041
1500.0	1666.667	0.367	0.204	0.108	0.038
1600.0	1777.778	0.349	0.193	0.102	0.036
1700.0	1888.889	0.332	0.183	0.096	0.034
1800.0	2000.000	0.317	0.173	0.091	0.032
1900.0	2111.111	0.303	0.165	0.086	0.030
2000.0	2222.222	0.290	0.158	0.082	0.029

DAMAGE 87/3.13

WEAPON RAI MODEL 500

AMMO 12.7x99 MATCH

24 x power scope installed.

DISPERSION ANGLE .0206867 degrees, .367763 NATO mils.

Range	Group Circle Width (mm)	Probability (0<p<.099) (m)			
		Body	Head	Hand	Bullseye
50.0	18.053	0.990	0.990	0.990	0.972
100.0	36.105	0.990	0.990	0.990	0.832
150.0	54.158	0.990	0.990	0.970	0.696
200.0	72.210	0.990	0.990	0.929	0.591
250.0	90.263	0.990	0.985	0.879	0.511
300.0	108.315	0.990	0.970	0.828	0.449
350.0	126.368	0.990	0.951	0.779	0.400

Range	Group Circle Width (mm)	Probability (0<p<.099) (m)			
		Body	Head	Hand	Bullseye
400.0	144.420	0.990	0.929	0.733	0.360
450.0	162.473	0.990	0.904	0.690	0.328
500.0	180.525	0.985	0.879	0.652	0.300
600.0	216.630	0.970	0.828	0.585	0.258
700.0	252.735	0.951	0.779	0.529	0.225
800.0	288.840	0.929	0.733	0.483	0.200
900.0	324.945	0.904	0.690	0.444	0.180
1000.0	361.050	0.879	0.652	0.410	0.164
1100.0	397.155	0.853	0.617	0.381	0.150
1200.0	433.260	0.828	0.585	0.356	0.138
1300.0	469.365	0.803	0.556	0.334	0.128
1400.0	505.470	0.779	0.529	0.314	0.120
1500.0	541.575	0.755	0.505	0.297	0.112
1600.0	577.681	0.733	0.483	0.281	0.106
1700.0	613.786	0.711	0.462	0.267	0.100
1800.0	649.891	0.690	0.444	0.254	0.094
1900.0	685.996	0.671	0.426	0.242	0.090
2000.0	722.101	0.652	0.410	0.232	0.085

DAMAGE 87/2.78

▼ AR 15A2 Delta HBAR

CARTRIDGE	5.56x45mm
OPERATION	Gas direct action
TYPE OF FIRE	Semiautomatic
RATE OF FIRE (SS)	45 rpm
MUZZLE VELOCITY	1000 m/s (3281 fps)
MUZZLE ENERGY	1977 J (1458 ft/lb)
SIGHTS	3- 9 power telescopic sight (primary), adjustable, aperture/post, range 800 m (backup)
FEED	20, 30, or 30/45 round removable box magazine
WEIGHTS:	
WEAPON (EMPTY)	4.536 kg
WEAPON (LOADED)	5.019 kg w/30 rds
MAGAZINE (EMPTY)	0.091 kg (20 rd), 0.117 kg (30 rd), 0.149 kg (30/45 rd)
MAGAZINE (LOADED)	0.335 kg (20 rd, 0.483 kg (30 rd), 0.698 kg (30/45 rd w/45 rds)
SERVICE CARTRIDGE	12.2 g
BULLET	4 g
LENGTHS:	
WEAPON OVERALL	99.1 cm
BARREL	50.8 cm
SIGHT RADIUS	50.1 cm

☞ continued

THE EDGE OF THE SWORD

STATUS In production
SERVICE Commercial sales

The HBAR, Heavy Barreled Automatic Rifle, is an interesting development from the M16A2 program. Initially, the M16A2 was to have a heavier barrel for its entire length but it was found that some accessories, most notably the M203 40mm grenade launcher, would not be able to clip onto the heavy barrel without modification. Because of the accessory problem, the full-length heavy barrel was dropped from the M16A2. In the HBAR model, the full length heavy barrel, 0.96 inch diameter up to the front sight, is returned to the M16A2 model with all of its advantages. The primary advantage is that the HBAR model can group its shots to 1 1/2 Minutes of Angle (MOA) against 2 to 3 MOA for the M16A2. The additional weight of the heavy barrel also adds to the stability and quick second-shot recovery of the weapon. The use of a telescopic sight as a standard sight also allows the DELTA HBAR to take advantage of the design's greater intrinsic accuracy. The high cheekpiece attached to the buttstock gives the shooter a solid head/cheek rest when using the telescopic sight. The unusual shape of the cheekpiece is dictated by the design of the rifle, with the cutout being needed to clear the cocking handle. As the civilian semiautomatic fire only version, the AR-15A2 Delta HBAR is receiving a good welcome from military match shooters as well as police departments because of its excellent accuracy. This accuracy results in the Delta HBAR being a practical sniper system out to approximately 300 meters.

WEAPON: AR15-A2 Delta HBAR
AMMO: 5.56x45 9 x power scope installed.
Dispersion angle: .0238733 degrees, .424414 NATO mils.

Range	Group Circle Width (mm)	Probability (0<p<.099) (m)			
		Body	Head	Hand	Bullseye
25.0	10.417	0.990	0.990	0.990	0.990
50.0	20.833	0.990	0.990	0.990	0.955
75.0	31.250	0.990	0.990	0.990	0.873
100.0	41.667	0.990	0.990	0.990	0.787
125.0	52.083	0.990	0.990	0.974	0.710
150.0	62.500	0.990	0.990	0.953	0.644
175.0	72.917	0.990	0.990	0.927	0.587
200.0	83.333	0.990	0.990	0.898	0.539
250.0	104.167	0.990	0.974	0.839	0.462
300.0	125.000	0.990	0.953	0.782	0.403
350.0	145.833	0.990	0.927	0.729	0.357
400.0	166.667	0.990	0.898	0.681	0.321
450.0	187.500	0.983	0.869	0.638	0.291
500.0	208.333	0.974	0.839	0.599	0.266

DAMAGE 39/0.67

RAI MODEL 500

AR15A2 Delta HBAR without magazine

CHAPTER 5

SHOTGUNS

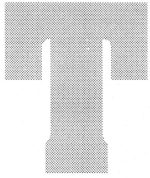

he combat shotgun has long been recognized as an effective close-in fighting weapon in the United States with some military units of the Civil War Confederate Cavalry being armed solely with sawed-off double-barrel 12 gauges. The U.S. has issued shotguns for combat duty since World War One and they were highly valued by troops in the Pacific

Theater of World War Two as well as in the jungles of Vietnam. Police forces throughout North America have also valued the shotgun for its great psychological as well as physical effect. With the possible exception of Italy, shotguns have long been ignored as combat weapons in Europe, but this attitude has been changing in recent years.

The primary reason for the popularity of the fighting shotgun is its great destructive potential and flexibility. The destructiveness is due to the shotgun being able to launch a swarm of projectiles for each shot fired with each sub-projectile having lethal potential. The projectiles gradually spread into a circular pattern as they travel from the muzzle of the weapon with the circle becoming larger as the distance increases. At longer ranges, above 40 meters for most weapons, the circular pattern is so large that only a few or one projectile would hit a man-sized target. Close in, (under five meters), the projectiles would be so closely packed together that they would strike as a single mass and do tremendous damage. The speed at which the pattern opens

over distance is determined by the barrel length and the amount of choke which the barrel has. The shorter a barrel is, the more rapidly the shot will spread, although not at the great rate depicted in modern cinema. A very short barrel will still have all of its projectiles strike as a single mass at close range, but the muzzle blast and recoil will be very great and cause the weapon to be difficult to control. Choke is the constriction at the muzzle of a shotgun's barrel and the amount of this constriction is the degree of choke. "No Choke" is referred to as a cylinder with the maximum construction being called "full choke." Any constriction tighter than full choke tends to damage the shot as it is fired in addition to it being forced outward by the pressure of the shot passing through. Between the two extremes of cylinder and full choke, there is improved cylinder and modified, with additional grades for specific applications. Most combat shotguns have relatively short barrels for quick handling plus cylinder choke for quick shot spread.

The most common type of shotgun used today is the pump or slide action weapon

which has seen wide use and acceptance. Some of the limitations of the pump action are its requiring two hands for use as well as its being difficult to operate in a prone position. The semiautomatic shotgun is becoming more common with its ability to be operated with one hand from almost any position. The fast firepower of the semiautomatic has also led to a new idea in shotguns: that of the machine shotgun which is capable of full automatic fire. This class of weapon is still relatively new, but has seen some field use in the hands of combat troops. The United States Navy's Close Assault Weapon System (CAWS) trials are an attempt to combine the massive firepower of a selective fire shotgun with a new family of ammunition, making it combat effective on a single target at a range of 150 meters. In combination with the new weapon is a requirement for it to be loaded from removable box magazines, greatly increasing the speed of reloading the weapon over the cumbersome tubular magazine style loaded with single rounds. ●

▼ Heckler & Koch HK 512

CARTRIDGE	18.5x70mmR
OPERATION	Gas
TYPE OF FIRE	Semiautomatic
RATE OF FIRE	(SS) 21 rpm
MUZZLE VELOCITY	350 m/s (1148 fps)
MUZZLE ENERGY	2571 J (1896 ft/lb), 214 J (158 ft/lb) per pellet
SIGHTS	Fixed, non-adjustable, U-notch/blade
FEED	7 round tubular magazine
WEIGHTS:	
WEAPON (EMPTY)	3.100 kg
WEAPON (LOADED)	3.548 kg
MAGAZINE (LOADED)	0.448 kg (7 rds)
SERVICE CARTRIDGE	64 g
BULLET	42 g (12 x 3.5 g)
LENGTHS:	
WEAPON OVERALL	102 cm
BARREL	46.3 cm
SIGHT RADIUS	30 cm
STATUS	In production

This is an Italian design by the Luigi Franchi company that is marketed by the Heckler and Koch company of Germany. The Model 512 has been primarily sold to German police organizations with over 500 being sold. The outline of the weapon follows standard lines with a fixed stock and extended magazine. The major difference between the HK 512 and the original Franchi PG 80 is the addition of a two-to-one shot diverter on the muzzle of the HK weapon. The shot diverter changes the pattern of the shot from a simple circle to a vertical oval twice as tall as it is wide. The pattern works out to an oval with a vertical spread of 80 cm and a horizontal spread of 50 cm at 20 meters when fired with buckshot. The use of a vertical rather than horizontal spread increase allows the shotgun to be used in a hostage situation where a target could be taken out with less risk to innocent bystanders, and by simply firing with the weapon held on its side, allows a much greater probability of a hit on a single target.

ASSESSMENT	50 cm at 20 m
WEAPON	H&K 512 w/Diverter
AMMO	18.5x70 00 Magnum
DISPERSION ANGLE	2.29153 degrees, 40.7383 NATO mils.

Range	Group Circle Width (mm)	Probability (0<p<.099) (m)			
		Body	Head	Hand	Bullseye
5.0	200.000	0.978	0.851	0.614	0.276
10.0	400.000	0.851	0.614	0.379	0.149
15.0	600.000	0.719	0.470	0.272	0.102

☞ continued

Range	Group Circle Width (mm)	Probability (0<p<.099) (m)			
		Body	Head	Hand	Bullseye
20.0*	800.000	0.614	0.379	0.212	0.077
25.0	1000.000	0.533	0.317	0.173	0.062
30.0	1200.000	0.470	0.272	0.147	0.052
35.0	1400.000	0.420	0.238	0.127	0.045
40.0	1600.000	0.379	0.212	0.112	0.040
45.0	1800.000	0.345	0.191	0.100	0.035
50.0	2000.000	0.317	0.173	0.091	0.032

* indicates range for which data was supplied

DAMAGE	12 pellets 14/1.20, 8 pellets 14/0.80, 4 pellets 14/0.40, 1 pellet 14/0.10

▼ SPAS-12

SPAS-12 set on semiautomatic with stock folded

CARTRIDGE	18.5x70mmR
OPERATION	Gas or manual pump action
TYPE OF FIRE	Semiautomatic or single shot repeater
RATE OF FIRE	(SS) 24 rpm
MUZZLE VELOCITY	385 m/s (1262 fps)
MUZZLE ENERGY	4032 J (2976 ft/lb), 336 J (248 ft/lb) per pellet
SIGHTS	Fixed, non-adjustable, aperture/blade
FEED	8 round tubular magazine
WEIGHTS:	
WEAPON (EMPTY)	4.354 kg
WEAPON (LOADED)	4.866 kg x@3
MAGAZINE (LOADED)	0.512 kg
SERVICE CARTRIDGE	64 g
BULLET	42 g (12 x 3.5 g)
LENGTHS:	
WEAPON OVERALL	71/93 cm
BARREL	46 cm
SIGHT RADIUS	37.9 cm
STATUS	In production
SERVICE	Commercial sales

☞ continued on next page

☞ *SPAS-12 continued*

COST $700

The SPAS 12 is a very unusual weapon both in appearance and action. SPAS stands for either Special Purpose Automatic Shotgun or Sporting Purpose Automatic Shotgun, depending on who the weapon is being sold to. The sporting purpose of this weapon is hard to see from its appearance as a massive weapon of very lethal intentions. The action of the SPAS can be switched from gas operated semiautomatic to pump action repeater by a simple action of the operator. When in the semiautomatic mode the weapon is capable of firing up to four rounds a second using the most powerful ammunition available. In the pump-action mode the act of operating the weapon can deter a situation and prevent escalation. In the pump action mode the SPAS can repeatedly fire rounds such as light shot or tear gas shells that would not have enough power to operate the weapon on semiautomatic. The barrel is threaded at the muzzle to accept a variety of accessories. The accessories include a grenade launcher for canister type grenades, an assortment of chokes, and a shot diverter much like the one on the HK 512 , but one which can be rotated to put the long axis of the pattern horizontal or vertical. The folding stock locks solidly into position either open or closed. With the stock closed the SPAS can be hung over the seat of a vehicle by rotating the hook attachment. This same hook attachment acts as an arm brace with the stock unfolded and allows the SPAS to be controllably fired with only one hand. The mechanism is complex and takes some getting used to, but the SPAS operates effectively though it is quite heavy for its type. The tubular magazine is loaded from underneath the weapon, just in front of the trigger guard. The manufacturer states a qualified operator can load the seven round magazine in 15 seconds, giving the SPAS a rate of fire of 25 to 30 rounds per minute.

WEAPON SPAS 12 w/Cylinder choke
AMMO 18.5x70 00 Magnum
DISPERSION ANGLE 1.69583 degrees, 30.1481 NATO mils.

Range	Group Circle Width (mm)	Probability (0<p<.099) (m)			
		Body	Head	Hand	Bullseye
5.0	148.000	0.990	0.924	0.724	0.353
10.0*	296.000	0.924	0.724	0.475	0.196
15.0	444.000	0.820	0.576	0.349	0.135
20.0	592.000	0.724	0.475	0.275	0.103
25.0	740.000	0.643	0.402	0.227	0.083
30.0	888.000	0.576	0.349	0.193	0.070
35.0	1036.000	0.521	0.308	0.168	0.060
40.0	1184.000	0.475	0.275	0.149	0.053
45.0	1332.000	0.436	0.249	0.133	0.047
50.0	1480.000	0.402	0.227	0.121	0.043

* indicates range for which data was supplied
DAMAGE 12 pellets 15/1.68, 8 pellets 15/1.12, 4 pellets 15/0.56, 1 pellet 15/0.14

▼ SPAS-15

CARTRIDGE	18.5x70mmR
OPERATION	Gas or manual pump action
TYPE OF FIRE	semiautomatic or single shot repeater
RATE OF FIRE	(SS) 30 rpm
MUZZLE VELOCITY	339 m/s (1111 fps)
MUZZLE ENERGY	2408 J (1776 ft/lb), 201 J (148 ft/lb) per pellet
SIGHTS	Fixed, non-adjustable, notch/post
FEED	6 round removable box magazine
WEIGHTS:	
WEAPON (EMPTY)	3.800 kg
WEAPON (LOADED)	4.410 kg
MAGAZINE (EMPTY)	0.226 kg
MAGAZINE (LOADED)	0.610 kg
SERVICE CARTRIDGE	64 g
BULLET	42 g (12 x 3.5 g)
LENGTHS:	
WEAPON OVERALL	92 cm
BARREL	40 cm
SIGHT RADIUS	52.2 cm
STATUS	Commercial sales

This is a modified version of the SPAS-12 intended primarily for military sales. The major change is the switch from a tubular magazine to a removable box magazine. Besides the obvious changes to accept the magazine, the gas operation system was placed over the barrel to shorten the distance that the shell must travel from the magazine to the barrel. The SPAS-12 system of semiautomatic and pump action is retained in the SPAS-15 and the mode of operation selected by a thumb switch on the top of the slide grip. The cocking handle for the semiautomatic action is the lever on top of the receiver, protected by the carrying handle. The bolt locks back after the last shot is fired and inserting a loaded magazine releases the bolt, loading the first round.

WEAPON SPAS 15 w/Cylinder choke
AMMO 18.5x70 00 Magnum
DISPERSION ANGLE 1.69583 degrees, 30.1481 NATO mils.

☞ *continued*

Range	Group Circle Width (mm)	Probability (0<p<.099) (m)			
		Body	Head	Hand	Bullseye
5.0	148.000	0.990	0.924	0.724	0.353
10.0*	296.000	0.924	0.724	0.475	0.196
15.0	444.000	0.820	0.576	0.349	0.135
20.0	592.000	0.724	0.475	0.275	0.103
25.0	740.000	0.643	0.402	0.227	0.083
30.0	888.000	0.576	0.349	0.193	0.070
35.0	1036.000	0.521	0.308	0.168	0.060
40.0	1184.000	0.475	0.275	0.149	0.053
45.0	1332.000	0.436	0.249	0.133	0.047
50.0	1480.000	0.402	0.227	0.121	0.043

* indicates range for which data was supplied

DAMAGE 12 pellets 14/1.08, 8 pellets 14/0.72, 4 pellets 14/0.36, 1 pellet 14/0.09

▼ PA-3/215

CARTRIDGE	18.5x70mmR
OPERATION	Manual pump action
TYPE OF FIRE	Single shot repeater
RATE OF FIRE	(SS)12 rpm
MUZZLE VELOCITY	305 m/s (1002 fps)
MUZZLE ENERGY	1953 J (1440 ft/lb), 163 J (120 ft/lb) per pellet
SIGHTS	None
FEED	3 round tubular magazine
WEIGHTS:	
WEAPON (EMPTY)	2.700 kg (2.300 kg w/o stock)
WEAPON (LOADED)	2.892 kg (2.492 kg w/o stock)
MAGAZINE (LOADED)	0.192 kg (3 rds)
SERVICE CARTRIDGE	64 g
BULLET	42 g (12 x 3.5 g)
LENGTHS:	
WEAPON OVERALL	47/71.5 cm
BARREL	21.5 cm
STATUS	In production

This is one of the smallest large caliber shotguns presently being produced in Europe. The action is a straightforward manual pump action developed from the pump system used in the SPAS-12. There is a large safety switch on the forward right hand side of the trigger guard that can be easily operated by the firing finger. The two pistol grips allow for good control of the PA3215 with a fast second round recovery. The muzzle of the PA3 is threaded to accept the full line of Franchi shotgun accessories, choke tubes, diverters, and a canister grenade launcher, though the recoil with its use would be severe. The folding stock locks into position, either open or closed, and may be easily removed to allow for maximum concealability of the weapon (such as under a coat during VIP protection). The psychological and physical effect of a shotgun is well known in the Americas but is just now being accepted in Europe. The PA3 design originates from Franchi in Italy where the shotgun has been used as a combat weapon for some years.

WEAPON	PA-3/215
AMMO	18.5x70 00 Magnum
DISPERSION ANGLE	1.91094 degrees, 33.9722 NATO mils.

Range	Group Circle Width (mm)	Probability (0<p<.099) (m)			
		Body	Head	Hand	Bullseye
5.0	166.776	0.990	0.898	0.681	0.321
10.0	333.552	0.898	0.681	0.435	0.176
15.0	500.328	0.782	0.533	0.317	0.121
20.0	667.104	0.681	0.435	0.248	0.092
25.0	833.880	0.599	0.367	0.204	0.074
30.0	1000.656	0.533	0.317	0.173	0.062
35.0	1167.432	0.479	0.278	0.151	0.054
40.0	1334.208	0.435	0.248	0.133	0.047
45.0	1500.984	0.398	0.224	0.119	0.042
50.0	1667.760	0.367	0.204	0.108	0.038

DAMAGE 12 pellets 12/0.96, 8 pellets 12/0.64, 4 pellets 12/0.32, 1 pellet 12/0.08

▼ Bernadelli B4 • B4/B

Bernadelli B4/B with stock extended

CARTRIDGE	18.5x70mmR
OPERATION	Gas/manual pump action (manual pump action)
TYPE OF FIRE	Semiautomatic/single shot repeater
RATE OF FIRE	(SS) 32 rpm
MUZZLE VELOCITY	350 m/s (1147 fps)
MUZZLE ENERGY	2571 J (1896 ft/lb), 214 J (158 ft/lb) per pellet
SIGHTS	Fixed, non-adjustable, notch/blade
FEED	3, 5, or 8 round removable box magazine
WEIGHTS:	
WEAPON (EMPTY)	3.45 kg (3.00 kg B4/B)
WEAPON (LOADED)	4.302 kg (3.852 kg B4/B)

MAGAZINE (EMPTY)	0.340 kg (8 rd)
MAGAZINE (LOADED)	0.852 kg (8 rd)
SERVICE CARTRIDGE	64 g
BULLET	42 g (12 x 3.5 g)
LENGTHS:	
WEAPON OVERALL	73/95 cm
BARREL	46 cm
SIGHT RADIUS	38.4 cm
STATUS	Under development

This is a pair of weapons developed for the military and police markets. The B4 model can be switched from a gas operated, semiautomatic mode to a manual pump action by a simple selection lever. The B4/B model is a manual pump action only weapon that is almost identical to the B4 model except for the missing gas operation parts, removing about 0.450 kg from the weight of the weapon. The B4 series has an aluminum alloy frame dark finished for a glare free surface. The barrel is of steel and the external diameter is such that the weapon can launch standard rifle grenades. The folding stock locks firmly in place, and when folded, lies along the right side of the weapon. The high profile sights combined with the stock design give a recoil that is in line with the shooter's shoulder, minimizing muzzle climb from recoil. The removable box magazine changes the loading time from the 15 seconds for a standard tubular 8 round magazine weapon to under two seconds for the box magazine, also holding eight rounds.

WEAPON	Bernadelli B4 w/Cylinder choke
AMMO	18.5x70 00 Magnum
DISPERSION ANGLE	1.69583 degrees, 30.1481 NATO mils.

Range	Group Circle Width (mm)	Probability (0<p<.099) (m)			
		Body	**Head**	**Hand**	**Bullseye**
5.0	148.000	0.990	0.924	0.724	0.353
10.0*	296.000	0.924	0.724	0.475	0.196
15.0	444.000	0.820	0.576	0.349	0.135
20.0	592.000	0.724	0.475	0.275	0.103
25.0	740.000	0.643	0.402	0.227	0.083
30.0	888.000	0.576	0.349	0.193	0.070
35.0	1036.000	0.521	0.308	0.168	0.060
40.0	1184.000	0.475	0.275	0.149	0.053
45.0	1332.000	0.436	0.249	0.133	0.047
50.0	1480.000	0.402	0.227	0.121	0.043

* indicates range for which data was supplied

DAMAGE 12 pellets 14/1.20, 8 pellets 14/0.80, 4 pellets 14/0.40, 1 pellet 14/0.10

▼ Benelli 121 M1

CARTRIDGE	18.5x70mmR
OPERATION	Recoil
TYPE OF FIRE	Semiautomatic
RATE OF FIRE	(SS) 28 rpm
MUZZLE VELOCITY	358 m/s (1175 fps)
MUZZLE ENERGY	2701 J (1992 ft/lb), 225 J (166 ft/lb) per pellet
SIGHTS	Fixed, non-adjustable, notch/blade
FEED	7 round tubular magazine
WEIGHTS:	
WEAPON (EMPTY)	3.450 kg
WEAPON (LOADED)	3.898 kg
MAGAZINE (LOADED)	0.448 kg (7 rds)
SERVICE CARTRIDGE	64 g
BULLET	42 g (12 x 3.5 g)
LENGTHS:	
WEAPON OVERALL	99.1 cm
BARREL	50.8 cm
SIGHT RADIUS	41.3 cm
STATUS	In production
SERVICE	Commercial sales
COST	$500

Utilizing a unique system of recoil operation, the Benelli is the fastest operating semiautomatic shotgun available and is found in the hands of the British SAS, amongst other organizations. The speed of operation is a direct result of the recoil operation that uses the inertia of the bolt carrier to unlock the rotating bolt after pressures have dropped to a safe level, but before the weapon has reached full recoil. An expert operator is able to fire all eight shots before the first empty shell has hit the ground, under one second. Another result of this recoil action is the excellent reliability of operation for which the system is noted. The requirement for a recoil spring extending into the stock prevents any type of folding stock from being fitted to the M121. The receiver separates into an upper and lower section, easing cleaning and maintenance. The stocks are of walnut and are found to be somewhat short for most U.S. users, a matter simply remedied by the addition of spacers and a recoil pad.

WEAPON	Benelli M121 w/Cylinder choke
AMMO	18.5x70 00 Magnum
DISPERSION ANGLE	1.69583 degrees, 30.1481 NATO mils.

Range	Group Circle Width (mm)	Probability (0<p<.099) (m)			
		Body	Head	Hand	Bullseye
5.0	148.000	0.990	0.924	0.724	0.353
10.0*	296.000	0.924	0.724	0.475	0.196
15.0	444.000	0.820	0.576	0.349	0.135
20.0	592.000	0.724	0.475	0.275	0.103
25.0	740.000	0.643	0.402	0.227	0.083
30.0	888.000	0.576	0.349	0.193	0.070
35.0	1036.000	0.521	0.308	0.168	0.060
40.0	1184.000	0.475	0.275	0.149	0.053
45.0	1332.000	0.436	0.249	0.133	0.047
50.0	1480.000	0.402	0.227	0.121	0.043

* indicates range for which data was supplied

DAMAGE	12 pellets 14/1.20, 8 pellets 14/0.80, 4 pellets 14/0.40 1 pellet 14/0.10

▼ Beretta M3P

M3P with stock extended

M3P with stock folded and magazine removed. Action is set to manual operation with bolt and slide to rear

CARTRIDGE	18.5 x 70mm R
OPERATION	Recoil or manual pump action
TYPE OF FIRE	Semiautomatic or single shot repeater
RATE OF FIRE	(SS) 30 rpm
MUZZLE VELOCITY	339 m/s (1111 fps)
MUZZLE ENERGY	2408 J (1776 ft/lb), 201 J (148 ft/lb) per pellet
SIGHTS	Fixed, non-adjustable, aperture/post

FEED	5 round removable box magazine
WEIGHTS:	
WEAPON (EMPTY)	3.210 kg
WEAPON (LOADED)	3.860 kg
MAGAZINE (EMPTY)	0.330 kg
MAGAZINE (LOADED)	0.650 kg
SERVICE CARTRIDGE	64 g
BULLET	42 g (12 x 3.5 g)
LENGTHS:	
WEAPON OVERALL	68.6/94.5 cm
BARREL	40.2 cm
SIGHT RADIUS	32.5 cm
STATUS	In production
COST	$700

The M3P is most notable for being the first box magazine-fed shotgun to reach production status with a major arms manufacturer. The magazine is of standard layout, specially reinforced to withstand the shock of recoil without tearing free of the weapon. The action of the M3P can be easily switched from semiautomatic to manual pump action by the use of a locking ring at the front of the forend. By pushing the forend forward and rotating the locking ring, the forend is locked in place, putting the weapon into the semiautomatic mode and giving a very high rate of fire with quick follow-up shots. With the forend unlocked, it reciprocates and operates the weapon as a pump action repeater, capable of using any available 12 gauge (18.5 x 70mm R) ammunition, including the lightest loads. The folding stock swings over the top of the receiver and locks in place to both act as a carrying handle and giving the weapon the shortest overall length for quick handling. The stock locks into the rear sight when folded and prevents use of the sights when in the folded configuration.

WEAPON	M3P w/Cylinder choke
AMMO	18.5x70 00 Magnum
DISPERSION ANGLE	1.69583 degrees, 30.1481 NATO mils.

Range	Group Circle Width (mm)	Probability (0<p<.099) (m)			
		Body	Head	Hand	Bullseye
5.0	148.000	0.990	0.924	0.724	0.353
10.0	296.000	0.924	0.724	0.475	0.196
15.0	444.000	0.820	0.576	0.349	0.135
20.0	592.000	0.724	0.475	0.275	0.103
25.0	740.000	0.643	0.402	0.227	0.083
30.0	888.000	0.576	0.349	0.193	0.070
35.0	1036.000	0.521	0.308	0.168	0.060
40.0	1184.000	0.475	0.275	0.149	0.053
45.0	1332.000	0.436	0.249	0.133	0.047
50.0	1480.000	0.402	0.227	0.121	0.043

DAMAGE	12 pellets 14/1.08, 8 pellets 14/0.72, 4 pellets 14/0.36, 1 pellet 14/0.09

▼ Striker

Striker shotgun with stock extended

CARTRIDGE	18.5x70mmR
OPERATION	Manual, spring loaded
TYPE OF FIRE	Semiautomatic double action
RATE OF FIRE	(SS) 24 rpm, 12 rds in 3 seconds, reload time 30 seconds
MUZZLE VELOCITY	362 m/s (1189 fps)
MUZZLE ENERGY	3612 J (2664 ft/lb), 301 J (222 ft/lb) per pellet
SIGHTS	Armson OEG
FEED	12 round cylinder
WEIGHTS:	
WEAPON (EMPTY)	4.200 kg
WEAPON (LOADED)	4.968 kg
MAGAZINE (LOADED)	0.768 kg (12 rds)
SERVICE CARTRIDGE	64 g
BULLET	42 g (12 x 3.5 g)
LENGTHS:	
WEAPON OVERALL	50/78 cm
BARREL	30 cm
STATUS	In production
SERVICE	Commercial sales
COST	$800

This unusual appearing weapon is a native design of South Africa and demonstrates a novel approach to enlarging a shotgun's magazine capacity. The Striker acts as a large revolver, firing in a semiautomatic mode and feeding from a spring wound drum. The result of this spring-assisted mechanical action is that the Striker will operate repeatedly, regardless of what load of shotshell is used. The enclosed rotating drum acts as the cylinder of an old style single action revolver, carrying all the ammunition in individual chambers. The drum rotates through the use of a radially wound spring and indexes on each pull of the trigger. As the drum does not finally align until the last ten percent of the trigger pull, accidental firings from dropping or careless handling are minimized. A drawback of the drum system is that each round has to be hand fed into an individual chamber while indexing the drum with the trigger while the safety is on. Each fired shell is also ejected by hand, using the long ejector rod on the right side of the barrel. The result of this is a twelve round weapon of excellent reliability that can fire all of its rounds in three seconds and be reloaded, empties ejected and fresh rounds inserted, in under thirty seconds. The design of the cylinder system prevents easily "topping up", that is reloading a partially empty cylinder, and this acts as something of a drawback in general combat conditions.

WEAPON Striker w/Cylinder choke
AMMO 18.5x70 00 Magnum
DISPERSION ANGLE 1.91094 degrees, 33.9722 NATO mils.

Range	Group Circle Width (mm)	Probability (0<p<.099) (m)			
		Body	Head	Hand	Bullseye
5.0	166.776	0.990	0.898	0.681	0.321
10.0	333.552	0.898	0.681	0.435	0.176
15.0	500.328	0.782	0.533	0.317	0.121
20.0	667.104	0.681	0.435	0.248	0.092
25.0	833.880	0.599	0.367	0.204	0.074
30.0	1000.656	0.533	0.317	0.173	0.062
35.0	1167.432	0.479	0.278	0.151	0.054
40.0	1334.208	0.435	0.248	0.133	0.047
45.0	1500.984	0.398	0.224	0.119	0.042
50.0	1667.760	0.367	0.204	0.108	0.038

DAMAGE 12 pellets 15/1.68, 8 pellets 15/1.12, 4 pellets 15/0.56, 1 pellet 15/0.14

▼ CAWS (HK)

CARTRIDGE	19.5x76mmB
OPERATION	Recoil
TYPE OF FIRE	Selective
RATE OF FIRE	(SS) 30 rpm (A) 60 rpm (CYCLIC) 240 rpm
MUZZLE VELOCITY	488 m/s (1600 fps)
MUZZLE ENERGY	4316 J (3183 ft/lb), 540 J (398 ft/lb) per pellet
SIGHTS	one power telescopic built into handle
FEED	10 round removable box magazine
WEIGHTS:	
WEAPON (EMPTY)	4.320 kg
WEAPON (LOADED)	5.299 kg
MAGAZINE (EMPTY)	0.189 kg
MAGAZINE (LOADED)	0.979 kg
SERVICE CARTRIDGE	79 g
BULLET	36.3 g (8 x 4.5 g)
LENGTHS:	
WEAPON OVERALL	86.2 cm
BARREL	46 cm
STATUS	Under development

This is one of the two primary candidates for the U.S. Close Assault Weapons System and is a cooperative design between Heckler and Koch for the weapon and Olin for the ammunition. Heckler and Koch have chosen a bullpup layout to give a short, maneuverable overall length while still allowing for a sufficient barrel length for high velocity. The action is recoil operated and carried inside a multi-piece, reinforced plastic shell. With the action sealed inside the shell, it is protected from dirt that could cause jams, greatly adding to the design's overall reliability. The magazine is located behind the pistol grip which slows reloading somewhat but not a significant amount. The selector switch is in the pistol grip where it can be reached by the operator's thumb. The original design was capable of full automatic fire and this is what the CAWS is known for. However, the new design is semiautomatic but offers full auto fire as an option. The ammunition developed by Olin is a specialized 12 gauge (19.5 x 76mm B) all-brass belted case of a much higher chamber pressure than normal shotgun ammunition. The intent of the belted case is to prevent its use in standard weapons as well as adding strength to the design. Several loads are being developed with the best known being an eight pellet load of 000 buckshot. The high velocity of the weapon gives the buckshot load an effective range of 150 meters, more than triple the normal range. The HK design is able to fire both the specialized 19.5 x 76mm B round, and with minor changes, fire 12 gauge 3 inch magnum loads for training. One of the several sight systems being considered is a 1 power optical sight built into the handle. The reticle of the optical sight is a black ring that is very fast to pick up on the target and sized so that it can also be used for rough range estimation.

Range	Group Circle Width (mm)	Probability (0<p<.099) (m)			
		Body	**Head**	**Hand**	**Bullseye**
80.0	1840.000	0.339	0.187	0.098	0.034
85.0	1955.000	0.323	0.177	0.093	0.032
90.0	2070.000	0.308	0.168	0.088	0.031
95.0	2185.000	0.294	0.160	0.083	0.029
100.0	2300.000	0.282	0.153	0.079	0.028
105.0	2415.000	0.271	0.146	0.076	0.026
110.0	2530.000	0.260	0.140	0.073	0.025
115.0	2645.000	0.250	0.134	0.069	0.024
120.0	2760.000	0.241	0.129	0.067	0.023
125.0	2875.000	0.233	0.124	0.064	0.022
130.0	2990.000	0.225	0.120	0.062	0.021
135.0	3105.000	0.218	0.115	0.060	0.021
140.0	3220.000	0.211	0.112	0.057	0.020
145.0	3335.000	0.204	0.108	0.056	0.019
150.0	3450.000	0.198	0.105	0.054	0.019

* indicates range for which data was supplied

DAMAGE 8 pellets 21/1.52, 5 pellets 21/0.95, 2 pellets 21/0.38, 1 pellet 21/0.19

▼ CAWS (AAI)

AAI CAWS with reflex sight and 12 rd magazine

CARTRIDGE 18.5x79mm
OPERATION Recoil
TYPE OF FIRE Selective
RATE OF FIRE (SS) 40 rpm (A) 90 rpm (CYCLIC) 450 rpm
MUZZLE VELOCITY 594 m/s (1950 fps)
MUZZLE ENERGY 3328 J (2454 ft/lbs), 423 & 366 J (7 @ 312 & 1 @ 270 ft/lbs) per pellet
SIGHTS Optical reflex sight w/backup adjustable, aperture/post iron sight
FEED 12 round removable box magazine
WEIGHTS:
WEAPON (EMPTY) 4.082 kg (3.600 kg w/o buttstock)
WEAPON (LOADED) 4.889 kg (4.407 kg w/o buttstock)
MAGAZINE (EMPTY) 0.303 kg
MAGAZINE (LOADED) 0.807 kg
SERVICE CARTRIDGE 42 g
BULLET 18.9 g (7 x 2.4 g, & 1 x 2.1 g)

WEAPON H&K CAWS
AMMO 19.5x76B 000 Buck
DISPERSION ANGLE 1.31775 degrees, 23.4266 NATO mils.

Range	Group Circle Width (mm)	Probability (0<p<.099) (m)			
		Body	**Head**	**Hand**	**Bullseye**
5.0	115.000	0.990	0.964	0.809	0.429
10.0*	230.000	0.964	0.809	0.563	0.245
15.0	345.000	0.890	0.669	0.424	0.171
20.0	460.000	0.809	0.563	0.339	0.131
25.0	575.000	0.734	0.484	0.282	0.106
30.0	690.000	0.669	0.424	0.241	0.089
35.0	805.000	0.612	0.377	0.211	0.077
40.0	920.000	0.563	0.339	0.187	0.068
45.0	1035.000	0.521	0.308	0.168	0.060
50.0	1150.000	0.484	0.282	0.153	0.055
55.0	1265.000	0.452	0.260	0.140	0.050
60.0	1380.000	0.424	0.241	0.129	0.046
65.0	1495.000	0.399	0.225	0.120	0.042
70.0	1610.000	0.377	0.211	0.112	0.039
75.0	1725.000	0.357	0.198	0.105	0.037

☞ continued

☞ continued on next page

☞ *AAI CAWS continued*

LENGTHS:
WEAPON OVERALL 98.4 cm (73 cm w/o buttstock)
BARREL 40.7 cm
SIGHT RADIUS 50 cm
STATUS Under development

The AAI CAWS candidate is developed from earlier research performed by AAI for a 20mm weapon. The round used by AAI is an all plastic cartridge case using eight flechettes as the projectile. Earlier use of flechette shotgun shells in Vietnam found that, though the flechettes would be more destructive than buckshot at ranges from 30 to 100 meters, at ranges closer than 30 meters, the flechette had not yet stabilized for point-first flight and would cause little lethal damage. The new round developed for the CAWS weapon utilizes a drag-cone stabilization that gives the projectiles point-first stable flight from the muzzle to the target. To give the weapon an effective range of 150 meters, the chamber pressure of the rounds are much greater than normal 12 gauge ammunition so that the new round is slightly too large to fit into a regular shotgun. Use of an adaptor however, allows the AAI-CAWS to fire standard 12 gauge buckshot ammunition. The design of the CAWS is along standard rifle lines with the line of recoil kept low and in line with the stock to lessen muzzle climb on full automatic. The result of the stock design, combined with the weapon's recoil operated action and effective muzzle brake, is to give the CAWS the felt recoil of an M16 rifle. Even with the stock removed, the AAI CAWS may be effectively fired. A special reflex optical sight has been developed for use with the CAWS for fast target acquisition in a combat situation. Standard iron sights are also fitted for backup. The twelve round box magazine and full auto fire capability gives the CAWS maximum close-in firepower with a reload time of five seconds for a fresh, loaded magazine.

WEAPON AAI CAWS
AMMO 18.5x79 Flechette
DISPERSION ANGLE 1.5278 degrees, 27.1609 NATO mils.

Range	Group Circle Width (mm)	Probability (0<p<.099) (m)			
		Body	Head	Hand	Bullseye
5.0	133.333	0.990	0.943	0.760	0.384
10.0	266.667	0.943	0.760	0.511	0.215
15.0	400.000	0.851	0.614	0.379	0.149
20.0	533.333	0.760	0.511	0.300	0.114
25.0	666.667	0.681	0.435	0.249	0.092
30.0*	800.000	0.614	0.379	0.212	0.077
35.0	933.333	0.558	0.335	0.185	0.067
40.0	1066.667	0.511	0.300	0.164	0.059
45.0	1200.000	0.470	0.272	0.147	0.052
50.0	1333.333	0.435	0.249	0.133	0.047
55.0	1466.667	0.405	0.229	0.122	0.043

☞ *continued*

Range	Group Circle Width (mm)	Probability (0<p<.099) (m)			
		Body	Head	Hand	Bullseye
60.0	1600.000	0.379	0.212	0.112	0.040
65.0	1733.333	0.356	0.197	0.104	0.037
70.0	1866.667	0.335	0.185	0.097	0.034
75.0	2000.000	0.317	0.173	0.091	0.032
80.0	2133.333	0.300	0.164	0.085	0.030
85.0	2266.667	0.286	0.155	0.081	0.028
90.0	2400.000	0.272	0.147	0.076	0.027
95.0	2533.333	0.260	0.140	0.072	0.025
100.0	2666.667	0.249	0.133	0.069	0.024
105.0	2800.000	0.238	0.127	0.066	0.023
110.0	2933.333	0.229	0.122	0.063	0.022
115.0	3066.667	0.220	0.117	0.060	0.021
120.0	3200.000	0.212	0.112	0.058	0.020
125.0	3333.333	0.204	0.108	0.056	0.019
130.0	3466.667	0.197	0.104	0.053	0.018
135.0	3600.000	0.191	0.100	0.052	0.018
140.0	3733.333	0.185	0.097	0.050	0.017
145.0	3866.667	0.179	0.094	0.048	0.017
150.0	4000.000	0.173	0.091	0.047	0.016

* indicates range for which data was supplied
DAMAGE 8 flechettes 11/0.87,

NOTE; There is a central flechette that has a slightly different mass than the rest of the flechettes in the load. To account for this different flechette, which has a slightly lower damage than the others, it is considered the only projectile to hit the target at maximum range.

5 flechettes 11/0.54,
2 flechettes, 11/0.21,
1 flechette 11/0.10

▼ Jackhammer Mark 3-A2

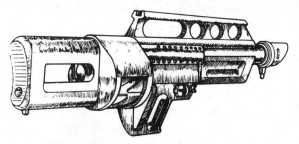

Jackhammer Mark 3 A2 showing ammunition cassette

CARTRIDGE 18.5x70mmR
OPERATION Gas
TYPE OF FIRE Selective

THE EDGE OF THE SWORD

RATE OF FIRE	(SS) 20 rpm (A) 40 rpm
	(CYCLIC) 240 rpm
MUZZLE VELOCITY	383 m/s (1256 fps)
MUZZLE ENERGY	3072 J (2268 ft/lb),
	256 J (189 ft/lb) per pellet
SIGHTS	fixed, non-adjustable, aperture/post
FEED	10 round removable drum
	magazine "cassette"
WEIGHTS:	
WEAPON (EMPTY)	3.871 kg
WEAPON (LOADED)	4.695 kg
MAGAZINE (EMPTY)	0.184 kg
MAGAZINE (LOADED)	0.824 kg
SERVICE CARTRIDGE	64 g
BULLET	42 g (12 x 3.5 g)
LENGTHS:	
WEAPON OVERALL	78.7 cm
BARREL	52.5 cm
SIGHT RADIUS	26 cm
STATUS	Under development

The Jackhammer is a new approach to solving the heating problem in a full automatic shotgun. When the heat from firing quickly builds up, such as during periods of rapid fire in combat or long bursts of full auto fire, the shotgun develops problems unique to the weapon. Most modern shotshells are made mainly of plastic for cost and waterproofing and the plastic can melt in a very hot chamber, acting as a glue and causing a very serious jam when another shell is chambered. In the HK and AAI CAWS, the ammunition is made either of metal or fiber-reinforced plastic and they do not have the melting round problem. The Jackhammer is intended to use standard shotgun shells which are carried in a cassette that acts as both magazine and firing chamber. The loaded cassette is placed behind the pistol grip in the bullpup design with the handguard in front of the pistol grip being pulled forward, then back to lock the round in place. When the weapon is fired, gas is tapped from the barrel to drive a piston and the barrel forward against a spring. The "Autobolt" attached to the barrel rotates the cassette half the distance to index a fresh round, and, as the spring drives the barrel rearward, finishes indexing a fresh round with the barrel. As the barrel inserts into the chamber and the opening casing seals the barrel, no gas leaks and the system runs efficiently. When the fired cases are removed with the used cassette, the waste heat goes with them, removing the heat problem from the weapon. Cassettes can be reloaded easily and reused. The trigger is of the progressive type with a slight pull giving semiautomatic fire and a long pull, full auto fire. A decocking/cocking lever is on the Jackhammer to allow the striker to be safely lowered on a loaded chamber and silently cocked immediately before use. The majority of the weapon and its cassettes are made of Rynite plastic for strength and light weight. The sights are of the notch-post type and are protected by the sides of the carrying handle. The inline design and operating system of the Jackhammer give it good control on full automatic fire.

WEAPON	Jackhammer Mark 3-A2
	w/Cylinder choke
AMMO	18.5x70 00 Magnum
DISPERSION ANGLE	1.69583 degrees, 30.1481 NATO mils.

Range	Group Circle Width (mm)	Probability (0<p<.099) (m)			
		Body	**Head**	**Hand**	**Bullseye**
5.0	148.000	0.990	0.924	0.724	0.353
10.0*	296.000	0.924	0.724	0.475	0.196
15.0	444.000	0.820	0.576	0.349	0.135
20.0	592.000	0.724	0.475	0.275	0.103
25.0	740.000	0.643	0.402	0.227	0.083
30.0	888.000	0.576	0.349	0.193	0.070
35.0	1036.000	0.521	0.308	0.168	0.060
40.0	1184.000	0.475	0.275	0.149	0.053
45.0	1332.000	0.436	0.249	0.133	0.047
50.0	1480.000	0.402	0.227	0.121	0.043

* indicates range for which data was supplied

DAMAGE 12 pellets 15/1.32, 8 pellets 15/0.88, 4 pellets 15/0.44, 1 pellet 15/0.11

▼ Remington 1100

CARTRIDGE	18.5x70mmR
OPERATION	Gas
TYPE OF FIRE	Semiautomatic
RATE OF FIRE	(SS) 16 rpm
MUZZLE VELOCITY	367 m/s (1205 fps)
MUZZLE ENERGY	2831 J (2088 ft/lb), 263 J (174 ft/lb)
SIGHTS	Adjustable, V-notch/blade
FEED	4 round tubular magazine
WEIGHTS:	
WEAPON (EMPTY)	3.175 kg
WEAPON (LOADED)	3.381 kg
MAGAZINE (LOADED)	0.206 kg (4 rds)
SERVICE CARTRIDGE	51.5 g
BULLET	36 g (9 x 4 g)
LENGTHS:	
WEAPON OVERALL	107.6 cm
BARREL	55.9 cm
SIGHT RADIUS	35.9 cm
STATUS	In production
SERVICE	Commercial sales
COST	$450

☞ continued on next page

☞ *Remington 1100 continued*

The Remington 1100 was the first successful gas operated semiautomatic shotgun to see wide commercial acceptance. The gas system utilizes a piston that surrounds the magazine tube and fits into a short chamber attached to the barrel. The piston has a short operating stroke that works from a metered amount of gas, tapped off the barrel. The result of this system of operation is that the magazine tube is able to be extended, eliminating the limitations of earlier gas systems. The action is also very fast operating and somewhat self adjusting, allowing the 1100 to reliably operate with a wide range of loads. In short barreled form, the Remington 1100 is very popular among combat shooters and police agencies, usually with an extended magazine. The placement of the action spring behind the receiver prevents the attachment of a folding stock.

WEAPON	Remington 1100 w/Cylinder choke	
AMMO	18.5x70 00 Magnum	
DISPERSION ANGLE	1.69583 degrees, 30.1481 NATO mils.	

Range	Group Circle Width (mm)	Probability (0<p<.099) (m)			
		Body	**Head**	**Hand**	**Bullseye**
5.0	148.000	0.990	0.924	0.724	0.353
10.0*	296.000	0.924	0.724	0.475	0.196
15.0	444.000	0.820	0.576	0.349	0.135
20.0	592.000	0.724	0.475	0.275	0.103
25.0	740.000	0.643	0.402	0.227	0.083
30.0	888.000	0.576	0.349	0.193	0.070
35.0	1036.000	0.521	0.308	0.168	0.060
40.0	1184.000	0.475	0.275	0.149	0.053
45.0	1332.000	0.436	0.249	0.133	0.047
50.0	1480.000	0.402	0.227	0.121	0.043

* indicates range for which data was supplied

DAMAGE   12 pellets 15/1.20, 8 pellets 15/0.80, 4 pellets 15/0.40, 1 pellet 15/0.10

▼ Remington 7188 • 7188 Mark I

Remington 7188 prototype

Remington 7188 Mark 1

Remington 7188 Mark 1 conversion kit for changing the Model 1100 to the 7188 configuration

Remington 7188 trigger group showing the selector switch behind the trigger set to the automatic fire position

CARTRIDGE	18.5x70mmR
OPERATION	Gas
TYPE OF FIRE	Selective
RATE OF FIRE	(SS) 28 rpm (A) 35 rpm (CYCLIC) 420 rpm
MUZZLE VELOCITY	381 m/s (1250 fps)
MUZZLE ENERGY	3048 J (2244 ft/lbs), 254 J (187 ft/lb) per pellet
SIGHTS	Fixed, non-adjustable, V-notch/blade
FEED	7 round tubular magazine
WEIGHTS:	
WEAPON (EMPTY)	3.657 kg (3.856 kg)
WEAPON (LOADED)	4.015 kg (4.304 kg)
MAGAZINE (LOADED)	0.448 kg (7 rds)
SERVICE CARTRIDGE	64 g
BULLET	42 g (12 x 3.5 g)
LENGTHS:	
WEAPON OVERALL	102.9 cm (104 cm)
BARREL	50.8 cm (51.4 cm)
SIGHT RADIUS	33.3 cm
STATUS	Out of production
SERVICE	Very limited U. S. service use (SEALS) and some law enforcement agencies

The Remington 7188 was a modification of the Remington 1100 for military use specifically as a selective fire weapon. Developed during the Vietnam war, the 7188 has the distinction of being the first successful, though limited, machine shotgun to see military use. British experience in Malaysia indicated that a full automatic shotgun would be of great use in a unconventional warfare situation and the 7188 was developed to test the theory. The standard Model 1100 was fitted with a modified trigger assembly and was otherwise unchanged. The trigger assembly has a switch in place of the safety that had a lever on the left hand side. The switch is rotated rearward for full automatic, forward for semiautomatic, and straight down for safety. The successful trials of the 7188 resulted in a limited number of 7188 Mark 1's being developed and manufactured. The Mark 1 is very much more military in appearance and intent. The barrel was fitted with rifle sights, a perforated handguard surrounded the upper part of the barrel, and a magazine tube extension was fitted to underneath the muzzle. The extension was also able to mount the M7 (M16 rifle) bayonet. A number of 7188 Mark 1's were made with the weapons having a dull parkerized finish, a rubber recoil pad, and plain walnut stocks. A further number of Mark 1 conversion kits were made consisting of the barrel assembly and the selective fire trigger mechanism. The conversion kit would allow any standard Model 1100 to be converted into a short barreled combat shotgun, capable of selective fire and having a seven round, (eight with one in the chamber), magazine capacity.

WEAPON Remington 7188 w/Cylinder choke
AMMO 18.5x70 00 Magnum
DISPERSION ANGLE 1.69583 degrees, 30.1481 NATO mils.

Range	Group Circle Width (mm)	Probability (0<p<.099) (m)			
		Body	Head	Hand	Bullseye
5.0	148.000	0.990	0.924	0.724	0.353
10.0*	296.000	0.924	0.724	0.475	0.196
15.0	444.000	0.820	0.576	0.349	0.135
20.0	592.000	0.724	0.475	0.275	0.103
25.0	740.000	0.643	0.402	0.227	0.083
30.0	888.000	0.576	0.349	0.193	0.070
35.0	1036.000	0.521	0.308	0.168	0.060
40.0	1184.000	0.475	0.275	0.149	0.053
45.0	1332.000	0.436	0.249	0.133	0.047
50.0	1480.000	0.402	0.227	0.121	0.043

* indicates range for which data was supplied

WEAPON Remington 7188 Mark I w/Modified choke
AMMO 18.5x70 00 Magnum
DISPERSION ANGLE 1.31775 degrees, 23.4266 NATO mils.

Range	Group Circle Width (mm)	Probability (0<p<.099) (m)			
		Body	Head	Hand	Bullseye
5.0	115.000	0.990	0.964	0.809	0.429
10.0*	230.000	0.964	0.809	0.563	0.245
15.0	345.000	0.890	0.669	0.424	0.171
20.0	460.000	0.809	0.563	0.339	0.131
25.0	575.000	0.734	0.484	0.282	0.106
30.0	690.000	0.669	0.424	0.241	0.089
35.0	805.000	0.612	0.377	0.211	0.077
40.0	920.000	0.563	0.339	0.187	0.068
45.0	1035.000	0.521	0.308	0.168	0.060
50.0	1150.000	0.484	0.282	0.153	0.055

* indicates range for which data was supplied
DAMAGE 12 pellets 15/1.20, 8 pellets 15/0.80, 4 pellets 14/0.40, 1 pellet 15/0.10

▼ Sidewinder Model SW-PC

CARTRIDGE	18.5x70mmR
OPERATION	Gas
TYPE OF FIRE	Semiautomatic
RATE OF FIRE	(SS) 20 rpm
MUZZLE VELOCITY	368 m/s (1208 fps)
MUZZLE ENERGY	2844 J (2100 ft/lbs), 237 J (175 ft/lb) per pellet
SIGHTS	Front bead
FEED	4 round tubular magazine
WEIGHTS:	
WEAPON (EMPTY)	2.948 kg
WEAPON (LOADED)	3.204 kg
MAGAZINE (LOADED)	0.256 kg (4 rds)
SERVICE CARTRIDGE	64 g
BULLET	42 g (12 x 3.5 g)
LENGTHS:	
WEAPON OVERALL	62.2 cm
BARREL	36.8 cm
STATUS	In production
SERVICE	Commercial sales
COST	$750

The Sidewinder is a conversion of the Remington 1100 to make it a more versatile weapon. The conversion centers around moving the action spring from behind the action to around the magazine tube behind the gas piston. The result of this movement of the spring is that the Sidewinder is able to be fitted with either a pistol grip or a telescoping stock. The SW-PC model of the Sidewinder is the shortest model available. Intended for situations where size is a major consideration but controlled rapid firepower is a need, the SW-PC has a short barrel with a normal sized magazine and a pistol grip. A quick detachable stud and rigid loop are fitted to the SW-PC so that it can be hung from a sling or on a shoulder harness underneath a coat. A special telescoping stock has been developed for the Sidewinder that is a very strong design and will stand up to the severest abuse. The U.S. Navy has adopted the Sidewinder for use by some of its unconventional warfare units. The stock adds 1.338 kilograms to the weight of the Sidewinder SW-PC.

WEAPON Sidewinder SW-PC w/Cylinder choke
AMMO 18.5x70 00 Magnum
DISPERSION ANGLE 1.91094 degrees, 33.9722 NATO mils.

Range	Group Circle Width (mm)	Probability (0<p<.099) (m)			
		Body	Head	Hand	Bullseye
5.0	166.776	0.990	0.898	0.681	0.321
10.0	333.552	0.898	0.681	0.435	0.176
15.0	500.328	0.782	0.533	0.317	0.121

☛ *continued on next page*

☞ *Sidewinder Model SW-PC continued*

Range	Group Circle Width (mm)	Probability (0<p<.099) (m)			
		Body	Head	Hand	Bullseye
20.0	667.104	0.681	0.435	0.248	0.092
25.0	833.880	0.599	0.367	0.204	0.074
30.0	1000.656	0.533	0.317	0.173	0.062
35.0	1167.432	0.479	0.278	0.151	0.054
40.0	1334.208	0.435	0.248	0.133	0.047
45.0	1500.984	0.398	0.224	0.119	0.042
50.0	1667.760	0.367	0.204	0.108	0.038

DAMAGE 12 pellets 15/1.20, 8 pellets 15/0.80, 4 pellets 15/0.40, 1 pellet 15/0.10

▼ Remington 870 P

Remington 870 P with stock extended

870 P with stock folded

CARTRIDGE	18.5x70mmR
OPERATION	Manual slide action
TYPE OF FIRE	Single shot repeater
RATE OF FIRE	(SS) 21 rpm
MUZZLE VELOCITY	358 m/s (1175 fps)
MUZZLE ENERGY	2701 J (1992 ft/lb), 225 J (166 ft/lb) per pellet
SIGHTS	front bead
FEED	7 round tubular magazine
WEIGHTS:	
WEAPON (EMPTY)	3.400 kg
WEAPON (LOADED)	3.848 kg
MAGAZINE (LOADED)	0.448 kg (7 rds)
SERVICE CARTRIDGE	64 g
BULLET	42 g (12 x 3.5 g)
LENGTHS:	
WEAPON OVERALL	77/102 cm
BARREL	50.8 cm
STATUS	In production
SERVICE	Commercial sales
COST	$400

The 870 was the first post World War II pump action design, developed by Remington and first sold in 1950. Using principles tested in earlier weapons, the 870 is particularly rugged and reliable. The action of the 870 has the bolt locking solidly to the barrel by a locking block through the barrel extension. With the locking block doing most of the work and the bolt acting as the housing, the receiver is made lighter than earlier designs but still very strong for the job it performs. The bolt fits on a slide that is moved by the twin action bars attached to the reciprocating forearm. The barrel of the 870 is locked to the weapon by a barrel ring that surrounds the magazine tube. The manner of barrel attachment allows for easily changed barrels and does not cover the end of the magazine tube. With the end of the magazine tube open, magazine extensions could be added and Remington started offering extended tube magazines in the mid 1960's using designs developed for the Remington 7188. In 1972 a significant accessory was developed for the 870, the folding stock. Originally only available to police and military agencies, the folding stock has a full pistol grip and a formed steel stock that folds over the top of the weapon with the buttplate pivoting to lie flat. The 870 P described in the data is the folding stock model with an extended seven round magazine, giving eight rounds with one in the chamber. The folding stock locks into position either open or closed and the weapon can be operated with the stock folded but the sights are blocked.

WEAPON	Remington 870 P w/Cylinder choke
AMMO	18.5x70 00 Magnum
DISPERSION ANGLE	1.69583 degrees, 30.1481 NATO mils.

Range	Group Circle Width (mm)	Probability (0<p<.099) (m)			
		Body	Head	Hand	Bullseye
5.0	148.000	0.990	0.924	0.724	0.353
10.0*	296.000	0.924	0.724	0.475	0.196
15.0	444.000	0.820	0.576	0.349	0.135
20.0	592.000	0.724	0.475	0.275	0.103
25.0	740.000	0.643	0.402	0.227	0.083
30.0	888.000	0.576	0.349	0.193	0.070
35.0	1036.000	0.521	0.308	0.168	0.060
40.0	1184.000	0.475	0.275	0.149	0.053
45.0	1332.000	0.436	0.249	0.133	0.047
50.0	1480.000	0.402	0.227	0.121	0.043

* indicates range for which data was supplied

DAMAGE 12 pellets 14/1.20, 8 pellets 14/0.80, 4 pellets 14/0.40, 1 pellet 14/0.10

▼ Remington 870 Mark I

CARTRIDGE	18.5x70mmR
OPERATION	Manual slide action
TYPE OF FIRE	Single shot repeater
RATE OF FIRE	(SS) 21 rpm
MUZZLE VELOCITY	358 m/s (1175 fps)

MUZZLE ENERGY	2701 J (1992 ft/lb),
	225 J (166 ft/lb) per pellet
SIGHTS	Adjustable, U-notch/blade
FEED	7 round tubular magazine
WEIGHTS:	
WEAPON (EMPTY)	3.600 kg
WEAPON (LOADED)	4.048 kg
MAGAZINE (LOADED)	0.448 kg (7 rds)
SERVICE CARTRIDGE	64 g
BULLET	42 g (12 x 3.5 g)
LENGTHS:	
WEAPON OVERALL	106 cm
BARREL	53.3 cm
SIGHT RADIUS	30.5 cm
STATUS	In production
SERVICE	U.S. Marines

In 1966, the U.S. Marine Corps put out a requirement for a new combat shotgun. The Remington 870 was modified to meet their requirements and was accepted as the best combination of firepower and reliability. The modifications include an extended seven round magazine tube with a large bayonet adaptor attaching the tube to the barrel of the muzzle. The adaptor allows the weapon to mount the M7 bayonet with the ring of the bayonet surrounding the end of the magazine tube. Rifle sights are attached to the barrel and sling swivels are also mounted on the weapon. All metal parts are either parkerized with a dull gray color or a black oxide finish. The walnut stock and forearm are finished with a plain oil finish that does not shine.

WEAPON	Remington 870 Mark I
	w/Modified choke
AMMO	18.5x70 00 Magnum
DISPERSION ANGLE	1.31775 degrees, 23.4266 NATO mils.

Range	Group Circle Width (mm)	Probability (0<p<.099) (m)			
		Body	Head	Hand	Bullseye
5.0	115.000	0.990	0.964	0.809	0.429
10.0*	230.000	0.964	0.809	0.563	0.245
15.0	345.000	0.890	0.669	0.424	0.171
20.0	460.000	0.809	0.563	0.339	0.131
25.0	575.000	0.734	0.484	0.282	0.106
30.0	690.000	0.669	0.424	0.241	0.089
35.0	805.000	0.612	0.377	0.211	0.077
40.0	920.000	0.563	0.339	0.187	0.068
45.0	1035.000	0.521	0.308	0.168	0.060
50.0	1150.000	0.484	0.282	0.153	0.055

* indicates range for which data was supplied

DAMAGE 12 pellets 14/1.20, 8 pellets 14/0.80, 4 pellets 14/0.40, 1 pellet 14/0.10

▼ Ithaca Model 37 M&P

Ithaca Model 37 M&P with parkerized finish

CARTRIDGE	18.5x70mmR
OPERATION	Manual slide action
TYPE OF FIRE	single shot repeater
RATE OF FIRE	(SS) 21 rpm
MUZZLE VELOCITY	358 m/s (1175 fps)
MUZZLE ENERGY	2587 J (1908 ft/lb), 216 J (159 ft/lb)
SIGHTS	Front bead
FEED	7 round tubular magazine
WEIGHTS:	
WEAPON (EMPTY)	3.040 kg
WEAPON (LOADED)	3.448 kg
MAGAZINE (LOADED)	0.448 kg (7 rds)
SERVICE CARTRIDGE	64 g
BULLET	42 g (12 x 3.5 g)
LENGTHS:	
WEAPON OVERALL	100.1 cm
BARREL	51.1 cm
STATUS	Out of production
SERVICE	Commercial sales
COST	$350

Next to the Remington 870, the Ithaca Model 37 is the most common shotgun found in U.S. police armories. First marketed in 1937, the Model 37 is made from a solid billet of steel machined for the receiver and most internal parts, resulting in great strength. The barrel is also made from a bar of solid stock first machined and then rotary forged, making an extremely strong barrel which is very resistant to damage. The action of the M37 utilizes bottom ejection giving the receiver one opening for both loading and ejection. With ejection going out the bottom, the weapon is easily used by right or left handed shooters. Generally, the action of the Model 37 is very reliable and positive in functioning but the bottom of the receiver has to be held above any obstacles to allow for clear ejection. A major point in the M37's design is the lack of a disconnector although one can be added as an option. The lack of a disconnector allows the weapon to fire when the bolt closes if the trigger is held back. The result of this is that the weapon can be rapidly fired by holding back the trigger and quickly working the action, giving the M37 the highest rate of fire for a pump action shotgun. In the late 1960's Ithaca recognized the need for extending the magazine capacity of the M37 and modified the weapon accordingly. The barrel is attached to the M37 by an interrupted thread at the breech and a lug that fits over the magazine tube, locked in place by a stud on the magazine cup. The method of barrel attachment requires the barrel lug to be moved further on the barrel to allow the

☞ *continued on next page*

☞ *Ithaca Model 37 M&P continued*

magazine tube to be extended. The model described in the data for military and police sales is the eight shot model with the long magazine tube holding seven rounds. The barrel of a given magazine length cannot be changed to one of a different length with the drawback giving a very strong magazine tube.

WEAPON Ithaca Model 37 M&P w/Cylinder choke
AMMO 18.5x70 00 Magnum
DISPERSION ANGLE 1.69583 degrees, 30.1481 NATO mils.

Range	Group Circle Width (mm)	Probability (0<p<.099) (m)			
		Body	Head	Hand	Bullseye
5.0	148.000	0.990	0.924	0.724	0.353
10.0*	296.000	0.924	0.724	0.475	0.196
15.0	444.000	0.820	0.576	0.349	0.135
20.0	592.000	0.724	0.475	0.275	0.103
25.0	740.000	0.643	0.402	0.227	0.083
30.0	888.000	0.576	0.349	0.193	0.070
35.0	1036.000	0.521	0.308	0.168	0.060
40.0	1184.000	0.475	0.275	0.149	0.053
45.0	1332.000	0.436	0.249	0.133	0.047
50.0	1480.000	0.402	0.227	0.121	0.043

* indicates range for which data was supplied

WEAPON Ithaca Model 37 M&P w/Full choke
AMMO 18.5x70 00 Magnum
DISPERSION ANGLE 1.16879 degrees, 20.7786 NATO mils.

Range	Group Circle Width (mm)	Probability (0<p<.099) (m)			
		Body	Head	Hand	Bullseye
5.0	102.000	0.990	0.976	0.846	0.469
10.0*	204.000	0.976	0.846	0.607	0.271
15.0	306.000	0.917	0.712	0.463	0.190
20.0	408.000	0.846	0.607	0.373	0.146
25.0	510.000	0.776	0.526	0.312	0.119
30.0	612.000	0.712	0.463	0.267	0.100
35.0	714.000	0.656	0.414	0.234	0.086
40.0	816.000	0.607	0.373	0.208	0.076
45.0	918.000	0.564	0.340	0.187	0.068
50.0	1020.000	0.526	0.312	0.170	0.061

* indicates range for which data was supplied

DAMAGE 12 pellets 14/1.08, 8 pellets 14/0.72, 4 pellets 14/0.36, 1 pellet 14/0.09

▼ Ithaca Stakeout

Ithaca Stakeout in 12 gauge

CARTRIDGE 15.6x70mmR (18.5x70mmR)
OPERATION Manual slide action
TYPE OF FIRE Single shot repeater
RATE OF FIRE (SS) 22 rpm
MUZZLE VELOCITY 346 m/s (1134 fps) (365 m/s <1199 fps>)
MUZZLE ENERGY 1790 J (1320 ft/lbs), 89 J (66 ft/lb) per pellet (2799 J <2064 ft/lbs>, 233 J (172 ft/lb) per pellet
SIGHTS Front bead
FEED 4 round tubular magazine
WEIGHTS:
WEAPON (EMPTY) 1.588 kg (2.268 kg)
WEAPON (LOADED) 1.756 kg (2.524 kg)
MAGAZINE (LOADED) 0.168 kg (0.256 kg) (4 rds)
SERVICE CARTRIDGE 42 g (64 g)
BULLET 30 g (20 x 1.5 g) (42 g <12 x 3.5 g>)
LENGTHS:
WEAPON OVERALL 58.4 cm
BARREL 33.7 cm
STATUS Out of production
SERVICE Commercial sales

The Stakeout is a line of modified M37 shotguns intended to give maximum firepower in a minimum sized package. Available in two calibers, 12 or 20 gauge, the Stakeout has the barrel shortened to just in front of the barrel lug with the weapon retaining the four round magazine tube. The pistol grip has two sling swivels, one at the top and one at the bottom. With a simple loop having a snap connector, the Stakeout can be slung from the shoulder underneath a coat or jacket and be quickly drawn into firing position. The strap underneath the operating slide prevents the hand from slipping in front of the muzzle while firing. The twenty gauge is much more controllable in a weapon of this size, with the twelve gauge giving a massive muzzle blast and recoil rise. The lighter recoil of the twenty gauge gives a much faster recovery time and allows quick engagement of multiple targets. The Stakeout is presently the only production version of what was referred to as a "Whippet" gun made in the U.S.A.

WEAPON Ithaca Stakeout w/Cylinder choke
AMMO 18.5x70 00 Magnum
DISPERSION ANGLE 1.69583 degrees, 30.1481 NATO mils.

Range	Group Circle Width (mm)	Probability (0<p<.099) (m)			
		Body	Head	Hand	Bullseye
5.0	148.000	0.990	0.924	0.724	0.353
10.0*	296.000	0.924	0.724	0.475	0.196
15.0	444.000	0.820	0.576	0.349	0.135
20.0	592.000	0.724	0.475	0.275	0.103
25.0	740.000	0.643	0.402	0.227	0.083
30.0	888.000	0.576	0.349	0.193	0.070
35.0	1036.000	0.521	0.308	0.168	0.060
40.0	1184.000	0.475	0.275	0.149	0.053
45.0	1332.000	0.436	0.249	0.133	0.047
50.0	1480.000	0.402	0.227	0.121	0.043

* indicates range for which data was supplied

DAMAGE (15.6x70) 20 pellets 11/0.60,
13 pellets 11/0.39,
6 pellets 11/0.18,
1 pellet 11/0.03

DAMAGE (18.5x70) 12 pellets 15/1.20,
8 pellets 15/0.80,
4 pellets 15/0.40,
1 pellet 15/0.10

▼ Ithaca MAG-10 Roadblocker

CARTRIDGE 19.7x89mmR
OPERATION Gas
TYPE OF FIRE Semiautomatic
RATE OF FIRE (SS) 16 rpm
MUZZLE VELOCITY 339 m/s (1112 fps)
MUZZLE ENERGY 4011 J (2958 ft/lbs),
79 J (58 ft/lb) per pellet
SIGHTS Front bead
FEED 2 round tubular magazine
WEIGHTS:
WEAPON (EMPTY) 4.870 kg
WEAPON (LOADED) 5.143 kg
MAGAZINE (LOADED) 0.273 kg (3 rds)
SERVICE CARTRIDGE 91 g
BULLET 71.4 g (51 x 1.4 g)
LENGTHS:
WEAPON OVERALL 106.4 cm
BARREL 55.9 cm
STATUS Out of production
SERVICE Commercial sales

COST $700

This is the largest caliber commercially made semiautomatic shotgun available today. Chambered for the 10 gauge 3 1/2 inch magnum round, the Roadblocker is a very large and heavy weapon. Intended for use at roadblocks where it would not be carried for long periods of time, the large shot load or slugs fired by the weapon would quickly disable fleeing vehicles. The gas system is made of stainless steel minimizing corrosion. The placement of the gas system at the front of the magazine tube limits the magazine capacity to two rounds, three with one in the chamber. Another aspect of the gas system is its counter-recoil design, called "countercoil" by the manufacturer. This accounts for some of the length of the system in the magazine tube but it is outweighed by the lowering of the recoil impulse.

WEAPON Ithaca Roadblocker w/Cylinder choke
AMMO 19.7x89 Magnum
DISPERSION ANGLE 1.69583 degrees, 30.1481 NATO mils.

Range	Group Circle Width (mm)	Probability (0<p<.099) (m)			
		Body	Head	Hand	Bullseye
5.0	148.000	0.990	0.924	0.724	0.353
10.0*	296.000	0.924	0.724	0.475	0.196
15.0	444.000	0.820	0.576	0.349	0.135
20.0	592.000	0.724	0.475	0.275	0.103
25.0	740.000	0.643	0.402	0.227	0.083
30.0	888.000	0.576	0.349	0.193	0.070
35.0	1036.000	0.521	0.308	0.168	0.060
40.0	1184.000	0.475	0.275	0.149	0.053
45.0	1332.000	0.436	0.249	0.133	0.047
50.0	1480.000	0.402	0.227	0.121	0.043

* indicates range for which data was supplied

DAMAGE (#4 Buckshot) 54 pellets 10/1.62,
36 pellets 10/1.08,
18 pellets 10/0.54,
1 pellet 10/0.03

DAMAGE (00 Buckshot) 18 pellets 12/1.44,
12 pellets 12/0.96,
6 pellets 12/0.48,
1 pellet 12/0.08

▼ Mossberg M500 ATP6 • M500 ATP8

CARTRIDGE 18.5x70mmR
OPERATION Manual slide action
TYPE OF FIRE Single shot repeater
RATE OF FIRE (SS) 18 rds (24 rds)
MUZZLE VELOCITY 376 m/s (1235 fps) (381 m/s <1250 fps>)

☞ continued on next page

☞ *Mossberg M500 ATP6 • M55 ATP8 continued*

MUZZLE ENERGY	2978 J (2196 ft/lb), 248 J (183 ft/lb) per pellet, (3042 J <2244 ft/lb>, 254 J <187 ft/lb> per pellet
SIGHTS	Front bead
FEED	5 round (7 round) tubular magazine
WEIGHTS:	
WEAPON (EMPTY)	2.950 kg (3.060 kg)
WEAPON (LOADED)	3.207 kg (3.508 kg)
MAGAZINE (LOADED)	0.320 kg (5 rds) (0.448 kg <7 rds>)
SERVICE CARTRIDGE	64 g
BULLET	42 g (12 x 3.5 g)
LENGTHS:	
WEAPON OVERALL	95.8 cm (100.9 cm)
BARREL	47 cm (50.8 cm)
STATUS	In production
SERVICE	Commercial sales
COST	$250 ($300)

The Mossberg M500 series is a standard-layout line of economically priced pump action shotguns. The basic M500 action has a bolt locked to a short barrel extension by a rising locking block. With the barrel and locking block absorbing the energy of firing, the receiver can be made of lightweight metal, and in the M500, the receiver is made from an aluminum aircraft-alloy forging. The bolt has twin extractors to insure positive extraction as well as twin action bars connecting the bolt to the operating slide. The lifter that transfers a shell from the magazine to the barrel is of a skeleton design to allow a misfeed to be quickly cleared and lifts the shell to a level in line with the chamber for a smooth feed. The barrel is held to the action by a lug that fits over the end of the magazine and locks into it by a threaded stud. The attachment of the barrel prevents magazines from being extended so Mossberg offers two magazine capacities, the ATP 6 with a five round capacity magazine, and the ATP 8 with a seven round magazine. To accommodate the magazine tubes, the ATP 6 model has an eighteen inch barrel and the ATP 8 has a twenty inch barrel. The safety on the M500 is placed at the top rear of the receiver for quick activation by the thumb of the shooter's hand.

WEAPON	Mossberg M500 w/Cylinder choke
AMMO	18.5x70 00 Magnum
DISPERSION ANGLE	1.69583 degrees, 30.1481 NATO mils.

Range	Group Circle Width (mm)	Probability (0<p<.099) (m)			
		Body	Head	Hand	Bullseye
5.0	148.000	0.990	0.924	0.724	0.353
10.0*	296.000	0.924	0.724	0.475	0.196
15.0	444.000	0.820	0.576	0.349	0.135
20.0	592.000	0.724	0.475	0.275	0.103
25.0	740.000	0.643	0.402	0.227	0.083

☞ *continued*

Range	Group Circle Width (mm)	Probability (0<p<.099) (m)			
		Body	Head	Hand	Bullseye
30.0	888.000	0.576	0.349	0.193	0.070
35.0	1036.000	0.521	0.308	0.168	0.060
40.0	1184.000	0.475	0.275	0.149	0.053
45.0	1332.000	0.436	0.249	0.133	0.047
50.0	1480.000	0.402	0.227	0.121	0.043

* indicates range for which data was supplied

DAMAGE	(ATP6) 12 pellets 15/1.20, 8 pellets 15/080, 4 pellets 15/0.40, 1 pellet 15/0.15
DAMAGE	(ATP8) 12 pellets 15/1.80, 8 pellets 15/1.20, 4 pellets 15/0.60, 1 pellet 15/0.15

▼ Mossberg M500 ATP6C • M500 ATP8C

Mossberg M500 ATP8C with black nylon sling

CARTRIDGE	18.5x70mmR
OPERATION	Manual slide action
TYPE OF FIRE	Single shot repeater
RATE OF FIRE	(SS) 18 rpm (24 rpm)
MUZZLE VELOCITY	376 m/s (1235 fps) (381 m/s <1250 fps>)
MUZZLE ENERGY	2978 J (2196 ft/lbs), 248 J (183 ft/lb) per pellet, (3252 J <2439 ft/lbs>, 368 J <271 ft/lb> per pellet)
SIGHTS	Front bead
FEED	5 round (7 round) tubular magazine
WEIGHTS:	
WEAPON (EMPTY)	2.600 kg (2.720 kg)
WEAPON (LOADED)	2.920 kg (3.168 kg)
MAGAZINE (LOADED)	0.320 kg (5 rds) (0.448 kg <7 rds>)
SERVICE CARTRIDGE	64 g
BULLET	42 g (12 x 3.5 g)
LENGTHS:	
WEAPON OVERALL	71.1 cm (76.2 cm)
BARREL	47 cm (50.8 cm)
STATUS	In production
SERVICE	Commercial sales
COST	$250 ($300)

To make the M500 series more maneuverable in the close confines of a modern car, Mossberg released the Cruiser model with a pistol grip instead of a shoulder stock. The pistol grip is easily attachable to any of the M500 weapons converting them to Cruiser configuration. To operate the safety, the grip has to be released for the thumb to reach the switch. There is a sling swivel mounted on the grip that allows the weapon to be slung at the side, within easy reach.

WEAPON Mossberg M500 Cruiser
w/Cylinder choke
AMMO 18.5x70 00 Magnum
DISPERSION ANGLE 1.69583 degrees, 30.1481 NATO mils.

Range	Group Circle Width (mm)	Probability (0<p<.099) (m)			
		Body	Head	Hand	Bullseye
5.0	148.000	0.990	0.924	0.724	0.353
10.0*	296.000	0.924	0.724	0.475	0.196
15.0	444.000	0.820	0.576	0.349	0.135
20.0	592.000	0.724	0.475	0.275	0.103
25.0	740.000	0.643	0.402	0.227	0.083
30.0	888.000	0.576	0.349	0.193	0.070
35.0	1036.000	0.521	0.308	0.168	0.060
40.0	1184.000	0.475	0.275	0.149	0.053
45.0	1332.000	0.436	0.249	0.133	0.047
50.0	1480.000	0.402	0.227	0.121	0.043

* indicates range for which data was supplied

DAMAGE (ATP6C) 12 pellets 15/1.20,
8 pellets 15/0.80,
4 pellets 14/0.40,
1 pellet 15/0.10

DAMAGE (ATP8C) 12 pellets 15/1.80,
8 pellets 15/1.20,
4 pellets 15/0.60,
1 pellet 15/0.15

CHAPTER 6

MACHINEGUNS

The development of the modern machinegun began in the middle 1800's with Dr. Richard Gatling's invention of a manually-operated repeating weapon. The Gatling gun used a number of rotating barrels, powered by a hand crank, for loading, firing, and extracting cartridges. Though the Gatling was used more as artillery (rather than the modern auto-weapon's role of direct support) it was a superbly practical design. In the 1960's when the armed services sought a high rate-of-fire design, the Gatling gun was reborn in the form of the Minigun and subsequent multi-barrel weapons.

Hiram Maxim is responsible for the creation of the first true machinegun, in which the power of the cartridge is used to operate the action. Weapons of this design were heavy, water-cooled guns, capable of sustained fire from long, linked-ammunition belts.

Between the wars, the invention of the Lewis gun and BAR introduced the concept of the light machinegun. A light machinegun is one that can be carried and operated by one man. During WW 2, the Germans established the general purpose machinegun concept with their MG-34 and 42. General purpose machineguns can be used as light MGs or mounted on tripods for sustained firing as a medium support machinegun. The world's major armies are presently armed with general purpose machineguns (the United States Army's M-60 is a typical example), and the trend is towards lighter calibers for individual use. ●

▼ AUG LSW (HBAR-T)

AUG LSW (HBAR-T) with bipod folded and 42 rd magazine

CARTRIDGE	5.56mm
OPERATION	Gas
TYPE OF FIRE	Selective
RATE OF FIRE	(SS) 40 rpm (A) 200 rpm
	(CYCLIC) 680 rpm
MUZZLE VELOCITY	958 m/s (3143 fps
MUZZLE ENERGY	1814 J (1338 ft/lb)
SIGHTS	Kahles ZF69 6 power telescopic sight
FEED	30 or 42 round removable box magazine
MOUNT TYPE	Bipod
WEIGHTS:	
WEAPON (EMPTY)	5.443 kg
WEAPON (LOADED)	6.114 kg w/42 rds
MAGAZINE (EMPTY)	0.142 kg (30 rd), 0.159 kg (42 rd)
MAGAZINE (LOADED)	0.508 kg (30 rd), 0.671 kg (42 rd)
SERVICE CARTRIDGE	12.2 g
BULLET	4 g
LENGTHS:	
WEAPON OVERALL	88.9 cm
BARREL	61 cm
STATUS	In production
SERVICE	Austrian military and commercial sales
COST	$1200

This is the light machinegun version of the AUG weapons system. Using the standard action/buttstock group, a special heavy barrel is mounted on the weapon with the barrel having a folding bipod mounted at the muzzle. The barrel is of a greater diameter than the standard AUG barrels with the additional metal acting as a heat sink, allowing for greater sustained fire. To take advantage of the greater fire potential, the HBAR AUG is normally used with the longer forty-two round magazine which is made of a translucent plastic, allowing the rounds to be seen. A specialized muzzle compensator is mounted on the heavy barrel to reduce recoil and minimize muzzle climb. The normal telescopic sight/receiver handle may be used on the HBAR but more often, a different receiver housing is used that has a standard telescope mount. When the weapon is using the scope mount receiver housing, the identification has a -T following the HBAR designation. The scope mounting will accept all standard sighting devices with the model listed in the data above using the 6 power ZF-69 telescopic sight offered by the manufacturer. Another aspect of using a high power telescopic sight is the advantage that can be taken of the inherent accuracy of the AUG's closed bolt firing, combined with the heavy barrel's stability.

ASSESSMENT	4.25 in @ 400 yds
WEAPON	AUG LSW
AMMO	5.56x45
	6 x power scope installed.
DISPERSION ANGLE	.0169103 degrees, .300627 NATO mils.

Range	Group Circle Width (mm)	Probability (0<p<.099) (m)			
		Body	**Head**	**Hand**	**Bullseye**
50.0	14.757	0.990	0.990	0.990	0.987
100.0	29.514	0.990	0.990	0.990	0.888
150.0	44.271	0.990	0.990	0.986	0.767
200.0	59.028	0.990	0.990	0.960	0.665
250.0	73.785	0.990	0.990	0.924	0.583
300.0	88.542	0.990	0.986	0.884	0.517
350.0	103.299	0.990	0.975	0.842	0.464
400.0	118.056	0.990	0.960	0.801	0.421
450.0	132.813	0.990	0.943	0.762	0.385
500.0	147.570	0.990	0.924	0.725	0.354
600.0	177.084	0.986	0.884	0.659	0.305
700.0	206.598	0.975	0.842	0.602	0.268
800.0	236.112	0.960	0.801	0.554	0.239
900.0	265.626	0.943	0.762	0.512	0.216
1000.0	295.140	0.924	0.725	0.476	0.196

DAMAGE 37/0.64

▼ FN-MAG

CARTRIDGE	7.62x51mm
OPERATION	Gas
TYPE OF FIRE	Full automatic
RATE OF FIRE	(A) 250 rpm (CYCLIC) 800 rpm
MUZZLE VELOCITY	840 m/s (2756 fps)
MUZZLE ENERGY	3429 J (2529 ft/lb)
SIGHTS	Adjustable, aperture/blade, range 1800m
FEED	Flexible metal disintegrating link (M13) belt
MOUNT TYPE	Integral bipod or tripod
WEIGHTS:	
WEAPON (EMPTY)	10.85 kg
WEAPON (LOADED)	13.844 kg w/100 rd belt

☞ continued on next page

☞ *FN-MAG continued*

WEAPON (MOUNTED & LOADED)
30.316 kg w/ tripod & 250 rds w/box
MOUNT 10.300 kg (tripod)
MAGAZINE (LOADED) 2.994 kg (100 rd belt), 9.166 kg
(250 rd belt w/box)
SERVICE CARTRIDGE 25.6 g
BULLET 9.8 g
LENGTHS:
WEAPON OVERALL 126 cm
BARREL 54.5 cm
SIGHT RADIUS 84.8 cm
STATUS In production
SERVICE Known to be in service with Argentina, Belgium, Canada, Cuba, Ecuador, India, Indonesia, Israel, Kuwait, Libya, Malaysia, Netherlands, New Zealand, Peru, Qatar, Sierra Leone, Singapore, South Africa, Sweden, Tanzania, Uganda, UK, USA, Venezuela, Zimbabwe, and commercial sales to over 75 countries.

This weapon, also known as the MAG-58, is the most popular general purpose machine gun used in the Western world today. Developed during the late 1950's, the MAG is a very rugged design with the receiver being made of milled slabs of steel solidly riveted together. Most of the internal parts are also machined from solid stock, resulting in a very strong weapon which is made with precision fitting of the parts. The barrel bore and parts of the gas system are chromium plated to minimize wear and corrosion. The gas system is easily and quickly adjusted by the gunner to give more operating power to the weapon, keeping it reliable in difficult conditions. The air-cooled barrel has an integral carrying handle that is also used to quickly change the barrel and maintain a sustained rate of fire without damaging accuracy. With the MAG firing from the open bolt position, the problem of cook-off is eliminated but the manufacturer still recommends changing the barrel every 200 rounds when firing at the maximum rate. The front sight is completely adjustable, allowing all the barrels of a specific weapon to be zeroed to that weapon's particular characteristics. The folding bipod is securely attached to the gas piston tube and locks securely in the open or closed position. When firing the MAG from the ground, the bipod is solidly attached to the gas piston tube and locks securely in the open or closed position. When firing the MAG from the hip, the bipod can be folded and in this position acts as a front handgrip. The wooden buttstock is removable, allowing the MAG to be used on a variety of vehicle mounts where overall length is a consideration. A very reliable and successful design, the MAG is finding wide sales with the world's militaries.

ASSESSMENT 10 inches @ 600 yards
WEAPON FN MAG
AMMO 7.62x51
DISPERSION ANGLE .0265085 degrees, .471262 NATO mils.

Range	Group Circle Width (mm)	Probability (0<p<.099) (m)			
		Body	Head	Hand	Bullseye
50.0	23.133	0.990	0.990	0.990	0.938
100.0	46.266	0.990	0.990	0.984	0.752
150.0	69.399	0.990	0.990	0.936	0.605
200.0	92.532	0.990	0.984	0.872	0.502
250.0	115.665	0.990	0.963	0.807	0.427
300.0	138.798	0.990	0.936	0.747	0.372
350.0	161.931	0.990	0.905	0.692	0.329
400.0	185.064	0.984	0.872	0.643	0.294
450.0	208.197	0.974	0.840	0.599	0.266
500.0	231.330	0.963	0.807	0.561	0.243
600.0	277.596	0.936	0.747	0.497	0.207
700.0	323.862	0.905	0.692	0.445	0.181
800.0	370.128	0.872	0.643	0.402	0.160
900.0	416.394	0.840	0.599	0.367	0.144
1000.0	462.660	0.807	0.561	0.338	0.130
1100.0	508.926	0.776	0.527	0.312	0.119
1200.0	555.192	0.747	0.497	0.290	0.110
1300.0	601.458	0.718	0.469	0.271	0.102
1400.0	647.724	0.692	0.445	0.255	0.095
1500.0	693.990	0.666	0.422	0.240	0.089

DAMAGE 50/0.38

▼ Minimi

Minimi (early model) with bipod extended and 200 rd belt container attached

CARTRIDGE 5.56x45mm
OPERATION Gas
TYPE OF FIRE Full automatic
RATE OF FIRE (A) 150 rpm (CYCLIC) 700–1000 rpm
MUZZLE VELOCITY 925 m/s (3034 fps)
MUZZLE ENERGY 1691 J (1247 ft/lb)

		Probability (0<p<.099) (m)			
Range	Group Circle Width (mm)	Body	Head	Hand	Bullseye
50.0	179.310	0.986	0.881	0.654	0.302
100.0	358.620	0.881	0.654	0.412	0.165
150.0	537.930	0.757	0.508	0.298	0.113
200.0	717.240	0.654	0.412	0.233	0.086
250.0	896.550	0.573	0.346	0.191	0.069
300.0	1075.860	0.508	0.298	0.162	0.058
350.0	1255.170	0.455	0.262	0.141	0.050
400.0	1434.480	0.412	0.233	0.124	0.044
450.0	1613.790	0.376	0.210	0.111	0.039
500.0	1793.100	0.346	0.191	0.101	0.035
600.0	2151.720	0.298	0.162	0.085	0.030
700.0	2510.340	0.262	0.141	0.073	0.025
800.0	2868.960	0.233	0.124	0.064	0.022
900.0	3227.580	0.210	0.111	0.057	0.020
1000.0	3586.200	0.191	0.101	0.052	0.018

SIGHTS Adjustable, aperture/post, range 1000 m

FEED 20, 30, or 30/45 round removable box magazine (M16), or flexible metal disintegrating link belt

MOUNT TYPE Bipod

WEIGHTS:

WEAPON (EMPTY) 6.875 kg (1.600 kg Spare barrel)

WEAPON (LOADED) 10.000 kg w/200 rds in box

MAGAZINE (EMPTY) 0.091 kg (20 rd), 0.117 kg (30 rd), 0.149 kg (30/45 rd), 0.277 kg (200 rd belt box)

MAGAZINE (LOADED) 0.335 kg (20 rd), 0.483 kg (30 rd), 0.698 kg (30/45 rd w/45 rds), 3.125 kg (200 rd belt w/box)

SERVICE CARTRIDGE 12.2 g

BULLET 4 g

LENGTHS:

WEAPON OVERALL 104 cm

BARREL 46.6 cm

SIGHT RADIUS 49.5 cm

STATUS In production

SERVICE US military and commercial sales

DAMAGE 36/0.62

▼ **Minimi-Para**

Recently adopted by the U.S. armed forces as their new squad level automatic weapon, the Minimi is a small light machinegun which is capable of either belt or magazine feed. Chambered for the 5.56 x 45mm NATO round, the Minimi is normally loaded with a 200 round container that clips underneath the weapon and feeds a metallic link belt into the feed well in the left side of the weapon. An alternate magazine well is underneath the belt feed opening and will accept any size M16 magazine. When a magazine is inserted, the belt feed mechanism is automatically disengaged and the weapon switches to feeding from the magazine. The gas operation system has two settings, one for normal operation and a second, allowing more gas to be tapped from the barrel, for additional power to function in adverse conditions. When changed to the adverse setting, the Minimi fires at a higher than normal rate of fire and this can put excessive wear on the weapon. The receiver is made from precision stampings for lightness with many of the parts being machined forgings to help lower costs and speed production. The barrel is chromium lined to limit corrosion and extend its service life. There is a quick release catch on the barrel as well as a carrying handle to speed barrel changes and increase sustained fire. The bipod will fold underneath the gas system and latch into the front handguard. Inside the removable handguard is a cleaning kit which is sufficient to maintain the weapon. Another feature is a removable triggerguard that allows the Minimi to be fired when the operator wears heavy gloves.

CARTRIDGE 5.56x45mm

OPERATION Gas

TYPE OF FIRE Full automatic

RATE OF FIRE (A) 150 rpm (CYCLIC) 700–1000 rpm

MUZZLE VELOCITY 866 m/s (2841 fps

MUZZLE ENERGY 1482 J (1093 ft/lb)

SIGHTS Adjustable, aperture/post, range 1000m

FEED 20,30,or 30/45 round removable box magazine or flexible metal disintegrating link belt

MOUNT TYPE Integral bipod

WEIGHTS:

WEAPON (EMPTY) 6.750 kg (1.470 kg Spare barrel)

WEAPON (LOADED) 9.875 kg w/200 rds w/box

WEAPON Minimi A

AMMO 5.56x45

DISPERSION ANGLE .205474 degrees, 3.65287 NATO mils.

☞ continued on next page

☛ *Minimi-Para continued*

MAGAZINE (EMPTY) 0.091 kg (20 rd), 0.117 kg (30 rd), 0.149 kg (30/45 rd), 0.277 kg (200 rd belt box)

MAGAZINE (LOADED) 0.335 kg (20 rd), 0.483 kg (30 rd), 0.698 kg (30/45 rd w/45 rds), 3.125 kg (200 rd belt w/box)

SERVICE CARTRIDGE 12.2 g

BULLET 4 g

LENGTHS:

WEAPON OVERALL 73.6/89.3 cm

BARREL 34.7 cm

SIGHT RADIUS 49.5 cm

STATUS In production

SERVICE Commercial sales

The Minimi-Para is a specially shortened version of the Minimi light machinegun intended for use by specialist troops and paratroopers. The barrel is shortened to the minimum length in front of the gas system and the flash suppressor refitted. The buttstock is replaced by a retractable metal stock to conserve length as well. Other than its shorter size, the Minimi-Para has all of the characteristics of the standard Minimi and operates in the same way. The Para may also be mounted on a light tripod for more accurate sustained fire.

WEAPON Minimi-Para
AMMO 5.56x45
DISPERSION ANGLE .205474 degrees, 3.65287 NATO mils.

Range	Group Circle Width (mm)	Probability (0<p<.099) (m)			
		Body	**Head**	**Hand**	**Bullseye**
50.0	179.310	0.986	0.881	0.654	0.302
100.0	358.620	0.881	0.654	0.412	0.165
150.0	537.930	0.757	0.508	0.298	0.113
200.0	717.240	0.654	0.412	0.233	0.086
250.0	896.550	0.573	0.346	0.191	0.069
300.0	1075.860	0.508	0.298	0.162	0.058
350.0	1255.170	0.455	0.262	0.141	0.050
400.0	1434.480	0.412	0.233	0.124	0.044
450.0	1613.790	0.376	0.210	0.111	0.039
500.0	1793.100	0.346	0.191	0.101	0.035
600.0	2151.720	0.298	0.162	0.085	0.030
700.0	2510.340	0.262	0.141	0.073	0.025
800.0	2868.960	0.233	0.124	0.064	0.022
900.0	3227.580	0.210	0.111	0.057	0.020
1000.0	3586.200	0.191	0.101	0.052	0.018

DAMAGE 33/0.58

▼ Heckler & Koch HK21E

HK21E with ammunition belt inserted and selector set on safe

CARTRIDGE 7.62x51mm

OPERATION Retarded blowback

TYPE OF FIRE Selective w/three round burst and full auto

RATE OF FIRE (SS) 40 rpm (A) 200 rpm (CYCLIC) 800 rpm

MUZZLE VELOCITY 840 m/s (2755 fps)

MUZZLE ENERGY 3428 J (2528 ft/lb)

SIGHTS Four power removable telescopic sight, range 600m or adjustable, aperture/post, range 1200m

FEED Flexible metal link belt

MOUNT TYPE Integral bipod and M1102 tripod

WEIGHTS:

WEAPON (EMPTY) 9.299 kg (9.948 kg w/scope) (2.200 kg Spare barrel)

WEAPON (LOADED) 12.293 kg w/100 rds (12.942 kg w/scope & 100 rds)

WEAPON (MOUNTED & LOADED) 22.493 kg w/100 rds (23.142 kg w/ scope & 100 rds)

MOUNT 10.200 kg

MAGAZINE (LOADED) 2.994 kg (100 rd belt)

SERVICE CARTRIDGE 25.6 g

BULLET 9.8 g

LENGTHS:

WEAPON OVERALL 114 cm

BARREL 56 cm

SIGHT RADIUS 68.5 cm

STATUS In production

SERVICE Mexico and commercial sales

COST $2350

This is the latest model of the HK21 series of light machineguns directly developed from the G3 rifle. The same roller delayed blowback system is used in the 21E as in all the major HK weapons with a considerable commonality of parts between the HK21E and the G3 series. The operation of the 21E is also of the standard Heckler and Koch pattern with additions to satisfy the role of light machinegun. The major addition, besides the belt feed, is the quick change barrel system. The very heavy barrel can be quickly unlocked and drawn to the rear of the barrel housing with the weapon being supported by the bipod attached to the front bearing. A vertical front grip is also attached to the bottom of the barrel housing as an assist for hip firing. The belt feed mechanism takes several types of metallic belts and is easily removable to allow attachment of accessories that enable the HK21E to use G3 rifle magazines. The new trigger mechanism allows for semiautomatic, three round controlled bursts, and full automatic fire to be selected. The pistol grip of the new trigger housing also holds a cleaning kit for weapons maintenance. To make use of the inherent accuracy of the HK system, the sight radius is lengthened from earlier designs and a new rear sight is fitted of the drum type, adjustable to 1200 meters. The receiver has also been lengthened by 94mm from earlier models, to add to the sight radius along with increasing weapon reliability. The unusual buttstock is designed to be held in the European manner. The accepted hold is for the left hand to hold the underside flat of the stock against the shoulder with the weight of the weapon being supported by the bipod.

WEAPON HK21E
AMMO 7.62x51
DISPERSION ANGLE .0118545 degrees, .210747 NATO mils.

Range	Group Circle Width (mm)	Probability (0<p<.099) (m)			
		Body	**Head**	**Hand**	**Bullseye**
50.0	10.345	0.990	0.990	0.990	0.990
100.0	20.690	0.990	0.990	0.990	0.956
150.0	31.035	0.990	0.990	0.990	0.875
200.0	41.380	0.990	0.990	0.990	0.790
250.0	51.725	0.990	0.990	0.975	0.713
300.0	62.070	0.990	0.990	0.954	0.646
350.0	72.415	0.990	0.990	0.928	0.590
400.0	82.760	0.990	0.990	0.900	0.541
450.0	93.105	0.990	0.983	0.871	0.500
500.0	103.450	0.990	0.975	0.841	0.464
600.0	248.280	0.954	0.784	0.536	0.229
700.0	289.660	0.928	0.732	0.482	0.200
800.0	331.040	0.900	0.684	0.438	0.177
900.0	372.420	0.871	0.640	0.400	0.159
1000.0	413.800	0.841	0.602	0.369	0.144
1100.0	455.180	0.813	0.567	0.342	0.132
1200.0	496.560	0.784	0.536	0.319	0.122
1300.0	537.940	0.757	0.507	0.298	0.113
1400.0	579.320	0.732	0.482	0.280	0.105
1500.0	620.700	0.707	0.459	0.264	0.099

DAMAGE 50/0.38

▼ Heckler & Koch HK23E

HK23E with bipod extended, ammunition belt inserted & selector set to safe

CARTRIDGE	5.56x45mm
OPERATION	Retarded blowback
TYPE OF FIRE	Selective w/three round burst and full auto
RATE OF FIRE	(SS) 40 rpm (A) 200 rpm (CYCLIC) 800 rpm
MUZZLE VELOCITY	950 m/s (3116 fps)
MUZZLE ENERGY	1783 J (1315 ft/lb)
SIGHTS	Four power removable telescopic sight, range 600 m or adjustable, aperture/post, range 1000 m
FEED	Flexible metal link belt
MOUNT TYPE	Integral bipod or M1102 tripod
WEIGHTS:	
WEAPON (EMPTY)	8.750 kg (9.399 kg w/scope) (1.601 kg Spare barrel)
WEAPON (LOADED)	10.174 kg w/100 rds (10.823 kg w/scope & 100 rds)
WEAPON (MOUNTED & LOADED)	20.374 kg w/100 rds (21.023 kg w/scope & 100 rds)
MOUNT	10.200 kg
MAGAZINE (LOADED)	1.424 kg (100 rds)
SERVICE CARTRIDGE	12.2 g
BULLET	4 g
LENGTHS:	
WEAPON OVERALL	103 cm
BARREL	45 cm
SIGHT RADIUS	68.5 cm
STATUS	In production
SERVICE	Commercial sales
COST	$2350

This is the latest version of the Heckler and Koch 23 machinegun series and is very similar to the HK21E. Aside from being physically smaller and chambered for the 5.56 x 45mm NATO round, the HK23E is much the same as the HK21E and operates in the same manner. The barrel does not protrude much past the end of the barrel housing and is fitted with a standard flash hider. The characteristics and improvements over earlier models are the same as for the 21E. The

☞ continued on next page

☞ HK23E continued

23E may be fitted to a tripod, fired from its own folding bipod, or hip fired in the same manner as the 21E.

WEAPON HK23E
AMMO 5.56x45
DISPERSION ANGLE .0118545 degrees, .210747 NATO mils.

Range	Group Circle Width (mm)	Probability (0<p<.099) (m)			
		Body	Head	Hand	Bullseye
50.0	10.345	0.990	0.990	0.990	0.990
100.0	20.690	0.990	0.990	0.990	0.956
150.0	31.035	0.990	0.990	0.990	0.875
200.0	41.380	0.990	0.990	0.990	0.790
250.0	51.725	0.990	0.990	0.975	0.713
300.0	62.070	0.990	0.990	0.954	0.646
350.0	72.415	0.990	0.990	0.928	0.590
400.0	82.760	0.990	0.990	0.900	0.541
450.0	93.105	0.990	0.983	0.871	0.500
500.0	103.450	0.990	0.975	0.841	0.464
600.0	124.140	0.990	0.954	0.784	0.405
700.0	144.830	0.990	0.928	0.732	0.359
800.0	165.520	0.990	0.900	0.684	0.323
900.0	186.210	0.983	0.871	0.640	0.293
1000.0	206.900	0.975	0.841	0.602	0.268

DAMAGE 37/0.63

▼ MG3 • MG 42/59

CARTRIDGE 7.62x51mm
OPERATION Short recoil
TYPE OF FIRE Full automatic
RATE OF FIRE (A) 250 rpm (CYCLIC) 700–1300 rpm
MUZZLE VELOCITY 820 m/s (2690 fps)
MUZZLE ENERGY 3268 J (2410 ft/lb)
SIGHTS Adjustable, U-notch/post, range 1200m
FEED Flexible metal non-disintegrating belt
MOUNT TYPE Bipod
WEIGHTS:
WEAPON (EMPTY) 10.523 kg
WEAPON (LOADED) 11.946 kg w/50 rds
WEAPON (MOUNTED & LOADED)
12.496 kg w/50 rds
MOUNT 0.550 kg (bipod)
MAGAZINE (LOADED) 1.423 kg (50 rds)
SERVICE CARTRIDGE 25.6 g
BULLET 9.8 g

LENGTHS:
WEAPON OVERALL 122.5 cm
BARREL 53.1 cm
SIGHT RADIUS 43 cm
STATUS In production
SERVICE Federal German forces, Austria, Chile, Denmark, Iran, Italy, Norway, Pakistan, Portugal, Spain, Sudan, Turkey, and commercial sales. Many WWII MG42s are still to be found in use almost anywhere in the world.
COST $2700

This weapon is a direct descendant of the German MG 42 developed during World War II. The MG 42 first used the roller-locking system that was later developed into the G3 rifle series but in the MG 42, the barrel is actually locked to the bolt by rollers and the system operates by short recoil with a gas assist at the muzzle. With the bolt to the rear, a handle at the right side of the barrel housing can be pushed forward and out so that the barrel will be withdrawn to the side and rear of the weapon in a very short time. This system of barrel change gives the operator the fastest changing time available without an assistant. In 1959, the new Federal German army adopted the MG 42 in 7.62 NATO as the MG 42/59. Later modifications resulted in the MG3 which has received wide sales and use. The 550 gram bolt of the MG3 results in a 1200 round per minute cyclic rate of fire and there is an optional 950 gram bolt available that reduces the cyclic rate to a more manageable 900 rounds per minute.

WEAPON MG3
AMMO 7.62x51
DISPERSION ANGLE .122495 degrees, 2.17768 NATO mils.

Range	Group Circle Width (mm)	Probability (0<p<.099) (m)			
		Body	Head	Hand	Bullseye
50.0	106.897	0.990	0.972	0.832	0.453
100.0	213.793	0.972	0.832	0.590	0.260
150.0	320.690	0.907	0.695	0.448	0.182
200.0	427.587	0.832	0.590	0.360	0.140
250.0	534.483	0.760	0.510	0.300	0.114
300.0	641.380	0.695	0.448	0.257	0.096
350.0	748.277	0.639	0.399	0.225	0.083
400.0	855.173	0.590	0.360	0.200	0.073
450.0	962.070	0.547	0.327	0.180	0.065
500.0	1068.967	0.510	0.300	0.163	0.059
600.0	1282.760	0.448	0.257	0.138	0.049
700.0	1496.553	0.399	0.225	0.120	0.042
800.0	1710.347	0.360	0.200	0.105	0.037
900.0	1924.140	0.327	0.180	0.094	0.033
1000.0	2137.933	0.300	0.163	0.085	0.030
1100.0	2351.727	0.277	0.150	0.078	0.027

☞ continued

Range	Group Circle Width (mm)	Probability (0<p<.099) (m)			
		Body	Head	Hand	Bullseye
1200.0	2565.520	0.257	0.138	0.072	0.025
1300.0	2779.313	0.240	0.128	0.066	0.023
1400.0	2993.107	0.225	0.120	0.062	0.021
1500.0	3206.900	0.211	0.112	0.058	0.020

DAMAGE 49/0.37

▼ Ultimax 100 Mark III

Ultimax Mark III on bipod with 100 rd drum magazine

CARTRIDGE	5.56x45mm
OPERATION	Gas
TYPE OF FIRE	Full automatic
RATE OF FIRE	(A) 150 rpm (CYCLIC) 500 rpm
MUZZLE VELOCITY	990 m/s (3248 fps
MUZZLE ENERGY	1938 J (1429 ft/lb)
SIGHTS	Adjustable, aperture/post, range 1000m
FEED	20, or 30 round box and 60 or 100 round drum magazine
MOUNT TYPE	Bipod
WEIGHTS:	
WEAPON (EMPTY)	4.420 kg (1.560 kg Spare barrel)
WEAPON (LOADED)	6.210 kg w/100 rds
WEAPON (MOUNTED & LOADED)	6.58 kg w/ bipod & 100 rds
MOUNT	0.370 kg
MAGAZINE (EMPTY)	0.091 kg (20 rd), 0.117 kg (30 rd, 0.255 kg (60 rd), 0.570 kg (100 rd)
MAGAZINE (LOADED)	0.335 kg (20 rd), 0.483 kg (30 rd), 0.987 kg (60 rd), 1.790 kg (100 rd)
SERVICE CARTRIDGE	12.2 g
BULLET	4 g
LENGTHS:	
WEAPON OVERALL	103 cm
BARREL	50.8 cm
SIGHT RADIUS	47.2 cm
STATUS	In production
SERVICE	Singapore armed forces, US Navy (SEALS), commercial sales

This completely new weapon is also the first venture into the light machinegun field by Chartered Industries of Singapore. Utilizing proven principals in a modern package, the Ultimax is a very light weight weapon of rugged and durable design with high firepower and easy handling. To eliminate difficulties in handling long belts of ammunition, the Ultimax uses a drum magazine with the largest holding 100 rounds. Since the weapon is chambered for the 5.56 x 45mm round, a large capacity drum is feasible without being too heavy or cumbersome. Besides the drum, slightly modified M16 magazines may also be used. Arguments that the drum prevents sustained firing are answered by the fact the drum can be changed by one man on the run in under five seconds and a drum pack, holding four 100 round drums, is only 14 inches long and weighs 7.20kg. The operation system is a straight forward gas system with the piston above the barrel to help keep the line of recoil low, assisting in controlling full automatic fire. The gas system also has an easily adjustable regulator that can increase power to operate the weapon in adverse conditions or cut the gas flow off to allow rifle grenades to be launched from the flash suppressor. The folding bipod is attached to the front of the receiver assembly and, when unfolded, allows the weapon to roll or swivel through a 30 degree arc. Another unusual feature is a bayonet lug on the barrel, allowing the Ultimax to mount the M7 bayonet from the M16 rifle. The overall design of the Ultimax results in a very stable, reliable weapon, capable of holding the burst of an entire magazine on a small target. The Ultimax 100 Mark III is the lightest 5.56mm machinegun available on today's market and the weapon is being closely examined by a number of elite units. With the quick-change barrel, an unusual accessory has become available: a suppressed barrel with a 14 inch effective length and an integral suppressor mounted on the muzzle, giving the barrel the overall length of a standard model. There is also a special 12 inch barrel available for the Ultimax which, when the removable buttstock is taken off, gives a very short handy weapon of unmatched firepower for its size.

ASSESSMENT	6.6 in group @ 100 yds (10 rds full auto)
WEAPON	ULTIMAX 100 Mk III
AMMO	5.56x45
DISPERSION ANGLE	.105042 degrees, 1.86742 NATO mils.

Range	Group Circle Width (mm)	Probability (0<p<.099) (m)			
		Body	Head	Hand	Bullseye
50.0	91.667	0.990	0.984	0.875	0.505
100.0	183.333	0.984	0.875	0.646	0.297
150.0	275.000	0.937	0.750	0.500	0.209
200.0	366.667	0.875	0.646	0.405	0.161
250.0	458.333	0.810	0.565	0.340	0.131
300.0	550.000	0.750	0.500	0.293	0.111
350.0	641.667	0.695	0.448	0.257	0.096

☞ *continued on next page*

☞ *Ultimax 100 Mark III continued*

Range	Group Circle Width (mm)	Probability (0<p<.099) (m)			
		Body	Head	Hand	Bullseye
400.0	733.333	0.646	0.405	0.229	0.084
450.0	825.000	0.603	0.370	0.206	0.075
500.0	916.667	0.565	0.340	0.188	0.068
600.0	1100.000	0.500	0.293	0.159	0.057
700.0	1283.333	0.448	0.257	0.138	0.049
800.0	1466.667	0.405	0.229	0.122	0.043
900.0	1650.000	0.370	0.206	0.109	0.038
1000.0	1833.333	0.340	0.188	0.099	0.035

DAMAGE 38/0.66

▼ CETMI Ameli

CETME Ameli with ammunition belt inserted and bipod extended

CARTRIDGE	5.56x45mm
OPERATION	Retarded blowback
TYPE OF FIRE	Full automatic
RATE OF FIRE	(A) 150 rpm (CYCLIC) 850–1200 rpm
MUZZLE VELOCITY	910 m/s (2986 fps)
MUZZLE ENERGY	1637 J (1207 ft/lb)
SIGHTS	Adjustable, aperture/post, range 1000m
FEED	Flexible disintegrating metal belt
MOUNT TYPE	Bipod
WEIGHTS:	
WEAPON (EMPTY)	6.151 kg (0.826 kg Spare barrel)
WEAPON (LOADED)	9.620 kg w/200 rds & box
WEAPON (MOUNTED & LOADED)	
	10.151 w/200 rds & box
MOUNT	0.531 kg
MAGAZINE (EMPTY)	0.322 kg (100 rd belt box), 0.621 kg (200 rd belt box)
MAGAZINE (LOADED)	1.746 kg (100 rds w/box), 3.469 kg (200 rds w/box)
SERVICE CARTRIDGE	12.2 g
BULLET	4 g
LENGTHS:	
WEAPON OVERALL	97 cm
BARREL	40 cm
SIGHT RADIUS	34.3 cm

STATUS In production
SERVICE Spanish military and commercial sales

The Ameli is a new design from CETME of Spain and greatly resembles a reduced MG3 (which is also produced by CETME). Internally, the Ameli uses the roller-delayed system of retarded blowback perfected by CETME and widely seen in the Heckler and Koch weapons. The frame of the weapon is made of stampings reinforced by plastic castings for the buttstock and pistol grip. The bolt and other internal parts are made from machined forgings with the result being an easily mass-produced weapon of low cost. An interesting feature of the Ameli is the barrel change mechanism. By grasping the front port of the upper carrying handle/rear sight, a catch may be unlocked, allowing the front part of the handle to rotate to the right, unlocking the barrel. By first pushing the barrel forward, it may be slid back from the right side of the barrel housing and a new barrel inserted in its place. Another interesting point of the Ameli is that by changing the firing pin carrier of the bolt (a simple procedure), the rate of fire can be changed to either 850 or 1200 rounds per minute, the rate of fire being inscribed on the body of the carrier. Metal ammunition boxes are available that hold either 100 or 200 rounds of ammunition. The Ameli is a very compact and reliable design, easily maintained in the field. The weapon strips down into 7 components including a 100 round ammunition box and these parts will fit inside a standard briefcase. The weapon can be assembled, loaded, and fired within 20 seconds of opening the case.

WEAPON CETMI Ameli
AMMO 5.56x45
DISPERSION ANGLE .154106 degrees, 2.73967 NATO mils.

Range	Group Circle Width (mm)	Probability (0<p<.099) (m)			
		Body	Head	Hand	Bullseye
50.0	134.483	0.990	0.941	0.757	0.381
100.0	268.966	0.941	0.757	0.508	0.213
150.0	403.449	0.849	0.611	0.376	0.148
200.0	537.932	0.757	0.508	0.298	0.113
250.0	672.415	0.678	0.433	0.247	0.091
300.0	806.898	0.611	0.376	0.210	0.077
350.0	941.381	0.555	0.333	0.183	0.066
400.0	1075.864	0.508	0.298	0.162	0.058
450.0	1210.347	0.467	0.270	0.146	0.052
500.0	1344.830	0.433	0.247	0.132	0.047
600.0	1613.796	0.376	0.210	0.111	0.039
700.0	1882.762	0.333	0.183	0.096	0.034
800.0	2151.728	0.298	0.162	0.085	0.030
900.0	2420.694	0.270	0.146	0.076	0.026
1000.0	2689.660	0.247	0.132	0.068	0.024

DAMAGE 35/0.61

THE EDGE OF THE SWORD

▼ L86A1

CARTRIDGE	5.56x45mm
OPERATION	Gas
TYPE OF FIRE	Selective
RATE OF FIRE	(SS) 40 rpm (A) 100 rpm (CYCLIC) 700–850 rpm
MUZZLE VELOCITY	970 m/s (3182 fps)
MUZZLE ENERGY	1859 J (1371 ft/lb)
SIGHTS	SUSAT four power telescopic sight (wt. 0.800 kg), or adjustable, aperture/blade, iron sights (wt. 0.300 kg)
FEED	20, 30, or 30/45 rd removable box magazine (M16)
MOUNT TYPE	Integral bipod
WEIGHTS:	
WEAPON (EMPTY)	6.400 kg w/SUSAT sight
WEAPON (LOADED)	6.883 kg w/SUSAT sight & 30 rds
MAGAZINE (EMPTY)	0.091 kg (20 rd), 0.117 kg (30 rd), 0.149 kg (30/45 rd)
MAGAZINE (LOADED)	0.355 kg (20 rd), 0.483 kg (30 rd), 0.698 kg (30/45 rd w/45 rds)
SERVICE CARTRIDGE	12.2 g
BULLET	4 g
LENGTHS:	
WEAPON OVERALL	90 cm
BARREL	64.6 cm
SIGHT RADIUS	33.5 cm
STATUS	In production
SERVICE	British military

Range	Group Circle Width (mm)	Probability (0<p<.099) (m)			
		Body	**Head**	**Hand**	**Bullseye**
50.0	134.483	0.990	0.941	0.757	0.381
100.0	268.966	0.941	0.757	0.508	0.213
150.0	403.449	0.849	0.611	0.376	0.148
200.0	537.932	0.757	0.508	0.298	0.113
250.0	672.415	0.678	0.433	0.247	0.091
300.0	806.898	0.611	0.376	0.210	0.077
350.0	941.381	0.555	0.333	0.183	0.066
400.0	1075.864	0.508	0.298	0.162	0.058
450.0	1210.347	0.467	0.270	0.146	0.052
500.0	1344.830	0.433	0.247	0.132	0.047
600.0	1613.796	0.376	0.210	0.111	0.039
700.0	1882.762	0.333	0.183	0.096	0.034
800.0	2151.728	0.298	0.162	0.085	0.030
900.0	2420.694	0.270	0.146	0.076	0.026
1000.0	2689.660	0.247	0.132	0.068	0.024

DAMAGE 37/0.65

▼ M60

M60 with bipod extended and ammunition belt inserted

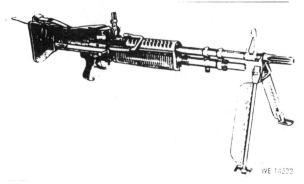

WE 14523

M60 with bipod and hinged buttplate extended

CARTRIDGE	7.62x51mm
OPERATION	Gas
TYPE OF FIRE	Full automatic
RATE OF FIRE	(A) 200 rpm (CYCLIC) 550 rpm
MUZZLE VELOCITY	855 m/s (2805 fps)
MUZZLE ENERGY	3553 J (2620 ft/lb)
SIGHTS	Adjustable, U-notch/blade, range 1100 m

The L86A1 is a slightly modified version of the L85A1 assault rifle and is intended to give supporting fire as a squad level automatic weapon. To fulfill its intended purpose, the L86A1 has a long heavy barrel to absorb some of the heat of firing. The barrel is covered along its bottom side by a long support to which a folding bipod attaches just below the muzzle. A slight change to the action allows the L86A1 to fire from the open bolt for additional cooling when fired on full automatic and to fire from the closed bolt position for greater accuracy when firing on semiautomatic. A vertical rear grip and folding shoulder support on the buttstock assist in stabilizing the weapon for full auto fire. In spite of the modifications, the L86A1 shares over 80 percent of its parts with the L85A1 rifle and is also issued with the SUSAT four power telescopic sight as standard equipment.

WEAPON	L86A1
AMMO	5.56x45 4 x power scope installed.
DISPERSION ANGLE	.154106 degrees, 2.73967 NATO mils.

☞ continued on next page

☞ *M60 continued*

FEED	Flexible disintegrating metal belt
MOUNT TYPE	Integral bipod or M122 tripod
WEIGHTS:	
WEAPON (EMPTY)	10.510 kg (3.740 kg Spare barrel)
WEAPON (LOADED)	13.504 kg w/100 rds
WEAPON (MOUNTED & LOADED)	
	20.304 kg w/100 rds
MOUNT	6.800 kg
MAGAZINE (LOADED)	2.994 kg (100 rds)
SERVICE CARTRIDGE	25.6 g
BULLET	9.8 g
LENGTHS:	
WEAPON OVERALL	110.5 cm
BARREL	56 cm
SIGHT RADIUS	54 cm
STATUS	In production
SERVICE	US military, Australia, Republic of Korea, Taiwan, and extensive commercial sales
COST	$2600

This is the standard general purpose machinegun used in the U.S. armed forces and has been made since the late 1950's. The M60 uses a straightforward gas operation system with a large gas cylinder and piston assembly attached to the barrel. The barrel is a quick change type but has some serious drawbacks. The gas cylinder and folding bipod are both attached to the barrel greatly increasing both the cost of the barrel as well as its weight. The bipod being attached to the barrel requires the weapon to be supported while the barrel is changed, normally needing an assistant gunner. The carrying handle is attached to the weapon with there being no sure grip on the hot barrel so a special asbestos mitten is issued with the spare barrel to aid in changing it. The feed system of the M60 uses a metallic link belt and is copied from the German MG 42. The operating rod/bolt system is also copied form a World War II German design, the FG-42. The large forearm assembly greatly assists in the M60 being hip fired and a strong operator is able to shoulder and fire the weapon like a rifle. The long length of service of the M60 has resulted in a number of improvements which have added to the strength and reliability of the weapon. Ammunition for the M60 is normally packaged in 100 round belts contained in a pack that can be attached to the left hand side of the weapon. The pack also has a shoulder strap allowing several to be easily carried by the gunner.

ASSESSMENT	15 inches @ 600 yards
WEAPON	M60
AMMO	7.62x51
DISPERSION ANGLE	.0397625 degrees, .70689 NATO mils.

Range	Group Circle Width (mm)	Probability (0<p<.099) (m)			
		Body	**Head**	**Hand**	**Bullseye**
50.0	34.699	0.990	0.990	0.990	0.844
100.0	69.399	0.990	0.990	0.936	0.605
150.0	104.098	0.990	0.974	0.840	0.462
200.0	138.797	0.990	0.936	0.747	0.372
250.0	173.497	0.988	0.889	0.666	0.310
300.0	208.196	0.974	0.840	0.599	0.266
350.0	242.895	0.957	0.792	0.544	0.233
400.0	277.595	0.936	0.747	0.497	0.207
450.0	312.294	0.913	0.705	0.457	0.187
500.0	346.993	0.889	0.666	0.422	0.170
600.0	416.392	0.840	0.599	0.367	0.144
700.0	485.791	0.792	0.544	0.324	0.124
800.0	555.189	0.747	0.497	0.290	0.110
900.0	624.588	0.705	0.457	0.263	0.098
1000.0	693.987	0.666	0.422	0.240	0.089
1100.0	763.385	0.631	0.393	0.221	0.081
1200.0	832.784	0.599	0.367	0.204	0.075
1300.0	902.183	0.570	0.344	0.190	0.069
1400.0	971.581	0.544	0.324	0.178	0.064
1500.0	1040.980	0.519	0.306	0.167	0.060

DAMAGE 51/0.38

▼ **M60E3**

M60E3 with long barrel

M60E3 fitted with short barrel

Conversion kit to change the M60 machinegun to the M60E3 configuration

CARTRIDGE	7.62x51mm
OPERATION	Gas
TYPE OF FIRE	Full automatic
RATE OF FIRE	(A) 200 rpm (CYCLIC) 600 rpm
MUZZLE VELOCITY	853 m/s (2800 fps) w/standard barrel, 823 m/s (2700 fps) w/short barrel
MUZZLE ENERGY	3541 J (2611 ft/lb) w/standard barrel, 3292 J (2428 ft/lb) w/short barrel
SIGHTS	Adjustable, U-notch/blade, range 1100m
FEED	Flexible disintegrating metal belt
MOUNT TYPE	Integral bipod or M122 tripod
WEIGHTS:	
WEAPON (EMPTY)	8.505 kg (8.392 kg w/short barrel) (2.126 kg Spare barrel <standard>, 2.013 kg Spare barrel <short>)
WEAPON (LOADED)	11.499 kg w/100 rds (11.386 kg w/short barrel & 100 rds)
WEAPON (MOUNTED & LOADED)	18.299 kg w/100 rds (18.186 kg w/short barrel & 100 rds)
MOUNT	6.800 kg
MAGAZINE (LOADED)	2.994 kg (100 rds)
SERVICE CARTRIDGE	25.6 g
BULLET	9.8 g

LENGTHS:	
WEAPON OVERALL	107.6 cm (93.7 cm w/short barrel)
BARREL	56 cm (42.1 cm)
SIGHT RADIUS	42.2 cm
STATUS	In production
SERVICE	US Navy and Marines, commercial sales
COST	$3200

This is a modified version of the M60 machinegun and is a considerably lighter and more flexible weapon. The large forearm of the M60 is replaced with a smaller forearm with a vertical grip for control. The bipod has been lightened and moved from the barrel and attached to the receiver on the same mounting that holds the forearm. The barrel has been considerably lightened and is of a smaller diameter with a redesigned flash hider. The carrying handle has been moved to the barrel where it can be used to change a hot barrel, eliminating the need for an insulated glove. There are two lengths of barrel available, one of standard length, and a shortened barrel with the front sight moved to just in front of the gas piston and the flash hider attached in front of the sight. In the U.S. Navy, which has adopted the M60E3, each weapon is issued with both a long and short barrel. The front sight is now adjustable allowing each barrel to be zeroed to an specific receiver, something that could not be done on the earlier M60. The

☞ continued on next page

☞ *M60E3 continued*

internal mechanism has been modified for additional safety as well as increased reliability, and a more comfortable pistol grip mounted on the trigger mechanism. The trigger guard has been changed so that it can be folded out of the way to allow the trigger to be pulled while wearing gloves. An upgrading kit is available to easily change a standard M60 to M60E3 specifications.

LMG field stripped with both belt feed with ammunition and magazine feed magazine

WEAPON	M60E3	
AMMO	7.62x51	
DISPERSION ANGLE	.0397625 degrees, .70689 NATO mils.	

Range	Group Circle Width (mm)	Probability (0<p<.099) (m)			
		Body	Head	Hand	Bullseye
50.0	34.699	0.990	0.990	0.990	0.844
100.0	69.399	0.990	0.990	0.936	0.605
150.0	104.098	0.990	0.974	0.840	0.462
200.0	138.797	0.990	0.936	0.747	0.372
250.0	173.497	0.988	0.889	0.666	0.310
300.0	208.196	0.974	0.840	0.599	0.266
350.0	242.895	0.957	0.792	0.544	0.233
400.0	277.595	0.936	0.747	0.497	0.207
450.0	312.294	0.913	0.705	0.457	0.187
500.0	346.993	0.889	0.666	0.422	0.170
600.0	416.392	0.840	0.599	0.367	0.144
700.0	485.791	0.792	0.544	0.324	0.124
800.0	555.189	0.747	0.497	0.290	0.110
900.0	624.588	0.705	0.457	0.263	0.098
1000.0	693.987	0.666	0.422	0.240	0.089
1100.0	763.385	0.631	0.393	0.221	0.081
1200.0	832.784	0.599	0.367	0.204	0.075
1300.0	902.183	0.570	0.344	0.190	0.069
1400.0	971.581	0.544	0.324	0.178	0.064
1500.0	1040.980	0.519	0.306	0.167	0.060

DAMAGE 51/0.38

LMG with magazine feed and 30 rd magazine, weapon has the lightweight barrel with compensator and no bipod

CARTRIDGE	5.56 x 45mm
OPERATION	Gas
TYPE OF FIRE	Full automatic
RATE OF FIRE	(A) 150 rpm (CYCLIC) 600 rpm
MUZZLE VELOCITY	840 m/s (2755 fps)
MUZZLE ENERGY	3428 J (2528 ft/lb)
SIGHTS	Adjustable, aperture/post
FEED	Flexible metallic disintegrating link belt or, with adaptor, 20, 30, or 30/45 round removable box magazine
MOUNT TYPE	Removable bipod
WEIGHTS:	
WEAPON (EMPTY)	4.912 kg (spare barrel 1.733 kg)
WEAPON (LOADED)	8.037 kg w/200 rds in box
WEAPON (MOUNTED & LOADED)	8.595 kg w/bipod & 200 rds
MOUNT	0.558 kg
MAGAZINE (EMPTY)	0.277 kg (200 rd belt box)
MAGAZINE (LOADED)	3.125 kg (200 rd belt w/box)
SERVICE CARTRIDGE	12.2 g
BULLET	4 g
LENGTHS:	
WEAPON OVERALL	97.1/107.3 cm
BARREL	55 cm
SIGHT RADIUS	54.1 cm
STATUS	Prototype

▼ 5.56mm LMG (The New Stoner)

LMG mounted on bipod with 200 rd belt box

This is the new light machinegun design out of Ares, Inc. in Port Clinton, Ohio and is referred to by some as the "New Stoner," after Eugene Stoner, president of Ares and chief designer of the weapon. Firing from the open bolt position, this LMG is a very rugged and lightweight design which is capable of a wide range of applications.

Normally fired from its removable bipod, the LMG is also usable as a heavy rifle with the bipod folded. A lightweight barrel with a large muzzle compensator that significantly lightens the weapon is available, but it also cuts down on sustained fire. By removing the feed cover and replacing it with an adaptor, the LMG is able to utilize any of the M16 type magazines. The stock layout aids in controllability when firing and is also adjustable in length to suit the firer. The forward portion of the rear sight base is an integral sight mount that allows many types of optical sights to be attached for use. The barrel is of the quick release type with a fixed headspace and an integral folding handle attached to assist in changing a hot barrel. The ammunition containers and links used are the same as those used by the MINIMI machinegun, giving this LMG easy access to ammunition which is already in the U.S. supply chain.

WEAPON	LMG				
AMMO	5.56x45				
DISPERSION ANGLE	.085351 degrees, 1.51735 NATO mils.				

Range	Group Circle Width (mm)	Probability (0<p<.099) (m)			
		Body	**Head**	**Hand**	**Bullseye**
50.0	74.483	0.990	0.990	0.923	0.579
100.0	148.966	0.990	0.923	0.722	0.351
150.0	223.448	0.967	0.818	0.574	0.251
200.0	297.931	0.923	0.722	0.472	0.195
250.0	372.414	0.871	0.641	0.400	0.159
300.0	446.897	0.818	0.574	0.347	0.134
350.0	521.379	0.768	0.518	0.306	0.116
400.0	595.862	0.722	0.472	0.274	0.103
450.0	670.345	0.679	0.434	0.247	0.092
500.0	744.828	0.641	0.400	0.226	0.083
600.0	893.793	0.574	0.347	0.192	0.070
700.0	1042.759	0.518	0.306	0.167	0.060
800.0	1191.724	0.472	0.274	0.148	0.053
900.0	1340.690	0.434	0.247	0.132	0.047
1000.0	1489.655	0.400	0.226	0.120	0.042

DAMAGE 32/0.57

▼ .50 M2HB

M2HB without tripod or mounts

CARTRIDGE	12.7x99mm
OPERATION	Recoil
TYPE OF FIRE	Selective

RATE OF FIRE	(SS) 70 rpm (A) 150 rpm (CYCLIC) 500 rpm
MUZZLE VELOCITY	930 m/s (3050 fps)
MUZZLE ENERGY	18539 J (13672 ft/lb)
SIGHTS	Adjustable, aperture/blade, range 2377m (2600 yds)
FEED	Flexible disintegrating link metal belt
MOUNT TYPE	M3 tripod
WEIGHTS:	
WEAPON (EMPTY)	38.100 kg
WEAPON (LOADED)	52.664 kg w/105 rds
WEAPON (MOUNTED & LOADED)	72.622 kg w/105 rds
MOUNT	19.958 kg
MAGAZINE (LOADED)	14.564 kg (105 rds)
SERVICE CARTRIDGE	115 g
BULLET	42.9 g
LENGTHS:	
WEAPON OVERALL	165.3 cm
BARREL	114.3 cm
SIGHT RADIUS	50.8 cm
STATUS	In production
SERVICE	USA and large commercial sales
COST	$6000

This is a massive weapon, just short of being in the machine-cannon class. Originally adopted in 1923 and modified to the M2 configuration in 1933, the M2HB has been improved several times during its service life and is presently the oldest operational design still seeing first line service. The M2 operates on the short recoil principle with the bolt locked to the barrel with the entire assembly moving backwards a short distance while recoiling. The bolt is unlocked by a cam and the barrel returns to battery while the bolt continues its rearward motion. While moving forward, the bolt recocks the firing pin, picks up a fresh loaded round and ejects the empty out the bottom of the receiver. A mechanism will lock the bolt to the rear after each shot, allowing semiautomatic fire if desired. If full automatic fire is desired, the mechanism may easily be locked out of operation and the bolt moves freely. A simple change of parts will allow the M2 to feed ammunition from the right or left sides. The cocking lever is also easily moved from one side to the other. The result of this is a simple mounting of twin M2's parallel to each other, one operating and feeding from the left side, the other from the right. The heavy barrel is unscrewed to change it and the headspace should be adjusted each time the barrel is changed. New weapons may have a quick change barrel system that uses a fixed headspace and this new option can be retrofitted to older weapons. The .50 M2 has a tremendous amount of power for a ground mounted weapon, but is quite heavy. The M2 must be fired from some type of mounting and a three man crew is able to move the weapon, tripod, and a limited amount of ammunition by man-packing it. Regardless of its drawbacks, the M2HB is a very powerful and almost unbelievably rugged weapon that will be seeing service for some years to come.

ASSESSMENT	18 inches @ 600 yards				
WEAPON	M2HB				
AMMO	12.7x99				
DISPERSION ANGLE	.0477465 degrees, .848827 NATO mils.				

Range	Group Circle Width (mm)	Probability (0<p<.099) (m)			
		Body	**Head**	**Hand**	**Bullseye**
50.0	41.667	0.990	0.990	0.990	0.787
100.0	83.333	0.990	0.990	0.898	0.539
150.0	125.000	0.990	0.953	0.782	0.403
200.0	166.667	0.990	0.898	0.681	0.321
250.0	208.333	0.974	0.839	0.599	0.266
300.0	250.000	0.953	0.782	0.533	0.227
350.0	291.667	0.927	0.729	0.480	0.198
400.0	333.333	0.898	0.681	0.435	0.176
450.0	375.000	0.869	0.638	0.398	0.158
500.0	416.667	0.839	0.599	0.367	0.143
600.0	500.000	0.782	0.533	0.317	0.121
700.0	583.333	0.729	0.480	0.279	0.105
800.0	666.667	0.681	0.435	0.249	0.092
900.0	750.000	0.638	0.398	0.224	0.082
1000.0	833.333	0.599	0.367	0.204	0.074
1100.0	916.667	0.565	0.340	0.188	0.068
1200.0	1000.000	0.533	0.317	0.173	0.062
1300.0	1083.333	0.505	0.297	0.161	0.058
1400.0	1166.667	0.480	0.279	0.151	0.054
1500.0	1250.000	0.456	0.263	0.141	0.050
1600.0	1333.333	0.435	0.249	0.133	0.047
1700.0	1416.667	0.416	0.236	0.126	0.045
1800.0	1500.000	0.398	0.224	0.119	0.042
1900.0	1583.333	0.382	0.214	0.113	0.040
2000.0	1666.667	0.367	0.204	0.108	0.038

DAMAGE 92/3.05

CHAPTER 7

GRENADES & GRENADE LAUNCHERS

Small pottery and metal jars were among the first hand-held weapons using black powder as an explosive. Though they have no definite date of invention, various hand-thrown bombs were in use by the 14th century.

Because of undependable performance, grenades had fallen out of use in the first quarter of the 1800's.

Before and during WW 1, there was a resurgence in the use of grenades. Now, every military group (and many paramilitary police) make use of the varied types of modern grenades: blast(offensive), fragmentation, smoke, incendiary, gas, stun, illuminating, and anti-tank.

The grenade launcher family of weapons includes rifle grenades, 30 mm/40 mm cartridge grenade launchers, and smoothbore shell launchers (usually for tear gas). Invented near the end of WW 1 to give greater grenade throwing range to the infantryman, rifle grenade launchers consist of a clamped tube or muzzle modification that directs the gas of a blank cartridge to drive the grenade, which has been slid over the launcher. Modern rifle grenades have a "bullet trap" at their base, allowing standard ball ammo to be used.

The more recent (1960's) launchers in 30 mm/40 mm actually fire a small shell from a rifled barrel. This sort of grenade has a far greater range and accuracy than the rifle-launched ones. The last type, tear gas guns, are the shortest-ranged weapons of the group. They use fin-stabilized projectiles because of their unrifled barrels. ●

▼ HG 78 (OFF HG 78)

HG 78 fragmentation grenade

TYPE	Fragmentation hand grenade (Blast/ concussion hand grenade)
FILLER	PETN
FUSE TYPE	Pull ring/lever, percussion
FUSE DELAY	4 seconds
WEIGHTS:	
ROUND	0.520 kg
FILLER	0.070 kg
EFFECTS:	
EFFECT	Blast and fragmentation @ 5,500 fragments (Blast and shock wave)
AREA OF EFFECT	15 m
LENGTHS:	
LENGTH	11.5 cm
WIDTH (DIAMETER)	6 cm
STATUS	In production
SERVICE	Austrian armed forces and commercial sales

This is an improved version of earlier designs and is presently the standard issue hand grenade for the Austrian armed forces as well as seeing good export sales. There are two versions of this grenade, the HG-78 fragmentation grenade and the OFF HG 78 offensive blast grenade with no fragmentation. In the HG 78, the plastic body is made of a cast matrix, holding 5,500 steel balls surrounded by a thermoplastic shell for physical strength. When the explosive filler detonates, the balls fly out at a high velocity as lethal fragments. The fragmentation is controlled by the type of explosive, an explosive waveshaper to control the detonation, and the strength of the matrix holding the balls. The small

size, 2.0 – 2.3mm diameter, and weight of the fragments also serve to limit their lethal range. At close ranges (5 meters or less), there are over 28 fragments per square meter, with no perforating fragments at 20 meters. The OFF HG 78 has a smooth outer shell and produces no fragments. The fuse is of the familiar bouchon pull ring and safety lever type with some noticeable improvements. The body of the fuse is cast plastic and has a number of retaining clips that hold the ring of the safety pin against the body of the fuse. The fly-off lever is shrouded over the top of the fuse and designed so that it must be released over a 50 degree arc to activate the fuse. The point of the safety pin is also covered by the fuse body, preventing it from snagging while being carried.

DAMAGE	174 Blast, MAX (100) Stun, Fragmentation 5/(2.28 MAX)

▼ HG 80

HG 80 mini fragmentation grenade (actual size)

TYPE	Miniature fragmentation hand grenade
FILLER	PETN
FUSE TYPE	Pull ring/lever, percussion
FUSE DELAY	4 seconds
WEIGHTS:	
ROUND	0.165 kg
FILLER	0.013 kg
EFFECTS:	
EFFECT	Blast and fragmentation @ 1,000 fragments
AREA OF EFFECT	10m
LENGTHS:	
LENGTH	7.6 cm
WIDTH (DIAMETER)	4 cm

STATUS In production
SERVICE Commercial sales

This is a miniaturized fragmentation grenade intended for use at close quarters such as house-to-house or in other situations where the power of a full sized grenade would be excessive. The body of the grenade is roughly the same size as the fuse assembly, making for a very compact package. A matrix holding 1,000 steel ball fragments 2.0–2.3mm in diameter forms the body. Over the matrix is a thermoplastic shell with three raised rings to indicate the type of grenade. The small size of the grenade limits the fragmentation density with there being 4.6 fragments per square meter at five meters but only 0.4 fragments per square meter at ten meters. The fuse is the same type as on the HG 78 grenade and has the same features.

DAMAGE 32 Blast, 22 Stun,
Fragmentation 5/(2.28 MAX)

▼ HE-RFL-35x40 BTU M262

CALIBER 22mm
TYPE Fragmentation rifle grenade w/bullet trap
MUZZLE VELOCITY 63 m/s (5.56mm rifle), 79 m/s (7.62mm rifle)
FILLER Composition B
FUSE TYPE F85 Impact nose fuse
FUSE DELAY None
WEIGHTS:
ROUND 0.385 kg
FILLER 0.054 kg
EFFECTS:
EFFECT Blast and fragmentation
AREA OF EFFECT 5 m
MINIMUM RANGE 15 m
MAXIMUM RANGE 300 m (5.56mm rifle), 400 m (7.62mm rifle)
LENGTHS:
LENGTH 28.8 cm
WIDTH (DIAMETER) 4 cm
STATUS In production
SERVICE Wide commercial sales

This is one member of a family of rifle grenades produced by MECAR of Belgium and widely sold throughout the world. The main advantage of the MECAR grenades is that they do not require the use of a special blank launching cartridge but may be launched with a bulleted round. The BTU in the grenade's designation indicates it is fitted with the Bullet Trap Universal which allows any regular ball round, either 5.56 or 7.62mm caliber, to be safely used to launch the grenade. The internal diameter of the tail assembly is 22mm which will fit over any NATO standard grenade launcher or flash suppressor for launching. The fuze arms on setback when the grenade is launched, has a built in safety that delays arming until the grenade has traveled at least five meters, and will not fully arm until the grenade has traveled 15 meters. After it is armed, the fuze will function on impact with the grenade's tail fins insuring a nose-first strike. The upper body of the M262 contains the explosive and the interior of the body is notched to provide controlled fragmentation of the body into about 300 fragments.

ASSESSMENT 30 cm @ 100 m
WEAPON HE-RFL M262
DISPERSION ANGLE .171887 degrees, 3.05578 NATO mils.

Range	Group Circle Width (mm)	Probability (0<p<.099) (m)			
		Body	Head	Hand	Bullseye
50.0	150.000	0.990	0.921	0.719	0.349
100.0*	300.000	0.921	0.719	0.470	0.193
150.0	450.000	0.816	0.571	0.345	0.134
200.0	600.000	0.719	0.470	0.272	0.102
250.0	750.000	0.638	0.398	0.224	0.082
300.0	900.000	0.571	0.345	0.191	0.069
350.0	1050.000	0.516	0.304	0.166	0.060
400.0	1200.000	0.470	0.272	0.147	0.052

* indicates range for which data was supplied

DAMAGE 109 Blast, 73 Stun,
Fragmentation 5/(2.28 MAX)

▼ HE-RFL LR BTU M287

CALIBER 22mm
TYPE Fragmentation rifle grenade w/ bullet trap and rocket assist
MUZZLE VELOCITY 39 m/s MAXIMUM VELOCITY 105 m/s
FILLER Composition B
FUSE TYPE Impact nose fuse
FUSE DELAY None
WEIGHTS:
ROUND 0.825 kg (7.62mm version) 0.780 kg (5.56mm version)
FILLER 0.158 kg
EFFECTS:
EFFECT Blast and fragmentation
AREA OF EFFECT 20m
MINIMUM RANGE 25 m
MAXIMUM RANGE 650 m
LENGTHS:
LENGTH 30.1 cm
WIDTH (DIAMETER) 5.5 cm
STATUS In production

☞ continued on next page

☛ *HE-RFL LR BTU M287 continued*

SERVICE Commercial sales

This is a rocket assisted long range rifle grenade intended to be a possible replacement for light mortars. The M287 uses the MECAR bullet trap, allowing standard rifles using ball ammunition to launch the grenade at low velocity. Immediately after launch, a rocket motor ignites and propels the grenade to a high velocity, greatly extending its range. The four fins which stabilize the grenade in flight are spring loaded and can be unfolded before firing or held in place by a light cylinder which slips off when the grenade is launched. The fuze starts to arm after it has traveled 15 meters from launch and is fully armed 25 meters from launch. The body of the grenade is internally serrated to control breakup of the casing into at least 500 fragments. The differences in weight between the 7.62 and 5.56 versions of this grenade have no bearing on the effectiveness of the weapon and both versions are roughly matched in range.

ASSESSMENT 12 m @ 700 m
WEAPON HE-RFL LR M287
DISPERSION ANGLE .98219 degrees, 17.4612 NATO mils.

Range	Group Circle Width (mm)	Probability (0<p<.099) (m)			
		Body	Head	Hand	Bullseye
50.0	857.143	0.589	0.359	0.199	0.072
100.0	1714.286	0.359	0.199	0.105	0.037
150.0	2571.429	0.256	0.138	0.071	0.025
200.0	3428.571	0.199	0.105	0.054	0.019
250.0	4285.714	0.163	0.085	0.043	0.015
300.0	5142.857	0.138	0.071	0.036	0.012
350.0	6000.000	0.119	0.062	0.031	0.011
400.0	6857.143	0.105	0.054	0.027	0.009
450.0	7714.286	0.094	0.048	0.024	0.008
500.0	8571.429	0.085	0.043	0.022	0.007
550.0	9428.571	0.078	0.040	0.020	0.007
600.0	10285.714	0.071	0.036	0.018	0.006
650.0	11142.857	0.066	0.034	0.017	0.006
700.0*	12000.000	0.062	0.031	0.016	0.005

* indicates range for which data was supplied

DAMAGE 320 Blast, MAX (100)
Stun, Fragmentation 5/(2.28 MAX)

▼ TYPE 241 BLINDING

TYPE Flash/Dazzle hand grenade
FILLER Magnesium based flash composition
FUSE TYPE Pressure initiating cap
FUSE DELAY 1.5 seconds
WEIGHTS:
ROUND 0.100 kg

EFFECTS:
EFFECT Brilliant flash of light, 5,000,000 candelas for .002 sec.
AREA OF EFFECT 20 m
LENGTHS:
LENGTH 12 cm
WIDTH (DIAMETER) 5 cm
STATUS In production
SERVICE French forces and commercial sales

This is an unusual grenade developed in France and sold commercially by the Ruggieri company. The grenade has a plastic body that does not fragment and a flash compound filler that does not cause blast damage. When the grenade fires, it creates an intense dazzling flash of light that lasts for a few hundredths of a second. The dazzle effect on a group of targets will last up to two minutes, preventing any sighted action on the part of the targets. The effects are temporary and wear off completely within a few hours. The fuze of the Type 241 is also unusual. A safety cap is removed from the top of the grenade, exposing a push button with a safety clip. Removing the clip allows the push button to be driven home and the grenade is thrown immediately as it will function 1.5 seconds after the button is pushed.

DAMAGE SPECIAL-Temporary blindness 10 to 120 seconds

▼ M67

TYPE Fragmentation hand grenade
FILLER Composition B
FUSE TYPE M213 pull ring/lever percussion
FUSE DELAY 4 seconds
WEIGHTS:
ROUND 0.390 kg
FILLER 0.180 kg
EFFECTS:
EFFECT Blast and fragmentation
AREA OF EFFECT 15 m
LENGTHS:
LENGTH 9 cm
WIDTH (DIAMETER) 6.4 cm
STATUS In production
SERVICE U.S. military

This is presently the standard issue fragmentation grenade of the U.S. Army. The round, baseball shape of the M67 is intended to make it easier to throw and more stable in flight. The thick casing of the body separates into a good number of fragments, but is not quite as effective as other methods of controlling fragmentation. The fuze is of the bouchon type with a safety lever, pull ring, and a safety clip. The safety clip is normally unsnapped from the fuze before use and the pull ring drawn out just before throwing.

DAMAGE 365 Blast, MAX (100)
Stun, Fragmentation 5/(2.28 MAX)

▼ M26A1

TYPE	Fragmentation hand grenade
FILLER	Composition B w/Tetryl booster
FUSE TYPE	M204A1 pull ring/lever percussion
FUSE DELAY	4–5 seconds
WEIGHTS:	
ROUND	0.454 kg
FILLER	0.156 kg (Comp. B), 0.009 kg (Tetryl)
EFFECTS:	
EFFECT	Blast and fragmentation
AREA OF EFFECT	15m radius
LENGTHS:	
LENGTH	9.9 cm
WIDTH (DIAMETER)	5.7 cm
STATUS	In production
SERVICE	US forces and widely copied abroad
COST	$5

The M26A1 is still in wide use with U.S. forces and militaries supported by the U.S. The body of the M26A1 is made up of a pair of stamped steel cups that surround the charge and fragmentation coil. The fragmentation coil is made up of a coil of square cross-sectioned wire that is notched to control breakup. To insure positive detonation of the relatively insensitive filler, there are several pellets of the more sensitive explosive Tetryl surrounding the detonator.

DAMAGE 333 Blast, MAX (100)
Stun, Fragmentation 5/(2.28 MAX)

▼ AN-M8 HC

TYPE	Burning type HC smoke hand grenade
FILLER	HC smoke composition type C
FUSE TYPE	M201A1 pull ring/lever percussion
FUSE DELAY	0.7–2 seconds
WEIGHTS:	
ROUND	0.680 kg
FILLER	0.539 kg
EFFECTS:	
EFFECT	Creates a dense cloud of white screening smoke
BURN TIME	105–150 seconds
AREA OF EFFECT	18x4x2m cloud
LENGTHS:	
LENGTH	14.5 cm
WIDTH (DIAMETER)	6.4 cm
STATUS	In production
SERVICE	US forces

This is a canister style, burning smoke grenade that is standard issue in the U.S. armed forces. The sheet steel canister body holds the smoke mixture and supports the fuze assembly. There are four tape covered holes in the cover of the body to emit the smoke created by the burning composition. The pyrotechnic composition produces a dense cloud of zinc chloride smoke that is heavy and spreads out over the ground, dissipating slowly. The smoke is relatively non-toxic but should not be breathed for long periods of time. The fuze is of the standard bouchon type with a pull ring and safety lever. It has a short delay and then fires a burst of hot particles into the starter mixture that ignites the HC smoke mixture.

▼ NICO Sound/Flash

TYPE	Stun hand grenade
FILLER	8 cardboard "thunderflash" submunitions filled w/pyrotechnic composition
FUSE TYPE	Pull ring/lever percussion
FUSE DELAY	2.5 seconds
WEIGHTS:	
ROUND	0.275 kg
PROJECTILE	0.022 kg per thunderflash
FILLER	0.010 kg per thunderflash
EFFECTS:	
EFFECT	8 flashes in a random pattern @ 1,000,000 candela and 175 db causing 5–15 seconds of disorientation
AREA OF EFFECT	10m

☞ *continued on next page*

☞ *NICO Sound/Flash continued*

LENGTHS:
LENGTH 12.8 cm
WIDTH (DIAMETER) 6 cm
STATUS In production
SERVICE Commercial sales

This is one of the earliest available stun grenades and was reportedly used by GSG-9 at the Mogadishu rescue. The grenade is a canister type, carrying eight submunitions that it ejects out of the top. The body of the grenade holds the fuze and acts as the carrier for the submunitions. It will cause no dangerous fragmentation when the grenade functions. When the pull ring is removed and the safety lever released, the bouchon type fuze ignites a short 2.5 second delay. At the end of the delay, the eight submunitions eject from the top of the body as the fuze and cover blow away. Each of the submunitions is a cardboard cased thunderflash that is self-propelled and has a very short fuze. Each of the thunderflashes flies off in a random pattern and flashes after a 0.5 second delay. The flashes are each 175 to 185 decibels and several hundred thousand candelas in intensity with the cardboard cases harmlessly disintegrating. The thunderflashes are carefully engineered to be above the temporary disabling level but not of such intensity as to cause permanent physical damage. The blast and shock causes temporary psycho- and physiological disorientation, preventing any voluntary acts on the part of those exposed to the effects. The total disorientation is of short term, five to fifteen seconds duration, and the effects completely disappear within a short time. The scattering effect of the submunitions gives the NICO grenades an impressive effectiveness zone of 10 meters radius.

DAMAGE SPECIAL 100 Stun within 10 meters

▼ M7A3 CS

TYPE Burning type canister CS gas hand grenade
FILLER CS/pyrotechnic smoke composition
FUSE TYPE M201A1 pull ring/lever percussion
FUSE DELAY 0.7–2 seconds
WEIGHTS:
ROUND 0.439 kg
FILLER 0.128 kg CS, 0.208 kg pyrotechnic mix
EFFECTS:
EFFECT Produces a large cloud of CS gas
BURN TIME 15–35 seconds
AREA OF EFFECT 240 M3, 18x4x4m cloud
LENGTHS:
LENGTH 14.5 cm
WIDTH (DIAMETER) 6.4 cm
STATUS In production

SERVICE US military and police agencies, wide commercial sales

M7A3 CS grenade

This is presently the standard CS gas grenade of the U.S. armed forces and is the most likely one to be encountered. A canister style, burning type grenade, the M7A3 has a bouchon type, pull-ring safety lever fuze at the top. The fuze has a two second delay when initiated after which it fires a charge of hot particles into the filler mixture. The filler consists of a pyrotechnic mixture made up of a type of nitrocellulose powder that produces a large amount of dense white smoke as it burns. The CS agent (Orthochlorbenzalmalononitrile) is a white powder contained in gelatin capsules spread throughout the pyrotechnic mixture. As the pyrotechnic mixture burns, it volatilizes the CS agent in the capsules and carries it in the smoke out of the escape holes in the bottom and top of the grenade canister. The gas cloud thins fairly quickly, and so can be seen through. However, the effects of the CS gas are still strong, even when the cloud is difficult to see. CS takes effect on an individual within a few seconds of exposure to a visible cloud. The effects include severe pain and burning of the eyes and mucous membranes of the nose, mouth, and throat. Stinging and burning of the skin also begins to occur. As exposure continues for 30 to 60 seconds, sneezing, dripping of the nose, coughing, and tightness of the chest takes place. Even longer exposure, 1 to 2 minutes, will cause the eyes to close involuntarily in roughly 90 percent of the individuals exposed. Breathing also becomes difficult with breaths being short and labored after a few minutes exposure. Many individuals may panic, so difficult does breathing appear to become. Symptoms disappear rapidly when a victim is removed to fresh air, usually within 5 to 10 minutes. Lethality is rarely a problem with CS gas unless it is used in a small enclosed space where death from suffocation becomes a real problem. One of the difficulties in using the M7A3 canister grenade is that while functioning, the exterior of the body may get as hot as 500 degrees, igniting possible combustibles.

▼ M25A2 CS

TYPE	Bursting type CS gas plastic hand grenade
FILLER	powdered CS1/talc mixture
FUSE TYPE	pull ring/plunger percussion
FUSE DELAY	1.4–3 seconds
WEIGHTS:	
ROUND	0.227 kg
FILLER	0.057 kg
EFFECTS:	
EFFECT	Instantneous release of CS gas cloud
AREA OF EFFECT	5m burst radius, 20x4m cloud downwind
LENGTHS:	
LENGTH	8.6 cm
WIDTH (DIAMETER)	7.4 cm
STATUS	In production
SERVICE	US forces

The M25A2 grenade was developed to allow CS to be used in situations where the danger of fire is too great to allow burning type canister grenades to be used. The bursting type M25A2 grenade also releases all of its chemical agent in an instantaneous cloud, giving the CS a more immediate effect and preventing any possible throwback of a burning CS canister. The body of the grenade is a hollow plastic sphere with a control core containing the fuze and detonator assembly. The fuze is a spring loaded plunger that sticks out of the top of the grenade and is retained by a sleeve held by a pull ring and cotter pin. With the pull ring removed, the sleeve may be held in place with the thumb of the throwing hand. If the sleeve is allowed to move, it becomes very difficult to replace the pull pin if desired. When the sleeve is released, the plunger is driven into the grenade by a spring and strikes a firing pin starting a two second delay. After the delay, the detonator fires, rupturing the plastic shell and spreading the agent filler. The filler consists of 95 percent CS powder and 5 percent silica gel to keep the filler from clumping. The visible cloud of agent starts with a diameter of about 10 meters but is quickly elongated by any wind. With a 12 to 18 mph wind, a single M25A2 grenade can make a CS cloud that covers more than 420 square meters and still has the major effective symptoms of the gas. The powdered agent will contaminate an area for several hours at least and a person walking through the area will stir up enough agent to quickly affect them.

▼ Kilgore/Schermuly

TYPE	Stun hand grenade
FILLER	Cardboard submunition containing photoflash composition
FUSE TYPE	Pull ring/lever percussion w/ejection charge
FUSE DELAY	1.5–2 seconds, . 0.5–1 second submunition fuse
WEIGHTS:	
ROUND	0.227 kg
PROJECTILE FILLER	0.034 kg

☞ *continued on next page*

☞ *Kilgore/Schermuly continued*

EFFECTS:

EFFECT	Blast and flash (stun), 1,000,000 candela and 175 db causing 5–15 seconds of disorientation
AREA OF EFFECT	10m
LENGTHS:	
LENGTH	10.9 cm
WIDTH (DIAMETER)	6.4 cm
STATUS	In production
SERVICE	Commercial sales

This is the original stun grenade first publicly seen when used by the SAS at the Princess Gate rescue. The grenade is roughly the same size and shape as an M26A1 fragmentation grenade but has a smooth plastic body with a flat bottom. The standard bouchon type fuze has a two second delay that starts after the safety lever is released. After the delay, a paper submunition is ejected from the base of the grenade where, after less than a second's delay, it detonates with a brilliant flash and loud report. In addition, the submunition creates a large cloud of dense white smoke that lingers for a length of time. The flash dazzles anyone looking at it and the loud report causes severe disorientation. Though the effects are short in duration, five to fifteen seconds, they effectively prevent any intentional act on the part of someone exposed to the blast. With the submunition being made of paper and detonating far, 2 or 3 meters, from the plastic grenade body, there is little damage the blast can do unless an individual is actually in contact with the submunition when it goes off. A drawback of this grenade is that the flash may set fire to fabric or other easily ignited material it contacts.

DAMAGE	SPECIAL 100 Stun within 10 meters

▼ M460 Thunderstrip

TYPE	Stun munition
FILLER	Magdex thunderflash stun mix
FUSE TYPE	Instadet pull ring/lever percussion w/6 m flashtube
EFFECTS:	
EFFECT	Blast and flash (stun)
AREA OF EFFECT	Approx. 4 meter radius
LENGTHS:	
LENGTH	30.5 cm
WIDTH (DIAMETER)	7.6 cm
THICKNESS	2.5mm
STATUS	In production
SERVICE	Commercial sales
COST	$40

This is a very thin, flat stun munition intended to be slipped under a door or through a slightly open window before firing. A slim 6 meter tube is attached to the M460 for firing. At the other end of the firing tube is a bouchon type fuze with a standard pull ring and safety lever. When the safety lever is released, the fuze fires a flash along the tube, detonating the thunder strip. As the strip is made of a rubberized material, there is no dangerous fragmentation.

DAMAGE	SPECIAL 100 Stun within 4 meters

▼ M465 Thunder Rod

TYPE	Stun munition
FILLER	Magdex thunderflash stun mix
FUSE TYPE	Pull ring/lever percussion
FUSE DELAY	1 second
EFFECTS:	
EFFECT	Blast and flash (stun)
AREA OF EFFECT	Approx. 4 meter radius.
LENGTHS:	
LENGTH	35.5 cm
WIDTH (DIAMETER)	1.7 cm
STATUS	In production
SERVICE	Commercial sales
COST	$35

This is another specialized stun munition manufactured by Accuracy Systems, Inc. and like the Thunder Strip, is intended to be inserted into a room before it is entered. The rod will fit through any 3/4 inch hole in a door, wall, or floor and is sized to slip through the hole left by a 12 gauge shotgun slug. At one end of the rod is a standard bouchon type fuze with pull ring and safety lever. To insure that the rod is completely inside the target area it is first inserted into the hole and the pull ring removed. When the rod is mostly inserted into the hole the safety lever can be released. When the lever is released, a small rocket fires, propelling the rod into the room where it detonates one second after the safety lever is released. The body of the Thunder Rod is made of a material that harmlessly disintegrates when it is fired and there is no dangerous fragmentation.

DAMAGE	SPECIAL 100 Stun within 4 meters

▼ Multi-Purpose Grenade MPG-120 (CS)

TYPE	Flameless "soft delivery" CS gas hand grenade
FILLER	CS powder
FUSE TYPE	Pull ring/lever percussion w/variable time delay
FUSE DELAY	2 or 5 seconds
WEIGHTS:	
ROUND	0.415 kg
FILLER	0.110 kg CS
EFFECTS:	
EFFECT	Instantly releases a cloud of CS gas

tenth of a second. The agent is a micro-particle sized CS dust that quickly creates a large active cloud of agent. Since the piston remains inside the grenade's body, no propellant gas escapes and the chances of fire are none. As the agent is ejected in such a short time, the grenade cannot be thrown back and there is no danger of fragmentation. The MPG may even be hand held and fired with the base pointing at the target. When the grenade functions, the agent will be expelled as a jet-like cloud at the target. The MPG is extremely safe and will not burn, even if the body is ruptured by striking the target before the propellant charge has fired.

MPG-120 CS grenade

AREA OF EFFECT	18x4m downwind cloud
LENGTHS:	
LENGTH	16.5 cm
WIDTH (DIAMETER)	8.1 cm
STATUS	In production
SERVICE	Commercial sales
COST	$20

This grenade was designed from its inception as a safe, flameless way of disbursing CS agent without danger to the operator or target. A very large, plastic, canister type grenade, the MPG (Multi Purpose Grenade) is unique, both in appearance and action. Having a red plastic body with ribbed sides makes the MPG easily recognizable, even in the dark. The fuze uses the familiar pull ring and safety lever but also has a selector switch for determining the time delay. The lever is pushed so that the pointer at its opposite end points at either the raised number 5 or 2 on the grenade's top for either a five or two second delay. The two second delay is used for most purposes with the five second delay used for rifle launching the grenade or dropping it from a helicopter. After the delay, a small propellant charge inside the grenade fires, driving a piston towards the bottom of the body. The pressure created by the piston blows out the rupture disk at the base of the grenade and the CS dust agent is ejected in about one

GRENADE LAUNCHERS

▼ NR 8111A1 FLY-K Mortar

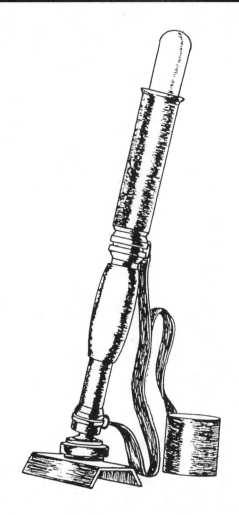

CALIBER	52mm
AMMUNITION TYPES	NR 802A2 HE-FRAG, XNR 210A1 SMK-WP, NR 409 ILLUM, NR 9114 GRAPNEL
OPERATION	Manual
TYPE OF FIRE	Single shot, muzzle loaded

☞ *continued on next page*

☞ *NR 8111A1 FLY-K Mortar continued*

RATE OF FIRE	(SS) 6 rpm
MUZZLE VELOCITY	90 m/s (295 fps)
SIGHTS	None
FEED	Single round
MOUNT TYPE	Hand held w/baseplate
WEIGHTS:	
WEAPON (EMPTY)	4.500 kg
WEAPON (LOADED)	5.250 kg
SERVICE CARTRIDGE	0.750 kg (NR 208A2 HE-FRAG)
PROJECTILE	0.750 kg
EFFECTS:	
EFFECT	Blast and fragmentation
AREA OF EFFECT	16 m radius
MINIMUM RANGE	200m (fuse arms after 45m)
MAXIMUM RANGE	600m
LENGTHS:	
WEAPON OVERALL	60.5 cm
BARREL	12.8 cm
STATUS	In production
SERVICE	Under evaluation by several armed forces, commercial sales

This is a unique grenade launcher that shares some of the characteristics of a light mortar. Also referred to as the FLY-K by the manufacturer, the NR 8111A1 uses a special propulsion system that results in a flashless, noiseless, smokeless firing signature, effectively a silenced mortar. Specifically, the FLY-K acts as a spigot mortar, that is, it has a rod over which the shell fits to launch and the short barrel has little practical effect beyond protecting the rod and shell. Inside the tail of the shells are special propulsion cartridges that are the heart of the FLY-K system. Each propulsion unit is shaped something like an inverted gun barrel with a sliding piston in place of a bullet. The rod, which also contains the spring loaded firing pin, fits up the tail against the piston. When the sleeve on the body of the launcher underneath the barrel is pushed down, it cocks the firing pin. As the sleeve is pushed further down, it releases the fixing pin which strikes a primer in the center of the piston in the propulsion cartridge. The primer ignites the propellant charge behind the piston and the expanding gas drives the piston violently against the rod, launching the shell. As the piston reaches the tail of the shell, a special detention ring slows and stops it before it can leave the end of the tail. With the piston caught inside the cartridge tube, all propellant gases remain inside the shell and all that is heard is a sharp "click" when the NR 8111A1 is fired. The spigot rod has three external ribs to help guide and center the round for firing. The range of the round is determined by the angle of the launcher and this can be set by using the simple bubble sight on the muzzle of the weapon which is graduated in hundreds of meters. Since the weapon does not need to hold in any pressure when firing, it is made of alloys to save weight. A simple curved baseplate is sufficient to support the weapon which is also

held by the operator while firing. The recoil of the FLY-K ammunition is severe and any attempt to fire the weapon without the baseplate being held firmly on the ground could result in severe injury to the operator or weapon. The NR 8111A1 is normally carried by one man along with a rucksack containing 10 rounds.

WEAPON	NR 8111A1
AMMO	NR 802A2 HE-FRAG
DISPERSION ANGLE	2.8642 degrees, 50.919 NATO mils.

Range	Group Circle Width (mm)	Probability (0<p<.099) (m)			
		Body	**Head**	**Hand**	**Bullseye**
200.0*	10000.000	0.073	0.037	0.019	0.006
250.0	12500.000	0.059	0.030	0.015	0.005
300.0	15000.000	0.050	0.025	0.013	0.004
350.0	17500.000	0.043	0.022	0.011	0.004
400.0	20000.000	0.037	0.019	0.009	0.003
450.0	22500.000	0.033	0.017	0.008	0.003
500.0	25000.000	0.030	0.015	0.008	0.003
550.0	27500.000	0.027	0.014	0.007	0.002
600.0	30000.000	0.025	0.013	0.006	0.002
650.0	32500.000	0.023	0.012	0.006	0.002
700.0	35000.000	0.022	0.011	0.005	0.002

* indicates range for which data was supplied

▼ NR 208A2 HE-FRAG

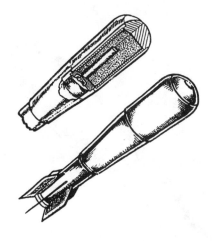

CALIBER	52mm
TYPE	High explosive fragmentation spigot mortar shell
MUZZLE VELOCITY	90 m/s (295 fps)
FILLER	Composition B

FUSE TYPE	Base, initiation on impact
FUSE DELAY	Instantaneous
WEIGHTS:	
ROUND	0.750 kg
PROJECTILE	0.750 kg
FILLER	0.135 kg
EFFECTS:	
EFFECT	Blast and fragmentation
AREA OF EFFECT	16m radius
MINIMUM RANGE	45m
MAXIMUM RANGE	600m
LENGTHS:	
LENGTH	33 cm
WIDTH (DIAMETER)	5.2 cm
STATUS	In production
SERVICE	Under evaluation

This is the major casualty producing round for the NR 8111A1 launcher. The fragmentation is from a coil of notched, square steel wire surrounding the explosive. A thermoplastic body and cap streamline the round. The fuze is at the base of the explosive and is armed only when the round is fired and has traveled about 45 meters. There are no external safeties to be removed and the round is slipped over the launching rod for use. the tail has four stabilizing fins and holds the propulsion cartridge.

DAMAGE 273 Blast, MAX (100) Stun, Fragmentation 5/(2.28 MAX)

▼ NR 209 Illuminating

CALIBER	52mm
TYPE	White parachute flare ejecting spigot mortar shell
MUZZLE VELOCITY	100 m/s (328 fps)
FILLER	Pyrotechnic composition
FUSE TYPE	Pyrotechnic delay, initiated on firing
FUSE DELAY	4 seconds
WEIGHTS:	
ROUND	0.605 kg
EFFECTS:	
EFFECT	Illuminates an area w/200,000 candelas
BURN TIME	25 seconds
AREA OF EFFECT	225m
MAXIMUM RANGE	450m
LENGTHS:	
LENGTH	41 cm
WIDTH (DIAMETER)	5.2 cm
STATUS	In production
SERVICE	Under evaluation

This is an illuminating shell for the NR 8111A1 that ejects a burning white magnesium parachute flare at altitude. The warhead holds the star flare and parachute in a plastic cylinder with the top of the shell covered with a pointed white cap. At the base of the warhead there is an ejection charge and a pyrotechnic delay fuze. The fuze is initiated when the round is fired, and after a built in delay, fires the ejection charge which both ejects and ignites the magnesium flare. The parachute slows the flare's fall until after the flare has burned out. The tail contains the FLY-K propulsion cartridge. The NR 209 is fired at a set angle which normally allows the shell to reach an altitude of 220 meters and a range of 450 meters before ejecting the flare. The flare will illuminate a 225 meter radius circle for 25 seconds with a central circle about 80 meters wide that is twice as well lit.

▼ XNR 210A1 WP Smoke

CALIBER	52mm
TYPE	Bursting type white phosphorus smoke spigot mortar shell
MUZZLE VELOCITY	85 m/s (279 fps)
FILLER	White phosphorus
FUSE TYPE	Base, initiated on impact
FUSE DELAY	Instantaneous
WEIGHTS:	
ROUND	0.600 kg
FILLER	0.060 kg
EFFECTS:	
EFFECT	Spreads burning phosphorus over burst area creating white smoke

☞ continued on next page

☞ *XNR 210A1 WP Smoke continued*

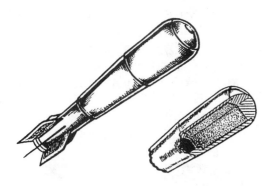

BURN TIME	20 seconds @ 2,700° C
AREA OF EFFECT	15m
MINIMUM RANGE	45m
MAXIMUM RANGE	600m
LENGTHS:	
LENGTH	33 cm
WIDTH (DIAMETER)	5.2cm
STATUS	Under development

This is a multi-use round with the primary effect being a rapid smoke screen. Since the white phosphorus filler burns at a high temperature and spreads fragments throughout the burst radius, the round also acts as an incendiary and casualty producing shell. The warhead is a simple molded plastic shell that contains the white phosphorus. The fuze is a base detonating type with a booster charge to shatter the casing and spread the phosphorus. The fuze detonates on impact and is not armed until the shell is fired and has traveled at least 45 meters. The tail is finned for stability and carries the FLY-K cartridge. The burning phosphorus creates a dense cloud of white smoke very rapidly but the smoke will quickly rise and the cloud only lasts about 40 seconds.

DAMAGE	Fragmentation 5/(2.28 MAX)
	Incendiary (6.84)

▼ NR 9114 Light Grapnel

CALIBER	52mm
TYPE	Grappling hook and line
MUZZLE VELOCITY	78 m/s (256 fps)
WEIGHTS:	
ROUND	3.9 kg w/line in case
PROJECTILE	0.650 kg

EFFECTS:	
EFFECT	Launches unfolding grappling hook attached to climbing line
MAXIMUM RANGE	37m @ 60 degrees inclination
LENGTHS:	
LENGTH	25 cm (41m rope)
WIDTH (DIAMETER)	21.2 cm (9mm rope)
STATUS	In production
SERVICE	Under evaluation and commercial sales

This is the most unusual "shell" fired by the NR 8111A1 as it consists of a multi-pronged grappling hook and rope. The round comes packaged in a canister that contains the grapnel and 41 meters of 9mm diameter nylon climbing rope. The grapnel is loaded like a standard round over the firing rod. The rope is attached to a shackle that slides to the end of the grapnel when it is fired. Launching at a 60 degree angle will give the grapnel a range of about 37 meters with a maximum altitude of about 15 meters. The light alloy grapnel is very strong and the tines are lightly padded with a foam coating. The tines have multiple hardened points and will unfold and dig in. The rope has a breaking strength of 2800 kilograms.

▼ HAFLA DM-34

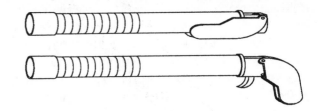

CALIBER	35mm
TYPE	Disposable incendiary/smoke grenade launcher
OPERATION	Manual
TYPE OF FIRE	Single shot
SIGHTS	None
FEED	Single round prepackaged
MOUNT TYPE	Hand held
FILLER	Red phosphorus
FUSE TYPE	Pyrotechnic initiated on firing

FUSE DELAY 2 seconds
WEIGHTS:
WEAPON (LOADED) 0.625 kg
FILLER 0.225 kg
EFFECTS:
EFFECT Spreads burning phosphorus over burst area creating a large smoke cloud igniting any combustible
BURN TIME 120 seconds @ 1,300° C
AREA OF EFFECT 5–8m (struck target), 15m long x 10m wide (self destruct)
MINIMUM RANGE 8m
MAXIMUM RANGE 70–80m
LENGTHS:
WEAPON OVERALL 44.5 cm
STATUS In production
SERVICE Federal German armed forces

Range	Group Circle Width (mm)	Probability (0<p<.099) (m)			
		Body	Head	Hand	Bullseye
10.0	400.000	0.851	0.614	0.379	0.149
20.0	800.000	0.614	0.379	0.212	0.077
30.0	1200.000	0.470	0.272	0.147	0.052
40.0	1600.000	0.379	0.212	0.112	0.040
50.0	2000.000	0.317	0.173	0.091	0.032
60.0	2400.000	0.272	0.147	0.076	0.027
70.0	2800.000	0.238	0.127	0.066	0.023
80.0	3200.000	0.212	0.112	0.058	0.020

DAMAGE Fragmentation 5/(2.28 MAX)
Incendiary (6.84)

This is in effect a launched incendiary/smoke grenade that comes packaged in its launcher. The firing handle is folded over the trigger at the rear of the launcher. Depressing a safety button allows the handgrip to rotate 90 degrees downward, locking to the rear and exposing the trigger. Until the grip is locked to the rear, the trigger cannot be pulled. When the trigger is pulled, an aluminum capsule containing the red phosphorus filler is ejected at the same time that the pyrotechnic fuze in the capsule's base is ignited. After the the fuze's two second delay, the projectile bursts, spreading red phosphorus over the burst area. Unlike white phosphorus, which ignites spontaneously on exposure to air, red phosphorus has to be ignited by outside means; the pyrotechnic fuze accomplishing this in the HAFLA. The fuze delay allows the capsule to travel 70 to 80 meters before it ruptures the case, spreading the filler over a 15 meter long, 10 meter wide oval. If the capsule should strike a target with a hard surface from 8 to 70 meters from the launcher, the capsule will burst with a brilliant flash and blinding smoke covering an area from 5 to 8 meters wide. Below 8 meters, the capsule does not have the velocity, nor has the fuze functioned long enough to burst the capsule and ignite the contents. The red phosphorus burns for two minutes, creating a large cloud of smoke that clears within a few minutes of the phosphorus burning out. The fragments burn at 1300 degrees C. and quickly ignite combustible materials. Three HAFLA's come packaged in a small belt pouch and the aluminum launchers are thrown away after firing. There are no sights on the launcher.

WEAPON HAFLA DM-34
DISPERSION ANGLE 2.29153 degrees, 40.7383 NATO mils.

▼ 40mm Granatepistole

Granatepistole with stock extended and rear sight raised for long range fire

Granatepistole with stock collapsed and sight folded

CALIBER 40x46mmR
AMMUNITION TYPES All 40mm low velocity ammunition
OPERATION Manual
TYPE OF FIRE Single shot, break open, single action
RATE OF FIRE (SS) 6 rpm
MUZZLE VELOCITY 76 m/s (249 fps)
SIGHTS Adjustable, square-notch/blade, range 350m
FEED Single round
MOUNT TYPE Shoulder fired
WEIGHTS:
WEAPON (EMPTY) 2.620 kg w/sling
WEAPON (LOADED) 2.852 kg w/sling & DM-41 rd
SERVICE CARTRIDGE 0.232 kg (DM-41 HE-frag)

☛ continued on next page

☞ *40mm Granatepistole continued*

PROJECTILE 0.176kg

EFFECTS:

EFFECT Blast and fragmentation, 700 2.25mm steel ball fragments

AREA OF EFFECT 5m

MINIMUM RANGE 14m

MAXIMUM RANGE 400m

LENGTHS:

WEAPON OVERALL 46.3/68.3 cm

BARREL 35.6cm

SIGHT RADIUS 34.2cm

STATUS In production

SERVICE Federal German forces and commercial sales

This is the German answer to the American 40mm M79 grenade launcher. This 40mm launcher replaces many rifle grenades in effect, and is more accurate in general. Using the High-Low pressure system, the weapon uses a small high pressure chamber inside the cartridge case to properly burn the propellant with a larger low pressure chamber that allows the gasses to expand and push the relatively large projectile at a lower velocity than otherwise obtainable. The low pressure push prevents the GrP from having too severe a recoil. Mechanically, the GrP is very simple to operate and acts somewhat like a break open shotgun. The locking lever, the upper of the two levers at the back, is pulled down and the barrel unlocks. The muzzle may then be pulled down opening the breech. Fired cartridge cases are removed by hand and the straight access to the barrel allows any length of round to be loaded as long as it is the proper caliber. The hammer is cocked by pulling down the longer of the two rear levers. The telescoping buttstock locks securely in the open or closed position. With the stock telescoped the launcher is able to fit in a special hip holster making it a very handy weapon. There is a simple flip sight for quick use up to 100 meters. Beyond that range, the ladder sight is unfolded, allowing accurate aiming at up to 350 meters.

WEAPON GRANATE PISTOLE

AMMO 40MM

DISPERSION ANGLE .391191 degrees, 6.9545 NATO mils.

Range	Group Circle Width (mm)	Probability (0<p<.099) (m)			
		Body	Head	Hand	Bullseye
50.0	341.379	0.893	0.672	0.428	0.172
100.0	682.759	0.672	0.428	0.243	0.090
150.0	1024.138	0.525	0.311	0.170	0.061
200.0	1365.517	0.428	0.243	0.130	0.046
250.0	1706.897	0.360	0.200	0.106	0.037
300.0	2048.276	0.311	0.170	0.089	0.031
350.0	2389.655	0.273	0.147	0.077	0.027
400.0	2731.034	0.243	0.130	0.067	0.023

▼ DM-41 HE-FRAG

CALIBER 40x46mmR

TYPE High explosive fragmentation low velocity grenade launcher shell

MUZZLE VELOCITY 76 m/s (249 fps)

FILLER Hexal 70/30

FUSE TYPE Point detonating nose fuse w/ self destruct, initiated on firing

FUSE DELAY 8 seconds for self destruct

WEIGHTS:

ROUND 0.232 kg

PROJECTILE 0.176 kg

FILLER 0.030 kg

EFFECTS:

EFFECT Blast and fragmentation, 700 2.25mm steel ball fragments

AREA OF EFFECT 5m

MINIMUM RANGE 14m

MAXIMUM RANGE 400m

LENGTHS:

LENGTH 9.9cm

WIDTH (DIAMETER) 4.3 cm

STATUS In production

SERVICE Federal German forces and commercial sales

This is an antipersonnel round for 40mm grenade launchers and was especially intended for use with the 40mm Granatepistole also produced by Heckler and Koch. The 40 x 46mm R round uses the standard high-low pressure system for propulsion with the primary attention being given to the projectile. A particularly complex fuze was developed for the DM-41 that is released by the setback created when the round is fired and arms from the centrifugal force of the round's spinning flight. The force of firing also ignites a delay fuze that burns for about four seconds elapsed time, roughly equivalent to a range of 400 meters. The self destruct feature of the fuze normally prevents any duds from occurring. Fragmentation is provided by a hemispherical plastic shell surrounding the explosive charge with 700 2.25mm steel pellets embedded in the plastic. Due to the small size of the projectile, combined with a relatively large fuze required for positive functioning, fragmentation has to be positive for efficient effect and the DM-41 easily matches this requirement.

DAMAGE 68 Blast, 45 Stun, Fragmentation 5/(2.28)

▼ ARMSCOR 6 rd 40mm

ARMSCOR 6 rd 40mm with buttstock extended and sight set to 0

CALIBER	40x46mmR
AMMUNITION TYPES	All low velocity 40mm grenades
OPERATION	Manual, spring loaded
TYPE OF FIRE	Semiautomatic, double action
RATE OF FIRE	(SS) 12 rpm
MUZZLE VELOCITY	76 m/s (250 fps)
SIGHTS	Adjustable, optical collimating occluded eye (Aimpoint)
FEED	6 round cylinder
MOUNT TYPE	Shoulder fired
WEIGHTS:	
WEAPON (EMPTY)	5.298 kg
WEAPON (LOADED)	6.666 kg w/6 rds
MAGAZINE (LOADED)	1.368 kg (6 rds)
SERVICE CARTRIDGE	0.228 kg (M381 HE)
PROJECTILE	0.172 kg
EFFECTS:	
EFFECT	Blast and fragmentation
AREA OF EFFECT	5m radius
MINIMUM RANGE	3m
MAXIMUM RANGE	400m
LENGTHS:	
WEAPON OVERALL	57.5/80.8 cm
BARREL	31 cm
STATUS	In production
SERVICE	South African forces and commercial sales

The ARMSCOR Multishot Grenade Launcher (MGL) is a native South African design for a multishot 40mm grenade launcher. The MGL has a rotating cylinder that holds six 40 x 46mm R grenades of any type as long as their overall length is under 120mm. An interesting mix of mechanical and gas operation, the MGL is very similar to the Striker shotgun. By pulling the cylinder axis pin (the small hook in front of the cylinder) forward, the rear pistol grip assembly can be rotated to the right exposing the chambers. The spring loaded cylinder is wound with the fingers inserted into the empty chambers. With the cylinder wound, the chambers may be loaded and the rear grip and plate rotated back into position. A thumb safety is just above the rear grip on the left hand side where it is switched down to fire. The trigger is double action, and cocks and releases the firing pin each time it is

pulled. When a grenade fires, a gas operated piston unlocks the cylinder and allows it to rotate a fresh round into battery. If a round should misfire, the trigger can be pulled again to attempt to fire the round. There is a release button on the side of the launcher that unlocks the cylinder and allows a fresh round to rotate into place. The folding stock has three positions into which it can lock: straight back for normal use, slightly angled for long range fire, and folded over the barrel for compactness. The MGL may be fired with the stock folded and the weapon held by both pistol grips. The sight normally used with the MGL is the ARMSON OEG single point sight. With the OEG both eyes are open and the sight superimposes a red dot on the target. The dot glows for use at night. The OEG is mounted on an adjustable bracket that can be set for range from 50 to 350 meters in 25 meter increments. The MGL can be aimed and fired at the rate of one round per second. The weapon cycles a new round in place in 0.3 seconds with the maximum aimed rate of fire being 12 rounds per minute.

WEAPON	ARMSCOR 6RD
AMMO	40MM
DISPERSION ANGLE	.859421 degrees, 15.2786 NATO mils.

Range	Group Circle Width (mm)	Probability (0<p<.099) (m)			
		Body	**Head**	**Hand**	**Bullseye**
50.0	750.000	0.638	0.398	0.224	0.082
100.0	1500.000	0.398	0.224	0.119	0.042
150.0	2250.000	0.287	0.156	0.081	0.028
200.0*	3000.000	0.224	0.119	0.062	0.021
250.0	3750.000	0.184	0.097	0.050	0.017
300.0	4500.000	0.156	0.081	0.041	0.014
350.0	5250.000	0.135	0.070	0.036	0.012
400.0	6000.000	0.119	0.062	0.031	0.011

* indicates range for which data was supplied

▼ BG-15

AKS-74 with BG-15 mounted under the front grip

CALIBER	40mm
AMMUNITION TYPES	HE long, HE short
OPERATION	Manual
TYPE OF FIRE	Single shot, muzzle loaded
RATE OF FIRE	(SS) 6 rpm
MUZZLE VELOCITY	53 m/s (175 fps)

☛ continued on next page

☞ *BG-15 continued*

SIGHTS	adjustable, V-notch/post, Range 420m	
FEED	Single round	
MOUNT TYPE	AKM(S)-47 or AK(S)-74 rifle	
WEIGHTS:		
WEAPON (EMPTY)	0.900 kg	
WEAPON (LOADED)	1.166 kg	
WEAPON (MOUNTED AND LOADED)	5.317 kg	
MOUNT	4.151 kg (AKS-74 w/30 rds)	
SERVICE CARTRIDGE	0.266 kg (HE long)	
EFFECTS:		
EFFECT	Blast and fragmentation	
AREA OF EFFECT	5m	
MINIMUM RANGE	5m	
MAXIMUM RANGE	450m	
LENGTHS:		
WEAPON OVERALL	27.9cm (69/93cm mounted)	
BARREL	14 cm	
SIGHT RADIUS	14.5 cm	
STATUS	In production	
SERVICE	Soviet forces	

Range	Group Circle Width (mm)	Probability (0<p<.099) (m)			
		Body	Head	Hand	Bullseye
50.0	500.000	0.782	0.533	0.317	0.121
100.0	1000.000	0.533	0.317	0.173	0.062
150.0	1500.000	0.398	0.224	0.119	0.042
200.0	2000.000	0.317	0.173	0.091	0.032
250.0	2500.000	0.263	0.141	0.073	0.025
300.0	3000.000	0.224	0.119	0.062	0.021
350.0	3500.000	0.196	0.103	0.053	0.018
400.0	4000.000	0.173	0.091	0.047	0.016

This is a relatively new weapon to the West with only a few captured examples coming out of Afghanistan. The BG-15 has been found mounted underneath the barrel of the AKS-74 rifle and cannot be fired unmounted. Capable of being mounted on any AK series rifle, the BG-15 has a clamp that latches over the barrel in front of the foregrip and under the gas cylinder. There is a very short pistol grip with a hole in it, possibly for the thumb, just behind the trigger. The trigger appears to be double action with a straight pull to the rear, cocking and firing the weapon. The rounds are unusual in that they are muzzle loaded with no retention in the barrel except for a slip fit. The high-low pressure system is used in a novel approach. The high pressure chamber is attached to the base of the round and holds the percussion primer in its center surrounded by 10 bleed holes. When the round is fired the propellant in the high pressure chamber ruptures a seal over the bleed holes and uses the breech end of the barrel as the low pressure chamber. The use of this system eliminates the need for a cartridge case but does give the BG-15 a reportedly heavy recoil. The short barrel is rifled for accuracy and the rounds have a pre-engraved band to engage the rifling. The sights are attached to the left side of the launcher where they can fold out of the way. The sight consists of a rod that can be angled according to an engraved range scale and has an adjustable post at one end and a simple aperture peep at the other.

WEAPON	BG-15
AMMO	40MM
DISPERSION ANGLE	.572953 degrees, 10.1858 NATO mils.

▼ HE long • HE short

HE (long) showing nose fuse cap

HE (short) showing pre-engraved rotating band and propellant chamber

CALIBER	40mm
TYPE	High explosive fragmentation
MUZZLE VELOCITY	53 m/s (175 fps)
FILLER	A-IX-1
FUSE TYPE	Nose fuse, initiated on impact
WEIGHTS:	
ROUND	0.266 kg (0.250 kg)
FILLER	0.036 kg (0.034 kg)
EFFECTS:	
EFFECT	Blast and fragmentation
AREA OF EFFECT	5m
MINIMUM RANGE	5m
MAXIMUM RANGE	300 m (420 m)
LENGTHS:	
LENGTH	11.8 cm (10.1 cm)
WIDTH (DIAMETER)	4.0 cm
STATUS	In production
SERVICE	Soviet forces

There are only two rounds presently known to be available for the BG-15 and both are casualty producing fragmentation rounds. The two rounds, one long and one short, have no difference in effect and their primary difference may be interpreted (from examination of the weapon's sights), to be in range. Examination gives the long round an effective range of 300 meters and the shorter, lighter round an effective range of 420 meters. The fuze is point detonating and fires on impact with an estimated minimum range of 5 meters. The explosive charge is relatively small, and so the grenade uses the notched wire coil system of controlled fragmentation which the Soviets are using with greater frequency today. The propellant charge is in an extended cylinder at the base of the shell and measures 25 x 14mm in both rounds. Immediately ahead of the shell's base is a band of four bore-riding gas retention rings tapped off by a pre-engraved rotating band. The shell would be loaded from the muzzle of the BG-15, being given a slight turn to align the rifling with the rotating band. The barrel is short enough that the round may be pressed home with the fingertips seating the propellant chamber into the cavity at the base of the barrel.

DAMAGE 81 Blast, 45 Stun,
Fragmentation 5/(2.28 MAX)

▼ Webley-Schermuly Anti-riot gun

Webley-Schermuly Anti-riot gun with sight raised

CALIBER	38 mm
AMMUNITION TYPES	L5A4 Baton, Mark 2 CS
OPERATION	Manual
TYPE OF FIRE	Single shot, break open, double action
RATE OF FIRE	(SS) 6 rpm
MUZZLE VELOCITY	79 m/s (259 fps)
MUZZLE ENERGY	334 J (246 ft/lb)
SIGHTS	Non-adjustable, aperture/post
FEED	Single round
MOUNT TYPE	Shoulder fired
WEIGHTS:	
WEAPON (EMPTY)	3.180 kg
WEAPON (LOADED)	3.350 kg w/L5A4 rd
SERVICE CARTRIDGE	0.170 kg (L5A4 plastic anti-riot baton)
PROJECTILE	0.107 kg
EFFECTS:	
EFFECT	Impact w/target
MAXIMUM RANGE	60m
LENGTHS:	
WEAPON OVERALL	82.8 cm

BARREL	37.3 cm
SIGHT RADIUS	48.8 cm
STATUS	In production
SERVICE	British forces and commercial sales

This is a shoulder fired smoothbore grenade launcher, widely used by the British forces and seeing good commercial sales. The general design is much the same as American tear gas guns: a simple break-open action resembling sporting shotguns. As the operating pressures of this type of weapon are low, the Webley-Schermuly is made of light weight alloys and precision forgings. The trigger mechanism is of the double action type with only a simple rearward pull needed to fire the weapon. A safety interlock and rebounding firing pin insure the weapon from accidental discharges. The rear sight is a simple bar mounted on the forward part of the buttstock that is raised for use. The sight bar has several apertures for different ranges with the furthest range being 150 meters. The weapon can fire all standard 37mm (1.5 inch) gas gun shells and is most often seen using baton or rubber bullet rounds. A major point in the weapon's favor is its flexibility for use. The barrel is easily removed and replaced with a short version. The stock is also removable, taking with it the long range sight and leaving the pistol grip. Removing the stock and changing the barrel results in the Schermuly pistol. There is a mounting available that lets the anti-riot gun in its long barreled version to be mounted in vehicle turrets in the place of a machine gun.

WEAPON	WEBLEY-SCHERMULY
AMMO	38MM
DISPERSION ANGLE	.264746 degrees, 4.70659 NATO mils.

Range	Group Circle Width (mm)	Probability (0<p<.099) (m)			
		Body	Head	Hand	Bullseye
10.0	46.207	0.990	0.990	0.984	0.752
20.0	92.414	0.990	0.984	0.873	0.502
30.0	138.621	0.990	0.936	0.747	0.372
40.0	184.828	0.984	0.873	0.643	0.295
50.0	231.034	0.963	0.808	0.562	0.244
60.0	277.241	0.936	0.747	0.497	0.208

▼ L5A4 Plastic Anti-Riot Baton

CALIBER	38mm
TYPE	Plastic bulleted baton round
MUZZLE VELOCITY	79 m/s (259 fps)
MUZZLE ENERGY	334 J (246 ft/lb)
FILLER	PVC plastic
WEIGHTS:	
ROUND	0.170 kg
PROJECTILE	0.107 kg

☞ continued on next page

☞ *L5A4 Plastic Anti-riot Baton continued*

EFFECTS:

EFFECT	Impact on target
MAXIMUM RANGE	60m

LENGTHS:

LENGTH	9.9 cm
WIDTH (DIAMETER)	3.8 cm
STATUS	In production
SERVICE	British military and police forces, wide commercial sales

This is the standard issue baton round with the British forces and replaces all earlier baton and rubber bullet rounds. The L5A4 launches a PVC cylinder from an aluminum cartridge case. The intent is to fire the round at the ground in front of rioters so that the ricochet will strike them in the legs and upper body.

▼ Schermuly pistol

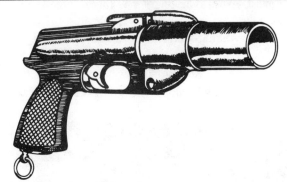

CALIBER	38mm
AMMUNITION TYPES	L5A4 Baton, Mark 2 CS Irritant
OPERATION	Manual
TYPE OF FIRE	Single shot, break open, double action
RATE OF FIRE	(SS) 6 rpm
MUZZLE VELOCITY	100 m/s (328 fps)
SIGHTS	None
FEED	Single round
MOUNT TYPE	Hand held

WEIGHTS:

WEAPON (EMPTY)	1.200 kg
WEAPON (LOADED)	1.410 kg
SERVICE CARTRIDGE	0.210 kg (Mark 2 CS)
PROJECTILE	0.107 kg

EFFECTS:

EFFECT	Produces a cloud of CS gas
AREA OF EFFECT	812 m3, 21.5x7x4 m cloud
MAXIMUM RANGE	150 m

LENGTHS:

WEAPON OVERALL	26.5 cm
BARREL	10.5 cm
STATUS	In production
SERVICE	British forces and commercial sales

This is the pistol version of the Webley-Schermuly anti-riot gun. Intended primarily as a signal flare launcher, the pistol may also be used to fire the Mark 2 CS round as well as the L5A4 baton round at close range. There are no sights on the pistol as it is simply pointed at a specific target. The action is the simple break open type with a double action trigger.

▼ Mark 2 CS Irritant Cartridge

CALIBER	38mm
TYPE	Burning type CS gas projectile for gas guns
MUZZLE VELOCITY	100 m/s (328 fps)
FILLER	CS/pyrotechnic composition
FUSE TYPE	Pyrotechnic, initiated on firing
FUSE DELAY	1.5–2.5 seconds

WEIGHTS:

ROUND	0.210 kg
PROJECTILE	0.107 kg
FILLER	0.098 kg

EFFECTS:

EFFECT	Produces a cloud of CS gas
AREA OF EFFECT	812 m3, 21.5x7x4m cloud
MAXIMUM RANGE	150m

LENGTHS:

LENGTH	12.2 cm
WIDTH (DIAMETER)	4 cm
STATUS	In production
SERVICE	British forces and commercial sales

This cartridge was designed to specifications supplied by the British military and is available for law enforcement use. The cartridge fires a burning type CS canister in the form of an aluminum capsule. The pyrotechnic fuze in the capsule's base is ignited on firing and has a 1.5 to .5 second delay. The capsule ignites after the delay, releasing CS smoke in a visible cloud through the base of the capsule. The round is improved over earlier versions and has an extended range and greater accuracy.

THE EDGE OF THE SWORD

▼ M79

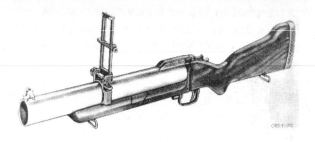

CALIBER	40x46mmR
AMMUNITION TYPES	All low-velocity 40mm grenades
OPERATION	Manual, break open
TYPE OF FIRE	Single shot
RATE OF FIRE (SS)	6 rpm
MUZZLE VELOCITY	76 m/s (250 fps)
SIGHTS	Adjustable, U-notch/blade, range 375m
FEED	Single round
MOUNT TYPE	Shoulder fired
WEIGHTS::	
WEAPON (EMPTY)	2.699 kg
WEAPON (LOADED)	2.927 kg
SERVICE CARTRIDGE	0.228 kg (M381 HE)
PROJECTILE	0.172 kg
EFFECTS:	
EFFECT	Blast and fragmentation
AREA OF EFFECT	5m radius
MINIMUM RANGE	3m
MAXIMUM RANGE	400m
LENGTHS:	
WEAPON OVERALL	73.7 cm
BARREL	35.7 cm
SIGHT	RADIUS 15.6 cm
STATUS	In production
SERVICE	Obsolete w/US forces, wide foreign usage and commercial sales
COST	$950

This was the first grenade launcher to use the high-low pressure system and it was first fielded by the U.S. military in the late 1950's. The basic design of the M79 was intentionally derived from single shot sporting shotguns allowing easy familiarity by new recruits. The breech is opened by pushing the locking lever on the top of the weapon to the right and pulling the barrel down, which partially extracts a fired casing, recocks the hammer, and resets the safety to safe. A fired case is removed by hand and a fresh round inserted into the chamber. Because of the low operating pressure the barrel is made of aluminum alloy and is rifled for accuracy with 6 narrow lands and wide grooves.

The buttstock has a high rear portion to allow good seating of the weapon when it is fired at a high angle for long range. A recoil pad is fitted to the stock though the M79 is not known for having excessive recoil. The flip-up rear sight is very tall when unfolded and somewhat prone to being damaged. There is a small fixed notch on the base of the rear sight that is used, when the sight is folded, for engaging targets of up to 100 meters range. When unfolded, the rear sight is adjustable for windage and elevation so that the weapon can be zeroed for a specific operator. There is a sliding notch that can be moved up or down on the sight to set for range. A scale is on the side of the sight for ranges from 75 to 375 meters in 25 meter increments. As the notch is moved for higher ranges, the sight automatically adjusts for drift. As the projectile spins with a right hand spin at 3,700 rpm, the tendency is for the shell to drift to the right; the automatic movement of the notch to the left compensates for this drift. A highly qualified operator rarely needs to use the sight for a group or close point target, as the slow flight and size of the projectile allows it to be seen in flight. Since the M79 is a break-open type action, any length of cartridge may be fitted into it, as long as the caliber is 40 x 46mmR.

ASSESSMENT	2m group @ 200m for zero
WEAPON:	M79
AMMO:	40MM
Dispersion angle:	.572953 degrees, 10.1858 NATO mils.

Range	Group Circle Width (mm)	Probability (0<p<.099) (m)			
		Body	**Head**	**Hand**	**Bullseye**
50.0	500.00	0.782	0.533	0.317	0.121
100.0	1000.00	0.533	0.317	0.173	0.062
150.0	1500.00	0.398	0.224	0.119	0.042
200.0*	2000.00	0.317	0.173	0.091	0.032
250.0	2500.00	0.263	0.141	0.073	0.025
300.0	3000.00	0.224	0.119	0.062	0.021
350.0	3500.00	0.196	0.103	0.053	0.018
400.0	4000.00	0.173	0.091	0.047	0.016

* indicates range for which data was supplied

▼ M203

CALIBER	40x46mmR
AMMUNITION TYPES	All low-velocity 40mm grenades
OPERATION	Manual
TYPE OF FIRE	Single shot, slide open
RATE OF FIRE (SS)	8 rpm
MUZZLE VELOCITY	71 m/s (235 fps)
SIGHTS	Adjustable quadrant, aperture/post, range 400m (primary), adjustable leaf, indicator/post, range 250m

(secondary)

FEED Single round

MOUNT TYPE Shoulder fired, mounted on M16 family rifle

WEIGHTS:

WEAPON (EMPTY) 1.361 kg

WEAPON (LOADED) 1.589 kg

WEAPON (MOUNTED AND LOADED)
5.655 kg w/M16A2 & 30 rds

MOUNT 4.066 kg (M16A2 w/30 rds)

SERVICE CARTRIDGE 0.228 kg (M381 HE)

PROJECTILE 0.172 kg

EFFECTS:

EFFECT Blast and fragmentation

AREA OF EFFECT 5m radius

MINIMUM RANGE 3m

MAXIMUM RANGE 400m

LENGTHS:

WEAPON OVERALL 40.5 cm (launcher only)

BARREL 30.5 cm

SIGHT RADIUS 12.9 cm (quadrant), 13.6 cm (leaf)

STATUS In production

SERVICE US military and wide commercial sales

COST $550

The major drawback of the M79 was its being a dedicated weapon with the grenadier carrying no other weapon than a pistol. The M203 was the final design in the development of a 40mm launcher that could be mounted underneath the barrel of the M16 rifle. Very light, the M203 is made up of lightweight alloys and fiberglass and can be mounted on any of the full-sized M16 series rifles. The barrel of the M203 is unlocked by pressing in a lever on the left side of the weapon above the center of the barrel and sliding the barrel forward against the stop. Any fired casing in the chamber is automatically extracted and ejected. A fresh round is inserted and the barrel slid back into battery to set the weapon for firing. There is a safety inside the trigger guard that, when it is on safe, blocks the inside the of trigger guard, preventing a finger from entering. There are two sights issued with the M203 the first, a simple leaf sight, folds up to use. Sighting with the leaf uses the front sight of the M16 rifle and is very quick to use. The leaf is graduated from 50 to 250 meters in 50 meter

increments. The second sight is a quadrant sight that mounts on the handle of the M16 on the left hand sight. The quadrant sight has a folding post and aperture and is adjustable for zero. For use, the quadrant sight is graduated in 25 meter increments from 50 to 400 meters. To use the M203, the rifle is held to the shoulder with the barrel of the 203 held by the left hand, while the right hand uses the magazine for a grip. The main advantage of the M203 is that, after the launcher is used, the grenadier has the 30 rounds of 5.56mm that are in the M16 rifle immediately available.

ASSESSMENT 5m group @ 200m for zero

WEAPON: M203

AMMO: 40MM

Dispersion angle: 1.43232 degrees, 25.4635 NATO mils.

Range	Group Circle Width (mm)	Probability (0<p<.099) (m)			
		Body	Head	Hand	Bullseye
50.0	1250.00	0.456	0.263	0.141	0.050
100.0	2500.00	0.263	0.141	0.073	0.025
150.0	3750.00	0.184	0.097	0.050	0.017
200.0*	5000.00	0.141	0.073	0.037	0.013
250.0	6250.00	0.115	0.059	0.030	0.010
300.0	7500.00	0.097	0.050	0.025	0.009
350.0	8750.00	0.083	0.043	0.022	0.007
400.0	10000.00	0.073	0.037	0.019	0.006

* indicates range for which data was supplied

▼ TALON

CALIBER 40x46mmR

AMMUNITION TYPES All low-velocity 40mm grenades

OPERATION Manual

TYPE OF FIRE Single shot, slide open

RATE OF FIRE (SS) 8 rpm

MUZZLE VELOCITY 71 m/s (235 fps)

SIGHTS Adjustable quadrant sight w/ Armson occluded eye optical sight, range 400m (primary), adjustable leaf, indicator/post, range 250m (secondary)

FEED Single round

MOUNT TYPE Shoulder fired, mounted on rifle w/ fitted mounting rail

WEIGHTS:

WEAPON (EMPTY) 1.360 kg

WEAPON (LOADED) 1.588 kg

WEAPON (MOUNTED AND LOADED)

	5.654 kg w/M16A2 & 30 rds
MOUNT	4.066 kg (M16A2 w/30 rds)
SERVICE CARTRIDGE	0.228 kg (M381 HE)
PROJECTILE	0.172 kg
EFFECTS:	
EFFECT	Blast and fragmentation
AREA OF EFFECT	5m radius
MINIMUM RANGE	3m
MAXIMUM RANGE	400m
LENGTHS:	
WEAPON OVERALL	38.1 cm
BARREL	30.5 cm
SIGHT RADIUS	13.6 cm (leaf)
STATUS	In production
SERVICE	Commercial sales

The M203 has been improved under the product improvement program of the U.S. military and the result has been named the Talon by the producing company. Operating in the same manner as the M203, the Talon has several improvements over the original weapon. A major change is the development of a quick release for the weapon combined with a universal mounting bar. By simple modifications to the mounting bar, it may be attached to a wide range of weapons including the AK-47 family, FN-FAL, G-3, G-41, AR-180, Galil, and a light folding stock for the launcher alone. Another modification is to the release system of the barrel. By pressing the barrel release, the barrel is slid forward to the stop as in the standard M203. By pressing the release a second time, the barrel may be slid forward an additional distance, allowing the loading of longer 40mm rounds developed for the M79. A replacement sight has been designed to take the place of the quadrant sight. The new sight mounts on the handle of an M16; other mounts are available for different weapons. The sight has an ARMSON OEG single point sight that is used with both eyes open and places a red dot on the target. The sight is adjustable for ranges from 50 to 400 meters in 25 meter increments. A special pistol grip stock is made for the Talon that allows it to be fired as a pistol, or with the folding stock opened, the weapon can be fired from the shoulder. With the stock folded over the weapon, the Talon pistol has a length of 45.7cm and a weight of 1.950 kilograms. Use of the mounting bar system has resulted in an unusual additional weapon that can be mounted under the M16. The Ithaca Stakeout model shotgun in 12 gauge will fit on the mounting rail when fitted with the proper brackets. This results in a pump-action shotgun riding underneath the M16. The obvious firepower is tremendous and is an especially good entry weapon for opening doors, using the shotgun for the hinges and lock while still having a fully loaded M16 at the ready. For the shotgun specifications, see Ithaca Stakeout under shotguns.

WEAPON:	TALON
AMMO:	40MM
Dispersion angle:	.859421 degrees, 15.2786 NATO mils.

Range	Group Circle Width (mm)	Probability (0<p<.099) (m)			
		Body	**Head**	**Hand**	**Bullseye**
50.0	750.00	0.638	0.398	0.224	0.082
100.0	1500.00	0.398	0.224	0.119	0.042
150.0	2250.00	0.287	0.156	0.081	0.028
200.0*	3000.00	0.224	0.119	0.062	0.021
250.0	3750.00	0.184	0.097	0.050	0.017
300.0	4500.00	0.156	0.081	0.041	0.014
350.0	5250.00	0.135	0.070	0.036	0.012
400.0	6000.00	0.119	0.062	0.031	0.011

* indicates range for which data was supplied

▼ M381 HE (M386 HE)

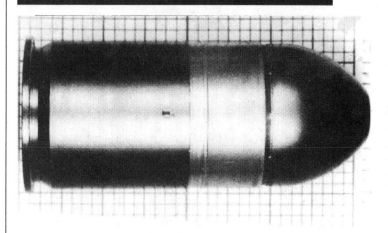

CALIBER	40x46mmR
TYPE	High explosive fragmentation grenade launcher shell
MUZZLE VELOCITY	76 m/s (250 fps)
FILLER	Composition B
FUSE TYPE	M552 (M551) point detonating, initiation on impact
FUSE DELAY	Instantaneous

WEIGHTS:
ROUND 0.228 kg (0.227 kg)
PROJECTILE 0.172 kg (0.171 kg)
FILLER 0.032 kg
EFFECTS:
EFFECT Blast and fragmentation
AREA OF EFFECT 5m radius
MINIMUM RANGE 3m (14m)
MAXIMUM RANGE 400m
LENGTHS:
LENGTH 9.9 cm
WIDTH (DIAMETER) 4.4 cm
STATUS In production
SERVICE US military and commercial sales

This is the most common round used in the 40mm grenade launcher. It is a fragmentation-type, casualty producing round. The heart of this, and of all the 40 x 46mmR family of grenades, is the aluminum cartridge case with the high-low pressure system. The cartridge case is made with a thick-walled propellant chamber, formed into the base of the casing and protruding into the low pressure area inside of the case. A thin-walled brass cup containing the propellant is inserted into the high pressure chamber and the base opening is sealed with an aluminum plug, holding the percussion primer. When the round is fired, the propellant, a double-base smokeless powder, burns creating a pressure of 35,000 psi inside the high pressure chamber. When the pressure reaches maximum, the brass cup ruptures, releasing the gas through the six bleed holes in the walls of the high pressure chamber into the low pressure chamber. In the low pressure chamber, the gas pressure has dropped to about 3,000 psi due to the larger area, and this pressure propels the projectile through the barrel with a softer shove than other systems would give. This shove, rather than a relatively sudden kick, allows the launcher to be shoulder fired with a heavy projectile without severe recoil. Propelling the projectile through the rifled barrel gives it a muzzle velocity of 250 feet per second with a right hand stabilizing spin of 3,700 revolutions per minute. The spin is what stabilizes the grenade in flight and also creates the forces necessary to arm the fuze. The fuze for a 40mm grenade is very complex for its size and it often makes up half of the grenade. In the M381 and M386 rounds, the only difference between them lies in the fuze. The fuze used in the M381 is the M552 point detonating fuze which arms from the centrifugal force of the projectile's spinning flight. The M381 projectile must travel 2.4 to 3 meters from the point of launch for the fuze to have spun enough to fully arm. The short arming distance makes the M381 round useful for house-to-house combat where it can be fired around a corner into a room and detonate when it hits the far wall. The drawback with the short aiming distance is that the grenade will arm while the firer is still in the area of the burst. If the armed round were to strike an object, the firer could easily be injured. To avoid this problem, the M386 uses the M551 fuze which is also point detonating and operates in the same manner

as the M552 fuze, but arms only after traveling at least 14 meters form the launcher. The M386 round is the more commonly issued round for standard troops because of its much longer safety zone. Both rounds have a small, ball-shaped grenade attached to the base of the fuze containing the explosive charge. The ball contains a spherical coil of rectangular steel wire, notched every quarter of an inch for fragmentation.

DAMAGE 65 Blast, 43 Stun, Fragmentation 5/ (2.28 MAX)

▼ M397A1 HE AIRBURST

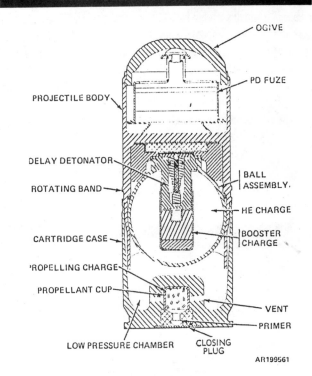

OGIVE
PROJECTILE BODY
PD FUZE
DELAY DETONATOR
BALL ASSEMBLY.
ROTATING BAND
HE CHARGE
CARTRIDGE CASE
BOOSTER CHARGE
PROPELLING CHARGE
PROPELLANT CUP
VENT
PRIMER
LOW PRESSURE CHAMBER
CLOSING PLUG
AR199561

CALIBER 40x46mmR
TYPE High explosive fragmentation grenade launcher shell w/rebound for airburst
MUZZLE VELOCITY 76 m/s (250 fps)
FILLER Octol
FUSE TYPE M536E1 point detonating w/ ejection charge and pyrotechnic delay, initiated on impact
FUSE DELAY 80 milliseconds
WEIGHTS:
ROUND 0.231 kg
PROJECTILE 0.175 kg
FILLER 0.032 kg
EFFECTS:
EFFECT Blast and fragmentation @ 2m

	above ground surface
AREA OF EFFECT	10m
MINIMUM RANGE	14m
MAXIMUM RANGE	400m
LENGTHS::	
LENGTH	10.3 cm
WIDTH (DIAMETER)	4.4 cm
STATUS	In production
SERVICE	US forces and commercial sales

As most fragmentation grenades detonate at ground level, much of the fragmentation is absorbed by the ground, and so, the round is less efficient. A much more effective round would detonate in the air as an airburst and this is what the M397A1 attempts to do. The projectile uses the M536E1 point detonating fuze which arms after 14 meters of travel. When the projectile strikes the ground, the fuze fires an ejection charge and ignites an 80 millisecond pyrotechnic fuze in the grenade. The grenade ball is blown into the air when the delay fuze detonates it about 5 feet above the ground. This grenade is especially effective in snow where other grenades would loose much of their force.

ASSESSMENT

DAMAGE	72 Blast, 48 Stun, Fragmentation 5/ (2.28 MAX)

▼ M433 HEDP

Diagram labels: OGIVE, M-550 LOT⊡⊡⊡, FUZE, PROJECTILE BODY, SHAPED CHARGE, COPPER CONE, ROTATING BAND, LOW PRESSURE CHAMBER, CARTRIDGE CASE, VENT, PROPELLANT CUP, CLOSING PLUG, PRIMER

CALIBER	40x46mmR
TYPE	High explosive fragmentation and

	armor penetrating grenade launcher shell
MUZZLE VELOCITY	76 m/s (250 fps)
FILLER	Composition A5
FUSE TYPE	M550 point initiating, base detonating, initiation on impact
FUSE DELAY	Instantaneous
WEIGHTS:	
ROUND	0.230 kg
PROJECTILE	0.174 kg
FILLER O	.045 kg
EFFECTS:	
EFFECT	Blast and fragmentation w/armor penetration
AREA OF EFFECT	5m radius, penetrates 5.1 cm steel
MINIMUM RANGE	14m
MAXIMUM RANGE	400m
LENGTHS:	
LENGTH	10.3 cm
WIDTH (DIAMETER)	4.4cm
STATUS	In production
SERVICE	US forces and commercial sales

This is a dual purpose impact type round intended to cause casualties from fragmentation, as well as penetrate up to 2 inches of steel. The cartridge case is a standard high-low pressure type with the projectile being particularly complex. The M550 fuze is the point initiating, base detonating type which arms from 14 to 27 meters from point of launch. When the round impacts, the fuze fires an RDX spitback charge which fires into the base of the explosive charge. The charge has a conical copper liner at its front to shape the blast into an armor piercing jet. This type of explosive charge is called a shaped charge and greatly increase the penetration effects of the rounds. The copper liner is vaporized into an armor piercing jet which actually causes the armor steel to flow away from it. The base and sides of the explosive charge are made up of serrated steel which fragments, giving the round its dual effect. Though the armor piercing jet is insufficient for heavy armored vehicles, it makes a very effective weapon against armored personnel carriers and other lightly armored targets.

DAMAGE	102 Blast, 68 Stun, Fragmentation 5/(2.28 MAX)

▼ M576 MP

CALIBER	40x46mmR
TYPE	Multiple projectile grenade launcher shell
MUZZLE VELOCITY	269 m/s (883 fps)

MUZZLE ENERGY 43 J (32 ft/lb) per pellet, 868 J (640 ft/lb) per round

FILLER 20 No. 4 buckshot (6mm dia.)

WEIGHTS:

ROUND 0.115 kg

PROJECTILE 0.059 kg (sabot w/pellets)

FILLER 0.024 kg (1.2 g ea.)

EFFECTS:

EFFECT Multiple projectiles on target

MAXIMUM RANGE 30 m

LENGTHS:

LENGTH 6.7 cm

WIDTH (DIAMETER) 4.4 cm

STATUS In production

SERVICE US forces and commercial sales

This is a multiple projectile "buckshot" round that effectively makes the 40mm launcher a large shotgun. Originally intended to give the M79 some close-in antipersonnel capability, the M576 round will also work in any single-shot 40 x 46mmR launcher. The round is very short and the projectile consists of a squat plastic cylinder. Inside the cylinder sabot is a small shot cup holding 20 number 4 buckshot and being sealed with a snap-off cap. As the round is fired setback (inertia) causes the shot cup to move backwards in the sabot disengaging the cap on the shot cup. As the projectile leaves the muzzle, the several drilled air scoops along the circumference of the sabot cause it to quickly lose speed. As the sabot falls away, the buckshot are free to continue on to the target. Due to the low pressure of the round, the shot does not have a very high velocity and so the maximum effective range is a short 30 meters, while tactical use of the round indicates a practical effective range of only 15 meters or so.

ASSESSMENT 99cm pattern @ 13.7m

WEAPON: M576 MP

AMMO: 40x46mm

Dispersion angle: 4.13856 degrees, 73.5743 NATO mils.

Range	Group Circle Width (mm)	Probability (0<p<.099) (m)			
		Body	Head	Hand	Bullseye
5.0	361.314	0.879	0.652	0.410	0.163
10.0	722.628	0.652	0.410	0.232	0.085
15.0	1083.942	0.505	0.296	0.161	0.058
20.0	1445.255	0.410	0.232	0.123	0.044
25.0	1806.569	0.344	0.190	0.100	0.035
30.0	2167.883	0.296	0.161	0.084	0.029

DAMAGE 8/.01 (0.04)(0.06)(0.09) per pellet

▼ M382 PRACTICE (M407A1 PRACTICE)

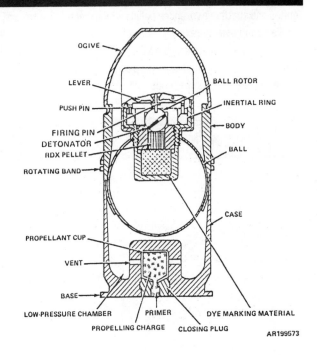

OGIVE
LEVER
PUSH PIN
FIRING PIN
DETONATOR
RDX PELLET
ROTATING BAND
PROPELLANT CUP
VENT
BASE
LOW-PRESSURE CHAMBER
PROPELLING CHARGE
PRIMER
CLOSING PLUG
DYE MARKING MATERIAL
BALL ROTOR
INERTIAL RING
BODY
BALL
CASE
AR199573

CALIBER 40x46mmR

TYPE Practice w/smoke puff indicator grenade launcher shell

MUZZLE VELOCITY 76 m/s (250 fps)

FILLER Yellow dye

FUSE TYPE M552 (M551) Point detonating, initiated on impact

FUSE DELAY Instantaneous

WEIGHTS:

ROUND 0.227 kg

PROJECTILE 0.171 kg

FILLER 4.54 g

EFFECTS:

EFFECT Puff of yellow smoke on impact

AREA OF EFFECT 1m

MINIMUM RANGE 3m (14m)

MAXIMUM RANGE 400m

LENGTHS:

LENGTH 9.9 cm

WIDTH (DIAMETER) 4.4 cm

STATUS In production

SERVICE US forces and commercial sales

These are both practice rounds and are ballistically matched to a high explosive round. The M382 matches the M381 HE round and uses the same M552 fuze. The M407A1 matches the M386 HE round and also uses the M551 fuze. When the rounds arm and then strike, the M382

THE EDGE OF THE SWORD

round fires the detonator of the fuze and releases a puff of dye that appears as a cloud of smoke. The M407A1 fuze fires a charge which ignites and shatters two smoke pellets which create a yellow puff of smoke to indicate the point of impact. As the rounds arm at the proper distances, 3 meters for the M382 and 27 meters for the M407A1, they can be used for practice in the place of the more expensive and dangerous high explosive rounds.

▼ M583A1 (WHITE), M661 (GREEN), M662 (RED) STAR PARACHUTE FLARES

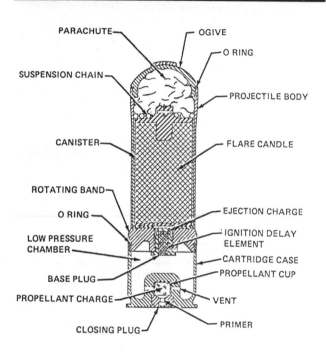

CALIBER 40x46mmR
TYPE Illuminating/signaling colored parachute flare grenade launcher shells
MUZZLE VELOCITY 76 m/s (250 fps)
FILLER Illuminating composition
FUSE TYPE Pyrotechnic, initiated on firing
FUSE DELAY 5 seconds
WEIGHTS:
ROUND 0.222 kg (M583A1), 0.213 kg (M661 & M662)
PROJECTILE 0.166 kg (M583A1), 0.168 kg (M661 & M662)
FILLER 0.093 kg (M583A1), 0.085 kg (M661 & M662)
EFFECTS:
EFFECT Ejects a burning parachute flare at altitude illuminating an area w/

90,000 cp (M583A1), 8,000 cp (M661), or 20,000 cp (M662)
BURN TIME 40 seconds
AREA OF EFFECT 100m
MAXIMUM RANGE 152-213m altitude
LENGTHS:
LENGTH 13.4 cm
WIDTH (DIAMETER) 4.4 cm
STATUS In production
SERVICE US forces and commercial sales

Each of these rounds fires a long projectile containing a single pyrotechnic star attached to a small parachute assembly. When the round is fired, a small pyrotechnic delay fuze is ignited from the propellant gases. After the four to five second delay, the round has reached an altitude of 500 to 700 feet and an ejection charge is fired by the fuze. The ejection charge ignites the flare candle and ejects it through the top of the aluminum projectile body. The flare lowers itself on a 20 inch wide parachute which slows its descent rate to about 7 feet per second. As the candle burns for about 40 seconds, it burns out well before the parachute reaches the ground. The body of the grenade is white with black markings and there is a raised letter on the plastic nose cap. The letter is W, R, or G, indicating either a white, red, or green flare and the raised letter can be felt with the fingers for identification at night.

▼ M713 (RED), M715 (GREEN), AND M716 (YELLOW) SMOKE GROUND MARKERS

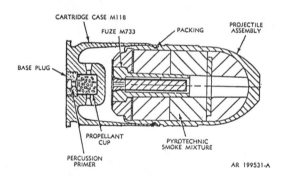

CALIBER 40x46mmR
TYPE Burning type colored smoke signaling grenade launcher shell
MUZZLE VELOCITY 76 m/s (250 fps)
FILLER Smoke composition
FUSE TYPE M733 base igniting fuse functioning on impact w/pyrotechnic delay backup fuse initiating on firing
FUSE DELAY 8-10 seconds (pyrotechnic backup)

WEIGHTS:
ROUND 0.222 kg
PROJECTILE 0.66 kg
FILLER 0.075 kg
EFFECTS:
EFFECT Produces a cloud of smoke on impact
BURN TIME 8 seconds
AREA OF EFFECT 622 m³ cloud
MINIMUM RANGE 15-45m
MAXIMUM RANGE 400m
LENGTHS:
LENGTH 9.9 cm
WIDTH (DIAMETER) 4.4 cm
STATUS In production
SERVICE US forces and commercial sales

These rounds are used to mark areas and indicate targets with colored smoke. The rounds are ballistically matched to the normal HE round so that the sights may be used with no special adjustment. The fuze is a combination pyrotechnic and mechanical which ignites when the round is fired, but will not fire the smoke mixture until the round has traveled 45 meters to centrifugally arm the fuze. On impact, the fuze ignites the smoke mixture and blows open an escape hole at the back of the round. If the impact is insufficient to fire the fuze, the pyrotechnic portion will ignite the smoke charge after a delay of 8 to 10 seconds. The color of the smoke is indicated by a colored band covering the nose of the round as well as markings along the body.

▼ **RP 707 CS**

CALIBER 40x46mm
TYPE Burning type CS gas irritant grenade launcher shell
MUZZLE VELOCITY 76 m/s (250 fps)
FILLER CS/pyrotechnic composition
FUSE TYPE Pyrotechnic delay, initiation on firing
FUSE DELAY 3 seconds
WEIGHTS:
ROUND 0.222 kg
PROJECTILE 0.180 kg
FILLER 0.007 kg CS, 0.023 kg pyrotechnic mix
EFFECTS:
EFFECT Produces a cloud of CS gas
BURN TIME 10 seconds
AREA OF EFFECT 249 m³
MAXIMUM RANGE 400m
LENGTHS:

LENGTH 10.2 cm
WIDTH (DIAMETER) 4.4 cm
STATUS In production
SERVICE Commercial sales

This is a burning type CS gas round produced by Dynamit Nobel in Germany for all 40 x 46mmR launchers. The RP707 round is the same general size and shape of a standard HE round so normal sight settings may be used. The high pressure chamber is replaced with a blank-loaded pistol cartridge and the entire round still uses the high-low pressure system. The pyrotechnic fuze in the base of the projectile ignites when the round is fired and has a delay of three seconds. When the delay is over, an ignition device fires which ignites the CS/pyrotechnic mix and also blows off the nose plug releasing the CS smoke. The body and nose of the projectile are made of heavy aluminum to allow the round to penetrate double-thick windows, wooden doors, and barricades. The round will penetrate 4cm of fiberboard at 100 meters.

▼ **RP 708 CS**

CALIBER 40x46mmR
TYPE Burning type CS gas irritant grenade launcher shell
MUZZLE VELOCITY 50 m/s (164 fps)
FILLER CS/pyrotechnic composition
FUSE TYPE Pyrotechnic, initiating on firing
FUSE DELAY 3 seconds
WEIGHTS:
ROUND 0.300 kg
PROJECTILE 0.245 kg
FILLER 0.024 kg CS, 0.066 kg pyrotechnic mix
EFFECTS:
EFFECT Produces a cloud of CS gas
BURN TIME 15 seconds
AREA OF EFFECT 756 m³
MAXIMUM RANGE 120 m
LENGTHS:
LENGTH 19.8 cm
WIDTH (DIAMETER) 4.4 cm
STATUS In production
SERVICE Commercial sales

This is another burning type CS round from Dynamit Nobel. The RP 708 is a much longer round than most other 40 x 46mm R rounds and normally has to be loaded into a break-open action such as the M79. The size of the round gives it an excellent CS capacity and it may be effectively used for riot control. The body of the projectile is made of a rubberlike plastic which prevents impact injuries as well as keeping the round from being picked up and thrown back, as the rubber melts quickly from the heat of burning. The cartridge uses the same blank pistol round and high-low pressure system of the RP 707 but with less than a third of the range. The pyrotechnic delays ignite the round three seconds after firing and opens a gas exit hole in the nose.

▼ 40 mm FERRET

CALIBER	40x46mmR
TYPE	Shattering type liquid CS gas irritant grenade launcher shell
MUZZLE VELOCITY	153 m/s (500 fps)
FILLER	Liquid CS gas mixture
FUSE TYPE	None, shatters after penetration
WEIGHTS:	
ROUND	0.120 kg
PROJECTILE	0.065 kg
FILLER	25 cc
EFFECTS:	
EFFECT	Contaminates an area with CS mist
PENETRATION	25mm pine board @ 10m, auto windshield @ 50m, hollow core (interior) door @ 100m
AREA OF EFFECT	127 m³
MAXIMUM RANGE	100m
LENGTHS:	
LENGTH	12.5 cm
WIDTH (DIAMETER)	4.4 cm
STATUS	In production
SERVICE	Commercial sales

The Ferret is a barricade penetrating, bursting-type CS round with little or no fragmentation potential and no possibility of fire. The round can be used in any 40 x 46mmR launcher that is capable of accepting its length. The casing is of polycarbonate plastic as is the projectile and the entire package is waterproof. The projectile is fin stabilized and is of a bore diameter that prevents it from engaging the rifling to a great extent but the round does spin in flight. The spin helps disseminate the payload of the round, 25cc of liquid CS agent enough to make untenable a 4,500 cubic foot space. The projectile shatters after penetration but will penetrate fully a given list of materials. The accuracy of the round is such that 90 percent of the rounds will group inside a 1 meter circle at 100 meters. A different sight picture is needed when the round is used with the M79 and a plastic slip-on front sight is supplied. When using the M203, the normal rifle sights are used.

▼ RUBBER IMPACT

CALIBER	40x46mmR
TYPE	Rubber baton grenade launcher shell
MUZZLE VELOCITY	60 m/s (197 fps)
MUZZLE ENERGY	323 J (238 ft/lb)
FILLER	Solid rubber
WEIGHTS:	
ROUND	0.231 kg
PROJECTILE	0.179 kg
EFFECTS:	
EFFECT	Unfolds into large X when fired and impacts with target
MINIMUM RANGE	10m
MAXIMUM RANGE	30 m
LENGTHS:	
LENGTH	14 cm
WIDTH (DIAMETER)	4.4 cm
STATUS	In production
SERVICE	Commercial sales

This is a baton type round designed to deliver a punishing but not damaging blow. The cartridge case is a standard 40 x 46mmR high-low velocity type. The projectile is a four-armed, right-angled cross that is folded under tension to a cylindrical form. The outer surfaces of the projectile are teflon coated to reduce bore friction. When fired, the arms unfold and the projectile takes up a cross-shaped form. The form of the projectile spreads the energy of its impact over a much larger area than conventional munitions of the type reducing the possibility of serious injury. The round is used at ranges of 10 to 30 meters for standing or running targets with target engagement within 10 meters only being used in cases of extreme urgency.

▼ MARK 19 MODEL 3

CALIBER	40x53mmR
AMMUNITION TYPES	All high velocity 40mm grenades
OPERATION	Blowback
TYPE OF FIRE	Selective
RATE OF FIRE	(SS) 30 rpm (A) 60 rpm (CYCLIC) 325-375 rpm
MUZZLE VELOCITY	244 m/s (800 fps)
SIGHTS	Adjustable, U-notch/blade, range 1500m
FEED	Flexible metal disintegrating link (M16/M16A1) belt
MOUNT TYPE	M3 tripod w/Mark 64 Mod 4 gun mount
WEIGHT:	
WEAPON (EMPTY)	34 kg
WEAPON (LOADED)	51.72 kg w/50 rd belt
WEAPON (MOUNTED AND LOADED)	81.203 kg w/ tripod mount & 50 rds
MOUNT	29.483 kg

MAGAZINE (LOADED) 17.72 kg (50 rd belt)
SERVICE CARTRIDGE 0.340 kg (M383 HE)
PROJECTILE 0.175 kg
EFFECTS:
EFFECT Blast and fragmentation
AREA OF EFFECT 15m
MINIMUM RANGE 1 8-36m
MAXIMUM RANGE 2200m
LENGTHS:
WEAPON OVERALL 102.8 cm
BARREL 41.3 cm
SIGHT RADIUS 3 6.5 cm
STATUS In production
SERVICE US and Israeli forces, commercial sales

The original Mark 19 was developed over a very short time in 1967 to provide riverine patrol boats in Vietnam with adequate firepower. It was improved and reissued in 1984. The Mark 19 Model 3 is a heavy machinegun capable of being tripod mounted and firing the 40 x 53mmR family of high-velocity grenades originally designed for helicopter guns. Using the blowback method of operation in combination with advanced primer ignition, the Mark 19 is operationally simple but mechanically complex. The ammunition is held in metallic disintegrating link belts that feed into the weapon from the left hand side. One of the cocking handles (there is one on each side) is drawn back twice to load the weapon. The bolt is locked to the rear and goes forward to fire the weapon. The movement of the massive (7.7kg) bolt changes the center of balance of the weapon considerably and normally requires a two-point mounting to allow accuracy with the weapon. The rounds fired use the high-low pressure system but are loaded to much higher velocities than the 40 x 46mm R rounds. Any attempt to fire the high velocity grenades in a low velocity weapon usually results in the destruction of the weapon and injury or death of the operator. Low velocity rounds could be fired in the Mark 19, but they would have to be singly loaded and would not operate the action. The major drawback of the Mark 19 is the weapon's size and weight as well as the bulk and weight of its ammunition. These drawbacks are considerably outweighed by the firepower of the Mark 19, especially when combined with the anti-armor and anti-personnel effects of the M430 HEDP round.

ASSESSMENT 8 x 23 m group @ 2000 m
WEAPON: MARK 19 MOD 3
AMMO: 40MM HV
Dispersion angle: .229183 degrees, 4.07437 NATO mils.

Range	Group Circle Width (mm)	Probability (0<p<.099) (m)			
		Body	Head	Hand	Bullseye
100.0	400.000	0.851	0.614	0.379	0.149

Range	Group Circle Width (mm)	Probability (0<p<.099) (m)			
		Body	Head	Hand	Bullseye
200.0	800.000	0.614	0.379	0.212	0.077
300.0	1200.000	0.470	0.272	0.147	0.052
400.0	1600.000	0.379	0.212	0.112	0.040
500.0	2000.000	0.317	0.173	0.091	0.032
600.0	2400.000	0.272	0.147	0.076	0.027
700.0	2800.000	0.238	0.127	0.066	0.023
800.0	3200.000	0.212	0.112	0.058	0.020
900.0	3600.000	0.191	0.100	0.052	0.018
1000.0	4000.000	0.173	0.091	0.047	0.016
1100.0	4400.000	0.159	0.083	0.042	0.015
1200.0	4800.000	0.147	0.076	0.039	0.013
1300.0	5200.000	0.136	0.071	0.036	0.012
1400.0	5600.000	0.127	0.066	0.033	0.011
1500.0	6000.000	0.119	0.062	0.031	0.011
1600.0	6400.000	0.112	0.058	0.029	0.010
1700.0	6800.000	0.106	0.054	0.028	0.009
1800.0	7200.000	0.100	0.052	0.026	0.009
1900.0	7600.000	0.095	0.049	0.025	0.008
2000.0*	8000.000	0.091	0.047	0.024	0.008

* indicates range for which data was supplied

▼ **M384 HE**

4.415 MAX

CTG 40MM HE M3
MM LOT [ ]

40 MM HE
CTG M384

CALIBER 40x53mmR
TYPE High explosive fragmentation high velocity grenade launcher shell
MUZZLE VELOCITY 244 m/s (800 fps)
FILLER Composition A5
FUSE TYPE M533 point detonating, initiation on impact
FUSE DELAY Instantaneous
WEIGHTS:
ROUND 0.340 kg
PROJECTILE 0.175 kg
FILLER 0.055 kg
BELT OF 50 17.72 kg

EFFECTS:
EFFECT Blast and fragmentation
AREA OF EFFECT 15m
MINIMUM RANGE 18-36m
MAXIMUM RANGE 2200m
LENGTHS:
LENGTH 11.2 cm
WIDTH (DIAMETER) 4.4 cm
STATUS In production
SERVICE US and Israeli forces, commercial sales
COST $5 ea

This is the high explosive, fragmentation round used for anti-personnel effects with the Mark 19 and other high velocity grenade launchers. The cartridge case is 53mm long, 7mm longer than the low velocity cartridge case which prevents the high velocity rounds from being chambered in the low velocity weapons unless the weapon is particularly worn. The high pressure chamber is quite large in order to hold the propellant charge and has six bleed holes into the low pressure chamber. The M533 fuze is point detonating and arms from centrifugal force. The grenade is fully armed after it has traveled 18 to 36 meters from point of launch. The high explosive charge is contained in a steel casing with internal serrations to assist fragmentation. Belted together with the M16A2 link, the rounds are normally packaged as a 48 round belt carried in the M548 metal box with the entire package weighing 24kg (53 lbs).

DAMAGE 124 Blast, 83 Stun, Fragmentation 5/(2.28 MAX)

▼ M433 HEDP

CALIBER 40x53mmR
TYPE High explosive fragmentation and armor penetrating dual purpose high velocity grenade launcher shell
MUZZLE VELOCITY 244 m/s (800 fps)
FILLER Composition B
FUSE TYPE M549 point initiating base detonating, initiation on impact
FUSE DELAY Instantaneous
WEIGHTS:
ROUND 0.340 kg
PROJECTILE 0.175 kg
FILLER 0.038 kg
BELT OF 50 17.72 kg
EFFECTS:
EFFECT Blast and fragmentation w/armor penetration

AREA OF EFFECT 5m radius, penetrates 5.1 cm steel
MINIMUM RANGE 18-30m
MAXIMUM RANGE 2200m
LENGTHS:
LENGTH 11.2 cm
WIDTH (DIAMETER) 4.4 cm
STATUS In production
SERVICE US and Israeli forces, commercial sales
COST $7 ea.

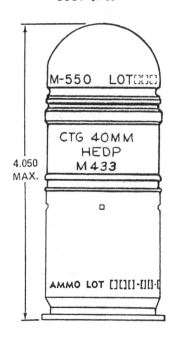

This dual purpose round has both an anti-personnel fragmentation effect as well as an armor penetration capability, and is considered the standard combat round for the Mark 19. The projectile is very much the same as the M433 low velocity round, but with a greater explosive capacity. The M549 point initiating base detonating fuze is used with the M430 and it arms from centrifugal force after the round has traveled 18 to 30 meters from the point of launch. When the fuze detonates, it fires a spitback charge which detonates the main charge. The main charge detonates, collapsing the copper cone at its front into an ultra-high velocity jet of molten metal that will penetrate 51mm (2 inches) of armor plate. The explosive also fragments the internally serrated steel projectile body giving the round an excellent antipersonnel effect. The primary target of this round would be armored personnel carriers whose armor it could penetrate while effecting any dismounted or otherwise exposed troops.

DAMAGE 77 Blast, 51 Stun, Fragmentation 5/ (2.28 MAX)

▼ M677 HE-T

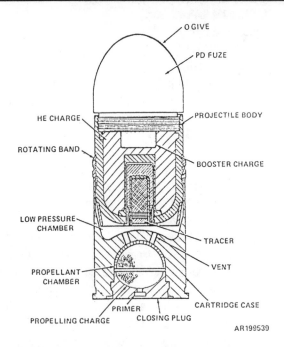

O GIVE
PD FUZE
HE CHARGE
PROJECTILE BODY
ROTATING BAND
BOOSTER CHARGE
LOW PRESSURE CHAMBER
TRACER
VENT
PROPELLANT CHAMBER
PRIMER
CLOSING PLUG
CARTRIDGE CASE
PROPELLING CHARGE

AR199539

CALIBER	40x53mmR
TYPE	High explosive fragmentation shell w/ tracer for high velocity grenade launchers
MUZZLE VELOCITY	244 m/s (800 fps)
FILLER	70/30 Cyclotol
FUSE TYPE	M533 point detonating, initiation on impact
FUSE DELAY	Instantaneous
WEIGHTS:	
ROUND	0.340 kg
PROJECTILE	0.175 kg
FILLER	0.045 kg
EFFECTS:	
EFFECT	Blast and fragmentation w/red tracer
BURN TIME	10 seconds (tracer)
AREA OF EFFECT	15m
MINIMUM RANGE	18-36m
MAXIMUM RANGE	2200m
LENGTHS:	
LENGTH	11.2 cm
WIDTH (DIAMETER)	4.4cm
STATUS	In production
SERVICE	US and Israeli forces, commercial sales

This is a high velocity anti-personnel grenade much like the M384 round. The M677 has a pyrotechnic tracer composition in the base of its projectile that ignites when the round is fired. The tracer burns for about 10 seconds with a bright red light, allowing the flight of the round to be tracked by the gunner or other observers.

DAMAGE	102 Blast, 68 Stun, Fragmentation 5/(2.28 MAX)

▼ ARWEN-37

CALIBER	37x112mmRb
AMMUNITION TYPES	AR1 Baton, AR2 CS, AR3 Baton/CS, AR4 Smoke, AR5 Penetrator CS
OPERATION	Manual
TYPE OF FIRE	Double action revolver
RATE OF FIRE (SS)	12 rpm sustained, 5 rds in 5 seconds
MUZZLE VELOCITY	76 m/s (250 fps)
MUZZLE ENERGY	232 J (171 ft/lb)
SIGHTS	Nonadjustable, aperture/indicator, range 100m
FEED	5 round open cylinder
MOUNT TYPE	Shoulder fired
WEIGHTS:	
WEAPON (EMPTY)	3.100 kg
WEAPON (LOADED)	3.820 kg w/5 rds
MAGAZINE (LOADED)	0.720 kg (5 rds)
SERVICE CARTRIDGE	0.144 kg (AR1)
PROJECTILE	0.080 kg
EFFECTS:	
EFFECT	Impact with target
MINIMUM RANGE	20m
MAXIMUM RANGE	100m
LENGTHS:	
WEAPON OVERALL	76/84 cm
BARREL	27.8 cm
SIGHT RADIUS	48 cm
STATUS	In production
SERVICE	Commercial sales
COST	$1000

The ARWEN (anti-riot weapon, Enfield), is a multi-shot tear gas gun designed to give security forces the ability to fire more than one round without having to pause and load. The ARWEN works on a straightforward mechanical principle firing a family of rounds developed for it. Feeding is from an open-sided cylinder with the five rounds being rotated into position and ejected by a spring-loaded sprocket. The rounds are loaded through the ejection port on the right side of the weapon and pressed against the sprocket which indexes one position for each round and winds the driving spring. The double action trigger pushes the bolt forward during the first half of its travel pressing the in-line round to seat against the barrel but not chamber. If the trigger is released before firing, the spring-loaded bolt is withdrawn, freeing the mouth of the cartridge from the barrel. Pulling the trigger fully fires the cartridge, and when the trigger is released, a fresh round indexes into place and the empty casing is ejected. The round is unsupported except at the mouth and base when fired and acts as its own chamber. The ARWEN is made from alloys and high strength plastics to keep its weight down. The rifled barrel has a foregrip adjustable to either side and a folding front sight. The rear sight is a simple folding peepsight attached to the trigger mechanism housing. Adjustment for range is done by sighting through the graduated scale on the transparent front sight. The buttstock is adjustable for six different lengths to fit a variety of operators.

ASSESSMENT Hit probability 100% @ 20m, 80% @ 100m, man sized target, average shooter
WEAPON: ARWEN 37
AMMO: 37MM
Dispersion angle: .343774 degrees, 6.11154 NATO mils.

Range	Group Circle Width (mm)	Probability (0<p<.099) (m)			
		Body	Head	Hand	Bullseye
10.0	60.000	0.990	0.990	0.958	0.659
20.0*	120.000	0.990	0.958	0.796	0.416
30.0	180.000	0.985	0.880	0.653	0.301
40.0	240.000	0.958	0.796	0.548	0.236
50.0	300.000	0.921	0.719	0.470	0.193
60.0	360.000	0.880	0.653	0.411	0.164
70.0	420.000	0.837	0.596	0.365	0.142
80.0	480.000	0.796	0.548	0.328	0.126
90.0	540.000	0.756	0.506	0.297	0.113
100.0	600.000	0.719	0.470	0.272	0.102

* indicates range for which data was supplied

▼ AR1 KINETIC ENERGY BATON

CALIBER 37x112mmRb
TYPE Plastic impact grenade launcher round
MUZZLE VELOCITY 76 m/s (250 fps)
MUZZLE ENERGY 232 J (171 ft/lb)
FILLER PVC plastic
WEIGHTS:
ROUND 0.144 kg
PROJECTILE 0.080 kg

EFFECTS:
EFFECT Impact with target
MINIMUM RANGE 20m
MAXIMUM RANGE 100m
LENGTHS:
LENGTH 11.2 cm
WIDTH (DIAMETER) 3.7 cm
STATUS In production
SERVICE Commercial sales
COST $13

This is a plastic baton round intended to strike a painful but not disabling blow at ranges from 20 to 100 meters. Unlike other baton or rubber bullet rounds, the AR-1 projectile is streamlined and shaped for better ballistic stability and accuracy. The cartridge case is aluminum and specifically designed for the ARWEN launcher. The propellant is held in a shortened .44 magnum cartridge case securely held in the base of the main casing. A simple flip-off cover seals the round from dirt or moisture and is removed before loading. The trajectory of the projectile is rather flat, making aiming easier. Within 20 meters, the impact of the plastic projectile could prove lethal.

▼ AR2 IRRITANT SMOKE CS

CALIBER 37x112mmRb
TYPE Burning type multiple source CS gas grenade launcher shell
MUZZLE VELOCITY 50 m/s (164 fps)
FILLER CS/pyrotechnic composition
FUSE TYPE Pyrotechnic, initiated on firing
FUSE DELAY 1 second
WEIGHTS:
ROUND 0.144 kg
PROJECTILE 0.080 kg
FILLER 0.016 kg
EFFECTS:
EFFECT Scatters 4 burning canister sub-munitions creating a cloud of CS gas
BURN TIME 12 seconds
AREA OF EFFECT 5m scatter radius, 135 m³ cloud
MAXIMUM RANGE 85-95m
LENGTHS:
LENGTH 11.2 cm
WIDTH (DIAMETER) 3.7cm
STATUS In production
SERVICE Commercial sales
COST $20

The AR-2 round launches a plastic projectile holding four CS canister submunitions. When the round is fired, the pyrotechnic delay fuze at the base of the projectile is ignited and burns for a one second delay. After the delay, the projectile bursts at about 85-95 meters maximum range scattering the ignited CS canisters over a five meter radius. The canisters burn for about 12 seconds, each releasing a white cloud of CS smoke.

▼ AR3 CRUSH-NOSE BATON

CALIBER 37x112mmRb
TYPE Plastic impact round w/ CS agent grenade launcher shell
MUZZLE VELOCITY 76 m/s (250 fps)
MUZZLE ENERGY 221 J (163 ft/lb)
FILLER PVC plastic/ powdered CS
WEIGHTS:
ROUND 0.116 kg
PROJECTILE 0.076 kg
FILLER 0.002 kg (CS)
EFFECTS:
EFFECT Releases CS cloud on impact w/ target
AREA OF EFFECT 1 0cm
MINIMUM RANGE 20m
MAXIMUM RANGE 50m
LENGTHS:
LENGTH 11.2 cm
WIDTH (DIAMETER) 3.7 cm
STATUS In production
SERVICE Commercial sales
COST $19

This is a variation of the AR-1 baton round. The nose of the projectile has been hollowed out and a quantity of CS powder installed under a styrofoam cap. When the round strikes, the nose shatters, spreading the CS over a small, 10cm area. The CS will affects the target struck, but will not contaminate a large area. As for the AR-1 round, the AR-3 should not be used on a target within 20 meters.

▼ AR4 SCREENING SMOKE

CALIBER 37x112mmRb
TYPE Burning type multiple source screeening smoke grenade launcher shell
MUZZLE VELOCITY 54 m/s (177 fps)
FILLER Pyrotechnic smoke composition
FUSE TYPE Pyrotechnic, initiated on firing
FUSE DELAY 1 second
WEIGHTS:
ROUND 0.178 kg
PROJECTILE 0.154 kg
FILLER 0.050 kg
EFFECTS:
EFFECT Scatters 4 burning canister

sub-munitions creating a cloud of white smoke
AREA OF EFFECT 5 m scatter radius, 420 m³ cloud
MAXIMUM RANGE 85-95m
LENGTHS:
LENGTH 11.2 cm
WIDTH (DIAMETER) 3.7 cm
STATUS In production
SERVICE Commercial sales
COST $19

This round is much like the AR-2 CS round but each of the four submunitions creates a dense cloud of white smoke. The smoke is non-toxic and is about three times as dense as the CS smoke from the AR-2 round. Functioning the same as the AR-2 round, the AR-4 is normally loaded with an HC smoke mixture for white smoke but other colors of smoke; red, orange, green, and blue, are available on special order.

▼ AR5 BARRICADE PENETRATOR

CALIBER 37x112mmRb
TYPE Penetrating, bursting type CS gas grenade launcher shell
MUZZLE VELOCITY 138 m/s (453 fps)
FILLER Powdered CS
WEIGHTS:
ROUND 0.130 kg
PROJECTILE 0.060 kg
FILLER 0.006 kg
EFFECTS::
EFFECT Penetrates target and releases CS gas cloud
PENETRATION Auto windshield @ 30m, 13mm plywood @ 40m, hollow core (interior) door @ 60m, double 5mm window pane @ 60m, single 5mm window pane @ 80m
AREA OF EFFECT 100 m³
MAXIMUM RANGE 80 m
LENGTHS::
LENGTH 11.2 cm
WIDTH (DIAMETER) 3.7 cm
STATUS In production
SERVICE Commercial sales
COST $19

This is a penetrating CS round with the projectile based on the streamlined one used in the AR-1 cartridge. The projectile will penetrate glass, wood, and other barricades and then shatter, spreading its CS powder throughout an area. The round will make uninhabitable an area of about 100 cubic meters.

CHAPTER 8

HEAVY WEAPONS

The class of heavy weapons are normally used to support the infantry when attacking strongly defended positions, or to destroy vehicles and aircraft. Most of them require a crew to carry the weapon and the ammunition supply, but can be fired by a single soldier. Included in this class are: recoiless rifles, light infantry mortars, anti-tank/anti-fortification rocket launchers, hand-held surface-to-air missiles, and light autocannon.

In WW 2 the Germans fielded the first of a new form of man-portable artillery—the recoiless rifle. This weapon was based on the *counterblast principle* (a design in which vented propellent gasses are used to balance the cannon's recoil). Despite their primary duties being replaced by grenade launchers and anti-tank missiles in the armies of major countries, recoiless rifles are still found in many Third World forces.

Among the forms of heavy weapon covered in this section is one of the oldest; the first mortars date back to the mid-1400's. A mortar's purpose is to launch a shell in a high arc over intervening obstacles, falling on the target from above. All modern mortars derive from the ideas of Sir Wilfred Stokes in 1915: a finned bomb with a firing charge is dropped down a smooth barrel. The charge ignites (launching the bomb) when it strikes a firing pin at the bottom. This is the most common type of mortar, and is referred to as a "drop-fire" weapon. Heavier artillery mortars are sometimes breech-loading or have rifled barrels for accuracy. ●

▼ 81mm L16 Mortar

81mm L16 Mortar showing traverse and elevation controls, portions of the sight are just visible above the traverse mechanism on left side of weapon

L16 Mortar, closeup of sight mounting on left side of bipod showing the M64 sight

81mm L16 Mortar setup for firing

CALIBER	81mm
AMMUNITION TYPES	L36A2 HE, L40 WP
OPERATION	Manual
TYPE OF FIRE	Single shot, muzzle loaded, drop fired
RATE OF FIRE	(SS) 15 rpm
SIGHTS	Adjustable quadrant type w/leveling vials and elbow scope.
FEED	Single round
MOUNT TYPE	Bipod w/baseplate
WEIGHTS:	
WEAPON (EMPTY)	12.7 kg (barrel)
WEAPON (MOUNTED)	37.85 kg w/bipod, baseplate, and sight
MOUNT	12.3 kg (bipod), 11.6 kg (baseplate)
SERVICE CARTRIDGE	4.2 kg (L36A2 HE)
EFFECTS:	
EFFECT	Blast and fragmentation
AREA OF EFFECT	34m radius
MINIMUM RANGE	166m
MAXIMUM RANGE	5650m
LENGTHS:	
WEAPON OVERALL	128 cm
BARREL	128 cm
STATUS	In production
SERVICE	British military as well as Austria,

Bahrain, Canada, Guyana, India, Kenya, Malawi, New Zealand, Nigeria, Norway, Oman, Qatar, United Arab Emirates, North Yemen, and the US army (as the M252)

This is a British developmed lightweight medium mortar that has also been adopted by the U.S. Army. The basic design of the weapon can be traced back to the Stokes 3 inch mortar of 1917 with the L16 operating in much the same manner. The weapon is made up of three major parts: the barrel, the bipod, and the baseplate with an optical sight mounting on the bipod. The barrel is made of high tensile alloy steel that maintains its strength at high temperatures. The bottom bolt of the barrel is deeply finned to increase the surface area available for cooling. At the base of the barrel is a ball joint which fits into the socket of the baseplate. The firing pin screws through the ball and protrudes into the breech. The baseplate gives the gun tube (barrel) a 360 degree rotation. The bipod is designed so that the legs can be adjusted to fit rough terrain. The elevation and traversing mechanisms are sealed against dirt and are relatively maintenance free. The clamp at the top of the bipod quickly attaches to the barrel and has a bracket to hold the sight. The sight is fully adjustable for range and elevation and quickly allows the gun tube to be properly angled and aligned to the right bearing. The mortar can be assembled and layed (aimed) within a minute by a three man crew that is properly trained. A single man can also lay and operate the L16 due, in part, to its light weight. The weapon is operated by dropping a prepared round, fin first, down the barrel of the aimed mortar. When the round hits the base, the fixed firing pin fires the shotshell-like ignition cartridge (primary charge) which in turn ignites any additional powder charges and launches the shell. The high angle of the ballistic arc of a mortar round allows it to clear intervening obstacles and drop almost vertically on a target. This ability to strike at targets that cannot be seen behind obstacles makes the mortar an indirect fire weapon (indirect fire weapons aim at targets which the gunner cannot see). To properly use the weapon, someone, usually a forward observer, must be able to see the target and communicate with the gun crew. The FO sees the impact of a round and tells the gun crew what corrections are necessary to hit the target. Though the L16 is light and can be carried by a three man crew, the ammunition itself is quite heavy, and a three man crew can normally carry only six rounds with the mortar.

ASSESSMENT   115x138m @ 4500m

▼ L36A2 HE with Mark 4 charge system

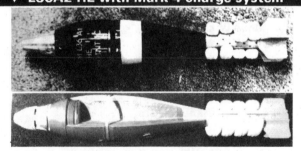

L36A2 high explosive mortar shell, cutaway view

CALIBER	81mm
TYPE	High explosive fragmentation mortar shell
MUZZLE VELOCITY	70–297 m/s (230–974 fps)
FILLER	60/40 RDX/TNT
FUSE TYPE	L127A2 nose fuse '63
WEIGHTS:	
ROUND	4.200 kg

FILLER	0.680 kg
EFFECTS:	
EFFECT	Blast and fragmentation
AREA OF EFFECT	34m radius
MINIMUM RANGE	166m
MAXIMUM RANGE	5650m
LENGTHS:	
LENGTH	47.2 cm
WIDTH (DIAMETER)	8.1 cm
STATUS	In production
SERVICE	Wide service

This is the standard high explosive round for use in the L16 mortar. The round is fin stabilized with a body made of spheroidal graphite and cast iron which shatters into efficient fragments when the filler detonates. The fuze is an adjustable impact type that can be set for an instant detonation or a slight delay so that the target is penetrated deeply before detonation. The fuze's safety pin is removed manually before the round is fired and the fuze arms from setback when the round launches. The round is bore safe and does not fully arm until it has left the gun tube. The tail contains the L33 primary cartridge which ignites the augmenting charges to increase the range of the rounds. As the mortar has a limited range of elevation and depression to further change the range of the round a variable charge system is used. The primary cartridge will give a range of from 100 to 500 meters, while if 6 additional charges are used, the range is 1,600 to 4,500 meters with 8 augmenting charges being the maximum.

DAMAGE	1377 Blast, MAX (100) Stun, Fragmentation 5/(2.28 MAX)

▼ L40 WP Smoke

81mm white phosphorous round with auxiliary charges

CALIBER	81mm
TYPE	Bursting type white phosphorus mortar shell
MUZZLE VELOCITY	70–297 m/s (230–974 fps)
FILLER	White phosphorus
FUSE TYPE	L127A2 nose fuse
WEIGHTS:	
ROUND	4.200 kg
FILLER	0.750 kg
EFFECTS:	
EFFECT	Spreads burning white phosphorus throughout the burst area creating a cloud of white smoke and igniting any combustibles
BURN TIME	120 seconds @ 2700° C

☞ *continued on next page*

☞ *L40 WP Smoke continued*

AREA OF EFFECT 20m radius
MINIMUM RANGE 166m
MAXIMUM RANGE 5650m
LENGTHS:
LENGTH 47.2 cm
WIDTH (DIAMETER) 8.1 cm
STATUS In production
SERVICE Wide service

This is a bursting-type white phosphorus smoke round with incendiary and antipersonnel effects. The L40 has the same ballistics and is handled in the same manner as the L36A2 high explosive shells. On impact, the fuze detonates a burster tube that opens the cast iron casing and spreads the phosphorus over the burst radius of 34 meters. White phosphorus ignites spontaneously on exposure to air. The burning phosphorus creates a dense white smoke cloud of phosphorus pentoxide which is only slightly toxic. The smoke, though dense and obscuring, is hotter than other screening smokes and so quickly rises away after the phosphorus has burned out. The burning temperature of the phosphorus gives it a very strong incendiary effect, allowing the L40 round to have a slight antimaterial effect. The phosphorus spreads as small burning particles and these will stick to an exposed individual, causing severe burns. This antipersonnel effect gives the L40 round a greater psychological impact than its actual effects merit.

DAMAGE Fragmentation 5/(2.28 MAX)
Incendiary (6.84)

▼ 30mm ASP

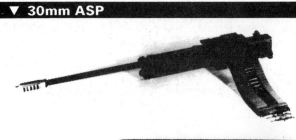

30mm ASP on the M3 tripod for ground use

CALIBER 30x113mmB
AMMUNITION TYPES M789 HEDP, M799 HEI, M788 TP
OPERATION Gas
TYPE OF FIRE Selective

RATE OF FIRE (SS) 40 rpm (A) 80 rpm
(CYCLIC) 400–450 rpm
MUZZLE VELOCITY 800 m/s (2624 fps)
SIGHTS Variable, reflex sight developed for ASP by Mcdonnell-Douglas
FEED Flexible disintegrating metal link (M29) belt
MOUNT TYPE M3 tripod
WEIGHTS:
WEAPON (EMPTY) 47.627 kg
WEAPON (LOADED) 80.347 kg
WEAPON (MOUNTED AND LOADED)
100.305 kg
MOUNT 19.958 kg
MAGAZINE (LOADED) 32.72 kg (80 rd belt)
SERVICE CARTRIDGE 0.351 kg (M789 HEDP)
PROJECTILE 0.237 kg
EFFECTS:
EFFECT Blast and fragmentation w/steel penetration
AREA OF EFFECT 5m radius, penetrate 7 cm+ steel
MINIMUM RANGE 150m
MAXIMUM RANGE 4000m
LENGTHS:
WEAPON OVERALL 202.7 cm
BARREL 132.1 cm
STATUS Under development
SERVICE Under evaluation

The ASP is an automatic, self powered machine cannon firing 30mm shells and capable of being mounted on any mounting that will accept the M2 HB .50 caliber machinegun, including the M3 tripod. The feed for the ASP is on the left side of the weapon and it uses the 30mm ammunition developed for the M230 Chain Gun used in the Apache gunship. The belted cannon shells give the ASP awesome firepower and this, combined with its easy mounting and relatively light weight, greatly adds to the firepower of ground troops. The gas operation system of the ASP is simple and particularly smooth in its action, giving the weapon a high reliability of operation. The short length behind the feed gives excellent balance to the ASP and allows it to be easily controlled from just its twin spade grips. There is no integral sight on the weapon and sighting systems are mounted as needed.

WEAPON ASP
AMMO 30MM
DISPERSION ANGLE .0795775 degrees, 1.41471 NATO mils.

Range	Group Circle Width (mm)	Probability (0<p<.099) (m)			
		Body	**Head**	**Hand**	**Bullseye**
100.0	138.889	0.990	0.936	0.746	0.371
200.0	277.778	0.936	0.746	0.496	0.207
300.0	416.667	0.839	0.599	0.367	0.143
400.0	555.556	0.746	0.496	0.290	0.110
500.0	694.444	0.666	0.422	0.240	0.089
600.0	833.333	0.599	0.367	0.204	0.074
700.0	972.222	0.543	0.324	0.178	0.064
800.0	1111.111	0.496	0.290	0.158	0.056
900.0	1250.000	0.456	0.263	0.141	0.050
1000.0	1388.889	0.422	0.240	0.128	0.045
1250.0	1736.111	0.355	0.197	0.104	0.036
1500.0	2083.333	0.306	0.167	0.087	0.030
1750.0	2430.556	0.269	0.145	0.075	0.026
2000.0	2777.778	0.240	0.128	0.066	0.023
2250.0	3125.000	0.216	0.115	0.059	0.020
2500.0	3472.222	0.197	0.104	0.053	0.018
2750.0	3819.444	0.181	0.095	0.049	0.017
3000.0	4166.667	0.167	0.087	0.045	0.015
3250.0	4513.889	0.155	0.081	0.041	0.014
3500.0	4861.111	0.145	0.075	0.038	0.013
3750.0	5208.333	0.136	0.071	0.036	0.012
4000.0	5555.556	0.128	0.066	0.034	0.012

▼ M789 HEDP

CALIBER	30x113mmB
TYPE	High explosive dual purpose armor penetrating cannon shell
MUZZLE VELOCITY	800 m/s (2624 fps)
FILLER	PBXN-5
FUSE TYPE	M759 Nose fuse initiating on impact
WEIGHTS:	
ROUND	0.351 kg
PROJECTILE	0.237 kg
FILLER	0.027 kg
EFFECTS:	
EFFECT	Blast and fragmentation w/steel penetration
AREA OF EFFECT	5m radius, 7 cm+ steel penetration
MINIMUM RANGE	150m
MAXIMUM RANGE	4000m

LENGTHS:	
LENGTH	20 cm
STATUS	In production
SERVICE	US military and commercial sales

This is a dual purpose round with both a fragmentation antipersonnel effect and an armor piercing shaped charge. The aluminum cartridge case saves weight with the raised belt adding strength to the base. The fuze arms by centrifugal force and detonates on impact. When the fuze detonates, it collapses the cone-shaped copper liner into an armor penetrating jet of metal and gasses. In addition, the explosion of the filler shatters the steel casing of the round into antipersonnel fragments. By the use of the shaped charge effect the projectile is not dependent on velocity for its armor defeating qualities and will penetrate over 5cm of steel all the way out to its maximum range.

DAMAGE 61 Blast, 41 Stun,
Fragmentation 5/(2.28 MAX)

▼ M799 HEI

CALIBER	30x113mmB
TYPE	High explosive incendiary cannon shell
MUZZLE VELOCITY	800 m/s (2624 fps)
FILLER	HE/incendiary mix
FUSE TYPE	M759 nose fuse initiating on impact
FUSE DELAY	Instantaneous
WEIGHTS:	
FILLER	0.043 kg
EFFECTS:	
EFFECT	Blast and fragmentation w/enhanced incendiary effect
AREA OF EFFECT	10m radius
MINIMUM RANGE	150m
MAXIMUM RANGE	4000m
LENGTHS:	
LENGTH	20 cm
STATUS	In production
SERVICE	US military and commercial sales

The M779 round is a high explosive round with both a fragmentation antipersonnel effect as well as an incendiary antimaterial effect. The incendiary effect is obtained by mixing a powdered pyrophoric metal such as zirconium with the explosive. When the fuze detonates the filler on impact with the target, the shell casing is shattered, providing the antipersonnel fragments. The heat of the explosion ignites the metallic

☞ *continued on next page*

☛ M799 HEI continued
particles mixed in with it and drives the burning particles out with the shock wave. The particles quickly ignite any available flammables. This type of round is particularly effective when used against aircraft.

DAMAGE 97 Blast, 65 Stun,
Fragmentation 5/(2.28 MAX)

▼ 90mm M67 Recoilless Rifle

ORD F1710

M67 recoiless rifle with bipod legs unfolded

CALIBER	90x414mmR
AMMUNITION TYPES	M371 HEAT, M590 Canister, XM591 HE
OPERATION	Manual
TYPE OF FIRE	Single shot, breech loaded
RATE OF FIRE	(SS) 5 rpm
MUZZLE VELOCITY	223 m/s (730 fps)
SIGHTS	M103 3 power telescopic sight, range 800m
FEED	Single round
MOUNT TYPE	Shoulder fired or mounted on built in folding tripod
WEIGHTS:	
WEAPON (EMPTY)	15.876 kg
WEAPON (LOADED)	20.072 kg
SERVICE CARTRIDGE	4.196 kg (M371 HEAT)
PROJECTILE	2.917 kg
EFFECTS:	
EFFECT	Heavy steel penetration, secondary blast and fragmentation
AREA OF EFFECT	Penetrates 20 cm+ steel 10m blast radius
MINIMUM RANGE	20m
MAXIMUM RANGE	2100m
LENGTHS:	
WEAPON OVERALL	134.6 cm
BARREL	134.6 cm
STATUS	In production (in S. Korea)
SERVICE	US military, many also still found in use throughout the world

The M67 is the largest shoulder fired recoilless cannon produced in the United States. In use since the 1950's for antitank purposes, the M67 has been replaced for that job by the wire guided missile, specifically, the M47 Dragon. With the advent of the light infantry unit, it, along with several other elite units, found the M67 an excellent house-to-house assault weapon for breaching walls, attacking bunkers, and antipersonnel use. The M67 uses the counterblast system to eliminate the recoil of firing. In a counterblast system, gasses from the fired round are vented to the rear of the weapon and accelerated through a venturi nozzle so that the effective recoil of the gas jet equals and cancels the recoil of the fired shell. The manually operated breechblock acts as the venturi nozzle, so it is a flared conical tube with a central support for the firing pin. Using the counterblast system results in a danger area behind the weapon where hot exhaust gasses, particles, and debris will cause casualties. The danger area of the M67 is cone shaped with its apex at the launcher. The blast spreads out in a 120 degree cone 90 feet long and 180 feet wide. The barrel of the M67 is steel and rifled for accuracy. The rear shoulder brace will unfold into two legs with the vertical front grip acting as the adjustable front leg of a tripod. The horizontal front grip holds the trigger and is connected to the spring-loaded firing pin by a long cable on the right side of the weapon. The telescopic sight has a graduated reticle for both range and movement of the target. There is a battery case that can be attached to the side of the telescope that will illuminate the reticle for firing at night. The M67 can be carried by one man but is normally used by a two man crew, one acting as the gunner and the other as the loader.

ASSESSMENT 3m square target @ 400m 100%

▼ M371 HEAT

M371A1 high explosive antitank round

CALIBER	90x414mmR
TYPE	High explosive antitank armor penetrating recoilless rifle shell
MUZZLE VELOCITY	223 m/s (730 fps)
FILLER	Composition B
FUSE TYPE	M530 Point initiating base detonating, initiation on impact
WEIGHTS:	
ROUND	4.196 kg
PROJECTILE	2.917 kg
FILLER	0.780 kg
EFFECTS:	
EFFECT	Heavy steel penetration, secondary blast and fragmentation
AREA OF EFFECT	penetrates 20 cm+ steel, 10m burst radius
MINIMUM RANGE	20m

MAXIMUM RANGE 2100m
LENGTHS:
LENGTH 70.6 cm
STATUS Out of production
SERVICE US military

This is the standard round for the M67 recoilless rifle. The M371 HEAT, High Explosive Antitank, round is fin stabilized and will penetrate a good deal of armor or concrete. The cartridge case is aluminum and has a plastic rupture disk in its base to allow gasses to escape through the rear venturi. The propelling charge is 21 ounces of propellant wrapped in a bag around the tail of the projectile. The long nose of the round serves a dual purpose. The piezoelectric crystal that detonates the charge is carried at the tip of the nose so that it contacts the target while the nose provides the proper stand-off for optimum armor penetration. The explosive charge has a large copper cone at its front that collapses into a jet when the charge is detonated. The body of the projectile is of steel and provides some fragmentation effect around the impact site.

DAMAGE 1580 Blast, MAX (100) Stun, Fragmentation 5/(2.28 MAX)

▼ M590 Canister

XM590EI canister round

CALIBER 90x414mmR
TYPE Muzzle activating canister flechette shell for recoilless rifle
MUZZLE VELOCITY 335 m/s (1100 fps)
MUZZLE ENERGY 28 J (21 ft/lb) each flechette
FILLER 2,300 finned flechette
WEIGHTS:
ROUND 3.279 kg
PROJECTILE 1.996 kg (Sabot w/flechettes)
FILLER 1.192 kg (flechettes 0.5 g ea)
EFFECTS:
EFFECT Releases a cone shaped swarm of flechettes starting 2.5m in front of the weapon
AREA OF EFFECT 300m cone, 42m wide at the base
MAXIMUM RANGE 300m
LENGTHS:
LENGTH 52.9 cm
STATUS Out of production

This canister round has the effect of turning the M67 into a 90mm shotgun. The M590 round fires a plastic and aluminum projectile designed to break up quickly upon leaving the muzzle of the weapon. When the plastic cap breaks up, the aluminum body quickly falls away leaving the approximately 2,300 eight grain, fin stabilized, steel flechettes to continue in a widening cone. Effective maximum range of the flechettes is 300 meters with the pattern being 42 meters wide at that range. From the point at which the flechettes are released, about 2.5 meters from the muzzle of the weapon, they expand in a cone with the cone widening about 7 meters for each 50 meters of range.

ASSESSMENT Any Man-sized target within the shot cone is struck unless it is behind cover
DAMAGE 6/.01 per flechette, 10 to 20 flechettes per target at least, 0.6 to 1.2 disruption per target

▼ XM591 HE

XM591 high explosive round

CALIBER 90x414mmR
TYPE High explosive fragmentation recoilless rifle shell
MUZZLE VELOCITY 145 m/s (475 fps)
FILLER Composition B
FUSE TYPE XM593 point detonating, initiating on impact
WEIGHTS:
ROUND 6.033 kg
PROJECTILE 4.990 kg
FILLER 0.953 kg
EFFECTS:
EFFECT Blast and fragmentation
AREA OF EFFECT 34m radius
MINIMUM RANGE 30m
MAXIMUM RANGE 2100m
LENGTHS:
LENGTH 67.9 cm
STATUS Out of production, limited number produced

This round is an attempt to give the M67 a greater antimaterial effect. Essentially, the round fires a modified 81mm high explosive mortar shell with a bore-riding sabot and extended tail. The body of the projectile is made of thick walled, pearlitic, malleable iron which shatters into splinters when the explosive charge is detonated. Fragmentation is dense and widespread for a heavy casualty effect and the large blast of the round is destructive to material. The low velocity gives the heavy projectile a limited range and few of these shells were made. A new interest has risen over this round as a possible wall breaching shell for house-to-house urban combat.

DAMAGE 1930 Blast, MAX (100) Stun, Fragmentation 5/(2.28 MAX)

▼ M202A1 FLASH

M202A1 Flash without ammunition clip

M202A1 Flash with 4 rd rocket clip fitted

CALIBER	66mm
AMMUNITION TYPES	M74 Incendiary, M96 CS
OPERATION	Manual
TYPE OF FIRE	Double action, multibarrel, repeating
RATE OF FIRE	(SS) 8 rpm
	(1 round per second for 4 rds)
MUZZLE VELOCITY	114m/s (375 fps)
SIGHTS	Optical reflex sight, range 500m
FEED	4 round clip
MOUNT TYPE	Shoulder fired
WEIGHTS:	
WEAPON (EMPTY)	5.216 kg
WEAPON (LOADED)	12.065 kg
MAGAZINE (EMPTY)	1.497 kg
MAGAZINE (LOADED)	6.849 kg
SERVICE CARTRIDGE	1.338 kg (M74 rocket)
PROJECTILE	1.275 kg
EFFECTS:	
EFFECT	Spreads burning TPA over burst radius
BURN TIME	8–9 seconds @ 1000° C
AREA OF EFFECT	20m radius
MINIMUM RANGE	9m
MAXIMUM RANGE	750m
LENGTHS:	
WEAPON OVERALL	68.6/88.3 cm
BARREL	68.6 cm
STATUS	In production
SERVICE	US forces

The M202A1 is intended as a replacement for the M9A1-7 and other flamethrowers. Using a four-round clip and having four tubes the M202A1 can place an incendiary rocket up to 750 meters away one round each second. The rectangular case of the weapon holds the firing mechanism, sights, and barrels for the rockets. Unloaded, the ends of the launcher fold up to cover the ends of the launch tubes. The sight and trigger handle also fold into the body of the weapon making a relatively compact unit. To fire, the ends are opened, trigger and sight unfolded and the firing pin mechanism extended from the rear. A loaded clip is slid into the rear of the launcher with the warheads fitting into the launch tubes and the retaining tubes at the clip latching onto the firing pin extension. The clip can be pressed into the body of the launcher by pressing a release. The rear cover will close over the clip and there is a wire handle attached to the clip to extend it for firing. The trigger mechanism is of the double action type with each pull of the trigger firing a fresh round. Each time the trigger is released, the firing mechanism rotates to the next tube. The open rocket tubes give no recoil when fired but there is a dangerous backblast area behind the weapon. The danger space of the backblast area is 15 meters long and 15 meters wide at its base. The launcher is made of fiberglass and aluminum and is considered to be semi-disposable with exception of the sight.

WEAPON	M202A1 FLASH
AMMO	66MM M74
DISPERSION ANGLE	1.26046 degrees, 22.4081 NATO mils.

Range	Group Circle Width (mm)	Probability (0<p<.099) (m)			
		Body	**Head**	**Hand**	**Bullseye**
50.0	1100.000	0.500	0.293	0.159	0.057
100.0	2200.000	0.293	0.159	0.083	0.029
150.0	3300.000	0.206	0.109	0.056	0.019
200.0	4400.000	0.159	0.083	0.042	0.015
250.0	5500.000	0.129	0.067	0.034	0.012
300.0	6600.000	0.109	0.056	0.028	0.010
350.0	7700.000	0.094	0.048	0.024	0.008
400.0	8800.000	0.083	0.042	0.021	0.007

▼ M74 Incendiary Rocket

M74 Incendiary Rocket 4 rd clip with restraining strap

M74 Incendiary Rocket with fins unfolded

CALIBER	66mm
TYPE	Bursting type incendiary rocket
MUZZLE VELOCITY	114 m/s (375 fps)
FILLER	TPA (Thickened Pyrophoric Agent-Triethylaluminium)
FUSE TYPE	M434 base detonating, initiating on impact
WEIGHTS:	
ROUND	1.338 kg
PROJECTILE	1.275 kg
FILLER	0.590 kg
4 ROUND CLIP (LOADED)	
	6.849 kg
EFFECTS:	
EFFECT	Spreads burning TPA over target area
BURN TIME	8–9 seconds @ 1000° C
AREA OF EFFECT	20m radius
MINIMUM RANGE	9m
MAXIMUM RANGE	750m
LENGTHS:	
LENGTH	54.6 cm
WIDTH (DIAMETER)	6.6 cm
STATUS	In production
SERVICE	US forces

This is the standard round of ammunition for the M202A1 Flash. The rocket consists of an M54 rocket motor with six spring loaded folding fins. The M236 warhead is attached to the motor by an adaptor which also contains the M34 base detonating fuze. The acceleration of firing releases a spring loaded rotor in the fuze. When the rotor has moved to the armed position, the detonator is in line with the firing pin and will fire on impact. On impact with the target, the detonator fires a burster which ruptures the casing of the warhead, spraying the filler over a 20 meter radius. The filler consists of TPA, triethylaluminum pyrophoric agent which ignites spontaneously on exposure to air. The TPA burns for 8 to 9 seconds at a temperature of 1000 degrees C. and will ignite any combustibles in the area. As the fuel in the rocket motor burns in 7 to 15 milliseconds, depending on the temperature, the fuel is consumed before the rocket leaves the launcher, preventing the operator from receiving injuries due to the exhaust. The rockets come packaged in a four-round clip for quick loading into the M202A1.

DAMAGE	Fragmentation 5/(2.28 MAX)
	Incendiary (6.84)

▼ M96 CS Rocket

CALIBER	66mm
TYPE	Bursting type CS gas rocket shell
MUZZLE VELOCITY	114 m/s (375 fps)
FILLER	CS2 powdered agent
FUSE TYPE	M34 base detonating, initiation on impact
WEIGHTS:	
ROUND	1.448 kg
PROJECTILE	1.385 kg
FILLER	0.700 kg
4 ROUND CLIP (LOADED)	
	7.037 kg
EFFECTS:	
EFFECT	Spreads powdered CS agent over area creating a large dust cloud
AREA OF EFFECT	12m burst radius, 9x64m cloud downwind of impact
MINIMUM RANGE	9m
MAXIMUM RANGE	750m
LENGTHS:	
LENGTH	53 cm
WIDTH (DIAMETER)	6.6 cm
STATUS	Under development
SERVICE	US forces

This is a bursting type CS rocket loaded in a four round clip for the M202A1 launcher. The round uses the same M54 rocket motor as the M74 round. The base detonating fuze arms after launch and detonates on impact. When the fuze fires, a burster ruptures the warhead spreading the CS dust in a large cloud. The cloud will drift with the wind, becoming much longer than it is wide. The M96 is a relatively new round with few reports on its use or effectiveness being available.

▼ 140mm RAW

XM-RAW launcher, unmounted with firing selector set to fire

CALIBER	140mm
AMMUNITION TYPES	HE
OPERATION	Manual

TYPE OF FIRE	Single shot disposable
MUZZLE VELOCITY	173 m/s (567 fps) max. velocity
SIGHTS	Uses aperture/post sights of M16 rifle
FEED	Single round prepackaged
MOUNT TYPE	M16 series rifle

WEIGHTS:

WEAPON (LOADED)	2.720 kg
WEAPON (MOUNTED AND LOADED)	6.355 kg w/M16A1 & 30 rds
MOUNT	3.635 kg (M16A1 rifle w/30 rds0

EFFECTS:

EFFECT	Blast and light fragmentation, creates a 36 cm hole in 20 cm thick double reinforced concrete
AREA OF EFFECT	10m blast radius
MINIMUM RANGE	10m
MAXIMUM RANGE	2000m

LENGTHS:

WEAPON OVERALL	30.5 cm
SIGHT RADIUS	50.1 cm (M16A1 rifle)
STATUS	Under development
SERVICE	Undergoing evaluation

The Rifleman's Assault Weapon (RAW) has been gradually developed over a number of years and is presently being tested by the U.S. military. The potential for the RAW system is great in that a small package easily used by the standard rifleman is equivalent in firepower to a 90mm recoilless rifle. The RAW launcher mounts on the standard M16 rifles and secures itself to the bayonet lug and flash hider. With the arming switch set to safe, the firearm can continue to be used with ball ammunition. When set to arm, the RAW projectile is launched when the rifle is fired. A small amount of gas is tapped from the muzzle to operate a firing pin inside the RAW launcher to fire the rocket. As the motor ignites, the exhaust is guided through two turbine nozzles which spin the mounting while the warhead is still attached. When the rocket motor reaches full thrust, it breaks away from the mounting while spinning. The spin received from the turbine stabilizes the projectile throughout its flight. The flight of the round is line-of-sight to 200 meters or, it may be fired on a ballistic arc out to 2000 meters. The most developed warhead at this time acts as a stand-off satchel charge since it contains 3 pounds of explosive and will blast a man sized hole through a concrete wall. Several other warheads are under development, including an armor piercing shaped charge.

WEAPON	140MM RAW
AMMO	HE
DISPERSION ANGLE	.166158 degrees, 2.95392 NATO mils.

Range	Group Circle Width (mm)	Probability (0<p<.099) (m)			
		Body	Head	Hand	Bullseye
50.0	145.000	0.990	0.928	0.731	0.359
100.0	290.000	0.928	0.731	0.482	0.199
150.0	435.000	0.827	0.583	0.355	0.138
200.0	580.000	0.731	0.482	0.280	0.105
300.0	870.000	0.583	0.355	0.197	0.071
400.0	1160.000	0.482	0.280	0.151	0.054
500.0	1450.000	0.409	0.231	0.123	0.044
600.0	1740.000	0.355	0.197	0.104	0.036
700.0	2030.000	0.313	0.171	0.090	0.031
800.0	2320.000	0.280	0.151	0.079	0.027
900.0	2610.000	0.253	0.136	0.070	0.024
1000.0	2900.000	0.231	0.123	0.064	0.022

DAMAGE 2756 Blast, MAX (100) Stun

▼ ARMBRUST (CROSSBOW)

Armbrust with stocks and sight extended for firing

Armbrust with transparent tube showing interior

CALIBER	67mm
AMMUNITION TYPES	HEAT
OPERATION	Manual
TYPE OF FIRE	Single shot disposable
MUZZLE VELOCITY	210 m/s (700 fps)
SIGHTS	Reflex optical, range 500 m
FEED	Single round prepackaged
MOUNT TYPE	Shoulder fired

WEIGHTS:

WEAPON (LOADED)	6.3 kg
PROJECTILE	1.0 kg

EFFECTS:

EFFECT	Penetrates steel, secondary blast and fragmentation
AREA OF EFFECT	penetrates 30 cm steel, 5m blast radius
MINIMUM RANGE	10 m

MAXIMUM RANGE 1500 m (300m max. effective)
LENGTHS:
WEAPON OVERALL 85 cm
BARREL 43.5cm
STATUS In production
SERVICE Commercial sales

The ARMBRUST (German for Crossbow) is actually a recoilless shell launcher using the countermass principle to eliminate recoil. The manner in which the ARMBRUST uses countermass also results in it having no smoke or flash, limited noise, and a minimal danger area behind the weapon. When the pistol grip and butt plate are unfolded from the tube, the weapon is ready to fire. The propellant charge is in the center of the firing tube with a cup shaped piston facing away from the charge on either side of the propellant. When the charge is fired, the front piston drives the fin stabilized shell out the front of the launcher. At the same time, the rear piston drives a mass of plastic flakes, the equivalent weight of the shell, out of the rear of the weapon. When the pistons reach the ends of the tube, they are caught and held, and because the pistons prevent the gas from slipping past them, all of the smoke and much of the noise is prevented from escaping. The countermass is made up of thousands of plastic flakes which quickly break apart and are harmless. The backblast is so limited that the ARMBRUST can be fired with a solid wall as close as 1 meter behind the operator with no danger. The sound of firing is equal to the firing of a .22 pistol and is very difficult to locate. The shell contains a standard style of shaped charge which is effective against most armored targets.

ASSESSMENT 99 cm group @ 150m, 122 cm group @ 250m
WEAPON ARMBRUST
AMMO HEAT
DISPERSION ANGLE .378151 degrees, 6.72269 NATO mils.

Range .	Group Circle Width (mm)	Probability (0<p<.099) (m)			
		Body	Head	Hand	Bullseye
50.0	330.000	0.901	0.685	0.439	0.178
100.0	660.000	0.685	0.439	0.251	0.093
150.0*	990.000	0.537	0.319	0.175	0.063
200.0	1320.000	0.439	0.251	0.134	0.048
250.0	1650.000	0.370	0.206	0.109	0.038
300.0	1980.000	0.319	0.175	0.092	0.032
350.0	2310.000	0.281	0.152	0.079	0.028
400.0	2640.000	0.251	0.134	0.070	0.024

* indicates range for which data was supplied
DAMAGE 986 Blast, MAX (100) Stun, Fragmentation 5/(2.28 MAX)

▼ M72A3 LAW

M72A3 LAW, extended for firing with sights raised

M72A3 LAW in carrying configuration

CALIBER 66mm
AMMUNITION TYPES HEAT
OPERATION Manual
TYPE OF FIRE Single shot disposable
MUZZLE VELOCITY 145 m/s (475 fps)
SIGHTS Nonadjustable, aperture/indicator, range 350m
FEED Single round prepackaged
MOUNT TYPE Shoulder fired
WEIGHTS:
WEAPON (EMPTY) 1.134 kg
WEAPON (LOADED) 2.132 kg
SERVICE CARTRIDGE 0.998 kg (M72A3 rocket)
PROJECTILE 0.694 kg
FILLER 60/40 Octol 0.304 kg
EFFECTS:
EFFECT Penetrates steel, secondary blast and fragmentation
AREA OF EFFECT penetrate 30.5 cm steel, 10m blast radius
MINIMUM RANGE 10m
MAXIMUM RANGE 1000m
LENGTHS:
WEAPON OVERALL 65.5/89.3 cm
BARREL 38.5 cm
SIGHT RADIUS 49 cm
STATUS In production
SERVICE US military and widely used throughout NATO
COST $150

The 66mm Light Antitank Weapon (LAW) was developed as a disposable antitank weapon of simple construction that could be issued to any infantryman, giving him an antiarmor capacity. The M72A3 rocket uses the same M54 motor as the M74 and M96 rockets with six spring-loaded fins that extend as soon as the rocket leaves the tube. The fuel in the M54 motor bums within 7 to 18 milliseconds, well before the rocket has left the launcher so that no exhaust will strike the operator. There is a danger area behind the launcher extending 15 meters behind the tube and 8 meters wide at its base. The LAW is prepared for firing by pulling a small ring pin at the rear of the weapon which releases the shoulder sling and both end caps. The collapsed launcher is extended until it locks in place. The hinged rear end cap acts as a buttplate to rest against the shoulder. The sights automatically pop up when the launcher is extended, with the rear sight being a simple peep sight and the front being a transparent plate with an aiming grid etched on it in black. The aiming grid accounts for range, windage, and speed of the target as well as having a stadia line for determining the range to a standard tank sized target (Soviet T-62). When the launcher is extended, the percussion firing mechanism is cocked and all that must be done is to release the safety before the weapon can be fired. Firing instructions are found etched on the side of each launcher in cartoon form. The M18A1 warhead uses a copper lined shaped charge for armor penetration. The light steel body of the warhead has little antipersonnel fragmentation effect but the detonation of the Octol explosive filler creates a sufficient blast front to damage anyone near the point of impact. The fiberglass and aluminum launcher tube is not intended to be reloaded and is discarded after firing.

ASSESSMENT 50% hit @ 140m, 75% hit @ 100m, 25% hit @ 200m (2.3x2.3m target)

WEAPON M72A2 LAW

AMMO HEAT

DISPERSION ANGLE 1.75884 degrees, 31.2683 NATO mils.

Range	Group Circle Width (mm)	Probability (0<p<.099) (m)			
		Body	Head	Hand	Bullseye
50.0	1535.000	0.391	0.220	0.117	0.041
100.0*	3070.000	0.220	0.117	0.060	0.021
150.0	4605.000	0.153	0.079	0.041	0.014
200.0	6140.000	0.117	0.060	0.031	0.010
250.0	7675.000	0.095	0.048	0.025	0.008
300.0	9210.000	0.079	0.041	0.020	0.007
350.0	10745.000	0.068	0.035	0.018	0.006

* indicates range for which data was supplied

DAMAGE 684 Blast, MAX (100) Stun, Fragmentation 5/(2.28 MAX)

CHAPTER 9

NIGHT VISION & SIGHTING DEVICES

ince the earliest days of warfare, man has sought the ability to act at night. But all known methods of illuminating the battlefield had the drawback of granting this capability to the enemy as well. This stalemate continued into the late '40s, when a series of technical breakthroughs gave the individual soldier the power to "see in the dark."

The first night vision weapon sights were Active Infrared devices, such as the T3 sight used on the M3 Carbine in Korea. A note: The majority of existing electronic weapon sights and vision devices can be divided into two types: *active*, a unit with its own illumination source (usually infrared), and *passive*, which depends on available ambient light sources to be amplified or filtered. Due to certain drawbacks in the performance of active systems (weather, size of unit, detectability), the trend since the mid-'60s has been towards passive sighting systems; most counterterrorist forces will be so equipped.

Today, research and production of passive devices is concentrated in the US, Great Britain, and Germany, while the USSR and former East Bloc militaries study and refine the older active systems.

Approximately fifteen years ago, a new discovery was made in the area of active sighting systems. Advanced development allowed laser projection units to be produced small enough, and light enough to be used for projectile weapon guidance. The laser sight's greatest advantage is its intimidation factor, because a target can be made aware that a marksman is "dead on" to him. ı

▼ NVS-700

NVS-700 starlight scope

TYPE	Passive Night vision weapon sight
WEIGHT	1.8 kg
LENGTH	29.2 cm
WIDTH	10.1 cm
MAGNIFICATION RNG	3.5 x 700 m (moonlight), 450 m (starlight)
POWER SOURCE	Two - AA Mercury batteries
OPERATING LIFE	60 hours
STATUS	In production
SERVICE	Military, police, and commercial sales
COST	$2,500

This is a second generation night vision sight which uses passive starlight means to allow a target to be seen at night. Used to create "near daylight" conditions for the user, the NVS-700 in effect multiplies available light thousands of times to allow the operator to see the target. Using available light is what gives this system a passive designation rather than active, which is used for the earlier infrared systems that had to illuminate the target. The system operates by available light being focused on the image intensifier tube. In the second generation system, the focused target light strikes a photosensitive screen where a small quantity of electrons are emitted from the opposite side of the plate. These emitted electrons are guided through minute glass fiber tubes, thousands of which are packed parallel to each other in what is called the microchannel plate (MCP). As the electrons travel down the channels, each time they collide with the wall of the channel, more electrons are released to also glide down the tube. It is this additional release of electrons that serves to "amplify" the available light. The emerging electrons from the MCP strike a second photoelectric screen which reproduces the visible light image that is represented by the electron stream. In the NVS-700, the image tube is 25mm in diameter, and shows a marked increase in strength and reliability over earlier first generation systems which are being removed from service. A major problem of first generation systems is "flaring" or "whiting out" when suddenly illuminated by normal light or even a muzzle flash from the weapon on which it is

mounted. Whiting out could take several minutes for the tube to recover from, or the tube could burn out completely. The second generation MCP systems have eliminated or greatly reduced this problem with white out recovery being only a few moments in the NVS-700 with its Automatic Brightness control. A daylight cover is available that allows the sight to be used and zeroed to the weapon in daylight. There are separate controls on the NVS-700 to allow the operator to adjust the focus to his eye as well as the brightness of either the tube or the reticle. The reticle appears as an illuminated red circle on the otherwise green image plate. The NVS-700 is relatively small and lightweight as well as being capable of mounting on any weapon system from rocket launchers to submachineguns. Though it cannot operate in total darkness, the NVS-700 allows a man sized target to be seen and engaged at 700 meters in moonlight and 450 meters in starlight. These ranges shorten accordingly by the amount of overcast in the sky, or cover that the target is under.

▼ M-909

M-909 night vision goggles

TYPE	Passive night vision goggles
WEIGHT	0.880 kg
LENGTH	16.5 cm
WIDTH	17.3 cm
HEIGHT	11.9 cm
MAGNIFICATION RNG	1 x 230 m, man sized object @ 1/4 moon
POWER SOURCE	2.7 volt mercury battery
OPERATING LIFE	20 hours
STATUS	Production
SERVICE	Military and commercial sales
COST	$3,000

These goggles are intended to give the wearer the ability to operate normally in near total darkness. With the goggles properly adjusted and worn, they are completely hands free in operation, allowing the wearer to drive or fly a vehicle, or operate a weapon. Each lens is adjusted for the individual eye and contains a 2nd generation-plus image intensifier tube. The 18mm tube contains a microchannel plate amplifier in wafer form to give a 20,000 gain over ambient light. For use when flying, a set of filters are available which block out instrument lights but allow vision through the windscreen. The drawback with this type of device is the limited peripheral vision along with the elimination of natural night vision. There is a special cutaway version of the M-909 goggles that are for use by pilots which greatly increase peripheral vision, but expose the glow of the eyepieces to outside observation. This glow is of no risk in an aircraft, but could result in an infantryman being observed at close range. For the ground user, the loss of peripheral vision is necessary to use the M-909 and they also make precise aiming of weapons difficult. The focus of the M-909 is easily adjustable down to a minimum of 30cm, allowing maps and control panels to be read. There is a small infrared light mounted between the lenses to illuminate maps for reading while not being visible to normal vision. A small switch must be held for the infrared light to be on preventing the light being left on and giving away a position.

▼ AIM-1

TYPE	Infrared laser aiming device
WEIGHT	0.255 kg
LENGTH	8 cm
WIDTH	3.5 cm
HEIGHT	5 cm
POWER SOURCE	Two AA 3.4V lithium batteries 'kN@d
OPERATING LIFE	12–85 hours
STATUS	Production
SERVICE	Commercial sales
COST	$150

The difficulty in aiming a hand held weapon while wearing night vision goggles has been largely eliminated with the development of this type of aiming device. The AIM-1 is a very small, solid-state laser that can be easily attached to most weapons; it projects an infrared beam that can only be seen by someone using a night vision device. Via a Gallium Aluminum Arsenide laser diode, the AIM-1 projects a spot on the target in the shape of a vertical line 2cm wide and 70cm tall at 100 meters. The adjustments on the laser allow the user to determine what point on the line will be the bullet's impact point, normally the top of the line is used. Being very small, the AIM-1 can be mounted on almost any weapon. The internal electronics are cast in plastic as a modular package making the AIM-1 virtually immune to most types of damage and easily repaired when damaged. There is both an on/off switch on the laser as well as a remote pressure switch that can fire the beam and be placed wherever on the weapon that the operator finds it most convenient. The AIM-1 also has a variable intensity switch, allowing the power of the laser to be increased for target identification. Even at maximum output and shortest battery life, the laser is of such a frequency and power that it is completely eye safe and does not require any special protection.

▼ LS 45

MP5SD5 with LS 45 laser sight with pressure switch on the pistol grip, no magazine and selector set to 3 rd burst

TYPE	Laser aiming device
WEIGHT	0.340 kg
LENGTH	19.1 cm
WIDTH	3.5 cm
HEIGHT	5.1 cm
RANGE	450 m (night), 50 m (bright day)
POWER SOURCE	Two standard (alkaline) 9V batteries
OPERATING LIFE	45 minutes continuous operation
STATUS	Production
SERVICE	Commercial sales
COST	$350

This is a visible light laser aiming system that projects a red dot on the target. The sight is adjustable so that the dot indicates the point of impact for the weapon. Using a Helium Neon gas laser, the LS 45 projects a relatively weak (1 milliwatt maximum), beam that cannot easily be seen, but creates a coruscating red dot that cannot be mistaken. If there is smoke, fog, or dust in the air, the beam is visible but the range is cut down considerably as the light reflects off particles in the air. There is a mounting bar on the base of the LS 45 that is adjustable to fit most standard telescopic sight mounts. The light weight and size of the LS 45 allows it to be mounted on pistols or almost any small arm. There is an open notch/post sight on top of the LS 45 (cast into the plastic body)to assist in rapid target acquisition. Properly adjusted, the red dot indicates the point of impact for most common combat ranges. The beam is straight and does not account for the ballistic arc of a specific round; this must be taken into account when the device is used at long ranges. There is a remote pressure switch that plugs into the LS 45 and activates the laser when pressure is applied. The back of the remote switch is covered in a velcro material that can be glued anywhere the operator desires on the weapon and still be easily removed. If the remote switch's plug is partially detached from the LS 45, it turns the device on until the plug is fully seated or removed. The LS 45 has a great intimidating effect on anyone who knows the device is trained on him, because the visible dot can be quite easily seen and is unmistakable as to its purpose.

APPENDIX "A": GLOSSARY

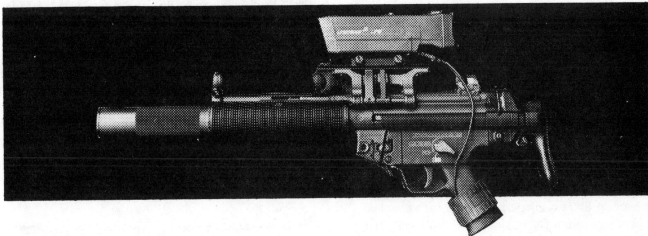

ASSESSMENT: This is the result of a firing test of the weapon, normally from a rest position unless otherwise stated. The measurement of the group size is from edge to edge of the bullets' holes, normally of a three to five shot group at a given range.

Example: 4 in @ 100 m indicates a group size of 4 inches (diameter of the circle which will enclose the group) at a range of 100 meters.

Where the Assessment of a weapon was not available from an actual firing test, the probable group size was calculated considering the type of weapon, sights, sight radius, and type of fire. Weapons where the assessment was calculated are indicated by the word "Assessment" being absent between the description of the weapon and the hit probability table.

Basic Load: This is a basic allowance of ammunition and magazines or other feed devices issued with a weapon. Basic Load is also a recommended amount of munition, such as hand grenades, to be carried.

Box Magazine: This is a removable box shaped, spring loaded ammunition feed device. Cartridges are held in the magazine by the feed lips that help guide them into the chamber of the weapon. The cartridges are pressed against the feed lips by the action of the spring loaded follower, a small platform on top of the magazine's spring. The box magazine is the most common feed device in semiautomatic and non belt-fed automatic weapons.

Burst Control: This is a mechanical limiter used on automatic weapons to set the number of rounds fired for each pull of the trigger. The number of rounds is set to prevent waste of ammunition on automatic fire.

Burst Radius: The radius of an area in which a munition has its effect. Within the radius, the munition has its primary effect, (i.e. fragmentation causes casualties, Smoke or Gas is at an effective concentration). Casualty causing munitions are considered to effect at least 50% of exposed personnel at the maximum distance of the radius with the percentage increasing closer to the function point of the weapon. The burst radius for smoke producing munitions is listed as the average size of the cloud under standard conditions.

Caliber:

(A) Caliber is the diameter of the inside of a rifle barrel stated in thousandths of an inch or in hundredths of a millimeter, (i.e. .308 Winchester, 7.62mm NATO).

(B) Caliber is commonly used to indicate the size and type of ammunition for which a particular weapon is chambered.

Chamber: The section of a firearm where the cartridge is seated to be fired.

Clip: A device used to hold a number of cartridges to facilitate loading a weapon. Also called a "stripper clip" or, in Great Britain, a "Charger." Sometimes used as a slang term for an ammunition magazine.

CN: The military abbreviation for one of the most commonly used tear gases, chloroacetophenone. Normally mixed with a smoke composition or dissolved in a solvent for use, CN causes immediate heavy production of tears, pain, and burning in the upper respiratory tract. In higher concentrations it also causes itching and burning of the skin. The effects of CN disappear within about 15 minutes of removal from exposure. CN is only slightly toxic and it would require at least a ten minute exposure to a very high concentration level to cause death. There have been no reported deaths from the use of CN.

Comp. B: Composition B is a powerful explosive used as a bursting charge in modern grenades and shells. The explosive is made of a mixture of 60% RDX, 39% TNT, with 1% of a wax desensitizer.

CS: This is the most powerful of the modern tear gases. CS is the military abbreviation for O-chlorobenzylmalononitrile. CS is normally mixed with a smoke producing compound for burning type munitions, with powdered talc, or as a 2% solution in kerosene for use as a liquid (Mace). CS causes extreme burning of the eyes with a copious flow of tears. The pain in the eyes increases with further exposure causing involuntary closing of the eyes. There is also increasing pain in the nose and throat with difficulty in breathing. Strong concentrations induce nausea and vomiting. The symptoms go away rapidly upon removal from exposure to clean air. Heavy concentrations of CS can be toxic though there have not been any reported deaths due to CS poisoning.

Double action: This is a type of firing action where a single pull of the trigger will both cock and fire the weapon. A double action weapon may also be fired single action that is, manually cocked and then fired. Some weapons are double action only and the action cannot be cocked manually.

Drum Magazine: This is a high capacity style magazine used primarily in automatic weapons. The drum style feeds rounds through a spiral built around the circumference of the drum. There is also a pan type drum magazine that lays flat across the top of the weapon's receiver. In the pan magazine, the cartridges are held flat across the radius of the magazine pointing to the center. Drum magazines are most often found on submachineguns with pans used more often on light machineguns.

EFF RNG: Effective range, the maximum range that an average qualified marksman can be expected to hit a standard target 50% of the time.

Feed Device: The feed device includes all the materials required to supply and feed ammunition to a weapon. The materials include all ammunition, belts, magazines, clips, ammunition boxes, or in some cases, loose rounds of ammunition.

Filler: The filler is the active agent in a grenade or shell. It can be, but is not limited to, explosives, chemical agents, smoke producers, flechettes, or inert materials.

Flechette: A small, fin stabilized dart used as a high velocity individual projectile or, in mass groups, as a "shotgun" like charge for a large bore weapon.

Full Automatic: In this type of fire the weapon uses the forces of firing (gas, recoil, blowback, etc.) to load, fire, extract, eject, and reload, continuously firing the weapon as long as there is ammunition and the trigger is pulled.

Gauge: The unit of measurement for shotgun bores. The gauge number is the number of pure lead balls of a given bore diameter that weigh one pound. Twelve 12 gauge lead balls would equal one pound.

HC: The military designation for a Hexachlorethane/Zinc dust mixture that burns to produce a harmless, dense grey-white smoke.

HE: The military abbreviation for High Explosive

HEAT: The military abbreviation for High Explosive Anti Tank. In the HEAT shell the power of the explosive is focused in a shaped charge to penetrate armor.

Integral (Internal) Magazine: This type of magazine is a permanent part of the weapon and cannot be easily removed. The magazine is often loaded through the use of a stripper clip.

Length: This is the overall length of a weapon. In the case of a folding stock weapon, the first number given is with the stock folded with the second being with the stock extended.

LMG: The military abbreviation for Light Machine Gun. A light machinegun often weighs between nine and fourteen kilograms and is fired from a bipod.

MAX RNG: Maximum range, the greatest distance a given projectile can fly, normally much greater than the effective range.

MG: The military abbreviation for Machine Gun.

MIN RNG: Minimum range, the shortest distance that a weapon will fully function. The distance traveled during the time it takes a projectile's fuse to Arm.

Munitions: All materials required to conduct offensive or defensive war including ammunition, weapons, transport, food, fuel, and clothing. The term is also used occasionally in place of Ordnance.

Muzzle Vel: Muzzle Velocity.

Ordnance: Military ammunition, explosives, combat vehicles, and weaponry.

Penthrite: Another term for the explosive PETN.

PETN: An abbreviation for Pentaerythritol tetranitrate, one of the most powerful explosives available. PETN has an R.E. of 1.66 compared to TNT.

Pyrotechnics: This is a type of ammunition including rockets, flares, and fireworks used for signaling, illuminating, or indicating targets.

Rate of Fire (RoF):

(SS) single shot: the number of aimed rounds that can be fired from a non-automatic weapon in one minute by an average qualified operator.

(A) Automatic: this is the recommended maximum practical rate of fire on full automatic. The practical rate includes time needed to change feed devices and to prevent overheating.

(Cyclic): The maximum rate at which an automatic weapon, given unlimited ammunition, could cycle (fire) in one minute. The cyclic rate is the maximum speed at which the weapons action can work.

Round: A complete piece of ammunition with all the parts needed to fire it. The projectile, a propellant, and igniter (primer) needed to fire a weapon once.

RDX: The military designation for the high explosive Cyclotrimethylenetrinitramine, also called cyclonite or hexogen. The term RDX is derived from the British Research Department formula X. A powerful explosive, RDX is used as the main ingredient for many plastic explosive compounds.

RPM: Rounds per minute.

SC: Star Cluster, a pyrotechnic that releases several, short burning length, stars as a signal.

Selective fire: This type of action allows the firer to choose between semiautomatic or automatic fire. In some modern designs, the selector may also have a burst-fire position in place of or in addition to full automatic fire.

Semiautomatic: Also referred to as autoloading. A semiautomatic weapon reloads itself automatically when fired but requires a pull of the trigger to fire each round.

Shaped Charge: In this type of explosive device, there is a hollow cavity in the explosive charge. When the charge is detonated, the cavity, often in the shape of a cone, focuses the blast of the explosive into a high speed jet of gases. The jet is moving at such speed that it pushes the steel of the target out of the way and can thereby penetrate a much greater thickness of steel than a simple explosive charge of equal weight.

Silencer: A silencer suppresses the noise of firing a bullet by slowing down the escape of the propellant gases. Though with a specially designed weapon, a silencer can be very effective, it cannot control the noise of the weapon's action or the supersonic crack of the bullet if it has a velocity greater than 1,130 feet per second. Due to a silencer having to work on the escaping gases, it cannot be easily fitted to a revolver because of the gases escaping through the gap between the cylinder and barrel. The term silencer is a popular though incorrect term, the proper term for this type of device is a suppressor.

Single Action: This type of action requires the hammer to be manually cocked into the firing position for each shot fired.

SP: Star Parachute, this pyrotechnic device is also referred to as a "Star shell" when fired from a mortar or other artillery. The round ejects a magnesium (white) or colored flare suspended from a parachute. The Star parachute shell is used for either illumination or as a signal with a red star parachute being an international distress signal.

Suppressor: Also Sound Suppressor, the technically correct term for a silencer. Since a silencer does not silence a weapon but only suppresses the sound of firing, suppressor is considered the correct term. This type of device is also called a sound moderator in parts of Europe.

Tetryl: A military designation for the high explosive Trinitrophenylmethylnitramine also called tetralite or pyronite.

TH3: The military designation of a specific mixture of thermite and oxidizers, generally referred to as thermate. TH3 burns at about 2,200 degrees centigrade and produces white hot molten iron as a byproduct.

TNT: The common abbreviation for the high explosive Trinitrotoluene. With TNT being widely used and easily purified to a specific grade, it is used as an international standard by which other explosives are measured.

Tubular magazine: This type of magazine holds the rounds in a spring loaded tube either underneath the barrel or in the buttstock of a weapon. A limitation of the tubular magazine is that it must use either flat tipped or rimfire rounds. If a standard primed pointed bullet round is used in a tubular magazine, the recoil of firing could drive the primer of one round onto the point of a bullet behind it firing the round in the magazine.

WP: The military abbreviation for White Phosphorus. White phosphorus ignites spontaneously on contact with air, burning with a hot flame and giving off dense clouds of smoke. Primarily used as a smoke producer, WP rapidly produces a dense cloud of white smoke but due to the heat of burning, the smoke rapidly rises.

APPENDIX "B":
METRIC-ENGLISH CONVERSIONS

Symbol	Multiply	By	To Get
C	Centigrade + 17.8	1.8	Farenheit
CM	Centimeters	0.3937	Inches
CM	Centimeters	0.0328084	Feet
CM	Centimeters	0.01	Meters
F	Farenheit - 32	5⁄9	Centigrade
Ft	Feet	30.48	Centimeters
Ft	Feet	0.3048	Meters
FPS	Feet per second	0.3048	Meters/second
Ft/Lb	Foot-pounds	0.1383	MKP
Ft/Lb	Foot-pounds	1.356	Joules
Gr	Grains	0.06480	Grams
Gr	Grains	0.000142857	Pounds
G	Grams	15.432	Grains
G	Grams	0.001	Kilograms
G	Grams	0.0352739	Ounces
G	Grams	0.0022046	Pounds
In	Inches	2.54	Centimeters
In	Inches	0.083333	Feet
In	Inches	0.0254	Meters
In	Inches	25.4	Millimeters
J	Joules	0.7376	Foot-pounds
Kg	Kilograms	15432.358	Grains
Kg	Kilograms	35.273962	Ounces
Kg	Kilograms	2.2046226	Pounds
Km	Kilometers	0.6213712	Miles
L	Liters	0.2641794	Gallons
L	Liters	33.81497	Ounces
L	Liters	1.056718	Quarts
M	Meters	3.2808399	Feet
M	Meters	39.37	Inches
M	Meters	1.0936133	Yards
M	Meters/second	3.2808399	Feet/second
Mi.	Miles	1.6093	Kilometers
MM	Millimeters	0.0032808	Feet
MM	Millimeters	0.03937	Inches
Oz.	Ounces	437.5	Grains
Oz.	Ounces	28.349523	Grams
Oz.	Ounces	0.0625	Pounds
Oz.	Ounces (Liquid)	0.0295727	Liters
Lb.	Pounds	7000	Grains
Lb.	Pounds	453.59237	Grams
Lb.	Pounds	0.4535923	Kilograms
Qt.	Quarts	0.9463264	Liters
Yd.	Yards	0.9144	Meters

THE EDGE OF THE SWORD

APPENDIX C:
Using Sword's Tables in Roleplaying Games

f you're planning to use **Edge of the Sword's** guns in your current RPG campaign, all you'll really need is the damage for the weapon (in your current system's statistics), and the accuracy modifiers (if any) that can be applied. These are listed in the table on page 212. The damage for each type of round (assumed to be a lead slug) is listed by round type and game system as well.

However, many people may find the extremely accurate tables for each Sword weapon very useful, and may even want to adapt their firearms combat to make use of these tables. The following adaptations allow game masters to convert the "handgun skills" of their current system into values which can use the Sword weapon accuracy tables.

One big advantage to this is that the common system allows you to have your Cyberpunk characters shoot it out with your Champions characters, while your Cthulhu character helps out the winning side...

Basic Sword System (Modified Percentile)

The Sword System breaks all marksmen into seven basic categories. Each category has a basic percentage chance of hitting at target under optimum conditions:

25%	**Familiar**
50%	**Marksman**
62%	**Sharpshooter**
75%	**Expert**
80%	**Sniper**
90%	**Competitive Shooter**
100%	**Olympic Class Shooter**

To use the Accuracy Tables, multiply the value of shooter by the percentage probability for that range and target. Example: You have a skill of 50 and are shooting for the body with a Styer GB. Range is 50 meters. On the table, percentage chance for a body shot at 50 meters

Range in meters

Statistical chance to hit

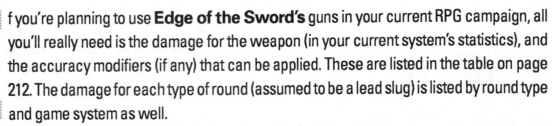

Range	Group Circle Width (mm)	Probability (0<p<.099) (m)			
		Body	Head	Hand	Bullseye
50.0	34.699	0.990	0.990	0.990	0.844
100.0	69.399	0.990	0.990	0.936	0.605
150.0	104.098	0.990	0.974	0.840	0.462
200.0	138.797	0.990	0.936	0.747	0.372
250.0	173.497	0.988	0.889	0.666	0.310
300.0	208.196	0.974	0.840	0.599	0.266
350.0	242.895	0.957	0.792	0.544	0.233
400.0	277.595	0.936	0.747	0.497	0.207
450.0	312.294	0.913	0.705	0.457	0.187
500.0	346.993	0.889	0.666	0.422	0.170

DAMAGE 51/0.38

Bullet test grouping

is 0.990. Multiplied by 50, this results in a 49.5% chance; rounded up this would be a 50% chance.

Percentile Based system (Call Of Cthuluhu™, others)

One of the most common types of system around, percentile based systems are fairly easy to convert to use in Sword. Use the character's skill (for the type of weapon: Handgun, Rifle or Shotgun) as a base. For example, if John Smith has a 20% in Handgun, and is firing a **Walther PP** at a cultist's **head** at a **range of 15 meters**, is probability number would be 0.990. Multiplied by his 20% handgun skill, John has a 19.8 or 20% chance.

Sounds like you've gone the long way around to get the same number, right? At some ranges, this is true. However, let's have John fire the same Walther at the same target at a range of 125 meters. The probability drops to 0.567, which gives John only a 11% chance to hit the same target. When you want to factor in absolute ranges, types of target size, and individual weapons, the Sword system gives you a greater amount of exactitude.

Hero System™ (OCV based)

In the Hero System, gun skill is normally determined by adding the character's OCV (Dexterity x3) plus levels of skill. Modifiers for range, weapons and/or maneuvers can also be added or subtracted. The target's Defensive Combat Value (DCV) is subtracted from this total to get the value the attacker must roll equal to or under in order to hit.

With this many angles, conversion of Sword to Hero is a bit of a bother (but the same is true for RTG's Interlock, so bear with us). To fit Hero into Sword's combat tables, first multiply the character's base Dexterity by 3 to determine his Base Handgun Skill. For example, a character with a 10 DEX would have a base 20% chance, 5% more than the "Familiar" category in Sword. At the highest possible DEX, a character would have a 60% base chance to hit in Sword (a little less than the "Sharpshooter" category.

Note that this is just raw na*tural* ability (one reason why Hero is a "superheroic" style game. You still need to add SKILLS into the mix. To do this, add an additional 3% for every level of actual Combat Skill the character has. Most Hero Skills range from 1 to 14, a spread of 3% to 42%. When stacked on top of the DEX number, this gives you a spread that tops out at 102 (or 60% DEX + 42% SKILL). Drop any value over 100% (the extra 2%) and you're even with the "Olympic class" shooter of Sword.

Sword works on the premise that people can't dodge bullets; hence, we've ignored the DCV factor entirely. Obviously, superheroes can dodge bullets. Therefore, in these cases, subtract the target's DEX times 3% from the attacker's total of DEX + SKILL. Additional modifiers for dodging, etc. are at a ratio of 3% for every DCV.

Interlock™ System (Cyberpunk 2020®, MEKTON II®)

Interlock skills are determined by adding a Weapon Skill, a Weapon

Modifier and a basic Reflex Statistic for a total value. This value is then compared to a To Hit Number based on the range of the target.

Here, the trick is to boil all these values down into a basic Gun Skill. You can toss out the Weapon modifier; it's factored into the Accuracy Table for each weapon. Simply add the Reflex, Weapon Skill and any targeting mods (for cyberwear, aiming, etc.). You should obtain a spread somewhere between 2 and 24. Multiply this value by 5 to obtain a Sword Basic Handgun Skill. Drop any value over 100% (the extra 2%) and you're even with the "Olympic class" shooter of Sword.

D20 Systems (AD&D™, others)

D20-based systems usually have no true firearms capacities. However, this can be worked around in two ways.

• Use the character's basic DEXTERITY. Multiply this value (normally a 1 to 20 value) by 5 to determine a basic Firearms skill. For example, with a Dexterity of 16, Thorvald Gunnerson would have an 80% Firearms Skill.

Now multiply this value by the Probability for the weapon, range and target. If Thorvald cuts loose with a Smith and Wesson 645 at 75 meters, aiming at an orc's head, he would have a 66% chance to hit. If the 1D20 system uses some type of weapon skills, you must determine the penalty for not having the skill, then subtract that from the Character's base DEXTERITY. If the Character chooses to Specialize, he would add the bonus received through this specialization to his Dexterity.

The big problem with this system is that it leaves your character with no way to improve, other than magically finding a ring that enhances Dexterity. There is another (better) way however.

Level can *also* be used to determine a handgunnery skill. Multiply the level by 5 to determine the basic Firearms Skill. Thus, As a 6th level character, Thorvald has a 30% Firearms Skill; at 8th level, he's at 40%; at 16th level he's up to 80.

1-10 skill systems (Twilight 2000™, etc.)

This system uses skill ratings from 1 to 10. The primary skills for using guns are Small Arms(Pistol) and Small Arms(Rifle). The base skill is doubled, halved or quartered, based on the range from the target, with the attacker rolling 1D10 under this skill number.

Most of the range factors of this system are factored directly into Sword's tables already. To make a skill conversion, you'll only need to convert the 1-10 skill ratings into a percentage; in this case, by multiplying the GDW system value by 10.

Mercenaries, Spies & Private Eyes™

In many ways, MSPE's system is not all that unlike the Sword tables; a base percentage is established based on range, target position and attacker position.

Add the character's DEX (3 to 18) and any points placed in the Firearms Skill (from 1 to 10) together. Multiply this value by 4 to determine the character's base weapon skill vis a vis Sword. Fit this value into the table and roll a percentage based on the range.

ABOUT THE DAMAGE TABLES

In most cases, damages are taken from the original statistics for each individual system. In cases where no actual game statistics existed, extrapolations were made, based on damages of similar weapons and information taken from the data within this compendium. To determine damage of a particular weapon, use the round type as a reference. Edge of the Sword projectile damage in the tables below is based on 4" of penetration (i.e., the average human arm).

The majority of the rounds listed in the tables are based on *standard ball* ammunition. Hollow point, semi-AP, KTW, Glaser safety and API rounds are not listed here; this is because each type of system treats these types of rounds in different fashions; to determine the effects of each type, use the individual game system's information.

Special Note: **AP** rounds are designed to penetrate armor. This means they do not usually cause a great deal of explosive damage. As the Compendium is designed to cover Man to Man combat, note that explosive damages vis a vis AP rounds will be quite small. Assume an AP round striking a man-sized target will result in the target being automatically blown apart.

HANDGUNS

Caliber	Edge of Sword	Cyberpunk®	Hero™ System	Call of Chuthulu™	Twilight 2000™	MSPE	D20 System
5.45x18mm USSR	0.52	1D6/2	1D6-1	1D6-2	1D6	1D6	1D6-1
5.7x17mmR (.22 Long)	0.16	1D6	1D6-1	1D6	1D6-1	1D6	1D4
7.65x17mmSR (.32 Auto)	0.28	1D6+1	1D6	1D8	1D6	2D6	1D4
9x17mm (.380 Auto)	0.40	1D6+2	1D6	1D8	1D6	2D6	1D4+1
9x18mm USSR	0.40	1D6+2	1D6	1D8+1	1D6	2D6+2	1D6
9x18mm Ultra/Police	0.44	2D6	1D6	1D8+2	1D6	2D6+2	1D6
9x19mm Nato Parabellum	0.64	2D6+1	1D6+1	1D10	1D6	3D6	1D6+1
9x19mmPT (Plastic Training)	0.20MAX	1D6+2	1D6	1D8+1	1D6	2D6+2	1D6
9x19mmR (.38 Special)	1.44	1D6+2	1D6	1D10	1D6	3D6	1D6-1
9x33mmR (.357 mag)	2.16	2D6+3	1D6+1	2D6+2	3D6	7D6+2	1D6+2
10.92x33mmR (.44 mag)	4.64	4D6	2D6	2D6+2	3D6	7D6+2	1D6+3
11.43x23mm (.45 Auto)	1.00	2D6+2	1D6+1	1D10+2	1D6	4D6+1	1D8

SUBMACHINEGUNS

Caliber	Edge of Sword	Cyberpunk®	Hero™ System	Call of Chuthulu™	Twilight 2000™	MSPE	D20 System
9x17mm	0.40	2D6	1D6	1D8	1D6	2D6	1D4+1
9x19mm	0.64	2D6+1	1D6+1	1D10	1D6	3D6+1	1D6+1
9x19mmPT	0.40MAX	2D6	1D6	1D8+1	1D6	2D6	1D6
11.43x23mm	1.12	2D6+2	1D6+1	1D10+2	1D6	4D6+3	1D8

BATTLE & ASSAULT RIFLES

Caliber	Edge of Sword	Cyberpunk®	Hero™ System	Call of Chuthulu™	Twilight 2000™	MSPE	D20 System
4.73x33mm Caseless	1.64	3D6	2D6-1	2D6	2D6	3D6+3	1D6
5x54mm Experimental	1.64	3D6	2D6-1	2D6	2D6	3D6+3	1D6
5,45x39mm USSR	2.00	3D6+3	2D6-1	2D8	2D6	3D6+3	1D6
5.56x45mm NATO	2.36	4D6	2D6	2D8	2D6	4D6	1D6
7.62x39mm USSR	1.06	5D6	2D6	2D6+1	3D6	7D6	1D8
7.62x51mm NATO	1.44	6D6+2	2D6+1	2D6+3	4D6	9D6+1	1D8

SNIPER RIFLES

Caliber	Edge of Sword	Cyberpunk®	Hero™ System	Call of Chuthulu™	Twilight 2000™	MSPE	D20 System
9x19mm	0.68	1D6+2	1D6+1	1D10	1D6	3D6+1	1D8
5.56x45mm	1.72	4D6	2D6	2D8	2D6	4D6	1D8
7.5x54mm (French)	1.44	6D6	2D6+1	2D6+3	4D6	9D6+2	1D8
7.62x51mm	1.64	6D6+2	2D6+1	2D6+3	4D6	9D6+2	1D8
7.62x54mm USSR	1.84	6D6+2	2D6+1	2D6+4	4D6	10D6+2	1D8
7.62x66mmB (.300 mag)	2.00	6D6+3	2D6+1	1D8+1D6+3	5D6	12D6+2	1D8

7.62x71mmB (.300 Weatherby)	2.72	6D6+3	2D6+1	1D10+1D8+3	6D6	30D6+3	1D8+3
8.58x71mm (.338/416 Rigby)	3.04	7D6	2D6+3	1D10+1D8+4	6D6	18D6+1	1D8+3
12.7x99mm (.50 Match)	11.12	4D10	3D6	2D10+4	8D6	48D6+1	1D10

MACHINEGUNS

Caliber	Edge of Sword	Cyberpunk®	Hero™ System	Call of Chuthulu™	Twilight 2000™	MSPE	D20 System
5.56x45mm	2.48	5D6	2D6	2D8	2D6	4D6	1D8
7.62x51mm	1.52	6D6+2	2D6+1	2D6+3	4D6	9D6+2	1D8
12.7x99mm (.50 MG)	12.20	4D10	3D6	2D10+4	9D6	44D6+3	1D10

SHOTGUNS (Multiple values are Damages at Close, Medium, Long, Extreme)

Caliber	Edge of Sword	Cyberpunk®	Hero™ System	Call of Chuthulu™	Twilight 2000™	MSPE	D20 System
15.6xmmR (20 ga.)	2.4/1.36/.72/.12	3D6/2D6/1D6	4XD6	2D6/1D6/1D3	6D6/1-5D6	8D6+2/1D6+1	1D10
18.5x70mmR (12 ga.)	4.8/3.2/1.6/.4	4D6/3D6/2D6	4xD6+1	4D6/2D6/1D6	9D6/1-7D6	8D6/4D6/2D6	1D10
18.5x79mm Flechettes (12ga Milspec/hi-pressure)	3.48/2.16/.84/.4	3D6/2D6/1D6	4xD6	3D6/1D6/1D6	7D6/1-7D6	8D6+2/1D6+1	1D8
19.5x76mmB (12ga Milspec/hvy. case)	6.08/1.8/1.52/.76	5D6/4D6/3D6	4D6+2	4D6/2D6/1D6	9D6/1-7D6	8D6/4D6/2D6	1D10
19.7x89mmR (10ga)	5.76/3.84/1.92/.32	6D6/5D6/4D6	5xD6	4D6+2/2D6+1/1D8	10D6/1-8D6	9D6/2D6+2/1D6+3	1D10

GRENADES (EXPLOSIVE DAMAGE)

TYPE	Edge of Sword†	Cyberpunk®	Hero™ System	Call of Cthulhu™	Twilight 2000™	MSPE	D20 System
HG78 (explosive)	B174/S100	5D6	6D6ex	2D6	C3/B6	20D6	1D6(x1D4)
HG 80 (explosive)	B32/S22	3D6	5D6ex	1D6-1	C2/B4	10D6	1D6-2(x1D4)
BTU M262 (rifle)	B109/S73	5D6	5D6ex	1D6	C7/B12	12D6	1D6(x1D4)
BTU M287 (rifle)	B320/S100	5D6	7D6ex	3D6	C3/B12	25D6	1D6(x1D4)
M67 (fragmentation)	B365/S100	7D6	7D6ex	3D6	C3/B12	25D6	1D6(x1D4)
M26A1 (fragmentation)	B333/S100	7D6	7D6ex	3D6	C3/B11	25D6	1D6(x1D4)
DM41 (40mm shell)	B68/S45	3D6	5D6ex	1D6	C1/B2	15D6	1D6(x1D4
HE Long/HE Short (Russian)	B81/S45	3D6	4D6ex	1D6	C1/B3	15D6	1D6(x1D4)
M381 (40mm HE shell)	B65/S43	3D6	5D6ex	1D6-1	C1/B2	11D6	1D8(x1D4)
M397 A1 (40mm shell)	B72/S48	4D6	5D6ex	1D6	C3/B12	15D6	1D8(x1D4)
M433 (40mm shell)	B102/S68	4D6	6D6ex	1D6+2	C3B12	12D6	1D8(x1D4)
M384 (40mm auto shell)	B124/S83	4D6	6D6ex	1D6+3	C3/B13	13D6	1D8(x1D4)
M430 (40mm auto shell)	B77/S51	4D6	5D6ex	1D6	C3/B12	15D6	1D8(x1D4)
M677 (40mm auto shell)	B102/S68	4D6	6D6ex	1D6+2	C2/B3	12D6	1D8(x1D4)
NR208 A2 (52mm shell)	B273/S100	6D6	7D6ex	2D6	C3/B9	20D6	1D8(x1D4)
All Incendiaries	individual entries	4D6x(4 turns)	6D6ex	2D6	C1/B12	20D6	1D8(x1D4)

HEAVY WEAPONS (EXPLOSIVE DAMAGE)

TYPE	Edge of Sword	Cyberpunk®	Hero™ System	Call of Cthuluhu™	Twilight 2000™	MSPE	D20 System
L36 A2 (81mm mortar [HE])	B1377/S100	10D10	12D6ex	6D6	C8/B28	72D6	1D8(x1D4)
M789 (30mm cannon [AP])	B61/S41	18D6	3D6+1ap	1D6	16D6 (ap)	36D6	1D8(x1D4)
M799 (30mm cannon [HE])	B97/S65	18D6	6D6ex	1D6	C1/B2	1D6+5	1D8(x1D4)
M371 (90mm recoil. rifle [AP])	B1580/S100	11D10	4 1/2D6ap	8D6	C4/B4	5D6x16	1D8(x1D4)
XM591 (90mm recoil. rifle [HE])	B1930/S100	12D10	12D6ex	8D6	C12/B34	72D6	1D8(x1D6)
RAW (140mm rocket [HE])	B2756/S100	13D10	15D6ex	11D6	C10/B28	5D6x25	2D6(x1D6)
Armbrust (rocket [AP])	B986/S100	10D10	4D6ap	4D6	C4/B4	5D6x20	1D8(x1D6)
M72A3 LAW (rocket [AP])	B684/S100	10D10	4D6ap	3D6	C3/B4	5D6x20	1D8(x1D6)

HOW THE DAMAGE WAS DONE

Damage ratings in Edge of the Sword are based on the tissue disruption caused by a projectile's impact and energy transfer. This is expressed as a two number formula: A/B; A= the total possible inches of penetration, B= the cubic inches of disruption per inch of penetration
example— 9mm NATO ball, 23/0.14

This formula can be calculated for any cartridge, provided certain statistics are known:

Total Damage= $[(Me \times CS)/10]* Bf$
Me=muzzle energy (ft/lbs)
CS=cross section of bullet (in²)
Bf= bullet factor (see chart)

Penetration= $(Mv \times Bdia)/BPf$
Mv= muzzle velocity (ft/sec)
Bdia= bullet diameter (thousandths/in)
BPf= bullet penetration factor (chart)

Read Penetration as #A, divide Total Damage by Penetration to get #B

Bullet Type	Bf	BPf
Pre-Fragmented (Glaser)	10	124
Lt. Jacketed Hollowpoint	5	59
Jacketed Hydra-shock	5	44
Copper-jkt. Hollowpoint	4.5	62
Tumbler	4.5	19
Hvy. Jacketed Hollowpt.	3.5	56
Lt. Jacketed Softpoint	3	119
Hollow Wadcutter	2.5	51
Semiwadcutter	2	22
Hvy. Jacketed Softpoint	1.5	43
Target Wadcutter	1	70
Roundnosed Lead	1	27
Full Metal Jacketed	1	1

How do I apply the damage? Disruption damage is calculated by multiplying #B by the thickness of the body area hit. Average thicknesses are as follows: Torso and Head=9in, Legs=6in, Arms=4in
The total rating of a cartridge would be written Penetration/Disruption (Disruption Arm) (Disruption Leg) (Disruption Torso-Head)
example—9mm Nato ball 23/.14 (.56) (.84) (1.26)
If a cartridge has less than 9in penetration then one of the damage ratings will be marked as the maximum damage the cartridge can deliver.
example—9mm Silvertip JHP 7/2.43 (9.72) (14.58) (17.01 MAX)

To utilize this information, the body's physical structure is represented by "body points" with Weak=150, Average=250, Strong=350. These points are then divided into regions calculated via human engineering studies:

Body Part	Body%	250pt average man
Head	8%	20
Neck	1%	3
Torso	37%	93
[zone 1]	[9%]	[23]
[zone 2]	[10%]	[25]
[zone 3]	[9%]	[23]
[zone 4]	[9%]	[23]
Shoulder (ea)	1%	3
Upper Arm (ea)	3%	8
Elbow (ea)	1%	3
Lower Arm (ea)	2%	5
Wrist (ea)	1%	3
Hand (ea)	1%	3
Thigh (ea)	10%	25
Knee (ea)	2%	5
Calf (ea)	3%	8
Ankle (ea)	1%	3
Foot (ea)	2%	5

Damage to part of a limb that equals or exceeds its body point rating renders that part (and all areas outward from that part) useless.

Damage to the Head or Torso area brings a chance of immediate death or unconsciousness:

Head Damage	Death%	Unconsciousness%
4.0	99%	99%
3.8	90%	99%
3.4	80%	99%
2.9	70%	99%
2.5	60%	99%
2.1	50%	99%
1.7	40%	99%
1.3	30%	76%
0.9	20%	48%
0.4	10%	24%

Torso Damage

Death%	Zone 1	Zone 2	Zone 3	Zone 4
99%	10	12.5	20	25
90%	9	11.2	18	22.6
80%	8	10	16	20.1
70%	7	8.7	14	17.3
60%	6	7.5	12	15
50%	5	6.3	10	12.5
40%	4	5	8	10
30%	3	3.7	6	7.5
20%	2	2.5	4	5
10%	1	1.3	2	2.5

In the case of multiple individual hits (i.e. automatic weapons) the damage is accounted for at the specific impact sites, but for overall body reaction, it is added together and applied as if it were a single hit striking the Torso in zone 2.

Wound shock effects are usually divided into unconsciousness and "knockdown," the body's nervous reflex reaction to the bullet wound. To determine shock effects, total the amount of damage recieved in a combat round and apply it to the following table:

Damage to cause

Knockdown	Unconsciousness	% Chance
34	51	99%
30.5	46	90%
27	41	80%
23.5	36	70%
20	31	60%
17	25.5	50%
13.5	20.5	40%
10	15.5	30%
7	10.5	20%
3.5	5	10%

Explosive weapons (grenades, rockets, etc.) are rated for damage in a different manner from projectiles. The ratings measure the "brisance" or shattering (and overpressure) effects of the explosion's blast wave on the body. This is combined with the stunning effects of the explosion's overwhelming assault on sight and hearing. The formula is two numbers: C/D; C=blast points, D=stun points

example—HG 78 frag grenade 174 Blast, 100 Stun

Both stun and blast points drop off at a rate of 50points/1m from point of impact.

Stun points are the direct percentage chance of being stunned and helpless for 2 to 8 seconds. Blast points are compared to the victim's body points on the following tables F90 & F91

Find the victim's body points in the left column, read right along the row until you reach the number on the table that is ≤ to the number of blast points inflicted, then read up to find the percentage chance of unconsciousness or death.

Fragmentation is expressed as a projectile disruption with an average damage quotient. All weapons produce the same fragmentation damage: 5/(2.28 MAX)

Incendiary weapons produce a fixed amount of damage per combat round.

Body Points	Chance of Death 10%	20%	30%	40%	50%	60%	70%	80%	90%	99%	**F90**
500	125	156	188	219	250	300	350	400	450	500	
450	113	141	170	198	225	270	315	360	405	450	
400	100	125	150	175	200	240	280	320	360	400	
350	88	110	132	154	175	210	245	280	315	350	
300	75	94	113	131	150	180	210	240	270	300	
250	63	79	95	110	125	150	175	200	225	250	
200	50	63	75	88	100	120	140	160	180	200	
150	38	48	57	67	75	90	105	120	135	150	
100	25	31	38	44	50	60	70	80	90	100	
50	13	16	20	23	25	30	35	40	45	50	

Body Points	Chance of Unconsciousness 10%	20%	30%	40%	50%	60%	70%	80%	90%	99%	**F91**
500	63	79	94	110	125	150	175	200	225	250	
450	57	71	86	100	113	137	158	181	203	225	
400	50	63	75	88	100	120	1140	160	180	200	
350	44	55	66	77	88	107	123	141	158	175	
300	38	48	57	67	75	90	105	120	135	150	
250	32	40	48	56	63	76	88	101	113	125	
200	25	31	38	44	50	60	70	80	90	100	
150	19	24	29	33	38	46	53	61	68	75	
100	13	16	20	23	25	30	35	40	45	50	
50	7	9	11	12	13	16	18	21	23	25	

▼ GRENADES & LAUNCHERS

▼ HEAVY WEAPONS

▼ PISTOLS

▼ SUBMACHINEGUNS